THE COLOUR LIBRARY BOOK OF

CAKE MAKING AND DECORATING

THE COLOUR LIBRARY BOOK OF

CAKE MAKING AND DECORATING

STELLA HARTWELL

COLOUR LIBRARY BOOKS

CLB 2136

This edition published 1988 by Colour Library Books Ltd
Godalming Business Centre, Catteshall Lane, Godalming, Surrey GU7 1XW

© Marshall Cavendish Limited 1988
Prepared by Marshall Cavendish Books Ltd
58 Old Compton St, London W1V 5PA

Typeset by Litho Link Limited, Welshpool, Powys
Printed in Hong Kong

ISBN 0 86283 602 6

CONTENTS

INTRODUCTION

Making and decorating your own cakes is great fun and is sure to impress your friends and family. Whether it is a perfect, feather-light sponge or a rich moist gâteau, it is very satisfying to know that the cake you set before them is all your own handiwork.

Once you have mastered the basic methods, you will find it is surprisingly easy to create impressive cakes. Even decorated cakes that appear very complicated at first glance are relatively easy once you understand the techniques of icing and piping decorations. *Cake Making and Decorating* is packed with all the know-how you need to become an expert.

The book contains a wide range of cakes, from simple all-in-one mixtures to elaborate iced celebration cakes, plus a whole selection of microwaved cakes. Each chapter has practical information explaining the method for making a particular type of cake, as well as the ingredients and equipment needed. Step-by-step instructions illustrate in detail the various techniques to help you achieve perfect results.

The book begins with all-in-one sponges, simple plain cakes with or without eggs, and yeast cakes made with both fresh and dried yeast. The chapter on cream cakes explains how to make such classics as a Victoria sponge and a Madeira cake, while the following chapter shows you how to transform light sponge cakes into decorative cakes with simple icings and easy piping techniques.

Small cakes are always popular, especially with children, and there is a chapter describing how to make lots of different small cakes in special tins or moulds, and how to cut out shapes from a large cake and decorate them with almond paste, icing, chocolate or sweets.

Children will also love the amazing selection of novelty cakes. No birthday party is complete without a special cake as the centrepiece and you can choose from such delights as a clown cake, a butterfly, maypole cake or merry-go-round to name but a few.

The chapter on special icings unravels the mysteries of frostings, which always look so impressive and are really simply to make yourself once you know how.

Melting method cakes, whisked sponges and rich fruit cakes are also explained in detail. Rich fruit cakes are the type most often used for celebration cakes and there are chapters on both simple celebration cakes – showing you how to make and use almond paste and royal icing – and elaborate celebration cakes such as a magnificently decorated wedding cake. Other special occasions call for different types of celebration cakes such as a key cake or an engagement cake, glamorous gâteaux or angel food cakes.

Finally there is a chapter on microwaved cakes, full of hints on how to make all kinds of cakes in the microwave, including a quick-version wedding cake and a delightful christening cake.

ALL-IN-ONE CAKES

Whether you fancy a light jam sandwich cake or a fruity tea-bread, the all-in-one method is the quickest and easiest way to make a cake.

All-in-one cakes differ from those made by other methods in that they are quicker and simpler to make. The basic ingredients are easy to remember: equal weights of self-raising flour, sugar, fat and eggs; plus 1 teaspoon baking powder to every 100 g [4 oz] self-raising flour. You simply put all the ingredients into a large mixing bowl and beat them together until they are light and slightly glossy. None of the usual laborious creaming or whisking of air into the mixture is needed. The extra baking powder does most of the work for you!

INGREDIENTS

Flour
Self-raising flour is always used for all-in-one cakes because it includes a calculated amount of baking powder. Soft and starchy, self-raising flour readily absorbs fat and produces a light crumbly texture which is just right for cakes.

Baking powder
The baking powder included in self-raising flour is not enough for all-in-one cakes, so extra is added. Baking powder is a raising agent. It reacts with liquid and heat to produce a gas which expands, making the cake rise as it cooks. Baking powder begins to act as soon as it becomes damp, so always store it in an airtight tin in a cool dry place.

Fat
Soft (sometimes called whipped or soft tub) margarine is tailor-made for this method. It beats to a beautifully even consistency when used straight from the refrigerator. You can use butter (for richer flavour) or ordinary margarine instead but these must be left to soften in a warm room for at least an hour before using so that they are easy to beat.

Sugar
Use caster or soft brown sugar because their fine crystals dissolve easily. Soft brown sugar gives a slightly richer, darker cake. Avoid granulated or Demerara sugar which give a coarse heavy texture.

Eggs
Eggs give colour and food value and help to bind (hold) ingredients together. They should be at room temperature, so be sure to remove them from the refrigerator an hour before you want to use them. Always use medium-sized eggs which weigh an average of 50 g [2 oz].

GETTING ORGANIZED

Mixing the ingredients is so quick that you leave this part until last. Having checked that you have all the ingredients and that they are at room temperature, turn on the oven, which will take 10-15 minutes to heat up. Unless your oven is a fan-assisted model, check that the shelf is in the correct position, in the centre of the oven.

Next fill a large mixing bowl with hot water so that it, too, will be at room temperature when you need it. Now choose and prepare the appropriate cake tin.

CAKE TINS

Successful baking depends to a considerable degree on using the correct size of tin. If the tin is too small, the mixture could overflow, the top might crack and form a peak or the cake may sink in the middle because it is not cooked right through. The depth is as

important as the diameter: the same quantity of cake mixture will physically fit into, say one 15 cm [6 in] deep round tin or two 18 cm [7 in] shallow round tins (called sandwich tins). But the cooking times will be different, so use the tin sizes as specified in recipes or remember to alter the cooking time (which is shown on the chart on page 13) if using alternatives.

Most cake tins are made of aluminium or tin, with or without a non-stick finish. Non-stick are more expensive but are often stronger and longer lasting.

The base and sides of all cake tins should be greased before the mixture is poured in, otherwise the cake may stick and prove difficult to turn out in one piece after cooking. (It is advisable to grease tins even when using a tin with a non-stick finish).

All tins, with the exception of fancy moulds, patty tins and non-stick tins must be greased, lined and then greased again. Fancy moulds and patty tins must be carefully greased.

Lining paper

Greaseproof paper is the cheapest and most widely used lining paper, but baking parchment, waxed paper or foil can be used instead. All lining paper, except baking parchment, must be greased after it has been put in the tin.

Cut the lining paper to size. Place it on the greased cake tin base, then grease the top of the paper so that the paper will peel away easily from the cake. If a deep tin or ring mould is used, you will need to line and re-grease the sides of the tin as well as the base.

Greasing

The fat needed for greasing is in addition to the fat needed for the recipe. It is possible to use hard fat to grease tins and lining paper, but it is more difficult to get an even coating. A flavourless oil, melted margarine or lard is better, and melted butter gives the cake crust good flavour.

Melt the fat gently in a saucepan, taking care it doesn't burn, then remove it from the heat. Dip a pastry brush into the melted fat (ideally you should keep one brush specifically for greasing) and thoroughly coat the base and sides of the tin, making sure no patches are left ungreased. Aim for a smooth, even film and don't leave any visible lumps or hardened fat or pools of oil – if the tin is over-greased the cake might have a crusty ring around the edges.

This glamorous Sherry layer cake is flavoured with sweet sherry and sandwiched together with sherry butter icing.

MAKING AND BAKING

In addition to the warmed mixing bowl and prepared cake tin already described, you will need:
- measuring equipment
- sieve
- wooden spoon
- spatula
- palette knife
- skewer
- wire rack

Accurate scales and measuring spoons are vital: one of the secrets of successful cake-making lies in the correct balance of ingredients.

The sieve can be either metal or plastic but it must have a fine mesh to sift the flour and baking powder together. This aerates the ingredients and ensures that the baking powder is evenly distributed.

A wooden spoon is best for beating the ingredients together once you have added eggs, sugar, fat and any flavouring. Stir vigorously with swift light movements. Don't skimp: it only takes 2-3 minutes to make the mixture slightly glossy and lighter in colour, and insufficient mixing may give your cake a speckled surface and coarse texture.

A rubber or plastic spatula is handy for transferring the mixture from the bowl to the cake tin and ensures you don't waste any of it.

A palette knife is useful for smoothing the surface of the mixture.

Baking time varies according to the recipe, the size of the cake and the idiosyncrasies of your particular oven. Don't be tempted to open the oven door before the end of the recommended cooking time as a rush of cold air can make the cake sink disastrously.

The cake is cooked when it is well risen, firm to the touch and light golden brown in colour. A way to test the cake is by inserting a fine, warmed skewer into the centre of it: the skewer should come out clean, that is, without any of the baking mix adhering to it.

Always leave your cake to stand in its tin for 3 minutes after it comes out of the oven – this is to allow the cake to shrink away from the tin. Then turn the cake on to a wire rack, because this allows a good circulation of air all round the cake, and leave it to become quite cold before storing or decorating. A large cake will take about 3 hours and a sandwich cake 1 hour to cool.

1 Place tin on lining paper and outline the size of the base in pencil.

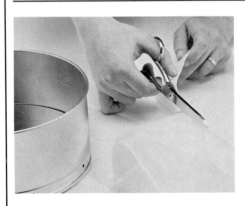

1 Cut lining for base. Cut a strip to go round tin. Make it 6 cm [2½ in] deeper than tin with a 2.5 cm [1 in] overlap.

1 Cut 16-20 strips of lining paper, 2.5 × 18 cm [1 × 7 in]. Grease tin.

PREPARING A SHALLOW [SANDWICH] TIN

2 Cut out the circle with scissors, just inside the pencil mark.

3 Grease base and sides. Position lining and grease again.

PREPARING A DEEP TIN

2 Make a 12 mm [½ in] fold along one long edge and crease. Snip diagonally to fold at 12 mm [½ in] intervals.

3 Grease sides and base of tin. Arrange strip with snipped edge on base. Place base lining in tin. Grease again.

PREPARING A 23 CM [9 IN] RING TIN

2 Push the strips into the tin so that they lie across the tunnel.

3 Overlap strips around inside of tin. Grease again.

MAKING ALL-IN-ONE CAKES

1 Sift the flour and baking powder into a large, warmed mixing bowl.

2 Add sugar, fat, eggs and any flavourings. Beat for 2-3 minutes.

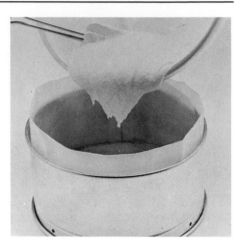

3 Scrape the mixture into a prepared cake tin with a spatula.

4 Smooth the top with a plastic spatula. Then bake.

5 Test the cake with a fine, warmed skewer. It should come out clean.

6 Allow the cooked cake to rest for 3 minutes to shrink from the tin.

STORING

Store cakes as soon as they are completely cold to prevent them from going stale. All-in-one cakes don't store as long as those made by other methods. Put cakes in an airtight tin, plastic container or well-sealed aluminium foil. Store for up to 3 days in a larder if they are un-decorated, or in a refrigerator if decorated.

Freezing

All-in-one cakes freeze for 6 months, but they must be airtight. Wrap closely in foil or pack in rigid containers. Open freeze decorated cakes to avoid damaging the icing.

7 Put wire rack on top of cake and carefully invert cake and rack.

8 Gently remove tin. Peel off lining paper and leave cake until cold.

GUIDE TO CAKE TINS

Weight of flour	Size of cake tin	Oven temperature	Baking time	No. of slices
100 g [4 oz]	one 15 cm [6 in] deep round	170°C [325°F] Gas 3	40-45 mins	8-10
	one 18 cm [7 in] shallow square	170°C [325°F] Gas 3	35-40 mins	16
	two 18 cm [7 in] sandwich	170°C [325°F] Gas 3	25-35 mins	6-8
	patty tins or paper cases	180°C [350°F] Gas 4	20-25 mins	18*
175 g [6 oz]	one 15 cm [6 in] deep square	170°C [325°F] Gas 3	1¼-1½ hours	9-15
	one 18 cm [7 in] deep round	170°C [325°F] Gas 3	1¼-1½ hours	10-12
	two 20 cm [8 in] sandwich	170°C [325°F] Gas 3	30-40 mins	12-16
	28 × 18 cm [11 × 7 in] shallow	170°C [325°F] Gas 3	30-40 mins	20-25
	oblong patty tins or paper cases	180°C [350°F] Gas 4	20-25 mins	24-30*
225 g [8 oz]	one 18 cm [7 in] deep square	170°C [325°F] Gas 3	1½-2 hours	15-20
	one 20 cm [8 in] deep round	170°C [325°F] Gas 3	1½-2 hours	12-16
	one 23 cm [9 in] ring	170°C [325°F] Gas 3	50-60 mins	16-20
	patty tins or paper cases	180°C [350°F] Gas 4	20-25 mins	36*

*number of cakes

FILLINGS FOR SANDWICH CAKES

Sandwich cakes are so called because they have a filling between layers of cake. Jam is probably the most popular filling, but there are lots of exciting and equally quick alternatives. Try some of the following:
● thick honey, marmalade or lemon curd.
● any soft thick fruit purée, such as apple.
● cream or curd cheese mixed with chopped pineapple or grated orange or lemon zest.
● mashed banana mixed with soft brown sugar and lemon juice to taste.
● two parts chocolate to one part butter, melted together.
● whipped cream on its own, or spread on top of jam, or mixed with orange or grapefruit segments, or flavoured with a little rum.

SLICING A DEEP CAKE IN HALF

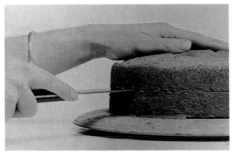

1 Place the cake on a wooden board. Use a large knife with a serrated edge. Crouch down so that your eye is level with cake.

2 Insert the tip of the blade into centre of cake. Turn the cake, keeping the knife straight and steady. Cut with a sawing action.

3 Separate the two halves, inverting bottom half so that the cut side is on the plate. Spread on prepared filling. Replace top half.

DECORATIONS AND ICINGS

Simple decorations are most attractive. A sandwich cake looks perfect with a dusting of sifted icing sugar or a pattern made by sifting through a doily. Unfilled sponges can be topped with glacé or butter-cream icing and a sprinkling of chopped nuts or chocolate drops to give contrasting texture and taste. Fruit cakes are best left plain.

Glacé icing

The simplest type of icing is given here. It is also known as water icing to distinguish it from a slightly more complicated version which is covered in another chapter. The method of making simple glacé icing is shown in the step-by-step pictures and instructions. The usual proportions are 2 tablespoons warm water to every 100 g [4 oz] icing sugar.

For flavoured glacé icing, simply use lemon, orange, pineapple or other fresh or canned fruit juice in place of the water.

For butter-cream icing

Allow 50 g [2 oz] butter at room temperature to every 100 g [4 oz] icing sugar. Flavour with one of the following: 25 g [1 oz] melted chocolate or 1 tablespoon cocoa powder; 2 teaspoons coffee and chicory essence or instant coffee powder; ½ teaspoon vanilla (or other flavour) essence; finely grated zest and juice of half an

orange or lemon; or 15 g [½ oz] chopped nuts. Add flavouring at the same time as the icing sugar.

ALL-IN-ONE LEMON CAKE

The all-in-one method is excellent for making simply-flavoured tea-cakes. Lemon gives a fresh flavour and its acidity helps the cake to rise.

For a really sumptuous cake, double the quantity of mixture. Divide between two prepared deep 20 cm [8 in] sandwich tins and bake for 1-1¼ hours. Sandwich the cold cakes with 6-8 tablespoons lemon curd. Use 175 g [6 oz] icing sugar and 3 tablespoons lemon juice for the glacé icing.

MAKES 10-12 SLICES
1 large lemon
175 g [6 oz] self-raising flour
½ teaspoon baking powder
175 g [6 oz] caster sugar
175 g [6 oz] soft margarine
3 medium-sized eggs

For the glacé icing:
125 g [4 oz] icing sugar
2 tablespoons freshly squeezed lemon juice

1 Heat oven to 170°C [325°F] Gas 3.
2 Fully grease and line an 18 cm [7 in] deep round cake tin and grease the paper.
3 Grate the zest of the lemon and squeeze 1 tablespoon of its juice.
4 Sift the flour and baking powder into a large warm mixing bowl.
5 Add the remaining ingredients and beat until glossy and light.
6 Turn the mixture into the prepared tin. Smooth the top with a palette knife.
7 Bake the cake for 1¼-1½ hours until cooked.
8 Remove the cake from the oven and allow it to rest for 3 minutes, then turn it out on to a wire rack and leave until completely cold.
9 To make the glacé icing, sift the icing sugar into a mixing bowl.
10 Warm the lemon juice, add to the icing sugar and beat for 3 minutes until shiny and thick enough to coat the spoon.
11 Pour icing on to cold cake and spread with a palette knife. Decorate with slices of crystallized lemon, if wished.

HANDY HINT

To avoid damaging a decorated cake when storing, place the cake on the inverted lid of the storage container and cover with the base.

HANDY HINTS

Cutting a sandwich cake
Don't press down on a sandwich cake when cutting, as this will cause the filling to ooze out. Let the knife do the work. Insert the point of a thin sharp knife into the centre and slice, pulling the knife towards you.

Making icing sugar
You can make your own icing sugar in seconds with an electric grinder. Use white granulated sugar and grind until powdery.

GLACÉ ICING

1 Sift icing sugar through a fine nylon or metal sieve into a bowl.

2 Beat in warm water, or any flavouring, and colouring.

3 Beat vigorously for 3 minutes until shiny and smooth.

4 Pour icing on to cake and spread with palette knife.

ICING SUGAR DECORATION

1 Place a doily on top of the cake and sift on icing sugar.

2 Gently lift the doily off the cake with the tips of your fingers.

BUTTER-CREAM ICING

1 Use the back of a wooden spoon to beat butter until very soft.

2 Sift in icing sugar and flavouring. Beat for 5 minutes until creamy.

SHERRY CAKE

Choose small flowers for frosting: wash and dry them, then brush with beaten egg white. Sprinkle with caster sugar and leave to dry. The flowers are for decoration only.

MAKES 10-12 SLICES
175 g [6 oz] self-raising flour
1½ teaspoon baking powder
175 g [6 oz] caster sugar
175 g [6 oz] soft margarine
3 medium-sized eggs
finely grated zest of 1 orange
2 tablespoons sweet sherry
2 tablespoons orange juice

For the sherry butter icing:
75 g [3 oz] butter, softened
225 g [8 oz] icing sugar, sifted
2 tablespoons sweet sherry

For the decoration:
frosted flowers

1 Heat the oven to 180°C [350°F] Gas 4. Grease and line two 4 cm [1½ in] deep, 18 cm [7 in] round tins and grease the paper.
2 Sift the flour and baking powder into a warm mixing bowl. Add the sugar, margarine, eggs and orange zest and beat with a wooden spoon for 2-3 minutes until evenly and smoothly blended.
3 Divide the mixture between the prepared tins and level each surface. Bake for 35-40 minutes, or until the cakes are springy to the touch.
4 Remove the cakes from the oven and leave for 3 minutes in the tins, then turn out on to a wire rack and leave until completely cold.
5 To make the icing, beat the butter

Glacé icing		Butter-cream icing	
Quantity of icing sugar used	**Size of cake covered**	**Quantity of icing sugar used**	**Size of cake covered**
100 g [4 oz]	15 cm [6 in] round 18 cm [7 in] round	75 g [3 oz]	15 cm [6 in] round
		100 g [4 oz]	18 cm [7 in] round 18 cm [7 in] square
175 g [6 oz]	18 cm [7 in] square 20 cm [8 in] round		
		175 g [6 oz]	20 cm [8 in] round
225 g [8 oz]	23 cm [9 in] round 23 cm [9 in] square 23 cm [9 in] ring	225 g [8 oz]	23 cm [9 in] round 23 cm [9 in] ring
(When weight of butter-cream icing is given in a recipe it refers to weight of icing sugar).			

until very soft, then slowly beat in the icing sugar. Continue beating until the mixture is pale and creamy, then beat in the sherry.

6 To assemble the cake, place one cake on a serving plate. Mix together the sherry and orange juice and spoon half evenly over the cake. Spread one-third of the icing over the cake, then top with the second cake. Sprinkle with the remaining sherry and orange mixture. Spread top with half of remaining icing, leaving a 5 mm [¼ in] border around edge. Mark a wavy pattern in the topping.

7 Place the remaining icing in a piping bag fitted with a small star nozzle and pipe a border of small rosettes around top edge of cake. Refrigerate for 20-25 minutes to firm. Just before serving, decorate with frosted flowers.

CHESTNUT CREAM GÂTEAU

MAKES 8-10 SLICES

100 g [4 oz] self-raising flour
1 teaspoon baking powder
100 g [4 oz] soft margarine
100 g [4 oz] caster sugar
2 large eggs
2-3 drops vanilla essence

For the filling:
250 g [8 oz] can chestnut spread

For the decoration:
275 ml [½ pt] whipping cream

1 Heat the oven to 170°C [325°F] Gas 3. Grease and line two 18 cm [7 in] sandwich tins and grease the paper.

2 Sift the flour and baking powder into a warm mixing bowl. Add the margarine, sugar, eggs and vanilla essence and beat with a wooden spoon for 1-2 minutes until evenly blended.

3 Divide mixture equally between the prepared tins and level each surface. Bake for 25-30 minutes until springy to the touch.

4 Remove the cakes from the oven and leave for 3 minutes in the tin, then turn out on to a wire rack and leave until completely cold.

5 To assemble the gâteau, put the chestnut spread into a bowl and stir with a fork until it is evenly mixed.

6 Slice each cake in half horizontally, then sandwich the layers together with the chestnut spread.

7 Whip the cream until it is standing in soft peaks, then spread over the top and sides of the cake to cover it completely. Serve the gâteau as soon as possible.

Variations

● For a special occasion, stir 2 teaspoons of brandy or rum into the chestnut spread. Just before serving, decorate the gâteau with sesame snaps or marrons glacés. Small packets of a single marron glacé are available at some Italian delicatessens.

HANDY HINT

Buying chestnut spread
Chestnut spread is a very sweet purée sold in tubes as well as cans.

JAM SANDWICH

This recipe is for a plain sandwich sponge cake, but you can make an exciting range of different sponges just by adding a few drops of concentrated essence or edible food dye to the basic recipe. Food dyes give colour but not flavour; most essences give both colour and flavour but some only flavour, so check your particular essence before using.

MAKES 6-8 SLICES

100 g [4 oz] self-raising flour
1 teaspoon baking powder
100 g [4 oz] soft margarine
100 g [4 oz] caster sugar
2 medium-sized eggs
3 tablespoons jam for filling
icing sugar for decorating

1 Heat the oven to 170°C [325°F] Gas 3.
2 Grease and line two 18 cm [7 in] round sandwich tins and grease the paper.
3 Sift the flour and baking powder into a warm mixing bowl. Add remaining ingredients and beat them thoroughly for 2-3 minutes until glossy and light.
4 Turn into the prepared cake tins and smooth the tops with a palette knife.
5 Bake in the centre of the oven for 25-35 minutes.
6 Remove from oven and cool for 3 minutes, then turn on to a wire rack and remove lining paper. Leave the cakes until cold.
7 Spread jam on one cake. Top with the other cake.

For a fresh-tasting lemon cake, add lemon zest to the basic recipe. If you want a golden colour, substitute butter for margarine.

Butter-cream icing has a thick, rich consistency which makes it a good filling as well as a topping. For chocolate butter-cream, either sift cocoa with the icing sugar or add melted chocolate.

To make an orange cake, use concentrated orange cordial. This gives a stronger colour and flavour than fresh orange juice. For colour alone, use edible food dye and add finely grated orange zest for an interesting texture.

Jam is traditionally used to sandwich thin cakes together. Use any flavour you like but choose a thick preserve, such as chunky marmalade, which gives greater contrast and looks nicer too!

For a coffee cake, use coffee and chicory essence — plain coffee essence will colour the mixture but won't flavour it. Alternatively, you can use instant coffee dissolved in a little milk or water.

There's no need to stick to jam as a filling. For a less sweet spread, try mashed bananas with unsweetened chestnut purée thinned with cream.

Transforming a plain sponge into an exciting cake is not difficult and can be great fun. Experiment with edible food dyes to colour your cake unusual shades. For extra interest, try adding chocolate dots to the basic recipe. These work well in a cake as they melt slightly but also retain their shape.

For a sophisticated filling, mix cream cheese with thick cream and spread generously.

To make a chocolate cake, use cocoa powder which both colours and flavours.

These are some of the many ingredients you can use to make easy all-in-one cakes.

ORANGE AND CHOCOLATE SQUARES

Placing spoonfuls of each different flavoured mixture alternately into each cake tin gives this cake a lovely marbled effect.

MAKES 16-18 SQUARES

175 g [6 oz] self-raising flour
1½ teaspoons baking powder
175 g [6 oz] soft margarine
175 g [6 oz] caster sugar
3 medium-sized eggs
1 tablespoon cocoa powder
2 tablespoons warm water
2 tablespoons concentrated
 orange cordial

For the butter-cream icing:
75 g [3 oz] butter, softened
175 g [6 oz] icing sugar
1½ tablespoons cocoa powder
1½ tablespoons concentrated
 orange cordial

1 Heat the oven to 170°C [325°F] Gas 3.
2 Grease and base line two 20 cm [8 in] square shallow tins. Grease the paper.
3 Sift the flour and baking powder into a warm mixing bowl. Add the margarine, sugar and eggs.
4 Beat with a wooden spoon for 2-3 minutes. Halve the mixture.
5 Blend the cocoa powder with the warm water and stir into one half of the mixture.
6 Beat the concentrated orange cordial into the other half.
7 Put the mixtures into the prepared tins in alternately-flavoured table-spoonfuls. Smooth top.
8 Bake for 25-35 minutes or until cooked.
9 Remove the cakes from the oven and leave in the tins for 3 minutes. Turn out on to a wire cooling rack and leave until completely cold.
10 To make the icing, beat the softened butter until light and fluffy. Then sift the icing sugar and beat together until well blended.

HANDY HINTS

Flavouring ideas

For chocolate mint squares, replace the concentrated orange cordial with green food colouring and peppermint essence.

For coffee and vanilla squares, substitute 2 tablespoons coffee and chicory essence for the cocoa and water in the cake, and a few drops of vanilla essence for the orange cordial. For the icing, use coffee and vanilla essence instead of the cocoa and orange cordial.

11 Halve the mixture. To one half, beat in cocoa powder blended with 2 teaspoons warm water.

12 To the other half, beat in the concentrated orange cordial.

13 Spread the orange icing over the surface of one cake. Put the second cake on top and spread with the chocolate icing. Cut into squares.

APPLE CAKES

The addition of apple purée gives a deliciously moist texture.

MAKES 36 SMALL CAKES
275 g [10 oz] self-raising flour
2 teaspoons baking powder
1½ teaspoons ground cinnamon
150 g [5 oz] soft margarine
225 g [8 oz] caster sugar
2 medium-sized eggs
275 ml [½ pt] thick apple purée, unsweetened
25 g [1 oz] raisins
2 red apples
lemon juice

1 Heat the oven to 180°C [350°F] Gas 4.

2 Sift the flour, baking powder and cinnamon into a warm bowl. Add remaining ingredients except red apples and lemon juice.

3 Beat together for 2-3 minutes. Divide mixture between 36 paper cases and place on baking trays.

4 Bake for 20-25 minutes

5 Remove the cakes from the oven and leave on a wire rack until completely cold.

6 Cut apples in quarters. Remove cores and cut into thin slices. Do not peel.

7 Dip slices in lemon juice. Decorate each cake with a slice of apple.

Variations
● Substitute another fruit purée for the apple: apricot, raspberry, blackberry and plum are all good. Decorate with glacé icing.
● Use chopped nuts, mixed peel, currants or sultanas in place of raisins.
● Replace ground cinnamon with nutmeg, mixed spice or cloves.

Moist apple cakes, tangy All-in-one lemon cake and Orange and chocolate squares are just some of the tempting tea-time goodies you can make with the all-in-one method. Simply flavoured icings are best. Let glacé icing dribble naturally down the sides of a deep cake, or spread soft butter-cream icing for a rich, melt-in-the-mouth topping.

FUDGY COFFEE CAKE

MAKES 8 SLICES

175 g [6 oz] self-raising flour
1½ teaspoons baking powder
175 g [6 oz] soft margarine
175 g [6 oz] light soft brown sugar
3 medium-sized eggs
1 tablespoon coffee and chicory essence
2-3 tablespoons apricot jam for filling

For the fudgy icing:
1 tablespoon coffee and chicory essence
2-3 tablespoons milk
40 g [1½ oz] soft margarine
few drops of vanilla essence
275 g [10 oz] icing sugar, sifted

1 Heat the oven to 170°C [325°F] Gas 3. Grease two 4 cm [1½ in] deep, 19 cm [7½ in] round sandwich tins. Line each base with greaseproof paper, then grease the paper.

2 Sift the flour and baking powder into a large warm bowl. Add margarine, brown sugar, eggs and coffee and chicory essence and beat with a wooden spoon for 1-2 minutes until evenly blended. Divide mixture equally between prepared tins and level each surface. Bake for 35-40 minutes, until springy to the touch.

3 Remove from the oven and leave for 3 minutes in the tin, then turn out on to a wire rack and leave until completely cold.

4 Sandwich cold cakes together with jam, then place on a wire rack with a plate underneath.

5 To make the icing, put the coffee and chicory essence, 2 tablespoons milk, margarine and vanilla into a small, heavy-based pan. Stir over low heat until the margarine has melted, then bring to the boil. Pour immediately on to the sifted icing sugar and beat with a wooden spoon until blended. If very stiff, beat in remaining milk.

6 Quickly spread the icing over the top and sides of the cake. Mark into wedges while the icing is still soft, then leave for about 30 minutes to set.

Variations

● Arrange a ring of mandarin orange segments around the edge, or pipe whirls of cream around the edge and top with mandarin orange segments.

Fudgy coffee cake can be served for tea or coffee time, or as a dessert. It is best eaten the day it is iced.

WALNUT LAYER CAKE

MAKES 8 SLICES

175 g [6 oz] self-raising flour
1½ teaspoons baking powder
175 g [6 oz] soft margarine
175 g [6 oz] light soft brown sugar
3 large eggs
50 g [2 oz] walnut pieces, chopped
2-3 drops vanilla essence

For the filling and topping:
350 g [12 oz] full-fat cream cheese
2 tablespoons clear honey
walnut halves

1 Heat the oven to 170°C [325°F] Gas 3. Grease and line a deep 19 cm [7½ in] round cake tin. Grease the paper.

2 Sift the flour and baking powder into a large warm bowl. Add the soft margarine, light brown sugar, eggs, chopped walnut pieces and vanilla essence and beat with a wooden spoon for 2-3 minutes until evenly blended.

3 Turn the mixture into the prepared tin and make a shallow hollow in the centre. Bake for about 1¼ hours until a fine, warm skewer inserted in the centre comes out clean.

4 Remove the cake from the oven and leave for 5 minutes in the tin, then turn out on to a wire rack and leave until completely cold.

5 To make the filling and topping, beat the cream cheese with a wooden spoon until smooth and creamy, then gradually beat in the honey. Chill the mixture until required.

6 Slice the cake horizontally into three equal layers, then use some of the cream cheese mixture to sandwich the layers together.

7 Spread the rest of the cream cheese mixture over the top of the cake, using a palette knife to make an attractive wheel pattern on the surface. Decorate with walnut halves.

Walnut layer cake makes a delicious dessert. Keep any left-over cake in the refrigerator.

COFFEE AND WALNUT RING

This delicious cake can be completely prepared in advance. The ring mould adds to its decorative appearance but you can cook the cake in an 18 cm [7 in] cake tin, in which case allow 10 extra minutes cooking time. You can use broken walnut pieces for the filling but you need walnut halves for decorating.

MAKES 8-10 SLICES

1 tablespoon milk
1 tablespoon instant coffee
100 g [4 oz] self-raising flour
1 teaspoon baking powder
100 g [4 oz] soft margarine
100 g [4 oz] caster sugar
2 medium-sized eggs

For the filling:
50 g [2 oz] walnut pieces
2 teaspoons instant coffee
4 teaspoons milk
100 g [4 oz] icing sugar
40 g [1½ oz] butter at room temperature

For the fudge icing:
2 tablespoons instant coffee
6 tablespoons milk
450 g [1 lb] icing sugar
50 g [2 oz] soft margarine or butter at room temperature
walnut halves for decorating

This Coffee and walnut ring is simple to make and decorate but the ring mould helps make it into something a little bit special.

1 Heat the oven to 170°C [325°F] Gas 3.

2 Grease a 20-23 cm [8-9 in] ring mould, line it with greaseproof paper and grease the paper.

3 Put the milk into a cup and stir in the coffee until it dissolves.

4 Sift the flour and baking powder together into a large warm mixing bowl.

5 Add the margarine and sugar to the bowl. Break in the eggs and add the coffee mixture. Beat with a wooden spoon for 2-3 minutes until glossy and light.

6 Turn the cake mixture into the prepared mould, being careful to distribute it evenly around the ring. Smooth the surface.

7 Bake for 35-45 minutes.

8 Remove the cake from the oven, cool for 3 minutes, then turn out on to a wire cake rack. Remove the lining paper and leave for a minimum of 1½ hours until cold.

9 Chop the broken walnuts for the filling with a sharp knife until reduced to small and even pieces.

10 To make the filling, dissolve the instant coffee in the milk.

11 Sift the icing sugar into a bowl. Add the butter, coffee mixture and nuts. Beat together for 2-3 minutes until well-mixed.

12 Cut the cake in half by pushing the knife through to the middle. Keep the knife steady and turn the cake all the way round until cut in two.

13 Invert the bottom half of the cake, and spread the filling on the firm browned side – the crumbs-side would stick to your knife. Sandwich the cake together again.

14 To make the icing, dissolve the instant coffee in the milk.

15 Half fill a saucepan with water and place a trivet or scone-cutter in it, and stand a mixing bowl on top. Set to heat. When the water is simmering gently, sift the icing sugar into the warmed mixing bowl.

16 Add the margarine (or butter) and coffee mixture, beat until the mixture is smooth. Remove from heat and leave to cool, beating occasionally until of a coating consistency.

17 Place cake on cooling rack over a tray. Pour icing over; shake to smooth the surface. If wished, repeat process with the icing that has collected in the tray.

18 Stud with a ring of walnut halves before the icing sets.

GINGER LAYER CAKE

MAKES 6-8 SLICES

100 g [4 oz] self-raising flour
1 teaspoon baking powder
100 g [4 oz] soft margarine
100 g [4 oz] caster sugar
2 large eggs

For the filling and decoration:
150 ml [¼ pt] whipping cream
8 tablespoons ginger marmalade
2 gingernut biscuits, coarsely crushed
   (optional)

1 Heat the oven to 170°C [325°F] Gas 3. Grease and line two 18 cm [7 in] round sandwich tins, then grease the paper.
2 Sift the flour and baking powder into a large warm bowl. Add the margarine, sugar and eggs and beat together with a wooden spoon for 2-3 minutes.
3 Divide the mixture equally between the prepared tins, level each surface and make a shallow hollow in the centre. Bake in the oven for 25 minutes until the cakes are springy to the touch.
4 Remove the cakes from the oven and leave for 3 minutes in the tins, then turn out on to a wire rack, remove the lining paper and leave until completely cold.
5 Cut each cake in half horizontally to make four layers altogether. Place each cake on a level surface and, with a long serrated-edged knife, score a line around the sides. Then cut the cake in half, using the scored line as your guide. Whip the cream until standing in soft peaks.
6 To assemble the cake, spread one layer with half the marmalade, place another layer on top and spread with half the cream.
7 Top with another layer and spread with the remaining marmalade.
8 Place the last layer, cut side down, on top and spread with the rest of the cream.
9 Sprinkle the crushed gingernuts around the top edge, if using. Serve within 1 hour, or chill in the refrigerator until ready to serve.

Ginger layer cake

Chequer cake

CHEQUER CAKE

MAKES 10-12 SLICES
175 g [6 oz] self-raising flour
1½ teaspoons baking powder
175 g [6 oz] soft margarine
175 g [6 oz] caster sugar
3 medium-sized eggs
few drops of red food colouring

For the filling and decoration:
4-5 tablespoons strawberry jam, sieved
    and warmed
75 g [3 oz] butter, softened
350 g [12 oz] icing sugar, sifted
3 tablespoons single cream
3-4 drops vanilla essence

1 Heat the oven to 170°C [325°F] Gas 3. Grease and line two 4 cm [1½ in] deep, 18 cm [7 in] round sandwich tins. Grease the paper.
2 Sift the flour and baking powder into a warm bowl. Add the margarine, sugar and eggs and beat with a wooden spoon for 2-3 minutes, to blend.
3 Spread half the mixture evenly in one prepared tin. Tint the remaining mixture pink, then spread evenly in the other tin. Bake for 30-35 minutes, until springy to the touch.
4 Remove the cakes from the oven and leave for 3 minutes in the tins,

then turn out on to a wire rack and leave until completely cold.
5 Place the cakes on a flat surface. Using a 10 cm [4 in] plain round cutter, cut out centre of each cake. Then remove centre of each cut out round with a 2.5 cm [1 in] plain round cutter. Brush the insides of rings with jam.
6 Place the medium-sized pink ring inside the large plain one, then fill the centre with the small plain ring. Reassemble remaining rings and round of cake to give the opposite colour scheme. Spread one cake with the rest of the jam, then place the other cake on top.
7 To make the icing, beat the butter until creamy, then gradually beat in the icing sugar, cream and vanilla essence.
8 Swirl the icing over the top and sides of the cake. Serve at once, or refrigerate for up to 2 days.

Variation
● For a Chocolate chequer cake, divide the sifted flour and baking powder between two bowls. Sift 1 tablespoon cocoa into one bowl. Divide the margarine, sugar and beaten eggs between the two mixtures. Spread one mixture in each tin, then bake and assemble as above.

DREAMY MOCHA GÂTEAU

MAKES 8 SLICES

100 g [4 oz] self-raising flour
1 teaspoon baking powder
100 g [4 oz] soft margarine
100 g [4 oz] caster sugar
2 eggs, beaten

For the filling and topping:
4 tablespoons chocolate spread
100 ml [3½ fl oz] milk, at room
    temperature
40 g [1½ oz] packet dessert topping mix
    with cream added
2 tablespoons powdered drinking
    chocolate
2 teaspoons coffee and chicory essence
1-2 tablespoons icing sugar, sifted
chocolate-flavoured sugar strands, to
    decorate

1 Heat the oven to 170°C [325°F] Gas 3. Prepare a 33 × 23 cm [13 × 9 in] Swiss roll tin. Cut a piece of greaseproof paper 2.5 cm [1 in] larger all round than tin. Fold edges over by 2.5 cm [1 in], crease and unfold. Place tin on paper and cut diagonally from each corner to corner of the tin. Grease the tin. Place the paper in the tin and overlap the cut corners so they fit neatly. Grease the lining paper.

2 To make the cake, sift the flour and baking powder into a large bowl. Add the soft margarine, caster sugar and eggs. Beat vigorously with a wooden spoon for 2-3 minutes until the mixture is smoothly blended.

3 Spread the mixture evenly in the prepared tin, then bake for 25 minutes until the cake is golden and the top springs back when gently pressed. Remove the cake from the oven and leave for 3 minutes in the tin, then turn out on to a wire rack and leave until completely cold.

4 To assemble the cake, trim the edges, then cut the cake lengthways into three equal pieces. Heat the chocolate spread in a small saucepan until softened, cool lightly and use to sandwich the cake layers on top of each other.

5 Pour the milk into a bowl. Sprinkle in the topping mix, drinking chocolate and coffee and chicory essence and whisk until stiff. Sweeten to taste with icing sugar.

6 Spread the mixture over the top and sides of the cake, then decorate the top with the sugar strands.

This Dreamy mocha gâteau can be served immediately or refrigerated for up to 8 hours.

ORANGE RING CAKE

If you do not want to make a greaseproof paper bag, drizzle chocolate over the cake from a metal spoon.

MAKES 12 SLICES

175 g [6 oz] self-raising flour
1½ teaspoons baking powder
175 g [6 oz] soft margarine
175 g [6 oz] light soft brown sugar
3 medium-sized eggs
finely grated zest of 1 orange

Orange ring cake

For the icing and decoration:
275 g [10 oz] icing sugar
finely grated zest of 1 orange
3 tablespoons orange juice
25 g [1 oz] plain dessert chocolate,
    broken into pieces
thin slices of orange (optional)

1 Heat the oven to 180°C [350°F] Gas 4. Thoroughly grease a 1.5 L [2½ pt] plain ring mould measuring 23 cm [9 in].
2 Sift the flour and baking powder into a large warm bowl. Add the margarine, soft brown sugar, eggs and orange zest, then beat with a wooden spoon for 2-3 minutes until blended. You can use a hand-held electric beater instead of a wooden spoon, but do not beat for longer than 1½-2 minutes. It is important not to overbeat the cake or it will rise unevenly and will have a heavy texture.
3 Turn the mixture into the prepared mould and level the surface. Bake for 35-40 minutes until a warm fine skewer inserted into the centre comes out clean.
4 Remove the cake from the oven and leave for 3 minutes in the ring mould, then run a palette knife around the sides to loosen the cake. Turn out on to a wire rack and leave until cold.
5 To make the icing, sift the icing sugar into a bowl. Add the orange zest and juice and mix with a wooden spoon until blended.
6 Place a large plate underneath the wire rack. Pour the icing over the top of the cake and quickly spread it over the sides with a palette knife. Leave the icing to set. Do not be tempted to transfer the cake to a serving plate until the icing is set or it will crack and the look of the cake will be spoilt.
7 Put the chocolate in a heatproof bowl set over a saucepan of gently simmering water. Heat gently until melted, stirring occasionally.
8 Put the melted chocolate into a greaseproof paper piping bag. Snip off the tip of the bag and pipe squiggly lines of chocolate over the iced cake. Leave until completely set. Just before serving, arrange orange slices in the centre of the ring if liked.

Variations

● Substitute finely grated zest of 1 lemon for the orange zest in the cake and also in the icing, and use 3 tablespoons lemon juice instead of the orange in the icing.
   Omit the chocolate and decorate the cake with jellied orange or lemon slices.

BANANA AND BRAZIL CAKE

If this cake is not iced, it will keep for up to 6 days stored in an airtight container. Allow time for the icing to set when you are ready to serve it.

MAKES 10 SLICES
100g [4 oz] self-raising flour
1 teaspoon baking powder
100 g [4 oz] soft margarine
100 g [4 oz] light soft brown sugar
2 medium-sized eggs
2 small bananas, mashed

For the icing:
1 tablespoon clear honey
75 g [3 oz] icing sugar, sifted
1-2 tablespoons cold water
25 g [1 oz] shelled Brazil nuts, coarsely
  chopped

1 Heat the oven to 170°C [325°F] Gas 3. Lightly grease and line an 850 ml [1½ pt] 450 g [1 lb] loaf tin. Grease the paper.
2 Sift the flour and baking powder into a large warm bowl. Add the margarine, sugar, eggs and mashed bananas, then beat with a wooden spoon for 1-2 minutes until evenly blended.
3 Turn the mixture into the prepared tin and level the surface. Bake for 1¼ hours until browned and firm to the touch. To test that the cake is cooked, insert a warmed fine skewer into the centre: it should come out free of any sticky uncooked mixture.
4 Cool the cake for 10 minutes, then turn out of the tin and carefully peel off the lining paper. Place the cake the right way up on a wire rack and leave to cool completely.
5 To make the icing, mix the honey into the icing sugar with a large metal spoon, then stir in just enough water to give a thick pouring consistency. Add the water a few drops at a time and mix well. If you do make the icing too thin, sift in a little extra icing sugar.
6 Place a plate under the wire rack. Spoon the icing over the top of the cake, allowing it to run down the sides. Leave for 10 minutes to firm slightly, then sprinkle with the nuts. Leave to set before cutting.

Variation
● Instead of Brazil nuts, use roughly chopped walnuts, almonds, hazelnuts or other nuts of your choice.

Banana and Brazil cake

Coffee gâteau

Freezing Coffee gâteau
Wrap the cold cakes separately, or with waxed paper between them. Seal, label and freeze for up to 4 months. Defrost at room temperature for 1-2 hours, then fill and decorate.

COFFEE GÂTEAU

MAKES 12 SLICES
225 g [8 oz] self-raising flour
2 teaspoons baking powder
225 g [8 oz] soft margarine
225 g [8 oz] caster sugar
4 medium-sized eggs
1 tablespoon cold strong black coffee

For the filling and decoration:
75 g [3 oz] unsalted butter, softened
175 g [6 oz] full-fat soft cheese
350 g [12 oz] icing sugar, sifted
2 teaspoons cold strong black coffee
175 g [6 oz] walnuts, chopped
14 walnut halves

1 Heat the oven to 180°C [350°F] Gas 4. Grease and line two 20 cm [8 in] sandwich tins, then grease the paper.
2 Sift the flour and baking powder into a large warm bowl. Add the soft margarine, caster sugar, eggs and coffee and beat for 2-3 minutes until blended and slightly glossy.
3 Divide the cake mixture equally between the prepared tins.
4 Bake for 25-30 minutes until just firm to the touch. Remove the cakes from the oven and leave for 3 minutes in the tin, then turn out on to a wire rack and leave until completely cold.
5 Meanwhile, make the filling, beat the butter and cheese together until light and fluffy. Beat in the icing sugar a tablespoon at a time until half has been incorporated, then beat in the coffee before adding the remaining icing sugar. Beat 50 g [2 oz] nuts into one-third of the butter-cream.
6 When the cakes are cold, sandwich the sponges together with the nut-flavoured butter-cream. Spread two-thirds of the plain butter-cream around the sides of the cake. Roll sides of the cake in remaining nuts.
7 Spread the remaining plain butter-cream on top of the cake. Smooth over the top with a palette knife, then make a zig-zag pattern all over the surface. Decorate with walnut halves.
8 Serve as soon as possible, or refrigerate, uncovered, overnight.

into a large warm bowl. Add the margarine, sugar, eggs and orange zest and beat for 2-3 minutes.

3 Turn the mixture into the prepared tin and bake for 1 hour until well risen, firm to the touch and light golden brown in colour and a fine warm skewer inserted into the centre comes out clean.

4 If the cake is not done, continue baking for up to 30 minutes, testing occasionally.

5 Remove from the oven and leave for 3 minutes in the tin, then turn out on to a wire rack and leave to cool.

6 Cut the cake in half horizontally. Whip the cream to the soft peak stage. Spread half the cream on the bottom layer and scatter half the chopped pineapple over the top.

7 Place the second layer of cake on top and spread with the remaining cream. Decorate with the remaining pieces of pineapple and the orange wedges.

SIMPLE FRUIT CAKE

An all-in-one fruit cake is much quicker to make than ordinary fruit cake, but takes about as long to bake. Extra flour is used to compensate for the addition of dried fruit and baking powder is omitted to give the fruit cake its characteristic dense texture.

MAKES 12-16 SLICES

350 g [12 oz] self-raising flour
175 g [6 oz] soft margarine
175 g [6 oz] soft brown sugar
3 medium-sized eggs
100 g [4 oz] dried apricots, chopped
175 g [6 oz] sultanas
100 g [4 oz] glacé cherries, halved

1 Heat the oven to 170°C [325°F] Gas 3.

2 Grease and fully line an 18 cm [7 in] deep, round cake tin and grease the paper.

3 Sift the self-raising flour into a warm mixing bowl. Add remaining ingredients.

4 Beat for 2-3 minutes.

5 Turn into the prepared tin and bake for 1½ hours.

6 Remove the cake from the oven and leave for 3 minutes in the tin, then turn out on a wire rack and leave until completely cold.

ORANGE PINEAPPLE SANDWICH

This delectable cake is sandwiched together with cream and topped with pineapple and orange slices and rosettes of cream.

MAKES 8-10 SLICES

225 g [8 oz] self-raising flour
2 teaspoons baking powder
225 g [8 oz] soft margarine
225 g [8 oz] caster sugar
4 medium-sized eggs
finely grated zest of 1 orange

For the filling and decoration:
275 ml [½ pt] double or whipping cream
50 g [2 oz] chopped fresh or canned
   pineapple
orange slices, cut into wedges

1 Heat the oven to 170°C [325°F] Gas 3. Grease and line a deep 20 cm [8 in] round cake tin. Grease the paper.

2 Sift the flour and baking powder

PLAIN CAKES WITHOUT EGGS

Plain cakes made without eggs are ideal for family teas – those occasions when you would like to provide something more than toast but don't feel justified in splashing out on anything very rich or fancy.

Plain cakes are at their very best shortly after they have come out of the oven, so there is no need to resist the temptation to cut into them while they are still warm and smelling deliciously inviting. Cut plain cakes into thick slices and spread them with plenty of creamy butter (plain cakes are also called tea-breads, probably for this reason) or, for a real treat, serve them with cream.

Plain cakes are made by the rubbing-in method and you will find it is not difficult to achieve perfect results every time. The proportion of fat to flour is half or less and no eggs are used so the results are economical, but certainly not dull, since the basic mixture can be adapted in innumerable ways by adding extra flavourings, such as spices, dried, fresh, canned or crystallized fruit, nuts, liquid flavourings or honey, syrups, treacles and jams.

The most important things to remember are to weigh your ingredients carefully and to handle the mixture lightly. These are the keys to success because they ensure the cake rises properly and has that characteristic open, light texture of a well-made plain cake.

In cakes made without eggs the raising agents used are chemical. These produce a gas, carbon dioxide, which expands on heating, so 'lifting' the cake. Air also expands on heating and, although it is not the main raising agent in rubbed-in cakes, the amount incorporated during the rubbing-in operation is valuable. So be sure to rub in lightly and evenly, and do all subsequent mixing lightly too – or you will expel the air again and the cake will not rise as it should.

BASIC INGREDIENTS

Flour

The texture of a good plain cake is described as 'tender'. This 'tender' texture can only be achieved by the use of a 'soft' flour, one which does not contain a high proportion of gluten. (Gluten is the elastic substance which develops and strengthens on beating, a property required for making bread but not for cakes.) On the domestic market it is seldom possible to buy a special, very low gluten flour (except for people on gluten-free diets) but plain white flour is perfectly suitable. If you want to give your cakes an even 'shorter' texture you can make a soft flour effectively at home by substituting cornflour for part of the flour in the ratio of one part cornflour to seven parts plain white flour. For example, where a recipe specifies 225 g [8 oz] plain white flour, use 200 g [7 oz] plain white flour and 25 g [1 oz] cornflour.

Never use strong white flour, brown flour or wholewheat because they would give the cake a heavy texture. And never use self-raising flour. Recipes vary in the amount and type of raising agent needed; self-raising flour contains a standard quantity and type of raising agent which might not be what is wanted.

Raising agents

As soon as the raising agents are mixed together in the presence of a liquid they begin to produce carbon dioxide. When they are heated the reaction speeds up and the gas bubbles expand, forcing the cake to rise. The mixture must therefore be baked as soon as it has been prepared so that it does not lose the raising effect of the gas

bubbles. The process continues steadily for some time which is why recipes give long cooking times even for quite small cakes.

Always measure carefully: an excess of raising agent will either give an uneven, coarse texture, or it will overstretch the gluten, causing the cake to collapse. Too much bicarbonate of soda will give a bitter taste. But, if there is insufficient raising agent not enough gas will be produced to aerate the mixture and the cake will be unappetizing.

Bicarbonate of soda can be used alone but it is usually used in conjunction with another acid substance, such as cream of tartar, sour milk, vinegar or black treacle, to produce a stronger reaction.

Baking powder: the commercial variety is a blend of two parts bicarbonate of soda to one part cream of tartar, with the addition of ground rice to help preserve the mixture. It is much better, and more economical, to make your own baking powder at home as you need it. Simply combine two parts bicarbonate of soda to one part cream of tartar and leave out the ground rice.

Salt
A little salt is added to bring out the flavour of the other ingredients.

Fat
The fat in a cake has several vital roles to play. It helps to tenderize or soften the gluten and starch in the flour, so contributing to that 'melt-in-the-mouth' texture. It traps the air bubbles which make the cake light and it helps to keep the cake moist.

Whichever fat you choose it should be at room temperature so that it can easily be rubbed in. If the fat is too hard or too soft the mixing will be uneven and the cake tough.

Butter: gives the best flavour but it is expensive. Also, it tends to become too soft and oily in warm conditions, or if handled too much.

Margarine: hard margarines are excellent, particularly those which contain some butter. They are less expensive

With its crunchy topping of flaked almonds, old-fashioned Honey tea-bread shows just how eye-catching a plain cake made without eggs can be!

than butter and remain firmer during use. Whipped margarines are not suitable because they are too soft.

Lard: should only be used in mixtures containing ingredients with strong distinctive flavours, such as spices. Lard is a 'pure' fat so you will need less of it than butter or margarine (reduce the quantity of fat given in the recipe by about a quarter, so where a recipe gives 100g [4 oz] butter use 80 g [3¼ oz] lard). As lard does not 'hold' air very well, the cakes will not have a really light, open texture.

Sugar

Sugar helps to improve the flavour, texture, appearance and keeping qualities of the cake. As with fat, sugar softens the gluten and gives a more tender cake. Used in the right proportions, sugar helps the cake to rise, but too much sugar softens the gluten so much that it is unable to support the risen shape and the cake will sink. Fat and sugar are usually present in equal amounts. If the sugar exceeds the fat the cake will be more tender and spongy. If the fat exceeds the sugar it will have a richer but closer texture.

Caster sugar is best as the many, small, sharp-edged crystals grate readily on the fat, aiding the rubbing-in process. Also, it dissolves easily during cooking.

Granulated sugar can be used but it will not mix in as efficiently because the crystals are rather coarse, and it will give a speckled appearance.

Soft brown sugar is sometimes used to add distinctive flavour and colour. Demerara sugar is not suitable because it is too coarse.

Liquid

Milk is usually used to bind the rubbed-in ingredients together. For a basic recipe using 225 g [8 oz] flour, 150 ml [¼ pt] milk is sufficient to bind the mixture to the right consistency. If additional liquid flavouring or fruit is used the milk is usually reduced to keep the balance of liquid to dry ingredients in correct proportion.

ADDITIONAL INGREDIENTS

Dry flavourings: when cakes are flavoured with certain powders, such as chocolate, an adjustment must be made to the amount of flour used, usually gram for gram (ounce for ounce), otherwise the cake will be dry and tough. Ground spices are used in such small quantities that this is not necessary. On the other hand, when fruit or nuts are added, the mixture must contain slightly less liquid than normal to make it stiffer so that it can support the weight of the additional ingredients and prevent them sinking.

Dried fruit: dried peaches, bananas, pears and figs can be used as well as the conventional currants, sultanas and raisins. Nearly all dried fruit purchased nowadays is cleaned and can virtually be used straight from the packet. Just

Drained canned fruit can be used to give plain cakes a lovely moist consistency.

take a quick glance to make sure that there are no stalks which would spoil the texture of the cake.

Fresh and canned fruit can be used and give cakes a lovely moist consistency. Prepare fresh fruit in the usual way for cooking, chopping it quite small. Always drain canned fruit well before using. Thick fruit purées add moisture and flavour.

Crystallized fruit can be added for extra sweetness, flavour and texture. Glacé cherries must be washed well in hot water to remove the heavy syrup coating or else they will sink. Drain them, then dry and chop finely: they are rather heavy and the cake structure will not be able to keep them suspended if they are too large. Ready-prepared candied peel is easily available – just check that there are no large pieces.

Nuts: all nuts should be shelled and chopped before using. For a slightly stronger nutty flavour, toast the nuts by spreading them in a single, even layer on a grill pan or shallow dish and grill under a moderately high heat. Turn the nuts frequently to ensure an even colour. They can also be browned in a moderate oven (180°C [350°F] Gas 4) provided that an eye is kept on them.

Liquid flavourings add extra colour as well as special flavours. When adding liquids you will have to adjust the proportions of the other ingredients accordingly. Too wet a mixture will give a close-textured, flat cake and any fruit present will sink to the bottom of the cake.

Honey, syrups and jam lend their own particular sweet flavour and can be used to replace some of the sugar. They will produce a closer-crumbed, moist cake with a better storing quality.

CHOOSING AND PREPARING BAKING TINS

Because the mixture must be cooked as soon as it has been prepared, always prepare the baking tin before you start making the cake itself.

Square or rectangular tins are generally used because plain cakes or tea-breads are usually sliced and buttered in the same way as bread.

Two types of rectangular tin can be used. Those with sloping sides and a base which is smaller than the top of the tin are called loaf tins. Sizes vary enormously and are not standardized.

LINING A SQUARE TIN

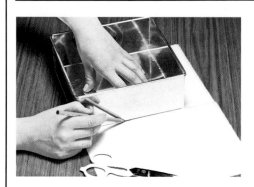

1 Place tin on lining paper and outline the size of the base in pencil. Cut out base lining with scissors, just inside pencil mark.

2 Cut a strip for each side of the tin. Make each strip 6 cm [2½ in] deeper and 2.5 cm [1 in] longer than the sides of the tin.

3 Make a 12 mm [½ in] fold along one of the long edges of each strip. Crease firmly. Snip diagonally to fold at 12 mm [½ in] intervals.

4 Grease sides and base of tin. Position strips with snipped edge on base. Position base lining paper. Grease again.

Don't worry if the measurements of your tin vary slightly from those recommended in the recipe: the precise size is not vital when making plain cakes without eggs.

You can also use a straight-sided rectangular tin, although these can be rather hard to obtain.

Square cake tins have straight sides. They are available in standard sizes. Some have a loose-bottomed base, which makes turning out the cooked cake easier, and some have a non-stick surface.

A round cake tin can be used instead of a square one. But remember that a square tin holds about the same amount of mixture as a round tin which is 2.5 cm [1 in] larger in diameter than the length of one side of the square tin. So if the recipe calls for a 20 cm [8 in] deep square tin you can use a 23 cm [9 in] deep round tin instead.

HANDY HINT

Greasing and lining the baking tin

The base and sides of your tin must always be greased before the cake mixture is poured in. (It is advisable to do this even when using a non-stick tin.)

If the recipe contains honey, treacle, syrup or jam you should also line and re-grease the tin. It is extremely difficult to fully line a loaf tin because it has sloping sides. Usually, therefore, just the bottom of the tin is lined. If you are using a square tin, it is worth taking the trouble to line the sides as well as the base.

OVEN TEMPERATURES

The cake assumes its final shape while it is in the oven, so just as much attention must be paid to the baking of the cake as to its making. Turn the oven to the recommended temperature before you start making the cake mixture, so that the right temperature will be reached by the time you need it.

It is extremely important to bake at the recommended temperature and shelf position because the heat not only expands the gas produced by the raising agents, but will also caramelize the surface sugar, giving a soft brown crust.

If the temperature is too high the cake will begin to cook and assume its final shape (the cooking term is to 'set') before it has risen. Setting starts from the sides and gradually moves towards the centre. If this occurs too quickly it produces a cake with a cracked peak in the centre and any fruit contained in the cake will sink. It also means that when the outside of the cake is ready the inside is still raw and, by the time the inside is cooked, the outside will be burnt.

If you bake at too low a temperature the raising agents will work but there will be insufficient heat to set the cake in its risen shape so that it will collapse and sink in the middle. Also a hard, sugary crust will form in the sunken shape.

As a general rule, the plainer or smaller the cake the hotter the oven should be. For larger or richer cakes the temperature will be reduced. Small cakes are baked in the hottest part of the oven, usually the top. Larger cakes, which require longer, slower cooking, are baked on the middle or lower shelves.

EQUIPMENT AND PREPARATION

When you have prepared the tin and heated the oven you can make the cake. For this you will need: measuring equipment, large mixing bowl, fine-meshed sieve, palette knife for cutting in the fat, metal spoon for folding in the milk and any additional ingredients, and a rubber spatula for scraping the prepared mixture into the bowl. Don't forget that you will also need oven gloves. (Those which have a magnet attached and can be fastened to the oven door save a frantic search for a glove at the vital moment when the cake is ready.) You also need a thin metal skewer for testing the cake and a wire rack or tray on which to cool the cake.

THE BASIC METHOD

Being organized is a great help towards good results so do all the weighing, measuring and any necessary preparation of additional ingredients such as fruit before you start to make the cake.

Always sift the flour together with the salt, powdered raising agents and any powdered flavourings such as spices, if used, into the mixing bowl. Sifting aerates the ingredients and ensures their even distribution.

Add the fat, which should be at room temperature, to the bowl and use a palette knife to cut it into the flour. When all the pieces of fat are pea sized and coated with flour, use your hands to rub the fat into the flour until the mixture resembles even-sized bread-crumbs. Remember that light stroking movements will give the best results. Lift the mixture high and let it trickle through your fingertips and fall back into the bowl.

Use a metal spoon to stir in the sugar. Make a hollow in the centre of the mixture, pour in the milk and add additional ingredients if used. Fold these ingredients into the rubbed-in mixture with a metal spoon. Use light, gentle movements to keep the mixture as airy as possible. On no account stir the mixture. Take the spoon right down to the bottom of the bowl, bring it up around the side of the bowl and then back to the centre, folding the mixture over (hence the technical term 'folding'). Repeat this action until the ingredients are just blended, and then stop: further folding would reduce the air content.

Scrape the mixture into the prepared tin with a rubber-bladed spatula. Plain cake mixtures are stiff and will not flow and adopt an even surface of their own accord. So use the spatula or the palette knife to smooth the top, making sure that the mixture is packed into the corners and sides of the tin before baking. If you are making a large cake, make a small hollow in the centre of the surface so that the cake will have an even surface when cooked.

MAKING PLAIN CAKES WITHOUT EGGS

1 Heat oven to recommended temperature. Sift flour, salt, powdered raising agents and any powdered flavourings into a mixing bowl. Sift all together to ensure an even distribution.

2 Cut fat into flour until the pieces are pea sized and coated with flour. Rub in until mixture resembles even-sized breadcrumbs, using the tips of your fingers.

3 Stir in sugar with a metal spoon. Make a hollow in the middle of the rubbed-in mixture, pour in milk and add any additional ingredients, if used.

4 To fold in the ingredients, use the spoon in a sweeping movement. Cut down to the bottom of bowl and bring spoon up round sides, using light gentle movements.

5 Fold again from the centre, turning the mixture over carefully. Do not use a stirring action. Stop when ingredients are incorporated as further folding would reduce the air content.

6 Scrape mixture into prepared tin and smooth the top. Make a slight hollow in the surface for large cakes so that it will be even when cooked. Bake.

7 At the end of baking time test by inserting a thin metal skewer into the middle of the cake. When ready it should come out clean with no hint of uncooked mixture on it.

8 Leave the cooked cake to stand in the tin to allow it to shrink away from the sides. Then run a palette knife around inside of rim between the lining paper and the tin.

9 Put a clean, dry tea-towel over the rack to avoid marking the surface of the cake. Turn the cake out, remove the lining paper and leave to cool completely.

At the end of baking time test that the cake is cooked by inserting a thin metal skewer into the middle of the cake – the skewer should come out clean.

Leave the cooked cake to stand in its tin for 3 minutes after it has come out of the oven to allow it to shrink slightly from the sides of the tin and to make turning out easier.

Run the palette knife around the inside rim of the tin to make sure that the cake is loose, then turn out on to a wire rack to cool.

SERVING SUGGESTIONS

Plain cakes made by the rubbing-in method are traditionally served un-decorated, simply cut into slices and spread with butter. This is particularly good if the cake is eaten while still slightly warm.

But there is no reason why you should not spend a little extra time to transform a plain cake into a more appealing 'special' treat. Allow the cake to become cold before decorating.

● Spread flavoured glacé icing thinly over the surface of the cooked cake. Edge the iced surface with crystallized fruit or whole nuts, or scatter slivers of stem ginger or chopped nuts over the surface.

STORING

Because of their crumbly, dry texture these cakes are best eaten really fresh and still warm from the oven. Should you be able to resist the temptation of eating it all at a sitting, a plain cake can be wrapped in greaseproof paper or kitchen foil and stored in an airtight tin or plastic box with a well-fitting lid for a maximum of 3 days.

These cakes should never be frozen because they become too dry.

Plain cakes are a family treat, eaten warm with butter. Date and walnut is deliciously moist because it contains treacle.

38

DATE AND WALNUT CAKE

Don't be deterred by the use of vinegar in this cake – it is added as a raising agent and not for flavouring purposes. The vinegar is added separately and last of all to prevent the possibility of it curdling the milk.

MAKES 900 G [1¾ lb] CAKE
125 g [4 oz] pressed dates
50 g [2 oz] walnuts
225 g [8 oz] plain flour
1 teaspoon bicarbonate of soda
pinch of salt
125 g [4 oz] butter or margarine
150 ml [¼ pt] milk
25 g [1 oz] black treacle
75 g [3 oz] caster sugar
2 tablespoons vinegar

1 Heat the oven to 170°C [325°F] Gas 3.
2 Grease and line a 15 cm [6 in] square tin and grease the paper.
3 Finely chop the dates and then chop the walnuts.
4 Sift the flour together with the bicarbonate of soda and salt into a large mixing bowl.
5 Add the fat and use a palette knife to cut it into the flour until the pieces are pea sized and coated with flour.
6 Rub the fat into the flour with your fingertips until the mixture resembles even-sized breadcrumbs.
7 Make a hollow in the centre of the mixture. Pour in the milk and add the treacle, sugar, dates and walnuts.
8 Using a metal spoon, fold the ingredients into the mixture until lightly blended. Add the vinegar then blend again. Do not stir.
9 Turn the mixture into the prepared tin. Bake for 1¼-1½ hours until a skewer inserted into the cake comes out clean.
10 Remove the cooked cake from the oven and allow to cool in the tin for 3 minutes.
11 Turn the cake on to a wire rack.
12 Remove the lining paper from the cake and serve warm or cold.

Variation
● For a currant and sultana cake use 75 g [3 oz] currants and 75 g [3 oz] sultanas plus 1 teaspoon mixed spice sifted with the flour.

DORSET APPLE CAKE

The juice which runs from the fruit during cooking makes this cake deliciously moist. Prepare the apples before you begin the cake.

This cake is particularly good if cut into wedges, while still slightly warm, and spread with cinnamon butter.

MAKES 700 G [1½ LB] CAKE
half a lemon
125 g [4 oz] cooking apples
225 g [8 oz] plain flour
2 teaspoons bicarbonate of soda
1 teaspoon cream of tartar
pinch of salt
125 g [4 oz] butter or margarine
125 g [4 oz] caster sugar
150 ml [¼ pt] milk

1 Heat the oven to 180°C [350°F] Gas 4.
2 Grease and line a 20 cm [8 in] sandwich tin. Grease the paper.
3 Grate the lemon zest.
4 Peel, core and chop the apples. Sprinkle the apples with a few drops of lemon juice to prevent discolouration.
5 Sift the flour, bicarbonate of soda, cream of tartar and salt into a bowl.
6 Add the fat and cut it into pea-sized pieces with a palette knife. Use your fingers to rub the fat into the flour until the mixture resembles even-sized breadcrumbs. Lightly stir in the sugar.
7 Make a hollow in the centre of the mixture and pour in the milk. Add prepared apples and lemon zest.
8 Fold in the ingredients with a metal spoon until just blended.
9 Scrape the mixture into the prepared tin and smooth over the top.
10 Bake the cake for 45 minutes until a skewer inserted into the cake comes out clean.
11 Allow the cooked cake to stand in the tin for 3 minutes then loosen and turn the cake on to a wire rack and leave to cool.

Variations
● Any fresh fruit may be substituted for the apples. Use an appropriate spice in place of the lemon zest.
● Use 125 g [4 oz] canned fruit, well-drained and chopped. For an extra special touch, replace 1 tablespoon milk with 1 tablespoon brandy, sherry or fruit-flavoured liqueur.

CARROT AND NUT CAKE

MAKES 16 SLICES

275 g [10 oz] plain flour
1 tablespoon baking powder
2 teaspoons ground mixed spice
125 g [4 oz] margarine
100 g [4 oz] shelled Brazil nuts, chopped
50 g [2 oz] pressed dates, chopped
175 g (6 oz) Muscovado sugar
120 ml [4 fl oz] unsweetened apple juice
225 g [8 oz] carrots, finely grated

For the decoration;
15 whole Brazil nuts
8 whole dried dates, halved and stoned
clear honey for glazing

1 Heat the oven to 180°C [350°F] Gas 4. Grease a deep 18 cm [7 in] square cake tin. Line the sides and base with greaseproof paper, then thoroughly grease the lining paper.

2 Sift the flour, baking powder and spice into a bowl. Add the margarine and use a palette knife to cut it into the flour until the pieces are pea sized and well coated with flour.

3 Rub the margarine into the flour with your fingertips until the mixture resembles even-sized breadcrumbs.

4 Make a hollow in the centre of the mixture. Fold in the nuts, dates, sugar and apple juice. Mix with a wooden spoon until well blended. Stir in the carrots, mixing well.

5 Turn the mixture into the prepared cake tin and level the surface. Arrange the whole Brazil nuts and halved dates in rows over the top.

6 Bake for about 1½ hours, or until a warm fine skewer inserted into the centre of the cake comes out clean. (Cover with greaseproof paper after 30 minutes baking to prevent overbrowning.)

7 Allow the cooked cake to stand in the tin for 15 minutes, then turn out of the tin and peel off the lining paper.

8 Place the cake the right way up on a large wire rack and brush the top with honey. Leave the cake to cool completely before cutting.

The Muscovado sugar for this Carrot and nut cake can be either the light or dark variety. The latter is sometimes called Barbados sugar.

ORANGE MARMALADE CAKE

This tasty, marmalade-topped cake is ideal for serving at tea time or coffee time. It has more sugar than fat, giving it a spongy texture.

MAKES 8-10 SLICES

250 g [9 oz] plain flour
1 teaspoon baking powder
½ teaspoon salt
½ teaspoon ground ginger
150 g [5 oz] caster sugar
100 g [4 oz] margarine, diced
200 g [7 oz] coarse cut orange marmalade
125 ml [4 fl oz] milk

1 Heat the oven to 190°C [375°F] Gas 5. Lightly grease a loose-based 18 cm [7 in] square tin, line sides and base with greaseproof paper, then grease the paper.

2 Sift the flour with the baking powder, salt and ginger into a bowl. Stir in the sugar. Add the margarine and use a palette knife to cut it into the flour until the pieces are pea sized and well coated with flour.

3 Rub the margarine into the flour with your fingertips until the mixture resembles even-sized breadcrumbs, then make a hollow in the centre.

4 Add 50 g [2 oz] marmalade and the milk and mix with a large metal spoon until thoroughly blended. Turn the mixture into the prepared tin and level the surface. Using a fork, gently spread the remaining marmalade over the top, to within 12 mm [½ in] of sides. (It will scorch if taken right to the edges.)

5 Bake the cake for 50-60 minutes, or until a warmed fine skewer inserted into the centre comes out with no uncooked cake mixture clinging to it. Cover the tin with greaseproof paper after 35 minutes baking to prevent the marmalade topping scorching.

6 Cool the cake for 5 minutes, then remove from the tin and carefully peel off the lining paper. Place the cake on a wire rack and leave to cool completely. The cake is ready for cutting once it is cold. For a more mellow flavour, wrap in foil and then store in an airtight container for 2-3 days (and up to 5 days).

Variations

● Try other marmalades, such as tangerine or lime. Ginger preserve can be used, but in this case omit the ground ginger. Plain wholemeal flour can replace the white flour and other ground spices, such as cinnamon, can be used instead of ginger.

Orange marmalade cake

8 Make a hollow in the centre of the mixture, add the sugar and milk and mix to a light and even consistency.
9 Turn into the prepared tin and smooth the surface.
10 Lightly press the prunes on top of the mixture, arranging them decoratively.
11 Spoon the butter mixture over the prunes. If the butter had begun to set, reheat it gently until runny.
12 Bake the cake in the oven for 40-45 minutes.
13 Use a skewer to test that the cake is cooked.
14 Allow the cooked cake to cool slightly before turning out on to a wire rack.
15 Remove the lining paper while the cake is still warm, cut into slices and serve immediately.

Variation

● For an apricot and almond cake , replace the prunes and walnuts. Pour boiling water over 125 g [4 oz] dried apricots and soak for two hours in a small saucepan. Bring the soaking liquid to the boil and simmer for 15 minutes, then drain. Replace the cinnamon with mixed spice and top the cake with apricots and flaked almonds.

HONEY TEA-BREAD

Here is an old-fashioned favourite with the sweet flavour of honey and a hint of spices.

MAKES 700 G [1½ LB] CAKE
225 g [8 oz] plain flour
½ teaspoon ground cinnamon
½ teaspoon mixed spice
1 teaspoon baking powder
pinch of salt
90 g [3½ oz] butter or margarine
50 g [2 oz] soft brown sugar
150 ml [¼ pt] milk
100 g [4 oz] clear honey
75 g [3 oz] finely chopped mixed peel
flaked almonds, to decorate (optional)

1 Heat the oven to 170°C [325°F] Gas 3.
2 Grease and line the base of a 20 × 10 cm [8 × 4 in] loaf tin and grease the paper.
3 Sift the flour, spices, baking powder and salt into a mixing bowl.
4 Using a round-bladed knife, cut the fat into the flour. Then rub it in with your fingertips until the mixture resembles even-sized breadcrumbs.

Alsace cake has a rich prune topping to contrast with the plain cake mixture underneath. Use canned prunes or substitute dried prunes, soaked and cooked. The ingredients for the topping are prepared before the cake is made so that there is the minimum of delay in getting it into the oven. The cake mixture itself is plain so a slightly higher than usual oven temperature is used.

ALSACE CAKE

MAKES 1 KG [2 LB] CAKE
For the topping:
425 g [15½ oz] canned prunes
50 g [2 oz] walnuts
25 g [1 oz] butter
¼ teaspoon ground cinnamon

For the cake:
225 g [8 oz] plain flour
1 teaspoon baking powder
½ teaspoon salt
100 g [4 oz] butter or margarine
225 g [8 oz] caster sugar
6 tablespoons milk

1 Heat the oven to 190°C [375°F] Gas 5.
2 Grease and line a 19 cm [7½ in] square tin and grease the paper.
3 Drain, stone and chop the prunes and set aside.
4 Chop the walnuts.
5 To make the topping, melt the butter gently in a small heavy-based saucepan. Remove from heat and stir in the cinnamon and walnuts.
6 Sift the flour, baking powder and salt into a bowl.
7 Using a round-bladed knife, cut the fat into the flour and then rub in with your fingertips.

5 Make a hollow in the centre and lightly and evenly fold in the sugar, milk, honey and mixed peel.

6 Scrape the mixture into the prepared tin with a spatula and smooth the surface.

7 Scatter the flaked almonds over the top if liked.

8 Bake the cake for 1¾-2 hours. Use a skewer to test whether the cake is cooked after 1¾ hours.

9 Remove the cake from the oven and leave in the tin for 3 minutes before turning out on to a wire rack. Serve either warm or cold.

Variation

●For banana honey cake, a deliciously moist variation, simply replace the peel with 125 g [4 oz] mashed bananas.

BOODLES RAISIN CAKE

This raisin cake contains a higher proportion of sugar, which gives it a spongy texture.

MAKES ABOUT 18 SLICES

450 g [1 lb] plain flour
3½ teaspoons baking powder
100 g [4 oz] margarine
225 g [8 oz] soft brown sugar
finely grated zest of 1 orange
450 g [1 lb] raisins, chopped
275 ml [½ pt] milk

1 Heat the oven to 170°C [325°F] Gas 3. Grease and line a deep 20 cm [8 in] round cake tin and grease the paper.

2 Sift the flour and baking powder into a large bowl. Add the margarine and use a palette knife to cut it into the flour until the pieces are pea sized and well coated with flour.

3 Rub the margarine into the flour with your fingertips until the mixture resembles even-sized breadcrumbs.

4 Make a hollow in the centre of the mixture. Stir in the sugar, orange zest and raisins, then gradually stir in the milk to make a stiff mixture.

5 Turn into the prepared tin and level the surface. Bake for 2¼ hours, or until golden and firm to the touch.

6 Turn the cake out onto a wire rack and peel off the paper. Leave to cool.

This fruit cake is a version of one that was served many years ago at Boodles club in London. The original fruit cake used to be served to club members with port at the end of a large lunch or dinner – the cake was intended to help absorb the excess alcohol!

PLAIN CAKES WITH EGGS

A dd eggs to plain cake mixtures and introduce richness and flavour to scrumptious large cakes and traditional buns and small individual cakes.

Now that you have learnt how very easy it is to make plain cakes without eggs (pages 32-43), plain cakes with eggs will be a simple triumph. Plain cakes with eggs are made by the same method and use the same ingredients, the only basic difference being the addition of eggs.

THE EFFECTS OF USING EGGS

Eggs immediately enrich a cake and give it a pleasant yellow colour. They also increase the food value because the fat in the yolk enriches the mixture. An added bonus to making

Fruit and nuts can be added to plain cakes with eggs, follow the outlines of proportions given in the chart on page 46.

plain cakes with eggs is that, because they are richer and therefore moister, they are less inclined to dry out. The eggs actually improve the cake's keeping qualities, so that you can bake a cake the day before it is required.

Eggs also act as a raising agent, trapping the air when they are beaten so that the cake will be good and light in texture. It is possible to make cakes using wholemeal flour if eggs are also included, because the eggs, together with the normal raising agents (baking powder, bicarbonate of soda and cream of tartar) can 'hold' the heavier flour much better.

INGREDIENTS

Ingredients, their preparation and uses for cake making are explained on page 32. For richer, moister cakes there are some modifications and exceptions to those instructions.

Flour

Like plain cakes without eggs, plain cakes with eggs require a 'soft' flour, that is, one that has a low gluten content to give the cake an even texture. (Gluten gives the dough elasticity – a property required more in bread making than in cakes.)

Plain white flour is suitable or even a mixture of plain flour and cornflour or plain flour and ground rice. The use of cornflour or ground rice gives a softer texture to the cake. When using cornflour or ground rice reduce the amount of flour used and make up the weight with one part cornflour or ground rice to seven parts flour.

Self-raising and wholemeal flour can be used, although they are not usually as effective because of the necessary adjustment of the raising agents. Never use strong flour as this will result in a heavy-textured cake that looks unattractive and will perhaps be inedible.

The flour you use (except for wholemeal) must be sifted before use. Wholemeal flour is only sifted when it is combined with a dry flavouring such as a ground spice. Sift the flour with the raising agent, salt and any spices used. When sifting wholemeal, stir the bran left in the sieve back into the flour.

Eggs

Eggs should always be as fresh as possible and used at room tempera-

ture. If you store your eggs in a refrigerator, remove them from the refrigerator at least one hour before using. Always use medium-sized eggs unless otherwise stated in a recipe. Beat lightly with a fork and add the eggs before the specified amount of liquid.

Liquid

The amount of liquid to be added will depend on the amount of fat used. It will also depend on any other 'runny' substances which are to be included, such as honey, syrups or jams. Milk is the best liquid to use as it increases the food value and the flavour, but an equal quantity of milk and water is an effective and cheaper alternative. The liquid is added to the mixture last of all.

As all the ingredients form such an integral part of each recipe, it is difficult to give specific proportions or the size and exact quantity of cakes the mixture will yield. The chart gives a general guide to proportions. Broadly speaking, a mixture made with 225 g [8 oz] flour will make one 15 cm [6 in] or 18 cm [7 in] cake or 6 to 8 small cakes.

Consistency

The main difference between a mixture intended for a large cake and one intended for small cakes (that is, buns baked on a baking sheet) is the consistency. This is determined by the amount of liquid included and must be varied to suit the type of cake you are making.

Unlike buns on a baking sheet, large cakes are shaped by the tin in which they are baked. A moist consistency, which gives maximum richness to the cake, is therefore possible. Small cakes may, of course, be baked in deep bun tins, when a moist consistency is feasible. The moulds will retain the spread of the mixture while cooking, and so the cakes will rise rather than spread outwards. However, cakes (buns) that are to be baked on a baking tray or sheet need to be of a stiffer consistency, because they are in no way contained and they might otherwise spread sideways while cooking, instead of rising.

A soft consistency is one that will easily drop off the spoon (moist but never runny or wet). A soft consistency is necessary for a large cake cooked in a tin. A stiffer consistency (made by adding less liquid) is one that will cling

Fruit purées

Fruit purées will add extra moisture to the cake mixture, but they are considerably stiffer than a liquid, and vary in stiffness according to the fruit and cooking method. Do not, therefore, simply replace the stated liquid element by purée. Omit the liquid and add the purée by degrees, a little at a time, checking on the consistency after each spoonful is incorporated. As soon as the correct consistency is reached, stop adding the purée.

Creating your own variations

By doing your sums correctly, you can use the flavouring ideas for large and small cakes. All these recipe ideas are based on 225 g [8 oz] flour, 75 g [3 oz] fat, 75 g [3 oz] sugar, 2 medium-sized eggs, 75-150 ml [3-5 fl oz] liquid and baking powder.

• For cherry cake wash 100 g [4 oz] glacé cherries and dry them on kitchen paper. Cut the cherries into quarters and dust lightly with a little flour to prevent them sinking to the bottom of the cake and ensure even distribution. Add them to the cake mixture after the sugar.

• For coconut cake replace 50 g [2 oz] of the flour with the same weight of desiccated coconut. This gives a lovely chewy texture.

• For coffee cake replace 2 tablespoons of the flour with instant coffee powder; sift flour and coffee powder together with 2 teaspoons of ground mixed spice. Add 50 g [2 oz] currants after the sugar.

• For chocolate cake replace 2 tablespoons of the flour with cocoa powder. Sift flour and cocoa powder with 1 teaspoon ground cinnamon. Add 50 g [2 oz] raisins after the sugar.

• Make citrus cake by adding the finely grated zest from 1 large orange or 2 medium-sized lemons, after the sugar. The lemon rind together with the egg gives this version a lovely sunny yellow colour.

• Make fresh fruit cake with oranges, pineapple, apricots, pears, apples or strawberries. Add 75 ml [3 fl oz] thick fruit purée after adding the sugar. For large cakes, 150 ml [¼ pt] of fruit purée must be added.

• For walnut and honey cake, finely chop 50 g [2 oz] walnuts and add these after the sugar. Warm a jar of clear honey and spoon 4 tablespoons honey, into the mixture after the walnuts.

to a spoon. This consistency is needed for small cakes not contained by a tin.

Flavouring the mixture

Any liquid or dry flavouring ingredient, added to the basic mixture, will alter the proportions and therefore the consistency of the mixture. When experimenting with your own combinations, follow the outlines of proportions given in the chart, but make the adjustments suggested in the following paragraphs, to maintain the basic balance.

Liquid

Liquid flavourings such as coffee essence, fruit juice, honey, treacle and syrup must be deducted from the liquid allowance. For example, if you add 50 ml [2 fl oz] of honey to 225 g [8 oz] flour, add only 25 ml [1 fl oz] milk for small cakes or 75 ml [3 fl oz] milk for large cakes.

Dry ingredients

Spices will not affect the consistency as they are added in relatively small quantities. However instant coffee, cocoa powder and desiccated coconut are added in accountable amounts that will affect the basic balance of the recipe. Their weight must therefore be deducted from the total amount of flour used.

EQUIPMENT

Equipment for cake making is described on page 10. Useful additions to this list are a spoon or fork for mixing small cakes. A large spoon is also handy for spooning the stiffer mixture (for small cakes) on to a baking sheet or tray. A second spoon will help to push the mixture off the first, on to the baking sheet or tray.

1 Heat oven to recommended temperature. Sift flour, salt, powdered raising agent and any powdered flavourings together.

5 Continue adding milk until the correct consistency is reached. A stiff mixture is needed for small cakes which are not baked in a tin.

Baking tins

Information on choosing and preparing tins for large cakes in round tins is covered on pages 8 and 9. Square, oblong and loaf tins are covered on page 35.

Remember that all tins must be greased and the bases and sides lined and re-greased. Loaf tins are greased but only the base is lined and re-greased.

Baking trays and sheets

Baking trays have raised edges on every side. Baking sheets have at least

BASIC PROPORTIONS FOR CAKES WITH EGGS

	Large cakes	Small cakes
flour (plain or wholemeal)	225 g [8 oz]	225 g [8 oz]
baking powder	2 teaspoons	2 teaspoons
salt	pinch	pinch
fat	50-75 g [2-3 oz]	50-75 g [2-3 oz]
sugar	50-75 g [2-3 oz]	50-75 g [2-3 oz]
fruit, nuts or other flavourings	50-100 g [2-4 oz]	50-100 g [2-4 oz]
eggs	1-2 medium-sized	1-2 medium-sized
liquid	150 ml [¼ pt]	75 ml [3 fl oz]

MAKING SMALL PLAIN CAKES WITH EGGS

2 Cut fat into flour until the pieces are pea-sized and coated with flour. Rub in until mixture resembles even-sized breadcrumbs.

3 Stir in sugar. Make a hollow in centre of the mixture and add lightly beaten egg. Stir into mixture, using a metal spoon.

4 Stir in milk, a spoonful at a time. Pull the mixture in from the sides of the bowl and work it into a stiff mixture with the spoon.

6 Place 6-8 spoonfuls of mixture on to prepared baking tray or sheet, spacing them 4 cm [1½ in] apart to allow for spreading. Bake.

7 At the end of baking time cakes should be browned and firm to the touch. Allow them to rest on the baking tray for 5 minutes.

8 Slide cakes on to a wire rack and leave to cool. The cakes may be eaten warm or left until completely cold. Serve split and buttered.

one edge with a raised side so theoretically the cooked cakes are easier to slide off. In practice, a baking tray is equally suitable, if you use it upside down. Make sure baking sheets or trays are adequately greased but there is no need to line with greaseproof paper.

Sheets or trays must be made of metal for adequate heat conduction. Ovenproof glass trays won't conduct the heat properly and will therefore result in a cake that is undercooked at the bottom. If you used glass and increased the length of cooking time, the results would still not be up to

standard as it is essential the cake mixture is immediately 'set' when it goes into the oven.

As a general rule, small cakes made with 225 g [8 oz] flour mixture will fit on to a 30 × 35 cm [12 × 14 in] baking sheet or tray, allowing enough room for the cakes to spread slightly.

OVEN TEMPERATURES

The basic importance of the correct oven temperature is discussed on page 36. Heat the oven 10 to 15 minutes beforehand and check that the shelf is

HANDY HINT

Freezing plain cakes
To freeze a baked cake, wrap tightly in freezer wrap as soon as it is completely cold and store in freezer for up to 6 months.

positioned in the right place before setting the oven. Changing a shelf position, once the oven is heated, can be tricky.

Large cakes cook best on the middle or just below middle shelf, while small cakes cook best on the middle or just above middle shelf. The oven temperature affects the final result of the cake, so it is essential that it is correct.

Small cakes need a hot oven 200°C [400°F] Gas 6, and should be baked for approximately 15 minutes. Large cakes are usually baked at 180°C [350°F] Gas 4. If the oven is too cool, a large cake will be close textured and heavy with a hard crust. It will possibly have sunk in the centre.

Small cakes, cooked in a cool oven will simply lose their shape, spread and run together. On the other hand, a scorching hot oven will cause large cakes to crack and form peaks, while small cakes will dry out and burn very quickly.

MAKING LARGE PLAIN CAKES WITH EGGS

Large cakes with eggs are made exactly like plain cakes without eggs. Follow the step by step instructions given on page 37 up to step 3. Then lightly beat the egg and add it after the sugar but before the milk.

Add sufficient liquid to obtain a soft, dropping consistency, that is, one that will drop off the spoon without any prompting. A mixture with insufficient liquid will result in a dry cake. Too much liquid, on the other hand, will result in an unbalanced consistency; the cake could take anything up to twice as long to cook.

MAKING SMALL PLAIN CAKES WITH EGGS

Position the oven shelf just above the centre of the oven and heat the oven to 200°C [400°F] Gas 6. Grease a baking sheet or tray with melted fat.

Make small plain cakes with eggs in the same way as described for large cakes, using the same quantities, to the point where the liquid is added. Stir in the lightly beaten egg and then add only sufficient liquid to obtain a stiff consistency, that is, one that will stick to the fork.

Using a tablespoon, scoop the cake mixture out of the bowl (roughly dividing it into six or eight) and, using a second tablespoon or your clean finger, push the mixture from the spoon on to the prepared baking sheet or tray. Take care to space each dollop of mixture about 4 cm [1½ in] apart on the baking tray or sheet. This spacing allows for expansion of the cakes as they cook.

In most cases a ragged appearance is part of their charm, so there is no need to smooth over the cake mixture on the tray. However small cakes with a smooth appearance can be achieved by shaping spoonfuls of the cake mixture into smooth balls with lightly floured hands.

Place the baking sheet or tray in the centre or just above centre oven and bake. The cakes are cooked when they are pale golden brown and feel firm to the touch. Remove cakes from the oven and leave on the tray for 5 minutes to rest. If you fail to rest the cakes they could disintegrate. After the brief cooling period, slide the cakes, using a palette knife, fish slice or spatula, on to a wire cake rack. The cakes may then be eaten warm or left until completely cold.

SERVING, STORING AND FREEZING

The addition of eggs to plain cakes means that the baked cake may be kept for up to 4 days if wrapped in greaseproof paper or foil and stored in an airtight tin or plastic box with a well-fitting lid. However, they are at their best if eaten warm or as soon as they are cold, then buttered. For special occasions, split and fill with fresh whipped cream and jam.

ROCK CAKES

MAKES 6-8 CAKES

225 g [8oz] plain flour
2 teaspoons baking powder
pinch of salt
½ teaspoon mixed spice
½ teaspoon freshly grated nutmeg
50 g [2 oz] butter
25 g [1oz] lard
75 g [3 oz] soft brown or white sugar
25 g [1 oz] chopped mixed peel
75 g [3 oz] mixed dried fruit
grated zest of half a lemon
1 medium-sized egg
150 ml [¼ pt] milk

1 Position oven shelf to just above

Adding liquid

As soon as the liquid is added to the dry ingredients, the cake(s) should be baked. If for some reason this can't be done, place the mixture in the bottom of the refrigerator. The cold will inhibit the raising agent. Don't delay baking for more than one hour.

centre and heat the oven to 200°C [400°F] Gas 6. Grease a 30 × 35 cm [12 × 14 in] baking sheet or tray.

2 Sift the flour, baking powder, salt and mixed spice into a large mixing bowl. Lightly stir in nutmeg.

3 Add the fats, cut into pea-sized pieces with a palette knife. Then rub in lightly until the mixture resembles even-sized breadcrumbs.

4 Using a fork, stir in sugar, mixed peel, dried fruit and lemon zest. Beat the egg in a cup with a fork and stir into the mixture.

5 Add the milk, a spoonful at a time, stirring and checking the consistency. Stop when the mixture binds together but still has a stiff consistency.

6 Roughly divide the mixture into six to eight portions in the bowl. Place spoonfuls of the mixture on to the prepared baking sheet or tray, spacing them 4 cm [1½ in] apart to allow for spreading.

7 Bake for 15 minutes or until cakes are pale golden brown and firm to the touch.

8 Remove from the oven and leave to cool for 5 minutes, on baking tray or sheet. Transfer to a wire rack and leave until warm or, if you prefer, cold.

Variations

● For ginger date cakes, replace the peel and dried fruit with 15 g [½ oz] finely chopped crystallized ginger and 90 g [3½ oz] chopped, stoned dates.

● For chocolate walnut cakes, replace 25 g [1 oz] of the flour with the same amount of cocoa powder. Omit the spices and lemon zest. Replace the fruit and peel with 100 g [4 oz] finely chopped walnuts. Add ½ teaspoon vanilla essence after the sugar.

RASPBERRY BUNS

MAKES 8 BUNS
225 g [8 oz] plain flour
2 teaspoons baking powder
pinch of salt
75 g [3 oz] margarine or butter
75g [3 oz] caster sugar
1 medium-sized egg
approximately 75 ml [3 fl oz] milk
3 tablespoons raspberry jam
1 small egg

1 Position the oven shelf to just above centre of oven and heat oven to 200°C [400°F] Gas 6. Grease a 30 × 35 cm [12 × 14 in] baking tray.

2 Sift flour, baking powder and salt into a large mixing bowl.

3 Add the fat and cut into pea-sized pieces using a palette knife. Rub in lightly until the mixture resembles even-sized breadcrumbs.

4 Stir in sugar. Beat the medium-sized egg in a cup with a fork and stir into the mixture.

5 Add the milk, a spoonful at a time, stirring and checking the consistency. Stop when the mixture binds together but still has a stiff consistency.

6 With lightly floured hands, divide the mixture into eight equal-sized pieces. Shape into smooth balls.

7 Make a hole in the centre of the top by gently pushing a clean, lightly floured finger or wooden spoon handle, two-thirds of the way down into the ball. On no account pierce the bottom of the bun.

8 Using a small spoon, spoon a little jam into each hole. Close up the hole by pinching the edges together to enclose the jam.

9 Place buns, jam hole facing downwards, on prepared baking tray, spacing them 4 cm [1½ in] apart to allow for spreading during cooking.

10 Beat the small egg in a bowl with a fork and brush each bun with beaten egg to glaze.

11 Bake for 15 minutes or until buns are golden brown, shiny and firm to the touch.

12 Remove buns from oven and leave to cool on tray for 5 minutes. Then transfer to a wire rack and leave to cool.

Variations

● For apricot buns, use thick apricot purée (made with dried apricots) to fill the buns instead of jam.

● For pineapple buns, place a small cube of fresh or drained, canned pineapple in each hole instead of the jam.

● For apple cinnamon buns, peel and core a medium-sized apple. Cut flesh into small pieces and dip into lemon juice to prevent discolouration. Place a piece of apple in each hole and sprinkle with a little ground cinnamon before closing the holes.

These traditional Rock cakes and Raspberry buns are best served fresh from the oven. Although raspberry is the traditional jam for these buns, you can use other flavours if wished.

WHOLEMEAL DATE LOAF

This wholesome tea-bread is made with wholemeal flour. Bake it in an 18 cm [7 in] round, deep cake tin.

MAKES ONE 900 G [2 LB] LOAF
125 g [4 oz] stoned dates
50 g [2 oz] walnuts
450 g [1 lb] plain wholemeal flour
5 teaspoons baking powder
1 tablespoon salt
½ teaspoon mixed spice
175 g [6 oz] butter or margarine
175 g [6 oz] caster sugar
2 medium-sized eggs
approximately 275 ml [½ pt] milk

1 Position the shelf just below centre of oven and heat the oven to 180°C [350°F] Gas 4. Grease the tin, then line and re-grease the base of a 900 g [2 lb] loaf tin.
2 Finely chop dates and walnuts.
3 Sift the flour, baking powder, salt and spice into a large, warmed mixing bowl. Tip any bran left in the sieve into the bowl and stir in.
4 Add the fat, cut into pea-sized pieces then rub in until the mixture resembles even-sized breadcrumbs.
5 Using a wooden spoon, stir in sugar, dates and walnuts.
6 Beat the eggs together in a cup with a fork and stir into the mixture.
7 Add the milk, a little at a time, stirring and checking the consistency. Stop when the mixture will easily drop from the spoon.
8 Using a spatula, scrape the mixture into the prepared tin and smooth top with the back of a metal spoon. Make a hollow in centre of cake to allow for rising.
9 Bake for 2 hours, or until a fine, warmed skewer inserted into the centre of the loaf comes out clean.
10 Remove from oven and leave to cool for 5 minutes.
11 Put a wire rack over top of cake and invert on to rack. Carefully remove tin. Peel off lining paper and leave to cool.

Variations

● For a banana loaf, replace the dates and walnuts with 450 g [1 lb] ripe, mashed bananas. Add this after the eggs with milk, if necessary, a little at a time and stop when the consistency is right.

● For a marmalade loaf, replace the dates and walnuts with 125 g [4 oz] thick-cut marmalade and the grated zest of one orange or one large lemon or lime. Add more milk, a spoonful at a time, if necessary.

● For hazelnut loaf, replace the dates and walnuts with 125 g [4 oz] chopped hazelnuts. Check that the consistency of the mixture is correct, gradually adding more milk, a spoonful at a time, if necessary.

CARAWAY CAKE

This traditional seed cake has a characteristic flavour of its own and an attractive speckled appearance.

MAKES ONE 700 G [1½ LB] CAKE
350 g [12 oz] plain flour
1 tablespoon baking powder

¼ teaspoon salt
125 g [4½ oz] margarine or butter
125 g [4½ oz] caster sugar
40 g [1½ oz] caraway seeds
2 medium-sized eggs
approximately 150 ml [¼ pt] milk

1 Position the shelf in the middle of the oven and heat the oven to 180°C [350°F] Gas 4.
2 Grease, line and re-grease an 18 cm [7 in] round, deep cake tin.
3 Sift the flour, baking powder and salt together into a large, warmed mixing bowl.
4 Add the fat, cut it into pea-sized pieces and rub in until the mixture resembles even-sized breadcrumbs.
5 Stir in the sugar and caraway seeds using a wooden spoon. Beat the eggs together in a cup with a fork and stir into the mixture.

6 Add sufficient milk, a tablespoonful at a time, stirring and checking consistency. Stop when the mixture drops easily from the spoon.
7 Using a spatula, scrape the mixture into the prepared tin and smooth the top with the back of a metal spoon. Make a hollow in centre of cake to allow for rising. (Making a slight hollow in the centre of the cake before baking ensures that the cake does not rise in a peak.)
8 Bake for 1½ hours, or until a fine, warmed skewer inserted into the centre of the cake comes out clean.
9 Remove from the oven and leave cake to cool in tin for 5 minutes.
10 Put a wire rack over the top of the cake and invert tin and rack. Place the rack on work surface. Gently and carefully remove tin. Peel off the lining paper and leave the cake to cool.

Caraway cake and Wholemeal date loaf are delicious tea-time treats.

51

FAMILY FRUIT CAKE

MAKES 8 SLICES

225 g [8 oz] self-raising flour
pinch of salt
150 g [5 oz] margarine, diced
100 g [4 oz] caster sugar
200 g [7 oz] dried mixed fruit
2 medium-sized eggs, lightly beaten
2-3 tablespoons milk

1 Heat the oven to 180°C [350°F] Gas 4. Grease a deep 18 cm [7 in] round tin. Line the sides and base with greaseproof paper, then grease the lining paper lightly.
2 Sift the flour and salt into a bowl. Add the margarine and rub it in with your fingertips, then stir in the sugar and dried fruit. Make a hollow in the centre.
3 Add the eggs and 2 tablespoons milk. Mix together with a fork, adding the remaining milk if necessary to give the mixture a dropping consistency. (To test the consistency, take some of the cake mixture on a spoon. Hold the spoon on its side and tap the handle gently against the rim of the bowl. The mixture should drop easily. If too stiff, add a little more milk and test again.)
4 Turn mixture into prepared tin and level the surface, then make a shallow hollow in the centre. Bake for about

Family fruit cake will keep for up to 2 weeks wrapped in kitchen foil or cling film in an airtight container.

1 hour, or until a warmed skewer inserted into the centre comes out clean.
5 Cool the cake for 10 minutes, then turn out of tin and peel off lining paper. Turn cake the right way up and leave on a wire rack to cool completely.

FRUITY SLAB CAKE

MAKES 12 SQUARES

350 g [12 oz] plain flour
1 tablespoon baking powder
1 teaspoon ground mixed spice
1 teaspoon salt
150 g [5 oz] margarine or butter, diced
150 g [5 oz] granulated sugar
100 g [4 oz] mixed dried fruit
50 g [2 oz] cut mixed peel
1 teaspoon black treacle
2 medium-sized eggs
225 ml [8 fl oz] milk

1 Heat the oven to 180°C [350°F] Gas 4. Lightly brush the inside of a shallow 27 × 18 cm [11 × 7 in] cake tin with melted margarine. Line the base and sides with greaseproof paper so that the paper extends about 2.5 cm [1 in] above the sides of the tin. Brush the paper with more melted margarine.
2 Sift the flour, baking powder, spice and salt into a large bowl. Add the margarine and rub it in with your

fingertips until the mixture resembles fine breadcrumbs.

3 Stir in the sugar, dried fruit, peel and treacle. Beat the eggs and milk together, then gradually stir them into the mixture, to give a soft dropping consistency.

4 Turn the mixture into the tin and level the surface. Bake for 45-50 minutes until golden and firm to the touch and a skewer inserted in the centre comes out clean.

5 Holding the greaseproof firmly, lift the cake on to a wire rack. When cool, but not cold, turn it over on to your hand and quickly peel off the greaseproof paper. Return the cake to the rack, the right way up.

6 Leave on the wire rack until cold, then serve cut into squares.

ICED APPLECAKE

MAKES 6-8 SLICES

225 g [8 oz] plain flour
2 teaspoons baking powder
½ teaspoon salt
75 g [3 oz] margarine or butter, diced
100 g [4 oz] caster sugar
50 g [2 oz] currants
1 medium-sized egg, lightly beaten
100 ml [3½ fl oz] milk

To finish:
2 dessert apples
25 g [1 oz] butter, melted
50 g [2 oz] caster sugar
¼ teaspoon ground cloves
50 g [2 oz] icing sugar, sifted
2-3 teaspoons lemon juice or water

1 Heat the oven to 200°C [400°F] Gas 6. Generously grease a loose-based, deep 20 cm [8 in] round cake tin.

2 Sift the flour, baking powder and salt into a bowl. Add the margarine and rub it in with your fingertips, then stir in the sugar and currants. Make a well in the centre.

3 Pour in the egg and milk and stir with a fork until evenly mixed. Turn the mixture into the prepared tin and level the surface.

4 Peel, quarter and core then thinly slice the apples. (Try to make the slices as even as possible and arrange them neatly, otherwise the finished cake will not look quite so attractive.) Arrange the slices, overlapping, in circles on top of cake mixture. Brush the apples with melted butter, then sprinkle with the caster sugar and ground cloves.

5 Bake the cake for about 50 minutes, until firm to the touch at the centre. Cool the cake for 5 minutes, then remove from the tin and place on a wire rack with a plate or tray underneath.

6 Blend the icing sugar with just enough lemon juice to give a smooth, thick icing. Using a metal spoon, drizzle the icing over the top of the cake, allowing it to run down the sides a little.

7 Leave the icing to set before cutting the cake into 6-8 wedges. The cake is best eaten while still warm. (It becomes less light and more crumbly as it cools.) The cake can also be served hot from the oven as a pudding, accompanied by custard or cream. In which case, omit the icing sugar and lemon juice.

Iced applecake can be eaten as a tea-time cake or a pudding.

YEAST CAKES

The short-time method is by far the easiest way of making bread. This same method can be applied to cake making. Yeast cakes are not just enriched forms of bread. They have all the qualities that you expect from a cake made in the usual way, but yeast is the raising agent not baking powder.

The name yeast cake suggests to most people, traditional tea-breads and buns. A true yeast cake, however, is neither of these. It is more like a traditional sponge cake, but still has something of the flavour and texture of a yeast-risen mixture.

A short-time enriched bread can be made by increasing the quantity of fat and by adding eggs but a yeast cake is more than this. It can best be described as a true cake, intended to be eaten on its own, and not a bread that would be eaten with other foods.

Yeast cakes are enriched by adding extra ingredients, chosen for their individual flavours and characteristics. These enrichments have the effect of softening the dough and, as a result, the yeast cake has a texture of a cake, rather than that of a bread.

BASIC INGREDIENTS

Flour

Strong plain flour is often used, as this gives both a good volume and texture to a yeast cake. Strong flour is rich in gluten and this will stretch and hold the valuable air bubbles. This gluten is strengthened by the kneading that is part of making most yeast doughs and helps to ensure an even rise. Plain flour may also be used.

A proportion of one of the brown flours can be used with strong white flour. The inclusion of brown flour will add variety and give interesting flavour combinations. Do not, however, use all brown flour, as the resulting cake would be extremely heavy with a close texture.

Other cereals

Certain cereals can be substituted for a proportion of the flour, to vary both flavour and texture. There are certain points to remember when using other cereals than wheat. One of the most important is that the additional cereals must be carefully measured and must replace a proportion of the wheat flour. Never substitute any cereal for the total weight of flour and never include the cereal in addition to the total weight of flour. Always remember to measure and calculate amounts, if you are altering a recipe to include any of the following cereals. Any miscalculation would produce an unbalanced effect.

The proportion of each cereal that you can use with strong plain flour is given below. Using more of these cereals would result in a heavy cake that would fail to rise properly. You can, of course, use less of the cereal than the proportion given here – and this will give a less pronounced flavour.

Oats add interest to a yeast cake, but as they contain very little gluten they should only be added in small quantities and only when you are using a strong plain flour. The proportion to use is up to 100 g [4 oz] to every 450 g [1 lb] of strong plain flour used.

Barley is coarsely ground to make a wholemeal flour called barley meal. This can be used in the preparation of certain yeast cakes. Use up to 175 g [6 oz] of barley meal per 450 g [1 lb] strong plain flour.

Rye flour when used in a yeast cake produces a close texture and, as a rule, makes the cake dry out rather quickly. Therefore, when rye flour is used in a recipe, precautions must be taken against the yeast cake drying out. Make sure that the fat content is always above 50 g [2 oz] per 450 g [1 lb] of mixed flours. The proportion of rye flour to use is up to 175 g [6 oz] per 450 g [1 lb] strong plain flour.

Semolina is a wheat product. It is the grains of wheat that are left after the sifting process known as bolting. Use up to 175 g [6 oz] semolina per 450 g [1 lb] strong plain flour.

Yeast and ascorbic acid

The raising agent for yeast cakes, as their name indicates, is yeast, either fresh or dried. The use of yeast as the raising agent distinguishes yeast cakes from cakes in which the raising agents are baking powder and/or eggs. Ascorbic acid is often used to speed up the raising processes when fresh yeast is used. The proportion is usually 25 g [1 oz] fresh yeast and 25 mg ascorbic acid per 225g [8 oz] flour but may vary according to individual recipes.

Liquid

Sufficient liquid must be added to bind the dry ingredients together. The amount of liquid used varies because the dough consistency alters according to the recipe used. As a rule, the liquid should never be more than 150 ml [¼ pt] per 225 g [8 oz] of whatever flour you use. This amount of liquid is generally enough to make a soft dough. You must remember that other enriching ingredients, such as eggs, will also provide a certain amount of liquid. The amount of liquid necessary will depend on the kind of flour and dry ingredients that are being used. Wholemeal and brown flours always absorb more liquid and, when they are combined with dry flavouring ingredients, they require a larger amount of liquid to bind them and make a manageable dough.

When the liquid is added, care must be taken to ensure that it is warm. This is necessary to help the yeast rise, giving it that warm atmosphere in which to grow and complete the work of raising the dough.

There are no hard and fast rules when it comes to deciding on what liquid to use. Warm water, milk or a mixture of the two are traditional, but others may be used quite satisfactorily. When you are feeling extravagant, top-of-the-milk or a thin cream can be used. These may be used in conjunction with warm water or milk but it is inadvisable to use all top-of-the-milk or cream, as they do not have the binding qualities that are essential.

Fruit-filled Savarin makes a delicious dessert – vary the fruit according to availability.

Use half water and cream or half milk and cream. Buttermilk, soured milk and plain yoghurt and soured cream, will give a richer flavour and texture.

Fats

Among other things, fats delay staling, and they are used in very small amounts in a short-time bread dough. For enriched dough the amount is increased and for a cake it is increased again.

Butter gives the best flavour, but butter and margarine or all margarine can be used successfully. Never use lard or dripping unless the recipe directs.

The maximum amount of fat to use is 225 g [8 oz] of fat per 450 g [1 lb] flour. This should be at room temperature, so remove from the refrigerator 30 minutes before it is required.

Eggs

Eggs are added to make an enriched yeast dough. For a yeast cake you will need more eggs than are necessary for an enriched bread. Eggs add colour, taste and enrich; they also help in the raising of the cake. Always use medium sized eggs (unless the recipe says otherwise), at room temperature. If you store eggs in the refrigerator, remove them at least one hour before they are required.

Sweeteners

High concentrations of sugar are never added directly to yeast, as this has the effect of killing off some of the yeast cells. Nevertheless, a yeast cake often uses large quantities of sugar to give the sweet taste we expect from a cake. The simplest way to include the sugar is to add it to the dry ingredients. It is usually added to the bowl after the fat has been rubbed in. Added like this it cannot detract from the yeast's rising qualities. The yeast liquid is then added to the mixture.

An alternative method is to make a plain dough and introduce the sweetness in the form of a filling, topping or icing. Some yeast cakes employ this method, using sticky sweet toppings. The conventional selection of toppings and icings can also be used on yeast cakes.

Honey, treacle and molasses are often used to sweeten a yeast cake. These sweeteners are not usually used as the sole sweetener, but are combined with sugar. The method of adding small quantities of syrup to the ingredients is very simple. Stir it into the dry ingredients and then add the yeast liquid and other liquid enriching ingredients, such as eggs. When the liquid sweetener is used in a large quantity, it is always advisable to mix it with the eggs before adding it to dry ingredients.

Salt

A small amount of salt is often added to bring out the flavour of the yeast cake. Measure the salt, taking care not to overdo the amount. Used in large amounts, salt will inhibit the rising action of the yeast.

FLAVOURINGS

Dry flavourings: coffee and cocoa powders can be used to flavour a yeast cake. Since these dry ingredients are generally used in significant amounts, an adjustment must be made to the amount of flour used. Reduce the flour by the exact weight of the coffee or cocoa powder used, or the resulting cake could be dry and tough. Ground spices are used in such small quantities that no reduction of flour is needed.

Dried fruit: mixed dried fruit, sultanas, currants and raisins all enhance a yeast cake. Try some of the more unusual dried fruit – apple rings, bananas, apricots, prunes, peaches or figs. A variety of these may be used with a complementary spice to bring out the flavour of the fruit. Up to 225 g [8 oz] of dried fruit can be added per 450g [1 lb] flour.

Crystallized fruit: any odds and ends of glacé or crystallized fruit can be used – the last few pieces of crystallized fruit or the few glacé cherries left in the tub. Alternatives are crystallized pineapple, pear, ginger, candied peel or any of the delicious tropical fruits that can be bought in a crystallized form.

Remember that these will add extra sweetness if they are added in larger quantities than 100 g [4 oz] per 450 g [1 lb] of flour. Wash them first in hot water to remove excess sugar and then dry and chop them before adding them to the dry ingredients.

Nuts: any type of nut can be used in a yeast cake provided it is chopped. When using nuts, cut down a little on the liquid; reduce it by approximately 5 teaspoons. This is because the mixture must be stiff enough to support the weight of the nuts. You will find, too, that the fat can be reduced slightly, because nuts tend to be rather oily.

EQUIPMENT

Cake tins

Almost any shape of cake tin will do for a yeast cake, but traditionally it is made in a round or square deep tin.

The tin size is most important, and it should on no account be too small. When you put the dough into the tin, it must come no more than two-thirds of the way up the tin. This is because the dough expands on the second rise to above the edges of the tin. As a guide, up to 450 g [1 lb] made up dough can be baked in a 20 cm [8 in] round tin, a 23 cm [9 in] ring or an 18 cm [7 in] square deep cake tin. A sandwich tin, 20 cm [8 in] in diameter, will take up to 225 g [8 oz] made up dough.

Other equipment

Always use a measuring jug for the liquid to ensure accuracy. You will also need a fork and a selection of spoons. A palette or round-bladed knife is needed for cutting in the fat. The mixing bowl must be large enough to permit rubbing in the fat easily. You will need a polythene bag large enough to contain your cake tin and greaseproof paper or parchment for lining the cake tin.

GETTING ORGANIZED

Short-time yeast doughs, the basis of a yeast cake, are as the name suggests, quick to make. A stop half way through the process can, if prolonged, produce poor results. Make sure your equipment is assembled before you start.

Cake tins must be lined, regreased and lined again. This can be done before you start making the dough if you wish, but there is a natural interruption when you are making a yeast dough, when the dough is put to rise for the first time. This delay can be profitably used for preparing the cake tin. If, however, you are lining a ring tin, leave yourself extra time, or prepare it before you start.

PREPARING THE DOUGH

Like all yeast doughs, yeast cakes must be made by the correct methods from carefully measured ingredients with careful timing.

When making yeast cakes, these rules must be followed with extra care because additional ingredients are being added. The fat, sugar and extra liquids and flavourings in yeast cakes alter the basic proportions of the dough. This increases the danger of things going wrong and means that, if you skip ahead instead of taking things in proper sequence, you could end up with an unmanageable dough.

Preparing the liquid

The yeast liquid is always prepared before anything else, so the first step is to heat the liquid. Brown flour absorbs more liquid than white but care must be taken not to prepare and then add too much – only sufficient to bind the dough together (unless otherwise stated in the recipe).

The temperature of the liquid should be just warm: try the finger test. If you are using cream or any liquid other than milk or water, do not heat the former. Heat the milk or water being used with them, then add the cream etc, to the warmed liquid.

Adding the raising agents

Yeast and its helper, ascorbic acid, are next added to the liquid. Crumble in the yeast and crush the ascorbic acid tablet to powder between two teaspoons before adding to speed up the rate at which they dissolve. Both are water soluble, but whisking with a fork will ensure no lumps or grains are left in the liquid.

Sifting the dry ingredients

Flour, salt and any powdered flavourings are sifted together into the mixing bowl. As well as aerating the mixture a little, this ensures that they are thoroughly mixed. Concentrations of salt or flavouring could result in an imbalance in different parts of the cake.

Incorporating the fat

Remember that the fat must be at room temperature before use, so make a rule to get it out of the refrigerator well before you warm the liquid for the yeast.

The fat is first cut then rubbed into the dry ingredients. This is quickly achieved since the proportion of fat is not high.

Adding sweetener

Add dry sweeteners and any additional flavourings before the liquids. Sugar is stirred into the rubbed-in mixture until there is no sign of lumps.

Syrup-type sweeteners when used in small quantities can be added directly to the rubbed-in mixture. Syrups are rarely used as the sole sweetening agent. If they are, however, they will be in comparatively large quantities and should be thinned down before adding to the dry ingredients. This ensures that the syrup does not form pockets of concentrated sweetness.

To thin a syrup, add the measured syrup to the beaten eggs then beat again. This means in effect that the syrup is added with the liquids in the next stage but one.

Adding fruit or nuts

Dried, fresh or crystallized fruit or chopped nuts are added to the dry ingredients with the sugar. Stir these in thoroughly before adding the liquid.

Adding the liquid and eggs

Add the yeast liquid all at once with the beaten eggs, as for other yeast doughs. Pull the dry ingredients into the liquid in the centre from the sides of the bowl until the dough forms.

Handling and rising

The kneading and rising processes are the same for a yeast cake as for bread made by short-time method. The dough is kneaded for a number of minutes, which may vary according to the ingredients. A dough hook may be used, as for breads, for cutting down the time, if longer kneading is called for. The dough is then usually put into a polythene bag in a warm place for 5-10 minutes for the first rising.

Putting the dough in the tin

For a round tin, shape the dough into a round and place it in the centre of the tin. For a square tin, shape the dough as you would a bread dough, tucking the ends under if necessary.

The main rise

The dough is then placed in the oiled polythene bag in a warm place until doubled in size. This takes a rather shorter time than bread – 30 minutes.

HANDY HINT

Using the correct tin

The importance of using the correct-sized cake tin has already been mentioned. If you have too much dough for your chosen tin – remember the dough will double in size – you must use another much larger tin or divide the dough.

The delay while the cake is rising for the first time gives you an opportunity to line, grease and regrease the tin as described on pages 11 and 35. After the first short rise, the dough is kneaded again to remove air bubbles. It is now ready to go into the tin.

Like bread, the cake dough should fit the tin neatly to ensure even rising.

MAKING A FRUIT YEAST CAKE

MAKES 900 G [2 lb] CAKE

225 ml [8 fl oz] milk
25 g [1 oz] fresh yeast
25 mg ascorbic acid
450 g [1 lb] strong plain flour
1 teaspoon salt
1 teaspoon mixed spice
75 g [3 oz] butter or margarine
75 g [3 oz] caster sugar
175 g [6 oz] mixed dried fruit
2 medium-sized eggs
1 tablespoon clear honey

1 Warm the milk and crumble into it the yeast and crushed ascorbic acid. Whisk.

2 Sift flour, salt and spice into a mixing bowl. Rub the fat into the flour until the mixture resembles breadcrumbs.

3 Stir in the sugar and dried fruit until well mixed. Beat the eggs in a separate bowl.

4 Make a well in the mixture and add the yeast liquid and eggs all at once. Stir the dry ingredients into the liquid.

5 Beat with a wooden spoon or dough hook of an electric mixer for 3 minutes.

6 Spread the dough into prepared tin. Put the tin in a greased polythene bag. Leave the dough to double in size, about 30 minutes.

7 Remove the tin from the bag and bake for 30-35 minutes until the cake is firm to the touch. Turn out cake on to a wire rack to cool.

8 Put the cake on a wire rack and brush over the top with clear honey to give a glazed effect.

OVEN TEMPERATURES

A hot oven is essential for a yeast cake for many reasons. The yeast is a living organism and, if it is put into a moderate oven or into one that is still warming up, the yeast could continue to live and grow. This would mean that the dough (which has already doubled during the rising period) would continue to rise, rather than set. As the cake is always baked in a tin, the dough would rise and flow over the edge. The shape of the cake would be spoilt and a very messy oven would result.

Temperatures of 200-220°C [400-425°F] Gas 6-7, are usual for baking yeast cakes. The higher or lower temperature is dictated by the method or the ingredients.

Cakes need between 30-45 minutes to bake, depending on temperature and ingredients.

CHOCOLATE CHIP CAKE

This unusual yeast cake has a spongy texture and is not in itself a sweet cake. The sweetness comes from the icing that is used to sandwich and top the cake.

This Chocolate chip cake is an unusual yeast cake – it has a spongy texture but is not in itself a sweet cake. The sweetness comes from the icing that is used to sandwich and top the cake.

MAKES 24 slices
225 ml [8 fl oz] milk
25 g [1 oz] fresh yeast
25 mg ascorbic acid
450 g [1 lb] strong plain flour
1 teaspoon salt
1 teaspoon caster sugar
2 medium-sized eggs
100 g [4 oz] chocolate chips

For the icing:
100 g [4 oz] butter
125 g [4 oz] caster sugar
50 g [2 oz] icing sugar
1 tablespoon sweetened condensed milk
50 g [2 oz] cocoa powder
25g [1 oz] ground almonds
1 teaspoon clear honey
2 tablespoons boiling water
50 g [2 oz] milk chocolate

1 Grease and line an 18 cm [7 in] cake tin. Grease the paper. Warm the milk and crumble into it the yeast and crushed ascorbic acid tablet. Whisk.

2 Sift flour and salt into a mixing bowl. Stir in the sugar and mix well.

3 Beat the eggs in a separate bowl. Make a well in the centre of the dry ingredients and add the eggs and yeast liquid. Stir the dry ingredients into the liquid then stir in the chocolate chips.

4 Beat with a wooden spoon or dough hook of an electric mixer for 3 minutes.

5 Spread the dough into the prepared tin. Put the tin in a lightly greased polythene bag and leave until the dough has doubled in size, 30 minutes.

6 Position the shelf in centre of oven and heat to 200°C [400°F] Gas 6. Remove the tin from the bag and bake the cake for 30-35 minutes until firm to the touch. Turn out of the tin on to a wire rack to cool.

7 To make the icing, place the butter and caster sugar in a bowl. Sift the icing sugar into the bowl and cream together until light and fluffy.

8 Beat in the condensed milk until smooth. Sift the cocoa powder into the bowl and add the almonds and honey plus the boiling water. Beat the ingredients together until incorporated.

9 Cut the cake into three equal-sized rounds. Spread one-third of the icing over the bottom layer of sponge and place the centre layer of cake on top.

10 Spread the centre layer with another third of the icing and place the top on the cake. Press down lightly.

11 Spread the remaining icing over the top of the cake to cover completely. Grate the chocolate and sprinkle this over the top.

Variation

Flavour the chocolate icing to taste with dark rum and decorate the top of the cake with walnut halves instead of chocolate.

RUM BABAS

Although the origin of rum baba is uncertain, many people do attribute its invention to a King Stanislas of Poland. One of the king's favourite stories was the fable Ali Baba: it is believed he called the cake after the story's hero.

MAKES 8

100 g [4 oz] strong plain flour
pinch of salt
1 teaspoon easy-blend dried yeast
50 ml [2 fl oz] hand-hot milk
2 small eggs, beaten
50 g [2 oz] margarine or butter, melted
 and cooled
25 g [1 oz] currants
plain flour, for dusting

For the syrup:
225 ml [8 fl oz] water
75 g [3 oz] granulated sugar
4½ teaspoons lemon juice
2 cloves
65 ml [2½ fl oz] dark rum

For the glaze and decoration
4 tablespoons apricot jam
1 tablespoon water
150 ml/¼ pint double cream, whipped
4 glacé cherries, halved
16 'diamonds' of angelica

1 Brush eight 9 cm [3½ in] individual ring tins with oil and dust lightly with flour, shaking off any excess.
2 Sift the flour and salt into a large bowl, then sprinkle in the yeast and stir well to mix.
3 In a separate bowl, mix together the milk, eggs and margarine and gradually beat into the flour mixture to make a smooth batter. Stir in the currants until well dispersed.
4 Spoon the batter into the oiled ring tins (it should not come more than one-third of the way up), cover with oiled polythene and leave in a warm place for 30 minutes until the batter has risen to the top of the ring tins.
5 Meanwhile, heat the oven to 200°C [400°F] Gas 6.
6 Uncover the babas and bake for 15 minutes more, until they are golden brown on top.
7 Turn the tins upside down on a work surface, leave for 10 minutes, then carefully ease the babas out of tins. Leave to cool slightly.
8 Meanwhile, prepare the syrup: put the water, sugar, lemon juice and cloves into a heavy-based saucepan. Heat until the sugar has dissolved, then bring slowly to the boil. Remove the syrup from the heat and stir in the rum.
9 Put the babas into a large shallow dish and prick them all over with a fine skewer. Pour over the hot syrup and leave for 30 minutes to soak up the syrup.
10 To make the glaze, sieve the jam into a small, heavy-based saucepan. Add the water and heat gently, stirring constantly, until the jam has melted. Remove glaze from heat and brush over the babas while still hot. Arrange babas on a serving plate or on individual plates.
11 To serve, spoon or pipe the whipped cream into the centre of each baba, then top with half a cherry and two 'diamonds' of angelica.

If you do not have the small ring tins for making Rum Babas, you can use 150 ml [¼ pt] dariole moulds instead.

SAVARIN

SERVES 8

75 ml [3 fl oz] milk
25 g [1 oz] fresh yeast
50 g [2 oz] granulated sugar
25 g [1 oz] butter, softened
2 large eggs, beaten
225 g [8 oz] strong plain flour
3 large egg yolks
150 ml [¼ pt] thick cream, whipped

For the syrup:
225 g [8 oz] granulated sugar
3 tablespoons brandy
3 tablespoons cointreau

For the filling:
1 banana, sliced
2 oranges, peeled and segmented
2 kiwi fruit, peeled and sliced
10 strawberries, hulled
10 white grapes, seeded
10 black grapes, seeded

For the glaze:
6-8 tablespoons apricot jam
1 tablespoon lemon juice

1 In a saucepan warm the milk until lukewarm, crumble the yeast over the milk and stir until dissolved.
2 Put the milk mixture into a large bowl and add the sugar, softened butter and the beaten eggs; sift in the flour. Mix well with one hand then add the egg yolks and mix to form a soft dough. Cover with cling film; leave in a warm place until doubled in size.
3 In the bowl, knead the savarin dough until is has returned to its original size.
4 Brush a 1.6 L [2¾ pt] savarin mould with melted butter and fill with the dough to one-third full. Cover with cling film and leave in a warm place to rise until the dough has filled the mould.
5 Meanwhile, heat the oven to 170°C [325°F] Gas 3.
6 Bake for 30-40 minutes or until golden brown.
7 Remove from the oven, allow to cool for 5 minutes in the tin, then turn out onto a wire rack to cool to lukewarm.
8 To make the syrup, put the sugar in a saucepan with 275 ml [½ pt] water, stir over a gentle heat until the sugar is dissolved, then bring to the boil for 5 minutes. Remove and add the brandy and cointreau.
9 Place the savarin on a flat serving dish the right way up and prick all over with a fork. Spoon three-quarters of the warm syrup evenly over the savarin, leave for 2-3 hours. Let the remaining syrup cool.
10 Put the fruit in a bowl and pour the cooled syrup over. Leave to macerate.
11 To make the glaze, combine the apricot jam with 2 tablespoons water and the lemon juice in a saucepan and heat until the jam is melted. Bring to the boil and then sieve to remove any lumps from the jam. Brush the glaze evenly over the savarin.
12 Spoon the macerated fruit into the centre; pipe the whipped cream decoratively around the savarin and serve.

BUTTERY YEAST CAKE

This yeast cake with a taste of butter is marvellous for serving with coffee.

MAKES 12 SLICES

500 g [18 oz] plain flour
25 g [1 oz] fresh yeast
75 g [3 oz] caster sugar
250 ml [9 fl oz] lukewarm milk
75 g [3 oz] butter, softened
150 g [5 oz] butter, melted
150 g [5 oz] icing sugar
1½ teaspoons ground cinnamon

1 Sift the flour into a warm bowl. Make a hollow in the centre.
2 Cream the yeast with 2 teaspoons of the sugar. Add 150 ml [¼ pt] of the milk and pour the mixture into the centre of the flour.
3 Cover the bowl with a clean cloth and set aside until the yeast starts to bubble, about 5 minutes.
4 Work the flour into the yeast mixture with a wooden spoon, adding the rest of the milk and sugar and the softened butter to form a dough. Knead the dough until it is smooth, shiny and blisters.
5 Butter and flour a deep roasting tin, about 33 × 28 cm [13 × 11 in]. Put the dough into the centre of the tin and press it out with your knuckles until it covers the bottom of the tin.
6 Cover the top of the tin lightly with a cloth and leave in a warm place until the dough almost doubles in bulk, about 1 hour.
7 Heat the oven to 190°C [375°F] Gas 5. When hot, bake the cake for about

30 minutes. While it is still hot, brush the cake with the melted butter and sprinkle with the icing sugar and ground cinnamon. Serve warm.

CRUMB-TOPPED CAKE

MAKES 12 SLICES

250 g [9 oz] plain flour
20 g [¾ oz] fresh yeast
2½ tablespoons caster sugar
125 ml [4 fl oz] lukewarm milk
4 medium-sized egg yolks
65 g [2½ oz] butter, melted
icing sugar for dusting (optional)

For the topping:
150 g [5 oz] plain flour
75 g [3 oz] caster sugar
1 tablespoon vanilla sugar (see right)
125 g [4½ oz] butter
finely grated zest of ½ lemon
1 teaspoon ground cinnamon
65 g [2½ oz] ground almonds

1 Sift the flour into a warm bowl and make a hollow in the centre. Cream the yeast in a small bowl with 1 teaspoon of the sugar. Stir in the milk and set aside.

2 As soon as the yeast begins to bubble, about 5 minutes, stir the mixture into the centre of the flour. Add the remaining sugar, the egg yolks and the butter. Mix with a wooden spoon, then knead until the dough is smooth, shiny and begins to blister.

3 Pat the dough into a ball, place in a lightly greased bowl, cover the top with a clean cloth and leave in a warm place until it is doubled in bulk, about 1 hour.

4 Meanwhile, butter and flour a baking tin measuring about 33 × 28 cm [13 × 11 in]. Rub together the topping ingredients until they are the consistency of rather coarse breadcrumbs, then reserve.

5 Knead the dough briefly, then place in the centre of the tin. Press the dough out with your knuckles until it covers the bottom of the tin. Sprinkle the topping over, cover the tin with a clean cloth and leave in a warm place to rise a second time, about 45-60 minutes or until doubled in size.

6 Heat the oven to 190°C [375°F] Gas 5. Bake the cake for about 40 minutes, or until the centre is firm when pressed with the fingertips. Allow the cake to cool in the tin.

7 Slice into rectangles for serving. Dust with icing sugar, if wished.

HANDY HINT

Vanilla sugar
To make vanilla sugar, simply leave a vanilla pod in a jar of sugar. It will soon have a lovely vanilla flavour.

Crumb-topped cake (left) is traditionally not very sweet – dust with a little icing sugar if wished. Buttery yeast cake (right) is marvellous for serving with coffee.

Yeast cake with fresh plums

YEAST CAKE WITH FRESH PLUMS

Although celebrated for sauerkraut, sausages and beer, Germany can also boast of much fine baking. This delicious plum cake is found all over Germany, where it is called Zwetschkendatschi. The base for the cake is often made with shortcrust pastry, but here yeast pastry is used because it soaks up the juice from the plums without becoming soggy and spoiling the texture of the cake.

MAKES ABOUT 16 SLICES

250 g [9 oz] strong plain flour
15 g [½ oz] fresh yeast
50 g [2 oz] icing or caster sugar
150 ml [¼ pt] lukewarm milk
60 g [2¼ oz] butter
1 medium-sized egg
1 medium-sized egg yolk
½ teaspoon finely grated lemon zest
700 g [1½ lb] plums, washed, dried and
    stoned
icing sugar, sifted
vanilla icing sugar, sifted (see Handy hint,
    page 63)
ground cinnamon

1 Sift the flour into a warm bowl. Cream the yeast with 1 teaspoon of the sugar in a cup. Add half the warm milk, sprinkle with a little of the flour and set aside until bubbles form on the surface. This will take about 10 minutes.
2 Meanwhile, melt the butter in a cup over hot water.
3 When the yeast is ready, make a hollow in the flour and pour in the yeast mixture.
4 Whisk together the rest of the lukewarm milk and melted butter and whisk in the egg and egg yolk: the temperature should be no more than lukewarm.
5 Whisk the egg mixture into the flour and yeast, then beat until the mixture is very smooth and blisters are just beginning to form on the surface. Mix in the lemon zest.
6 Grease and flour a deep baking dish or roasting tin, about 28 cm [11 in] square. Turn the dish or tin to coat, then tip out the loose flour.
7 Put the dough in the centre of the prepared dish and press it out with your fingers until it covers the bottom of the dish completely.
8 Halve or quarter the plums according to their size and cover the dough closely with the plums, cut side down and slightly overlapping.
9 Cover the dish or tin with a cloth and leave the dough to rise in a warm place away from draughts for about 1 hour.
10 Heat the oven to 200°C [400°F] Gas 6. When the dough has risen to about twice its original height, put the dish in the oven and immediately lower the oven temperature to 190°C [375°F] Gas 5.
11 Bake for 45 minutes, then lower the temperature to 180°C [350°F] Gas 4 and bake for another 15 minutes, or until golden brown.
12 Dust the cake with icing sugar and ground cinnamon while still hot. When warm, mark the cake into slices with a sharp knife.

GÂTEAU ESTEREL

MAKES 6 SLICES

1 tablespoon dried yeast
175 g [6 oz] butter
4 large eggs
225 g [8 oz] caster sugar
225 g [8 oz] plain flour
pinch of salt
8 tablespoons orange marmalade
225 g [8 oz] plain chocolate
1 tablespoon cointreau

For the syrup:
100 g [4 oz] granulated sugar
3 tablespoons cointreau

1 Heat the oven to 200°C [400°F] Gas 6.

2 In a small bowl, sprinkle the yeast into 4 tablespoons lukewarm water. Cover and leave to stand in a warm place for 6 minutes, then stir until dissolved.

3 Melt the butter in the top pan of a double boiler. Lightly grease a 20 cm [8 in] savarin mould with a little of the melted butter and dust with flour.

4 In a bowl, whisk the eggs and sugar until light and fluffy. Sift the flour with the salt and fold into the egg and sugar mixture with a large metal spoon.

5 Fold in the remaining melted butter and dissolved yeast mixture. Pour the mixture into the prepared mould and bake for 10 minutes.

6 Lower the oven temperature to 180°C [350°F] Gas 4 and bake the cake for a further 25 minutes, or until golden brown. Unmould on to a wire rack and leave to cool.

7 Meanwhile, to make the syrup, dissolve the sugar in 250 ml [8 fl oz] water in a small saucepan over a low heat. Bring to the boil and boil until the temperature reaches 108°C [220°F], about 10 minutes. At this point 2 teaspoons dipped into the syrup will form a short thread when pulled apart.

8 Remove from the heat, flavour with cointreau and leave to cool.

9 Cut the cake in half horizontally and moisten the cut sides of both halves with the syrup, reserving 3 tablespoons. Spread the cut sides with orange marmalade and re-form the cake.

10 Melt the chocolate in the top part of a double boiler over gently simmering water, add the reserved syrup and the cointreau, beating with a wooden spoon until smooth.

11 Place the cake on a serving platter, cover with the chocolate mixture and using a palette knife spread the chocolate evenly over the top.

Gâteau Esterel makes an impressive treat.

STRAWBERRY CRUMB CAKE

MAKES 24 SLICES

150 ml [¼ pt] milk
40 g [1½ oz] fresh yeast
25 mg ascorbic acid
350 g [12 oz] strong plain flour
1 teaspoon salt
50 g [2 oz] semolina
100 g [4 oz] butter or margarine
100 g [4 oz] soft brown and caster sugar, mixed
100 g [4 oz] candied peel
100 g [4 oz] sultanas
3 medium-sized eggs

For the topping:
75 g [3 oz] plain flour
50 g [2 oz] butter
50 g [2 oz] soft brown sugar
50 g [2 oz] chopped walnuts
100 g [4 oz] strawberry jam or preserve

1 Warm the milk to blood heat and test with a finger. Crumble the fresh yeast into the milk.
2 Crush the ascorbic acid tablet between two teaspoons and sprinkle into the milk. Whisk with a fork until the yeast has dissolved.
3 Sift the flour, salt and semolina into a large bowl.
4 Add the butter or margarine to bowl. Use a round-bladed knife to cut in the fat until all the pieces are pea-sized.
5 Rub the fat into the flour until the mixture resembles even-sized breadcrumbs.
6 Stir in the sugar mixture, the candied peel and sultanas.
7 Make a well in the centre of the dry ingredients. Beat the eggs lightly and add the yeast liquid and eggs. Mix together until the ingredients bind.
8 Beat with a wooden spoon or the dough hook of an electric mixer for 3 minutes until the dough is a soft dropping consistency.
9 Fully grease and line a 20 cm [8 in] square deep tin and grease the paper. Spread the mixture into prepared tin.
10 Put the tin into a polythene bag. Tie loosely and place the tin in a warm place until the dough has doubled in size, about 30 minutes.
11 Position the shelf in the centre of oven and heat to 200°C [400°F] Gas 6.
12 Meanwhile, place the flour for the topping in a bowl. Cut the butter into the flour until the pieces are pea-sized.

13 Rub the fat into the flour until the mixture resembles even-sized breadcrumbs. Stir in the sugar and walnuts.
14 When the dough is ready, remove the tin from the polythene bag and very lightly spread strawberry jam over the surface of cake. Sprinkle evenly with the rubbed-in mixture.
15 Bake for 30-35 minutes until cake feels firm to the touch. Remove cake from oven and remove from tin. Leave to cool, upright on a wire rack.

APRICOT KUCHEN

MAKES 12 SQUARES

125 ml [4 fl oz] milk
25 g [1 oz] fresh yeast
25 mg ascorbic acid
225 g [8 oz] strong plain flour
1 teaspoon salt
125 g [4 oz] desiccated coconut
50 g [2 oz] semolina
50 g [2 oz] butter or margarine
half a lemon
75 g [3 oz] caster sugar
1 medium-sized egg

For the topping:
425 g [15 oz] can apricots
50 g [2 oz] plain flour
25 g [1 oz] caster sugar
50 g [2 oz] butter
½ teaspoon ground cinnamon

1 Measure the milk carefully and warm it to blood heat. Test with a clean finger. Crumble the yeast into the milk.

2 Crush the ascorbic acid tablet between two teaspoons and add. Whisk the yeast liquid with a fork until completely dissolved.

3 Sift the flour and salt into a large bowl. Stir in 75 g [3 oz] desiccated coconut and all the semolina.

4 Add the fat and cut into the flour with a round-bladed knife until the pieces are pea-sized.

5 Rub the fat into the flour until the mixture resembles even-sized breadcrumbs.

6 Grate the zest from the lemon and stir this and the sugar into the dry ingredients.

7 Lightly beat the egg. Make a well in the centre of the dry ingredients and add the egg and the yeast liquid. Mix together until the mixture begins to bind together.

8 Turn out the dough on to a lightly floured surface and knead for 5 minutes, until the dough is smooth.

9 Place the dough in a lightly greased polythene bag and tie loosely. Place the dough on a baking sheet in a warm place for 10 minutes.

10 Meanwhile, lightly grease a Swiss roll tin.

11 Remove the dough from the polythene bag and flatten with the knuckles. Knead for 1 minute, until smooth.

12 Flatten dough to an oblong shape to roughly fit the tin. Place the dough in the tin and press out to fit the tin evenly.

13 Return tin to polythene bag, tie top loosely and place in a warm place until dough has doubled in size, about 30 minutes.

14 Position oven shelf to centre and heat oven to 200°C [400°F] Gas 6.

15 Meanwhile, for the topping, drain the syrup from the can of apricots. Dry the apricots on kitchen paper and roughly chop. Reserve.

16 Place the remaining topping ingredients in a bowl. Cut the fat into the flour until all the pieces are pea-sized.

17 Rub the fat into the flour until the mixture resembles breadcrumbs. Do not worry if the mixture is a little moist.

18 Remove the tin from the polythene bag. Scatter chopped apricots and remaining coconut over the dough. Sprinkle the rubbed-in mixture evenly over the apricots.

19 Bake for 35-40 minutes until the cake is firm to the touch. Carefully remove it from the tin. Remove the lining paper and cool the right way up, on a wire rack. Cut into squares to serve.

Serving a Strawberry crumb cake (left) turns tea-time into a special occasion. Apricot kuchen (right) is a soft yeast cake originating from Germany where it is still extremely popular. The cake is delicately flavoured with lemon, and the topping is a wonderful mixture of apricots, spices and coconut covered with a thin crunchy layer.

CREAMED SPONGE CAKES

The creaming method is used for the widest choice of cakes – rich in butter, sugar and eggs with a light, yet lusciously moist, texture. This chapter shows how to make some favourite tea-time classics, including a feather-light Victoria sponge and a buttery rich Madeira cake.

Rich cakes contain a higher proportion of fat and sugar than plain cakes. To incorporate these satisfactorily, a different method of preparation is used. The traditional way to make rich cakes is by the creaming method. Equal quantities of fat and sugar are vigorously beaten together with a wooden spoon until light and fluffy. This is known as 'creaming' to distinguish it from beating with a whisk. Eggs are then beaten in and, lastly, the flour is gently folded in.

Many of the same cakes can be made using the quicker all-in-one technique described on pages 8-31, but the extra time spent on the creaming method pays dividends. With the all-in-one method extra baking powder is used as the raising agent. With the creaming method, air is beaten in to raise the cake. Thorough creaming is therefore very important. The air expands on heating, forcing the cake to rise.

Cakes made by the creaming method have far better keeping qualities. Moreover, the actual process of creaming produces a far finer texture.

INGREDIENTS

Flour

Self-raising or plain flour, or occasionally a mixture of the two, are used for creamed cakes. The choice depends on the type of cake being made, but it must be a soft flour because this absorbs fat well and gives the cake a deliciously light, soft texture.

Strong flour is not suitable as it gives too coarse a texture to the cake. Use the type of flour specified in recipe and always sift the flour. Sifting not only aerates the flour, but it also removes any lumps which will cause an unevenly blended mixture.

Baking powder

If plain flour is used, a chemical raising agent (usually baking powder) is used to help the cake rise. The amount needed will depend upon the proportion of eggs to flour. As the number of eggs increases, the amount of chemical raising agent needed will decrease. Baking powder must be accurately measured.

Salt

A pinch of salt is sometimes added to bring out the flavour of the other ingredients. Sift it with the flour.

Fat

Butter is by far the best choice as it gives the richest flavour and a lovely golden colour to the cake. Although expensive, it is well worth using for those cakes which contain little or no additional flavourings.

Hard margarine is less expensive to use but will not give such a good flavour as butter. Hard margarines are best used for cakes which have pronounced flavours such as spices.

Whipped margarines are the most economical of all the fats to use and will give an extremely light result. Unlike butter or hard margarine, whipped margarine contains no water, so approximately one-fifth less is used.

Sugar

Caster sugar should be used as its fine crystals dissolve easily when creamed

with the fat. Coarse sugars such as granulated and Demerara are not suitable because they do not dissolve when creamed with the fat and will give a speckled appearance.

Eggs

Eggs make the cake light, give it a good flavour and a moist, soft texture. Eggs should always be medium sized unless the recipe states otherwise, and are used at room temperature. If you store eggs in the refrigerator, you should remove them at least one hour before they are going to be used.

Liquids

The eggs in the recipe contain a high proportion of water, so this contributes to the liquid in the cake mixture. The amount of liquid needed in addition will depend on the proportion of fat and sugar used.

In some cases, a small proportion of extra liquid is added to a cake and this may be either milk or water. The liquid must be at room temperature.

The liquid added to a rich cake mixture should be just enough to produce a soft dropping consistency. This consistency is one that is moist enough to drop easily from a spoon when the mixture is lifted above the bowl. A dropping consistency, however, is a good deal stiffer than a pouring consistency and should not be confused with it, or a consistency resembling batter.

FLAVOURINGS

Liquid flavourings

Liquid sweeteners, such as honey or golden syrup, may be used in place of some or all the sugar. Liquid sweeteners will give a moister, denser

Bake a cake that is as light as air with a deliciously rich flavour.

cake, as well as a hint of their own flavours.

Flavouring essences are very often used but should be used with extreme caution as their flavour is deceptively strong. Never use them straight from the bottle, but add them drop by drop. Flavouring essences should be added before the eggs.

Powdered flavourings

Ground spices are a convenient and easy way to give a cake a subtle flavour. Cocoa powder is used when a rich chocolate flavour is required. Instant coffee and liquid coffee also make delicious cakes. Unless otherwise stated, the amount of flour will have to be reduced by the same amount as the powdered flavouring.

Always sift the powdered flavouring with the flour to ensure an even distribution in the mixture. If using self-raising flour, the cocoa is best dissolved in a little hot water. This is then allowed to cool before it is beaten into the creamed fat and sugar mixture. Instant coffee, if powdered, can be sifted with the dry ingredients,

but if in granules it should also be dissolved in a little hot water before adding to the creamed mixture.

Flour substitutes

Ground rice or cornflour can both be used to give a shorter, melt-in-the-mouth texture to cakes. The same rules apply to these as to powdered flavourings.

PREPARING CAKE TINS

For success, rich cake making relies on the application of a simple set of rules. One very important rule is that you choose and prepare the baking equipment before you start preparing the cake so that there is no delay between the making and the baking. Choose shallow tins for cakes you intend to eat immediately because a shallow tin bakes a cake quickly. Use deep, round or square tins for fruit cakes or cakes with good keeping qualities.

The selection and preparation of large round and ring tins are discussed on pages 10-11; large square tins on

Having all the ingredients ready before you start baking is the recipe for success when using the creamed method for cakes.

GUIDE TO PROPORTIONS FOR CREAMED CAKES

plain flour	100 g [4 oz]	175 g [6 oz]	225 g [8 oz]
baking powder	½ teaspoon	1 teaspoon	1 teaspoon
salt	large pinch	large pinch	large pinch
fat	100 g [4 oz]	175 g [6 oz]	225 g [8 oz]
sugar	100 g [4 oz]	175 g [6 oz]	225 g [8 oz]
eggs	2 medium-sized	3 medium-sized	4 medium-sized
liquid	1-2 tablespoons	2 tablespoons	1-3 tablespoons*

*individual recipes may vary slightly

page 35.

Sandwich tins are usually base lined, as shown on pages 10-11. However, to give a Victoria sandwich a professional touch, dust the ungreased insides of the tins with equal quantities of sugar and rice flour. This gives the cake an appetizing sugary crust.

OTHER EQUIPMENT

Once the tin(s) are prepared, the next step is to collect together the equipment for making the cake.

The correct proportions for rich cakes are important, so you will need accurate scales and measuring spoons. In addition to these you will also need a sieve and bowl for the dry ingredients and a bowl and whisk for the eggs. Unless you have an electric mixer, you will need a wooden spoon for the creaming of the fat and sugar. Wooden spoons come in all sizes, so choose one that is easy to manage; a large cumbersome spoon will prove difficult and make the creaming process heavy going.

Choose a large mixing bowl for creaming the fat and sugar together, so that these can be vigorously beaten without the mixture overflowing. A rubber spatula is handy for scraping the mixture down the side of the bowl and it is also the best tool for turning the cake mixture into the prepared tin with the minimum of waste. You will need a metal spoon for folding in the flour and a palette or round-bladed knife for levelling the mixture in the tin. Oven gloves and a wire rack are necessary for turning the cake out of the tin once it is baked.

OVEN TEMPERATURES

Always heat the oven to the recommended oven temperature. This means heating the oven 20 minutes before the cake is to be baked, and is usually the first step when baking a cake. If a cake is put into the oven before it has reached the correct temperature the rise will be uneven.

It is very important that you bake cakes at the temperature given in the recipe. If the oven temperature is too low, the cake will have a heavy texture and will sink in the centre. Too hot an oven will result in a cake that forms a peak and cracks. A very hot oven will cause the sugar to caramelize and produce a hard, tough crust.

Large cakes without fruit should be baked at 180°C [350°F] Gas 4. Cakes cooked in sandwich tins need the same temperature. The temperature for small cakes will depend on the individual recipe to a certain extent but the average temperature is 190°C [375°F] Gas 5.

Oven positions

The position in the oven depends on the size and type of cake. When baking two sandwich cakes bake them on the same shelf, close together but not touching. If your oven is heated from the back, place the tins side by side. If it is heated from the sides, position one tin towards the back of the oven and the other towards the front. Always check that there is a gap of at least 2.5 cm [1 in] between the sides of the oven and the sides of the tins. If this is not done, the hot air will not be able to circulate freely and the results will be 'half-baked'!

Shelf positions

Large plain cakes should be baked on a shelf in the centre of the oven. Small cakes and sandwich cakes just above the centre of the oven.

MAKING A VICTORIA SPONGE SANDWICH

MAKES 18 CM [7 IN] CAKE
175 g [6 oz] self-raising flour
175 g [6 oz] butter or margarine
175 g [6 oz] caster sugar
3 medium-sized eggs
2 tablespoons milk
3 tablespoons raspberry or strawberry jam
icing or caster sugar to dredge

1 Put shelf above centre and heat oven to 180°C [375°F] Gas 4. Prepare two 18 cm [7 in] sandwich tins.

OR place the fat and sugar in a bowl and cream together with a hand-held electric whisk.

4 Whisk the eggs lightly then beat into the mixture, a little at a time, beating well after each addition.

5 With a rubber spatula scrape the mixture down sides of the bowl and off the spoon. Beat mixture again.

8 Bake for 25-30 minutes. Test by pressing lightly with fingertips. The cakes should be springy but firm.

9 Remove from oven if ready. A well-cooked cake should shrink from the sides of the tin. Cool 30 seconds.

10 Turn out cakes on to tea-towel. Remove paper and then turn right way up on to wire rack to cool.

2 Sift flour into a bowl and reserve. Put softened butter or margarine in mixing bowl and beat until light.

3 Add sugar to the fat and cream it with a wooden spoon until light in colour and fluffy in texture.

6 Fold in the flour, one-third at a time, using a figure-of-eight action. Add milk for a soft dropping consistency.

7 Divide the mixture equally between the two prepared tins. Level the top with a palette knife.

11 When cold, place one cake on serving plate and spread upper surface with jam.

12 Then dredge surface of remaining sponge liberally with caster or icing sugar. Place on top of other cake.

MAKING SMALL CAKES

Small cakes are ideal for icing and the same rules apply as to larger cakes, though small cakes are not usually filled.

Small cakes are easily made with the basic rich sponge mixture and may be baked in greased 6-, 9- or 12-hole bun tins or foil cases. If you are prepared to pay for convenience, buy paper cases. These need no greasing, but can only be used once.

Do not overfill the paper cases or bun tins. A heaped teaspoon of mixture in each case is quite enough. Nor is it necessary to spread the mixture evenly. It will expand on baking to fill the space.

If using paper cases, arrange these first on a baking sheet or tray. A fairly hot oven temperature, 190°C [375°F] Gas 5, is needed but cakes are baked for only 15–20 minutes just below the centre shelf.

MAKING A CREAMED CAKE

Assembling ingredients

Start by assembling all the ingredients listed in the recipe. Then prepare the baking tin(s). Make sure that the oven shelves are positioned correctly and heat the oven to the required temperature.

The ingredients should be used at room temperature and this will make preparation much easier. This means removing items from the refrigerator one hour before you start cake making. Whichever fat you are using remove it from the refrigerator one hour before it is required; rock hard fat is extremely difficult to cream. On the other hand, never try short cuts, such as heating the fat to soften it, because this will only result in an oil which is impossible to cream properly. Use eggs at room temperature. If they are used when very cold, this could have a curdling effect when they are added to the creamed fat and sugar mixture. Remove eggs from the refrigerator before they are going to be used.

Preparing additions

Prepare additional flavouring ingredients before the cake mixture is made. Chop nuts or fruit if required, wash crystallized fruit, or dissolve cocoa powder or coffee granules.

Sifting the dry ingredients

Sift the flour, raising agent and any dry flavouring ingredient into a medium-sized bowl ready for use later. The sifting initiates the aerating process, trapping the air as it falls from the sieve into the bowl.

Creaming fat and sugar

Measure the softened fat into the mixing bowl. This is then creamed, which gives the method its name. The aim is to work air into the mixture by blending the fat with a wooden spoon. This initial creaming releases the flavour of the butter, which will eventually be distributed throughout the finished cake, and makes sure that the cake is light in texture.

Creaming by hand: stand the bowl containing the fat on a damp cloth, as this prevents the bowl from slipping. Using a wooden spoon, beat the fat against the side of the bowl until it is light in colour and creamy in texture. All lumps of butter must be dispersed. The changing colour of the fat, from its

natural colour to a lighter shade, is a visual indication that it is sufficiently creamed and ready for the next stage.

Adding sugar: beat in the measured amount of sugar, all in one go. Using the same vigorous action, cream the ingredients together for 7-10 minutes or until the mixture no longer feels gritty and is light in colour and fluffy in texture. The change in colour, texture and volume is a direct result of air being incorporated. During this creaming period the mixture will increase in bulk.

During the creaming action, it is wise to stop from time to time and scrape the mixture off the spoon and down the sides of the bowl. If this is not done, undissolved sugar crystals will gather around the sides of the bowl. This will result in the baked cake being streaky or speckled in appearance.

Creaming with a mixer: when using a hand-held or table electric mixer, there is no need to beat the fat first. Simply place the fat and sugar in a mixing bowl and beat at the speed recommended by the manufacturer.

Additional flavourings

Crystallized fruit makes a delicious chewy addition. Make sure that any thick coating of sugar on the fruit is removed before using or the fruit will sink in the cake mixture. Wash the fruit under hot water, drain and dry completely then toss lightly in flour. Glacé cherries and mixed peel are popular, but finely chopped angelica and stem ginger are also excellent. When using glacé cherries, always halve them because whole cherries are too heavy to be supported by the cake mixture.

Nuts impart their own rich flavour, and give a moist, chewy texture. Always use the nuts as directed in the recipe, and check whether they should be used ground, chopped or whole. When ground nuts are used, a corresponding reduction of the amount of flour is made.

Caraway seeds are the traditional flavouring for seed cake. Use only as directed in the recipe as their flavour is surprisingly strong.

The classic Victoria sponge is a popular tea-time treat. The basic mixture is wonderfully versatile, and can be flavoured in many different ways.

• For a lemon sandwich, beat in the grated zest of 1 lemon before adding eggs. Sandwich the cakes together with 3-4 tablespoons lemon curd. Spread the top with lemon curd. Decorate with lemon jelly slices.

• For a chocolate sandwich, blend 1½ tablespoons cocoa powder with 2 tablespoons hot water; allow to cool slightly, then beat into the mixture before adding the eggs. Sandwich the cakes together with jam and a layer of lightly whipped cream. To finish the cake: sift a little icing sugar over the top of the cake, then decorate by piping a lattice of melted chocolate cake covering over the top. Plain dessert chocolate can also be used.

• For an orange sandwich, beat in the grated zest of 1 orange before adding the eggs. Sandwich the cakes with marmalade or cream. If liked, whip 150 ml [¼ pt] whipping cream until it will hold its shape; spread some of the cream over the top of the cake, then use the remainder to pipe rosettes around the edge. Top each rosette with a drained canned mandarin orange segment. Fresh orange segments can be used but canned mandarins are daintier and juicier.

• For a coffee and hazelnut sandwich, blend 2½ teaspoons instant coffee powder with 1 tablespoon boiling water; allow to cool slightly, then beat into the mixture before adding the eggs. Sandwich the cakes together with 3-4 tablespoons chocolate hazelnut spread. Cover the top with chocolate hazelnut spread and decorate with toasted skinned hazelnut kernels.

• For a coconut sandwich, add 2-3 drops of vanilla essence when beating in the eggs. Sandwich the cakes together with 3-4 tablespoons red cherry jam. Blend 100 g [4 oz] sifted icing sugar with 1 tablespoon warm water and use to ice the top of the cake. While the icing is still soft, scatter the top thickly with desiccated coconut; arrange sliced glacé cherries around the top edge.

Using an electric hand-held or table mixer cuts down on the time taken to cream the fat and sugar together.

Adding liquid flavourings

Flavouring essences, if used, are added at this stage. Beat them into the mixture so that their flavour is evenly distributed throughout the cake. If citrus zest is used, this is added at this stage.

Adding eggs

The next stage is to add the eggs and this requires careful attention. Eggs contain approximately two-thirds water and this must be completely absorbed into the fat and sugar.

If the amount of sugar used in the recipe is less than 225 g [8 oz] the eggs must be lightly whisked together before they are added, otherwise the eggs can quite happily be added one at a time, directly to the creamed mixture. Whichever way the eggs are added, the mixture must be beaten thoroughly after each addition.

Curdled eggs: if the eggs are added all at once or if they are used directly from the refrigerator, there is the danger that the mixture will curdle. This means that the fat and liquid in the mixture separates. You can see when this happens because, instead of a creamy, smooth texture, the mixture will become lumpy and appear grainy. Curdling is undesirable because a curdled mixture holds less air than a smooth one and therefore produces a heavy cake.

Provided that the eggs are added correctly and used at the right temperature, there is no reason why curdling should occur. If, despite your precautions, the mixture shows signs of curdling, add a little of the sifted flour with the quantity of egg. Curdling can sometimes happen when the last egg is added and in this case, stand the bowl containing the mixture in a bowl of hot water and beat very hard until the mixture assumes its smooth and creamy texture again.

When all the egg has been incorporated, scrape down the spoon and sides of the bowl with a spatula and beat again, very briefly, to ensure even mixing.

Madeira cake is a fairly rich cake with a soft texture and a top domed with fine cracks.

Adding the flour

The flour is added to the creamed mixture using a technique known as folding. This is quite different from beating or whisking which is unsuitable for cake mixtures because the brisk action strengthens the gluten in the flour and makes a tough cake. The object of folding one ingredient into another is to blend them together without losing volume. The folding action also aerates the mixture, helping the cake to rise.

Always add the flour to the creamed mixture. Using a metal spoon, add a third of the flour at a time to the creamed mixture, then use a figure-of-eight action to incorporate the flour into the mixture as lightly as possible. Repeat until it has all been incorporated.

Further additions

Further flavouring ingredients such as dried fruit and nuts may be added once the flour is incorporated. Use as light a hand as possible. At this point it may be necessary to add a small amount of liquid in the form of water or milk, to obtain the right consistency. Do this only where the recipe indicates or if by some chance the mixture is exceptionally stiff. The cake mixture should, at this stage, be of a soft dropping consistency.

BAKING

Using a spatula, scrape all the mixture down from the side of the bowl and then into the prepared tin(s). Smooth over the surface of the mixture with a palette knife, so that the mixture is level and will rise evenly in the tin. Bake on the appropriate shelf, making sure that the correct oven temperature is reached before putting the tin in the oven.

TESTING THE CAKE

Because the temperatures of individual ovens vary, baking times should be used as a guide, so it is always important to be sure that the cake is cooked through. Always wait until the end of the minimum baking time to have a look. Opening the door too early, before the cake has time to 'set', causes a sudden rush of cold air to enter the oven. This is a prime cause of cakes dipping in the centre.

To test a plain sponge follow these four golden rules.
● The cake should be evenly browned and well risen.
● The cake should have shrunk away from the sides of the tin.
● There should be no sound of bubbling (of uncooked mixture) when the cake is held to the ear.

• The mixture should feel firm but springy when lightly touched with a fingertip. If any impression of your fingertip remains, the cake will need a little longer baking.

COOLING

Rich cakes should be turned out to cool on a wire rack. Leaving a rich creamed cake in the tin would result in an unpleasant soggy cake.

Allow the cake to stand in the tin to let it shrink away from the sides. Leave sandwich cakes for approximately 30 seconds and other types of cakes for 5-10 minutes.

Carefully run a palette knife around the inside of the tin, between the cake and the side of the tin, to ease the cake away. Place a folded tea-towel over the top of the cake and turn the cake tin and tea-towel upside down, holding on to both. Put down the tea-towel with the inverted cake on it, left off the tin and peel away the lining paper and discard it. Place the wire cooling rack on top of the cake and turn over again, so that the cake is sitting the right way up. Leave until completely cold.

STORING AND FREEZING

Wait until the cake is completely cold for either storing or freezing. Plain, undecorated rich cakes will store successfully for up to 6 days in an airtight tin. Alternatively, they can be wrapped securely in cling film or foil and stored in a cool larder.

MADEIRA CAKE

This English cake was very popular during the 19th century and was traditionally served with a glass of Madeira wine – hence its name. Homemade Madeira cake is lighter, and has a much more 'spongy' and crumbly texture than commercial varieties.

MAKES 12 SLICES

100 g [4 oz] plain flour
100 g [4 oz] self-raising flour
pinch of salt
175 g [6 oz] butter, softened
175 g [6 oz] caster sugar
2-3 drops of vanilla essence
3 large eggs, lightly beaten
2 tablespoons milk
2 thin slices candied citron peel

1 Heat the oven to 170°C [325°F] Gas 3. Grease a deep 18 cm [7 in] round cake tin, line the sides and base with greaseproof paper, then lightly grease the paper.
2 Sift the flours with the salt. Reserve.
3 In a separate bowl, beat fat until soft and light. Add the sugar and cream together until pale and fluffy, then beat in vanilla essence. Add the eggs, a little at a time, beating thoroughly until blended after each addition.
4 Fold in the sifted flours, then stir in milk. Turn the mixture into the prepared tin and level the surface.
5 Bake the cake for 1 hour, then gently arrange citron peel on the top. (The top may have cracked slightly.) Return to the oven for a further 15 minutes, or until firm to the touch and a warmed fine skewer inserted into the centre comes out clean.
6 Cool the cake for 10-15 minutes, then turn out of the tin and peel off the lining paper. Place the cake the right way up on a wire rack and leave to cool completely. Madeira cake will keep for 2-3 weeks in an airtight container in a cool place.

Variations

• For a rich seed cake, omit the citron peel and add 2 teaspoons of caraway seeds to the sifted flour.
• For a cherry cake omit the citron peel, flavour the cake with a few drops of almond essence. Wash and dry 100 g [4 oz] halved glacé cherries and toss in 15 g [½ oz] of the measured amount of flour. Add the halved glacé cherries when all the flour has been incorporated by carefully folding them into the mixture.
• Chop 75 g [3 oz] walnuts coarsely and mix them with the sifted flour. Omit the citron peel and add the grated zest of one small lemon to the creamed butter and sugar mixture. Fold the nuts into the mixture with the flour.
• To make a ginger cake, omit the citron peel. Sift ½ teaspoon ground ginger with the flour and add 100g [4 oz] drained, rinsed, dried and coarsely chopped stem ginger when all the flour has been folded into the mixture.
• For a melt-in-the-mouth almond cake, omit the citron peel. Use only 175 g [6 oz] flour and add 25 g [1 oz] ground almonds and 25 g [1 oz] ground rice to the sifted flour. Flavour the mixture with ½ teaspoon almond essence.
• To make a coconut cake, omit the citron peel and add 100 g [4 oz] desiccated coconut to the sifted flour.

Frozen cakes:
Rich spice cakes and those containing flavouring essences can be frozen for up to 2 weeks, longer than that and the flavours of the spices will deteriorate.

Filled sandwich and layered cakes can be frozen for up to 2 months. Freeze them unwrapped then wrap and pack them into plastic containers to protect the decoration. When ready to serve them, unwrap them immediately after removing frozen from the freezer or the decoration will stick to the wrapper as the cake thaws. Rich cakes usually take 3-4 hours to thaw at room temperature but can be thawed overnight in the refrigerator.

Cherry cake is one of the many exciting variations of the delicious Madeira cake.

COFFEE CAKE

With morning coffee or afternoon tea, this traditional cake is a tried and tested favourite for the whole family to enjoy.

MAKES 8 SLICES

175 g [6 oz] self-raising flour
175 g [6 oz] butter or margarine
175 g [6oz] caster sugar
3 medium-sized eggs
25 g [1 oz] walnuts, finely chopped
1 tablespoon instant coffee powder
1 tablespoon hot water

For the icing:
100 g [4 oz] butter
175 g [6 oz] icing sugar, sifted
1½ teaspoons instant coffee powder
8 walnut halves

Coffee adds something special to cakes. This coffee cake has instant coffee in both the cake and the icing.

1 Heat the oven to 190°C [375°F] Gas 5. Grease and line two 18 cm [7 in] sandwich tins. Grease the paper.
2 Sift the flour into a mixing bowl and reserve.
3 Put the fat into a large mixing bowl and beat until soft and light. Add the sugar, then cream the ingredients together until light and fluffy.
4 Beat in the eggs gradually, beating well after each addition, then slowly fold in the flour and nuts.
5 Mix the instant coffee powder with the hot water and stir gently into the cake mixture.
6 Divide the mixture between the two prepared tins and bake for 20 minutes, or until firm and springy to the touch.
7 Leave the cakes to cool in the tins for 30 seconds, then turn out on to a wire rack, remove the lining paper and leave to cool completely.

8 To make the icing, cream the butter until soft, then beat in the sugar and coffee until all the ingredients are well mixed together.

9 Use half the icing to sandwich the cake layers together and spread the remainder over the top, swirling it with a fork. Decorate with the walnut halves.

OLD-FASHIONED SEED CAKE

This old-fashioned seed cake is made from a traditional Madeira mixture with caraway seeds added.

Traditionally a round cake, this variation is made in a loaf tin so that it can be cut into slices or thick finger shapes. Serve, unbuttered, with either tea or coffee and it will be enjoyed by family and friends alike.

MAKES 12 SLICES
100 g [4 oz] plain flour
100 g [4 oz] self-raising flour
pinch of salt
175 g [6 oz] butter
175 g [6 oz] caster sugar
3 large eggs, lightly beaten
2 tablespoons milk
2 teaspoons caraway seeds
2 tablespoons sugar, to finish

1 Heat the oven to 170°C [325°F] Gas 3. Grease a 1.75 L [3 pt], 1 kg [2 lb] loaf tin. Line the tin with greaseproof paper, then grease the paper.
2 Sift the flours with the salt into a bowl and reserve.
3 Put the fat in a mixing bowl and beat until soft and light. Add the sugar and cream together until pale and fluffy. Add the eggs, a little at a time, beating the mixture thoroughly after each addition.
4 Fold in the sifted flours, then stir in milk. Add the caraway seeds and gently fold them in, making sure they are evenly distributed. Turn the mixture into the prepared tin and level the surface, then make a shallow hollow in the centre. Sprinkle the sugar over the top.
5 Bake for 1-1¼ hours, or until firm to the touch and a warmed fine skewer inserted into the centre of the cake comes out clean. Check the cake after 1 hour's baking. Cover with greaseproof paper, if necessary, to prevent overbrowning. Unlike sponges, this cake does not rise evenly, so do not worry if the top peaks and cracks slightly. It is a traditional feature of the cake.
6 Cool the cake for 10-15 minutes, then turn out of the tin and peel off the lining paper. Place the cake the right way up on a wire rack and then leave to cool completely before slicing and serving. The cake (or any left-over slices) will keep for 2-3 weeks stored in an airtight tin or other container in a cool place.

Enjoy Old-fashioned seed cake at tea-time or coffee-time.

Frosted walnut layer cake is iced with a deliciously soft frosting which spreads easily and should be used as soon as made. Make sure the cake is cool and ready before you prepare the frosting. Use 2 teaspoons instant coffee powder dissolved in 2 teaspoons water if you have no coffee and chicory essence. It is best to decorate the cake on the day you intend to serve it.

FROSTED WALNUT LAYER CAKE

MAKES 900 G [2LB] CAKE
175 g [6 oz] plain flour
1 teaspoon baking powder
pinch of salt
175 g [6 oz] butter or margarine
175 g [6 oz] soft brown sugar
2 teaspoons coffee and chicory essence
3 medium-sized eggs
50 g [2 oz] walnuts
2 tablespoons milk (optional)

For the frosting:
1 medium-sized egg white
175 g [6 oz] caster sugar
2 tablespoons cold water
pinch of cream of tartar

For the decoration:
walnut halves

1 Heat the oven to 180°C [350°F] Gas 4.
2 Grease and fully line a deep 15 cm [6 in] round cake tin. Grease the lining paper.
3 Sift flour together with the baking powder and salt into a bowl. Reserve.
4 Put the fat in a large mixing bowl and beat until soft and light. Add the sugar and cream the ingredients together until light and fluffy. Scrape down the spoon and the sides of the bowl with a spatula.
5 Add the coffee and chicory essence, a little at a time, beating well after each addition.
6 Whisk the eggs lightly together and add gradually to creamed mixture, beating well after each addition. If any signs of curdling occur add a little of the sifted flour.
7 Scrape down the spoon and sides of the bowl and beat the mixture again briefly. Coarsely chop the 50 g [2 oz] walnuts.
8 Gently fold in the sifted flour until completely incorporated. Fold in chopped walnuts. If necessary, add enough milk to give a soft dropping consistency.
9 Put mixture into the prepared tin and smooth over the surface with a palette knife. Bake for 1-1¼ hours until well risen and evenly browned.
10 Allow cake to cool in tin for 5 minutes before turning out. Allow cake to cool completely on a wire rack.
11 Cut the cold cake horizontally into three equal layers, then place the bottom layer on a wire rack.

orange essence and a few drops of orange food colouring before beating over a pan of hot water and before the mixture thickens.

BUTTERFLY CAKES

MAKES ABOUT 15 CAKES

100 g [4 oz] self-raising flour
2 medium-sized eggs
100 g [4 oz] butter or margarine
100 g [4 oz] caster sugar

For the butter-cream icing:
50 g [2 oz] butter, softened
100 g [4 oz] icing sugar
few drops of pink food colouring

1 Heat oven to 190°C [375°F] Gas 5. Place 15 paper baking cases on a baking sheet.
2 Sift the flour into a bowl and reserve. Place the eggs in a small bowl and whisk together lightly.
3 Place the fat into a bowl and beat with a wooden spoon until light and creamy. Add the sugar and beat until light and fluffy.
4 Beat in the eggs a little at a time, beating well after each addition. Fold in the flour using a metal spoon.
5 Divide the cake mixture between the paper baking cases, put approximately 1 heaped teaspoon of the mixture in each paper case.
6 Bake just below the centre of the oven for 15 minutes, until cakes are golden brown.
7 Transfer cakes to a cooling rack to cool. Meanwhile make butter-cream icing according to the recipe on page 14, using given quantities. Colour with a few drops of colouring.
8 When the cakes are completely cold, cut a thin slice, horizontally from the top of each cake, cut each slice in half and place the halved 'tops', cut side facing down, on a cooling rack.
9 Sift a little plain icing sugar to just coat the tops of the cakes. Put a generous swirl of butter-icing on to the centre of each cake with a teaspoon or pipe on icing.
10 Replace two halves of cake cut from the top on to each cake, to represent butterfly wings. Press them gently into the butter-icing so that they are secure.
11 Repeat with the remaining cake tops. Put any remaining icing between the two 'butterfly wings' or pipe decoratively.

12 To start making the frosting, put all the frosting ingredients in a large bowl and beat lightly together with a table mixer or hand-held electric whisk until mixed together.
13 Place the bowl over a pan of hot, but not boiling, water. Beat for 7-10 minutes if using a hand whisk, or 2-3 minutes if using a hand-held electric whisk, until the frosting stands in soft peaks.
14 Spread a scant quarter of the frosting over the bottom layer of cake, then place the middle layer on top. Spread a further scant quarter of the frosting over the centre layer and top with the remaining layer of cake.
15 Quickly spread the remaining frosting on to the top of the cake, using a small palette knife, and spread down the side.
16 Swirl the frosting decoratively with the palette knife. Decorate the top with walnut halves.

Frosting variations
● For caramel frosting, use Demerara instead of caster sugar.
● For lemon frosting, add 1 teaspoon lemon juice before beating over a pan of hot water and before the mixture thickens.
● For orange frosting, add a few drops of

Of all the small sponge cakes there are to make, Butterfly cakes are perhaps the best known and the most popular with the younger members of the family.

CHOCOLATE AND COFFEE CAKE

MAKES 6-8 SLICES

200 g [7 oz] self-raising flour
25 g [1 oz] cocoa powder
2 teaspoons instant coffee powder
200 g [7 oz] butter
200 g [7 oz] caster sugar
4 medium-sized eggs, beaten

For the butter icing:
100 g [4 oz] butter
100 g [4 oz] icing sugar, sifted
2 tablespoons cocoa powder
1 teaspoon coffee essence
2 tablespoons boiling water
flaked almonds

1 Heat the oven to 190°C [375°F] Gas 5.
2 Grease and line two 18 cm [7 in] sandwich tins. Grease the paper.
3 Sift the flour with the cocoa and coffee powder and reserve.
4 Put the fat into a mixing bowl and beat until soft and light. Add the sugar and cream together until pale and fluffy. Beat in the eggs a little at a time. Add the eggs slowly and beat the mixture very thoroughly to prevent it curdling. If the mixture starts to look grainy instead of smooth and creamy, add a spoonful of the flour with the next addition of beaten egg. Fold in the flour mixture.
5 Divide the mixture between the prepared tins and make a hollow in the centre of each mixture to prevent peaking.
6 Bake the cakes for 30 minutes, or until they are firm and a skewer inserted into the centre comes out clean. Cool for 5 minutes in the tins, then turn the cakes out on to wire racks to cool completely.
7 To make butter icing, beat the butter with the icing sugar. Dissolve the cocoa powder and coffee essence in the boiling water and beat them into the butter.
8 Trim the top of the bottom cake. Use a long-bladed knife with a sharp serrated edge, cutting with a sawing action, to trim the top of the bottom cake so that it is level.
9 Spread the bottom cake with some of the butter icing, place the other cake on top and spread it with the remaining icing.
10 Just before serving, decorate the cake with flaked almonds.

Chocolate coffee cake freezes beautifully: wrap each layer in heavy duty foil or cling film and freeze for up to 6 months. Defrost in the wrappings at room temperature for about 2 hours. Finish, ice and decorate the cake just before serving.

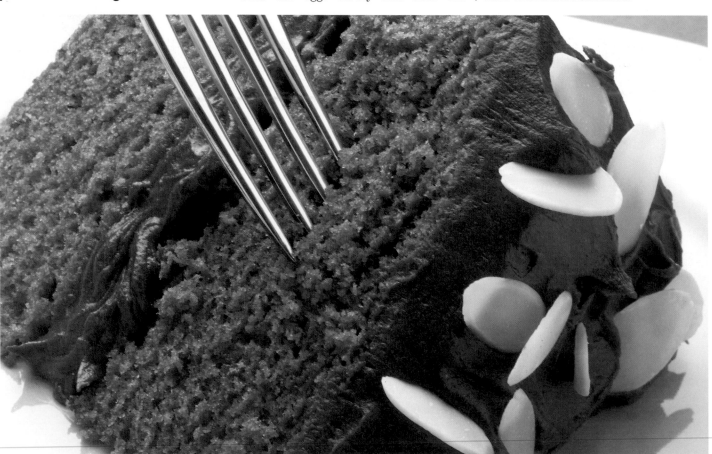

RASPBERRY CREAM CAKE

MAKES 6-8 SLICES

100 g [4 oz] self-raising flour
100 g [4 oz] butter or margarine
100 g [4 oz] caster sugar
1-2 drops of vanilla essence
2 large eggs
icing sugar to dredge

For the filling:
150 ml [¼ pt] thick cream
100 g [4 oz] raspberries
4-6 tablespoons raspberry jam

1 Heat the oven to 170°C [325°F] Gas 3. Grease and line two 18 cm [7 in] sandwich tins. Grease the paper.
2 Sift the flour into a large bowl. Reserve.
3 Put the fat in a mixing bowl and beat until soft and light. Add the sugar and cream until light and fluffy. Beat in the vanilla.
4 Whisk the eggs lightly, then beat into the creamed mixture, beating after each addition.
5 Gently fold in the sifted flour until completely incorporated.
6 Divide the mixture equally between the prepared tins and smooth over the surfaces with a palette knife. Bake for 25-30 minutes until just firm.
7 Leave the cakes to cool in the tins for 30 seconds, then turn out on to a tea-towel. Remove the paper lining and turn the right way up on to a wire rack to cool.
8 Meanwhile whip the cream until thick. Lightly crush the raspberries and fold them into the whipped cream.
9 When the cakes are cold, place one cake on the serving plate and spread the surface with jam, then with the raspberry cream mixture.
10 Spread the remaining jam over the underside of the remaining sponge, then cut it into six to eight wedges. Carefully position the wedges, jam-side down and slightly apart, on top of the raspberry filling: cut a thin strip off the last wedge, so that it fits in place.
11 Dredge the surface of the sponge wedges with icing sugar.

This luscious cake, with its raspberry and cream filling, makes a real tea-time special.
If fresh raspberries are unavailable, use 100 g [4 oz] defrosted frozen raspberries, or 200 g [7 oz] canned berries, that have been well drained.

Spicy marmalade cake has marmalade in both the cake and the filling, giving it a delicious flavour.

SPICY MARMALADE CAKE

MAKES 8-12 SLICES
350 g [12 oz] self-raising flour
1 teaspoon ground cinnamon
½ teaspoon freshly grated or ground nutmeg
¼ teaspoon ground cloves or ground mixed spice
175 g [6 oz] margarine
175 g [6 oz] golden syrup
5 tablespoons thin-cut marmalade
2 large eggs
about 50 ml [2 fl oz] milk
25 g [1 oz] dark soft brown sugar

For the filling:
6-8 tablespoons thin-cut marmalade

1 Heat the oven to 180°C [350°F] Gas 4. Grease and line a deep 23 cm [9 in] round cake tin. Grease the paper.
2 Sift the flour with the spices into a bowl and set aside.
3 In a large mixing bowl, beat the margarine until fluffy; add the golden syrup and beat until smoothly blended, then beat in the marmalade. Add the eggs, one at a time, beating well after each addition.
4 Using a large metal spoon, fold in the sifted flour, adding enough milk to give a stiff consistency.
5 Spread the mixture evenly in the prepared tin and make a deep hollow in the centre. Scatter the dark sugar over the top.
6 Bake the cake for 1 hour or until a warmed fine skewer inserted into the centre comes out clean. Leave the baked cake in the tin for 5 minutes, then turn it out on to a wire rack and peel off the lining paper. Turn the cake the right way up and leave on the wire rack to cool completely.
7 Cut the cold cake horizontally into three equal layers and sandwich back together with the marmalade.

SAFFRON HONEY CAKE

MAKES 8 SLICES

6 saffron strands
4 tablespoons milk
175 g [6 oz] plain flour
1 tablespoon baking powder
100 g [4 oz] butter or margarine, softened
50 g [2 oz] caster sugar
2 tablespoons clear honey
2 medium-sized eggs, lightly beaten
50 g [2 oz] cut mixed peel
75 g [3 oz] sultanas

For the icing:
10 saffron strands
1 tablespoon boiling water
200 g [7 oz] icing sugar
1-2 tablespoons lemon juice

1 Heat the oven to 180°C [350°F] Gas 4. Grease a deep 18 cm [7 in] round cake tin, line sides and base with greaseproof paper; grease the paper.
2 Crush the six saffron strands for the cake between your fingers and put into a small, heavy-based saucepan with the milk. Bring just to the boil, then remove from heat and leave to stand for 20 minutes.

3 Sift the flour with the baking powder and reserve.
4 Put the fat in a mixing bowl and beat until soft and light. Add the sugar and honey and cream together until pale and fluffy. Beat in the eggs, a little at a time, adding 1 tablespoon sifted flour if mixture shows signs of curdling. Fold in the sifted flour.
5 Strain the saffron milk, then stir into cake mixture, 1 tablespoon at a time. Fold in the peel and sultanas. Turn mixture into the prepared tin.
6 Bake for 65 minutes, or until a warmed fine skewer inserted into the centre comes out clean.
7 Meanwhile, put the 10 saffron strands for the icing into a small bowl with the boiling water and leave to stand until required.
8 Cool the cake for 5 minutes, then turn out of the tin and peel off the lining paper. Turn cake right way up and leave it on a wire rack to cool.
9 Sift the icing sugar into a large bowl and stir in 1 tablespoon lemon juice. Strain the saffron water, then stir into the icing until evenly coloured. Stir in remaining lemon juice if necessary, to give a thick pouring consistency.
10 Place a large plate under the rack. Pour icing over cake, smooth with a palette knife and leave to set.

Saffron honey cake is topped with a distinctive saffron-flavoured icing.

CRISPY LEMON SLICES

MAKES 16 SLICES

75 g [3 oz] margarine or butter
100 g [4 oz] caster sugar
grated zest of 1 lemon
2 eggs, separated
100 g [4 oz] self-raising flour, sifted
150 g [5 oz] natural yoghurt
40 g [1½ oz] cut mixed peel

For the topping:
100 g [4 oz] caster sugar
juice of 1 small lemon

1 Heat the oven to 180°C [350°F] Gas 4. Grease a 28 × 18 cm [11 × 7 in] Swiss roll tin with margarine.
2 Beat the margarine, sugar and lemon zest together until pale and fluffy. Add the egg yolks, one at a time, beating thoroughly after each addition.
3 Using a large metal spoon, fold in the sifted flour alternately with the natural yoghurt. Fold in the cut mixed peel.
4 Stiffly whisk the egg whites and fold them into the cake mixture, using a large, clean metal spoon to cut through the mixture.

5 Turn the mixture into the greased tin and spread it evenly. Bake for 30 minutes until the cake is a light golden colour and just firm to the touch when pressed lightly.
6 Meanwhile, to make the topping, mix together the caster sugar and lemon juice in a bowl to make a thin paste.
7 Let the baked cake stand in the tin for a few seconds, then carefully turn it out on to a wire rack and immediately spread the lemon paste over the surface. (The paste sinks in to make a crispy top.)
8 Leave the cake until quite cold before cutting into 16 rectangles. Serve the slices the day they are made as they soften if stored.

Variation

● For a special treat, you can easily turn these slices into the 'mimosa cakes' shown in the picture. Make up only half the amount of lemon paste. Cut the baked cake in half lengthways and spread one half with lemon paste. When the cakes are cold, spread the plain half with lemon curd and place the other half on top. Cut into eight pieces. Decorate each slice with crystallized mimosa balls and 'diamonds' of angelica.

Crispy lemon slices can easily be turned into fancy 'mimosa cakes'.

NUTTY CHOCOLATE TRIANGLES

MAKES 8

75 g [3 oz] plain flour
25 g [1 oz] cocoa powder
½ teaspoon baking powder
pinch of salt
75 g [3 oz] margarine
75 g [3 oz] light soft brown sugar
75 ml [3 fl oz] golden syrup
2-3 drops of vanilla essence
2 eggs

To finish:
3 tablespoons hazelnut chocolate spread
chopped roasted hazelnuts

1 Heat the oven to 180°C [350°F] Gas 4. Grease an 18 cm [7 in] square tin, about 2.5 cm [1 in] deep. Line the base with greaseproof paper, then lightly grease the paper.
2 Sift flour, cocoa, baking powder and salt into a bowl and reserve.

3 Put the fat in a mixing bowl and beat until soft and light. Add the sugar and syrup and cream together until pale and fluffy, then beat in the vanilla.
4 Beat in the eggs, one at a time, adding 1 tablespoon flour mixture with each egg. Stir in the remaining flour mixture with a wooden spoon, then beat briefly until smooth and evenly blended.
5 Pour mixture into prepared tin, level the surface, then make a hollow in the centre. Bake for 30-35 minutes, or until springy to the touch. (Cover with greaseproof paper towards end of baking to avoid overbrowning.)
6 Cool the cake for 5 minutes, then run a palette knife around the sides, turn out on to a wire rack and peel off lining paper. Turn the cake right way up and leave it to cool completely.
7 To finish, trim off crusty edges, then cover top of cake with hazelnut spread. Cut the cake into four squares then cut each square in half diagonally to make eight triangles.
8 Decorate the tops of the chocolate triangles with chopped roasted hazelnuts.

These delicious Nutty chocolate triangles make a mouthwatering coffee-time treat.

DECORATIVE SPONGE CAKES

Celebrations merit something extra – a special and beautifully decorated cake is often just the answer. This chapter shows you how to make cakes with exciting coloured interiors and how to ice and decorate cakes for amazing and professional-looking visual effects.

Some of the nicest cakes are those that are the simplest to make. They are then decorated to make them into something special. The Victoria sponge made by the creaming method, described on page 72, is the perfect base for a wide variety of fancy cakes. Rich sponge is ideal for icing; its light, spongy texture combines well with sweet, rich fillings and icings. Perhaps the most important factor of all is that it stores well. It can therefore be made in advance – leaving you plenty of time for the decorating.

This chapter shows you just what can be done to make eye-catching cakes. The Victoria sponge mixture can be used in two ways. The sponge itself can be multi-coloured. For marbled cakes prepared mixture is divided and the portions coloured (and flavoured) differently. The different coloured sponges are then baked in a single tin.

Alternatively, the different coloured cake mixtures can be baked separately and then the cooled sponges are cut and assembled together in a formal pattern. When completed, the cake is iced or coated, so that the colours inside come as a surprise when the cake is cut.

The secret of multi-coloured cakes is hidden inside. The decorative effect will only be visible once the slice of cake is on an individual tea plate.

Another, perhaps more spectacular way of decorating a cake is to ice the exterior. This chapter shows you the professional way to go about icing; how to handle the equipment; how to do feather icing; how to decorate the sides of a cake as well as the top. It also helps you with a selection of decorative patterns, so that you, too, can make a cake beautiful enough to win first prize at any baking show.

Chequered cakes

These traditional cakes are made from rich sponge mixture which is divided in two. One portion is usually left plain and the other is coloured and sometimes flavoured. The best known of these cakes is Battenburg. The sponges are baked in a single tin, which is cleverly divided lengthways by a strip of greaseproof paper (known as a wall), which separates the two mixtures. To make a Battenburg you will need a 28 × 18 cm [11 × 7 in] Swiss roll tin.

After baking, the cold sponge is cut lengthways and reassembled with jam so that, when cut, the individual slices will be chequered. The outside of the cake is encased with marzipan for a Battenburg.

Marbled cake

This cake acquired its name because the sponge has the effect of marble with different colours running through it in a random pattern. The basic uncooked cake mixture is divided into portions and the portions are then coloured with food colouring. For a sophisticated touch, the colouring is married up with an appropriate flavour. The flavour is achieved by adding food essence or a natural ingredient, such as grated citron zest or chopped nuts.

The choice is entirely up to you, but some obvious colour and flavour combinations are orange colour with orange zest, yellow with lemon zest, plain with vanilla, pink with raspberry or strawberry, green with almond or pistachio, coffee and chocolate powders will give a dark sponge. You can also try more sophisticated ideas; a touch of orange in a sponge coloured and flavoured with chocolate is excellent. Additions can also be made sparingly to one of the sponge mixtures, for example walnuts to coffee sponge. Follow the ideas and proportions for additions given on page 69. A recipe for marbled cake is given here as guidance. You can then experiment with your own colours and flavours.

Marbled cakes are simplicity itself to make. After the sponge has been divided and coloured, the different sponge mixtures are put together in the same tin. A skewer is then inserted and swirled through to give a marbled effect.

PREPARING A CAKE FOR ICING

An extra bit of care in preparing the cake before you fill and decorate it makes all the difference between an adequate result and a simply splendid

one. It is worth taking the trouble to make sure the cake is in good condition before you start!

Use cold sponge
The first rule is to make sure that the cake is completely cold. Any icing applied to a warm cake will certainly melt. Bear in mind that it is not advisable to decorate a cake which is only just cold, because it tends to be too soft to handle. Purists insist that the cake should be at least 12 hours old, but this is a matter of convenience. If you want to, save time by making the cake one day, storing it overnight wrapped in cling film or foil, then decorate it the next day.

Level the surface
The second rule is that the surface of the cake for icing must be level. It is both difficult to ice a cake with a peaked surface and also looks unsightly and spoils the effect after you have gone to trouble in the baking.

Even if you have followed all the rules for baking that should produce a

A simple sponge can be turned into something spectacular by covering the top with a layer of chocolate caraque dusted with icing sugar.

MAKING A BATTENBURG CAKE

SERVES 10
225 g [8 oz] self-raising flour
4 large eggs

225 g [8 oz] butter or margarine
225 g [8 oz] caster sugar
few drops of vanilla essence

few drops of red food colouring
apricot jam
225 g [8 oz] marzipan
caster sugar

1 Heat oven to 190°C [375°F] Gas 5. Grease and line a 28 × 18 cm [11 × 7 in] Swiss roll tin, drawing the grease-proof into a pleat. Re-grease.

2 Sift the flour into a bowl. Whisk eggs together lightly in a small bowl. Place the butter or margarine in a mixing bowl and beat until light and creamy.

3 Add the sugar and cream it with the fat until light and fluffy. Beat in a few drops of vanilla essence. Beat in the eggs, a little at a time.

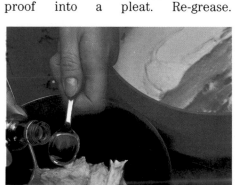

4 Fold in the flour and place half of the mixture in a separate bowl. Add a few drops of pink food colouring and beat well. Place mixture down one side of tin.

5 Place plain cake mixture down other side of prepared tin. Smooth both mixtures. Bake just above centre of oven for 45-50 minutes until golden brown.

6 Turn cakes on to a wire rack to cool. Cut each cake in half lengthways. Trim the cakes so that they are all exactly the same size.

7 Spread the sides of the cake with the jam and stick them together, alternating the colours. Press together. Spread outside of cake with jam.

8 Sprinkle the board liberally with caster sugar and roll out marzipan to an oblong 30 × 25 cm [12 × 10 in]. Spread with jam. Place the cake length on the marzipan.

9 Wrap the marzipan around the cake, seal the join and trim the edges. Pinch the top edges together to form a pattern and criss-cross the top with a sharp knife.

level surface, but still find the cake peaks, then do not be put off. There are ways to deal with this. For large cakes, place the cake on a level surface. Slice the 'peak' from the surface of the cake horizontally with a long-bladed sharp knife, using a sawing motion. Brush away any loose cake crumbs, using a pastry brush. Repeat if there is still a peak, until the cake is level.

Cakes baked in sandwich tins do not, however, require the same treatment if the surfaces are slightly uneven. Simply turn them upside down. If, on the other hand, they are very peaked, then follow the same procedure as for the larger cakes. Always brush away the loose crumbs

caused by slicing the cake.

Fillings

Unless you are making a particularly buttery cake, you will need to add extra flavour and moistness to a large basic cake with a filling. If you do not own sandwich tins in which to bake the cake, it may be made in a deep round or square tin. The cake is then sliced horizontally, as shown on page 13, for filling. Fillings are spread on to layers to sandwich a cake, they add both moisture and a contrast of texture and flavour. Butter icing, crème au beurre or a fresh thick cream can all be used. Recipes for butter-cream icing are given on page 14 and for crème au beurre on pages 252-253.

Battenburg sponges of two or more colours may appear complicated, but they are extremely easy to make at home.

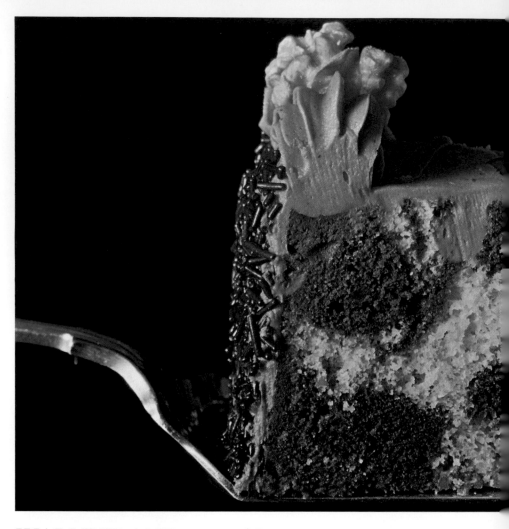

WALNUT AND CHOCOLATE MARBLE CAKE

The secret of this cake is revealed when the cake is cut to show the interesting 'marble look' of the two different coloured cake mixtures. It is a beautifully moist cake that the children will be unable to resist.

MAKES 10-12 SLICES

225 g [8 oz] self-raising flour
pinch of salt
50 g [2 oz] cocoa powder
175 g [6 oz] butter or margarine
175 g [6 oz] caster sugar
4 medium-sized eggs
50 g [2 oz] chopped walnuts

For the decoration:
225 g [8 oz] chocolate butter-cream icing
   (see page 14)
4 tablespoons chocolate vermicelli
8 walnut halves

1 Heat the oven to 180°C [350°F] Gas 4. Grease and fully line a deep, 18 cm [7 in] round cake tin. Grease the paper.

2 Sift the flour and salt into a bowl and reserve. Sift the cocoa powder into a second bowl and mix it to a thick paste with a little hot water. Put this aside to cool.

3 Place the butter or margarine in a mixing bowl and beat with a wooden spoon until soft and light. Add the sugar and cream together until light and fluffy.

4 Whisk the eggs lightly together and add gradually to the creamed mixture, beating well after each addition so that the mixture does not curdle.

5 Gently fold in the sifted flour until completely incorporated. Transfer half of the mixture into another bowl.

6 Add the walnuts to one part of the cake mixture. Stir in until completely incorporated.

7 Add the chocolate paste to the other half of the cake mixture and beat together, until the paste is evenly distributed throughout the mixture.

8 Place the two mixtures in the prepared tin in alternate heaped teaspoons until both mixtures are used up.

9 Smooth over the surface with a palette knife. Swirl through the mixture with a skewer, briefly and with a light hand.

10 Bake for 45-50 minutes until cake is cooked. Leave the cake to cool in the tin for 10 minutes before turning out. Cool.

11 Place a generous third of the chocolate butter-cream icing in a piping bag or pump fitted with a shell or star nozzle.

12 Spread the sides of the cake with half remaining butter-cream icing to completely cover. Smooth with a palette knife.

13 Sprinkle the chocolate vermicelli on to a large piece of greasproof paper.

14 Hold the top and bottom of the cake between the palms of your hands and carefully roll the iced side of the cake in the vermicelli to coat evenly.

15 Place the cake on a serving plate. Carefully spread the remaining icing from the bowl smoothly over the top of the cake.

16 Pipe a border of shells or stars around the top outer edge of the cake. Decorate the shells or stars with the walnut halves.

ICING EQUIPMENT

With the correct basic equipment, piping decorative shapes is not as complicated as it at first appears. Piping icing also requires patience and know-how about the various kinds of equipment that you can use. These include an icing pump, the piping bags, which may be bought, or disposable ones made of greaseproof paper at home, plus a selection of tubes and nozzles.

Icing pump

An icing pump resembles a hyperdermic syringe and more often than not is called a piping syringe. Pumps are available in plastic and metal and consist of a cylinder with a detachable plunger at one end. This descends into the tube, forcing out the icing in the cylinder through a detachable nozzle or tube, situated at the opposite end to the plunger. An icing pump can be a little awkward to handle if you are a beginner because it takes a bit of getting used to.

Investing in an icing pump means you are buying a set which usually includes the syringe with plunger, the nozzles and tubes. It should be stressed that the icing pump is best used with a thick icing such as a butter icing or crème au beurre. If you tried to use a thin glacé icing in an icing pump, it would run through.

MAKING A GREASEPROOF PAPER PIPING BAG

1 Cut a 25 cm [10 in] square from greaseproof paper. Fold this across diagonally, to make two triangles.

2 With base line facing away bring left-hand corner of the base up to meet the top of the triangle.

3 Holding the two points at the top together, bring up the right-hand corner to wrap it around the back so that the right corner meets top of the triangle to form a cone.

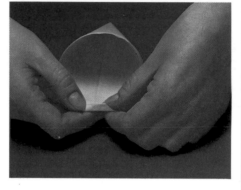

4 Fold the three corners (now all at the top) towards the inside of the cone. This prevents the bag from springing open.

5 Cut off the point of the piping bag to fit the size of the chosen nozzle or tube. Slip this into the bag to point out the bottom.

6 Holding the bag in one hand at an angle, fill it no more than half full with a teaspoon. Fold the top of the bag down to secure for use.

Piping bag

The alternative to the pump is a forcing bag which, as the name suggests, is a bag through which icing is forced. The bag looks like an elongated triangle and may be made from nylon, cotton, plastic or greaseproof paper with an opening at the point of the triangle. The chosen icing nozzle is slipped into the bag when empty and sticks out of the opening so that icing will pass through it. A bag can be filled with any consistency of icing.

For beginners at icing, an icing bag is a good investment as it is easier to use. The icing bags on sale come in varying sizes, with appropriate nozzle sizes. There are several important points to consider, to save you time and money when purchasing. If you intend to pipe a little but often, then it is best to learn how to make grease proof paper piping bags and invest in a medium or large commercial piping bag for bigger jobs.

Greaseproof piping bag

The main difference between a bought piping bag and a greaseproof paper one (which is equally as good and less expensive) is that a paper piping bag takes slightly less icing and can only be used once, for one batch of icing. The bag is made, the nozzle selected and fitted and and icing is inserted inside ready to use. But once that batch of icing is used, it is inadvisable to undo the bag and try to refill it.

If you are using different coloured icings for one cake, you can make several greaseproof paper piping bags. It is essential to make them all before you start, making sure that you have the correct size of nozzle or tube in each. Bought piping bags or pumps can easily be washed and dried if more than one colour icing is being used. This can, however, be a time consuming process, but can be speeded up when you have a selection of bags or pumps to hand.

The nozzles

Strictly speaking a nozzle is a metal or plastic tube through which the icing passes from the bag (or pump) on to the cake. A nozzle is cone shaped, with a pattern cut from the pointed end of the cone. When the icing is being forced through this decorative point, it produces a pattern – a star, a leaf, a shell or whatever – depending on the

ASSEMBLING AN ICING PUMP

1 Screw chosen nozzle or tube into the collar and screw the collar into the end of the icing pump.

2 Fill the icing pump two-thirds full with icing. Hold icing pump with the left hand.

3 Hold the plunger in the right hand and insert into top of icing pump. Secure it in place.

ASSEMBLING AND FILLING
A NYLON PIPING BAG

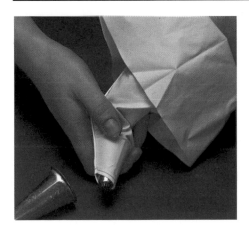 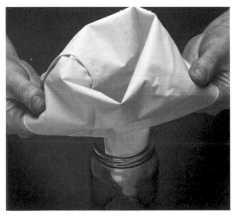 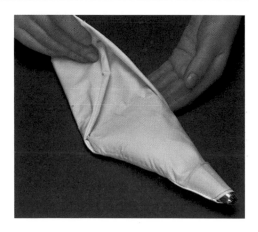

1 Slip chosen nozzle or tube into bag to project through the hole. Fold back outside of top of piping bag.

2 Place assembled bag inside a tall jar with the folded rim of the bag resting on the rim of the glass.

3 Half fill the bag with icing. Fold over icing bag to reach icing and twist, forcing out any trapped air.

nozzle you have chosen, for the particular decoration you need.

If the cone gives a plain thread of icing then it is called a tube, but is depends on the manufacturer as to what brand name it bears. Plain tubes are used for straight lines, trellis or writing and dots of icing.

If you are using a greaseproof paper piping bag to pipe threads of icing, there is no need to use a tube. Simply snip off the pointed end of the bag.

How much you cut off from the tip of the bag will determine the size of the thread of icing. Always cut away a little less than you think you need, so as to be on the safe side. If the hole is not big enough, you can always cut off more.

Whether you invest in metal or plastic nozzles or tubes they should be kept scrupulously clean. If any icing is allowed to remain in the cone, it will harden (after a period of time) and

block the cone the next time you use it. If the same nozzle or tube is going to be used to pipe different coloured icings consecutively, then it is essential that the cone is absolutely clean, so that the different colours are not allowed to mingle.

Simple piping techniques
Piping pumps and piping bags are virtually used in the same way with the same nozzles and designs.

PIPING LINES

1 Hold the bag or pump fitted with a plain tube at a 45° angle to the surface to be iced, about 12 mm [½ in] above.

2 Press out the icing carefully, lifting the pump or bag up slightly, so that the icing falls on to the cake.

3 Continue pressing the icing until the line is complete. To end the line, lower the tube to touch the cake.

PIPING FEATHER ICING

1 Pour glacé icing on to top of cake and spread over evenly with a round-blade or palette knife.

2 Pipe parallel lines of contrasting colour across the iced surface approximately 12 mm [½ in] apart.

3 Quickly draw the point of a knife or a fine skewer through the piped lines in alternating directions.

PIPING A TRELLIS

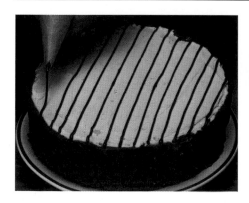

1 Cover the surface of the cake with straight parallel lines.

2 Pipe a 'ladder' of parallel lines at right angles on top.

USING A PIPING BAG

Before you start, make sure that there is no way that the icing can escape from the top of the bag while you are pressing it out through the other end. If the bag is made from greaseproof, fold down the top securely until it reaches the icing. With other piping bags, twist the folded top until you reach the icing.

Hold the filled piping bag in your right hand, so that the bag rests in the palm of the hand and your thumb is pressed on to the top of the bag securing the twist or fold that you have previously made. Bring your fingers around the bag so that you are holding it firmly. Your left hand is free to direct the bag if the pattern requires.

Using an icing pump

The body of the pump is held in the right hand with the nozzle or tube facing the surface to be iced and the left hand is used to depress the pump, thus forcing out the icing.

PIPING ICING

Piped icing can look as good as it tastes. Butter icing, crème au beurre and glacé icing are all suitable for piping and they complement the texture of the butter sponge. Plain or flavoured icings can be used.

Very rarely will you come across a recipe or see a cake where an icing of any description is piped straight on to a bare sponge. Generally speaking, each kind of icing is piped on to a cake

Quantities* of butter-cream icing for 18 cm (7 in) sandwich cake	
*amount of icing sugar used, not total weight	
For filling	75 g [3 oz]
For a topping	75 g [3 oz]
To coat the sides	175 g [6 oz]
To coat the sides and top or fill	225 g [8 oz]

which is already covered with icing of the same type. Thus, butter icing is usually piped on to butter icing and glacé icing on to glacé icing. However, butter icing can be piped on to a base of glacé icing as long as the icing underneath has had time to set.

The icing you choose to pipe should first and foremost be free from any lumps of undissolved sugar or flavouring (if used), as a lump will block the nozzle or tube. The second requirement is that the icing should be thick and firm if it needs to keep its shape on the cake. Glacé icing is usually of a coating consistency but by using less liquid it can be piped.

DECORATING THE SIDE OF A CAKE

1 Brush the side of the cake only with apricot jam glaze, or coat with butter-cream icing.

2 Sprinkle the decoration of your choice on to a large sheet of greaseproof paper.

3 Hold the cake firmly with the palm of one hand on the base and the other on the top.

4 Roll the cake evenly in the decoration to coat. For a square cake, press each side in turn.

FEATHER ICING

This very pretty way of using glacé icing (see page 14) is a lot less complicated than it appears. Use the quantities of glacé icing given in the chart on page 16.

Feather icing is only applied to the top of a cake and uses one batch of glacé icing, with a portion reserved (usually a third) which is coloured or flavoured to produce the decoration known as 'feathering'. This method of icing is unusual because it is the only occasion where the piped decoration is added while the base icing (or covering) of glacé icing is still soft.

Start by making a medium-sized paper bag and fitting it with a small plain tube.

Make the icing following the guide to quantities given on page 14. Once the icing is made, transfer a scant third of it to a separate bowl. At this point cover both bowls with a damp clean cloth to prevent the icing from drying and forming a crust. Colour the scant third of icing with a few drops of edible food colouring to contrast with, or complement, the colour of the icing over the cake. The cake covering may be plain and the decoration coloured or vice versa, or both may be coloured.

Fill the piping bag with the scant third of icing ready to use. Then, pour the remaining icing over the top of the cake and quickly spread over the surface to completely and evenly cover it. Quickly pipe parallel lines across the surface of the icing, approximately 12 mm [½ in] apart.

Draw the point of a knife or a fine skewer through the piped lines making alternate strokes in opposite directions. Wipe the blade of the knife or the tip of the skewer clean in between each stroke.

DECORATING THE SIDE OF A CAKE

Many professional-looking effects are surprisingly easy to achieve at home. This chapter concentrates on the simplest ways to decorate the sides of a cake.

The first rule is that the sides of the cake must always be done before the top is decorated.

Decorating with icings
The easiest way to decorate the side of a cake is to totally cover it with a thick

icing such as a butter icing or crème au beurre. Glacé icing can be used, but this is more difficult. Glacé icing is best used where the entire cake is to be covered so that the icing runs from the top of the cake and down the sides. Glacé icing may be spread on to the side of the cake, but the procedure is a messy one because it tends to dry out very quickly.

Simple ways with thick icing

• Use a round-bladed knife or a small palette knife and spread the entire surface of the side of the cake with a layer of icing. Using the knife, place the straight side of the blade against the side of the icing and draw it completely around the cake.
• Spread the entire surface of the side of the cake with icing. Smooth the icing with a round-bladed knife or palette knife. Take a fork and, starting at the base of the cake, draw the prongs of the fork up the side of the cake. Continue to work from the base to the top of the cake until you meet your first marking.
• This 'forking' can be done imaginatively by waving the line being drawn with the fork.

Additional decorations

While a simple covering of a thin or thick icing suits the majority of cakes, others look exciting when covered with additional decorations, for example coconut, nuts and chocolate.

To stick the decorations to the side of the cake, the side must be either brushed with a thin coating of sieved apricot jam glaze or an icing. Choose the decoration to complement the filling and topping, and make sure that the decorations you choose are of a suitable size and will easily adhere to the cake sides. Bear in mind the size and shape of the cake and keep decorations in proportion.

For a professional touch choose any of the following. Chocolate vermicelli, chopped nuts and desiccated coconut are the most popular choice of decoration. Nuts can also be used plain, flaked, nibbed or toasted. Finely crushed praline, caramel or biscuits or grated chocolate are also excellent.

The amount you need will depend on the size of the cake and how thick you want the decoration to be. As an approximate guide, 2-3 tablespoons is sufficient to cover the side of an 18 cm [7 in] round or square cake.

PIPING SHELLS

1 Hold pump or bag fitted with a 'shell' or 'star' nozzle at a 45° angle to the surface to be iced.

2 Hold the nozzle close to the cake and press out a blob of icing on to the surface of the cake.

3 Pull the nozzle down and away sharply to taper the end of the blob.

4 Pipe the next 'shell' directly on to the end of the tapered shell.

PIPING STARS

1 Use a 'star' or 'rosette' nozzle. Hold the bag or pump vertically, close to the cake surface.

2 Using short squeezes of the bag or plunges of a pump, press out icing. Lift off quickly.

SUPER DECORATED CAKES

Here are some suggestions for dressing up a simple Victoria sandwich cake. Quantities given are for an 18 cm [7 in] cake. Instructions for making the cake are given on page 72. The chart on page 97 gives the quantities of butter-cream icing needed. You will notice that when this is used to coat the sides and fill or top the cake the amount is slightly reduced. This means that it is spread a little thinner – otherwise the results would be too sickly. If decoration is to be piped, allow an extra 50 g [2 oz] icing. Butter-cream icing or crème au beurre may be used in the following cakes.

• For a special chocolate cake, bake a chocolate flavoured sandwich. When cold, sandwich together with 2-3 tablespoons black cherry jam or preserve. Coat the sides with butter icing and roll in chocolate vermicelli to coat. Ice the top of the cake smooth with chocolate butter icing. To decorate, pipe 6-8 swirls of butter icing around the edge of the cake and top each with a piece of glacé cherry.

Alternatively, cover the top with a layer of chocolate caraque and then dust with a small quantity of sifted icing sugar.

• For praline cake, sandwich, then spread the sides of the cake with lemon butter icing. Roll the side of the cake in a mixture of finely crushed praline and toasted, chopped almonds (which have been mixed together). Spread the top of the cake smooth with lemon butter icing and decorate with a border of piped shells. Sprinkle some more of the praline and nut mixture over the surface.

• Make this dinner party special. Bake a ginger flavoured cake. When cold, sandwich with a ginger flavoured crème au beurre. Use a little syrup from a jar of stem ginger to flavour this. Coat the top and side of the cake with more of the same crème au beurre, and smooth with a palette knife. Just before serving fill 6-8 bought brandy snaps with cream and arrange them decoratively over the top of the cake, to fan out from the centre. Place a small piece of stem ginger in each cream-filled brandy snap.

Serve this decorated ginger-flavoured sponge as a dinner party dessert.

FONDANT ICING

Fondant icing can be used to cover a sponge cake, or it can be modelled into decorations for the top of the cake. A sugar thermometer is essential for this icing as the sugar has to be heated to the point where it will be opaque and white when firm.

COVERS THE TOP OF A 22 CM [8½ IN] CAKE

450 g [1 lb] granulated sugar
150 ml [¼ pt] water
25 ml [1 fl oz] liquid glucose or ½ teaspoon
    cream of tartar
icing sugar for dusting

To finish the fondant:
50 g [2 oz] granulated sugar
flavouring (see below)
sifted icing sugar (if necessary)
food colouring (optional)

For the apricot glaze:
3 tablespoons apricot jam

1 Put 450 g [1 lb] sugar and 150 ml [¼ pt] water in a large, heavy-based saucepan and dissolve the sugar over a low heat. You may find that you get a rim of sugar round the pan above the level of the liquid. If so, dip a pastry brush in cold water and wipe any sugar crystals down into the syrup.
2 Bring the syrup to the boil. Meanwhile add the glucose (or the cream of tartar dissolved in 1 teaspoon water) to the syrup. Boil steadily for 10-15 minutes until it reaches 115°C [240°F].
3 Remove the pan from the heat, let the bubbles subside, then pour the syrup slowly into a heatproof bowl. Leave for about 1 minute until a skin forms on the top.
4 Using a wooden spoon, work the icing in figure-of-eight movements until it becomes white and firm.
5 Dust your hands with icing sugar and knead the icing until it is smooth.
6 Pack the fondant into a small bowl, cover with a damp cloth and leave for 1 hour. Then either use immediately, or wrap the fondant in waxed paper and keep in an airtight container until needed. It will keep for up to a year.
7 To use the icing for covering a cake, you will need to add a little sugar syrup to make it soft and flowing. To make this, dissolve 50 g [2 oz] sugar in 125 ml [4 fl oz] water in a small pan over a low heat. Bring it to the boil and boil until the temperature reaches 105°C [220°F], about 10 minutes.
8 Warm the fondant in a double boiler, adding 2-3 tablespoons sugar syrup and a flavouring. Heat, stirring, until the icing is the consistency of thick cream. (If the icing becomes too runny, add a little sifted icing sugar to correct it.) Add colouring if you wish.
9 Place the cake on a wire rack over a baking sheet. For the apricot glaze, sieve the jam into a small pan add 1 tablespoon water and heat gently. When the jam has melted let it stand a moment or two, then brush the warm glaze over the cake and leave to cool.
10 Pour the fondant icing over the top of the cake and smooth it to the edge with a palette knife.

● All liquid flavourings should be added to the icing at step 8, with a little of the sugar syrup, not after the syrup otherwise the fondant will be too runny. However, when using chocolate flavouring the cocoa should be added after the sugar syrup.
Vanilla: use 1 teaspoon vanilla essence.
Chocolate: use 2-3 tablespoons cocoa powder, sifted.
Coffee: use 1 tablespoon instant coffee dissolved in 1 teaspoon boiling water.
Lemon or orange: use 2-3 teaspoons lemon or orange juice and ½ teaspoon grated zest.

MOULDED ROSES

MAKES ABOUT 12 ROSES
½ quantity fondant icing
100-350 g [4-12 oz] icing sugar, sifted
few drops of food colouring
1 egg white, lightly beaten (optional)

1 To prepare the fondant icing for modelling, break off 25 g [1 oz]. (Keep the rest of the fondant covered). Knead it with your fingers to make it malleable, then sift a little icing sugar and knead again.
2 Add your chosen colouring a drop at a time. Continue kneading and sifting in sugar until you reach a good modelling consistency and the icing is evenly coloured.
3 Roll the prepared fondant into a long sausage about 12 mm [½ in] wide and cut it into 12 mm [½ in] pieces. Roll one piece into a ball. Lightly dust a piece of cling film with icing sugar, fold it and slip in the ball.
4 With the back of a spoon and using a stroking movement, work the paste

MODELLING ROSES FROM FONDANT

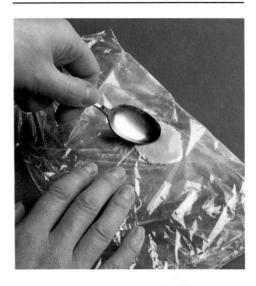

1 Roll the paste into 12 mm (½ in) balls, and insert into dusted cling film. Work paste to a petal shape, thin close to you, thicker at the top.

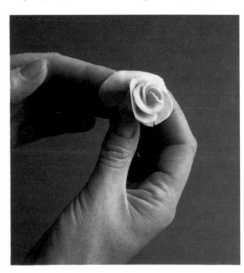

2 Dry petals for 10 minutes before assembly, then roll the first petal for the bud centre. Wrap petals round the bud, thick edge downward.

MAKING CHOCOLATE LEAVES

Using an artist's brush, coat the underside of clean rose leaves with melted chocolate. Chill until firm, then peel away the rose leaf.

into a petal shape. The petal is modelled upside down. The top edge of the petal, closest to you, should be very thin. The base of the petal is left thicker. Peel off the cling film.

5 Roll the petal gently with your finger to form the centre of the flower. Trim the base. If the fondant petal flops, this means the icing is too wet, so work in more icing sugar.

6 Make five-seven more petals in the same way for the outside of the flower. Leave to dry for 10 minutes.

7 Wrap the petals round the base, overlapping the joins. If you find the petals do not stick, use a little lightly-beaten egg white to stick them on. Make further roses in the same way. Leave to set for 1 hour before sticking them to the cake with dabs of icing.

CHOCOLATE LEAVES

MAKES 12-15 LEAVES

50 g [2 oz] plain chocolate
12-15 small fresh rose leaves

1 Break up the chocolate and melt it in a bowl over a pan of hot but not boiling water. Meanwhile, wash and dry the rose leaves.

2 Coat the underside of each leaf with melted chocolate, using an artist's paint brush. Place the coated leaves in the refrigerator to harden.

3 Just before you wish to use them, peel away the rose leaves.

CREAMY DECORATIVE ICING

This icing is easy to work and is ideal for making flowers and leaves for a sponge cake. It sets, so that the flowers can be arranged on the cake, but never becomes hard. It keeps in the freezer for up to a year, so you could make up a batch and use it as needed to make flowers and leaves for decorating. Do not use it for covering the cake as the taste is not particularly exciting. Use fondant icing or butter-cream icing for the basic cake icing and for sticking on the decorations.

MAKES 800 ML [1½ PT]

225 g [8 oz] hard white vegetable fat
150 g [5 oz] butter
550 g [1¼ lb] icing sugar
1 teaspoon almond essence
few drops of food colouring

1 Place the vegetable fat in a bowl with the butter and cream them together until smooth.

2 Sift in the icing sugar, a little at a time, mixing well after each addition.

3 Add the almond essence and beat the mixture until it is light and fluffy. Add a few drops of food colouring and mix well. Chill in the refrigerator for 1 hour before piping.

SUGAR LEAVES

MAKES ABOUT 20 LEAVES

⅙ quantity creamy decorative icing (see left)
1 drop of green food colouring

1 Tint the icing with green food colouring. If you own a leaf nozzle fit this in a piping bag. If you do not, make a paper cone and cut the top to resemble a nib. (It is possible to cut a small 'nib' first and make half a dozen small leaves and then to cut the nib bigger and go on to make larger leaves.)

2 Cut 20 pieces of greaseproof or silicone paper, each 5 cm [2 in] square. Stand the piping bag in a tumbler and turn down the top if you are using a fabric bag. Fill the bag three-quarters full with icing and close the top.

3 Guide the bag with your forefinger and curve the rest of your fingers around the bag. Hold the tip at 45° to the paper and pipe the icing with a slight up and down motion to make a crinkled edge. Pipe the leaves in varying sizes from 2.5-4 cm [1-1½ in] long. Release the pressure and lift the nozzle to complete each leaf. Place the leaves on a baking sheet in the refrigerator and leave them for a minimum of 2 hours to set.

4 About 1 hour before serving, attach the leaves to the cake with dabs of icing.

YELLOW WILD ROSES

MAKES ABOUT 5 LARGE AND 15 SMALL ROSES

⅓ quantity creamy decorative icing (see left)
few drops of yellow food colouring
few drops of red food colouring
few drops of green food colouring

102

From left: iced sponge cakes decorated with Yellow wild roses, Sugar leaves and Chocolate leaves.

1 Cut 20 pieces of greaseproof or silicone paper, each 5 cm [2 in] square. Stick the first one to an upturned jam-jar bottom with a dab of icing.

2 Divide the icing in half and set one half aside in a bowl covered with a clean damp cloth. To make large yellow roses, tint the other half with 3-4 drops of yellow colouring. Reserve 1 tablespoon of icing for the rose centres. Put a large rose petal nozzle into a piping bag, stand the bag in a tumbler, and turn down the top if you are using a fabric bag. Fill the bag three-quarters full with icing and close the top.

3 Guide the bag with your forefinger and curve the rest of your fingers round the bag. Holding the wide end of the nozzle at a 45° angle and turning the jam-jar with the other hand, press out the icing to make a round petal on the paper. It should be about 20 mm [¾ in] across. Make five petals in all, meeting in the centre to make a round flower about 4 cm [1½ in] diameter. As the roses are completed remove them to a baking sheet in the refrigerator and leave them to set.

4 To make small wild roses, colour the second quantity of icing with 2-3 drops each of yellow and red food colouring. Reserve 1 tablespoon icing for the centres.

5 Use the same size nozzle and pipe the small rose petals in the same way as the larger ones, but keep the size of the roses to 20 mm [¾ in] diameter. Place the roses in the refrigerator to set.

6 To make the centre of the large roses, add red colouring to the reserved icing. Fit the piping bag with a plain nozzle and carefully pipe five dots in the centre of each large rose.

7 To make the centres of the small roses, add a drop of green food colouring to the reserved icing. Using the same nozzle, pipe five orange dots in the centre of each small rose. Chill the roses for a minimum of 2 hours until set.

8 About 1 hour before serving, attach the roses to the cake with dabs of icing.

CRYSTALLIZED FLOWERS

CANDIES 6 OR MORE FLOWERS
1 large egg white
fresh flowers, such as apple blossoms, cherry blossoms, primroses or rose petals
caster sugar

1 Lightly beat the egg white.

2 Make sure the flowers or petals are dry. Carefully brush them all over with the lightly beaten egg white with an artist's paint brush. Be sure to coat the flowers or petals thoroughly as any exposed parts will darken and wilt. Do not coat too thickly or the caster sugar will adhere in lumps.

3 Sprinkle the flowers or petals with caster sugar, completely covering the surfaces. Leave them to dry, then dust again with caster sugar. Shake off excess sugar. The flowers will keep for up to 2 days.

SMALL CAKES

A series of delectable small cakes can be made from rich sponge mixture. These may be plain or fancy. They may be cut from a larger cake or baked separately, but all will prove irresistibly tempting.

Small cakes are easy to handle and are popular with children and adults alike. They are infinitely adaptable and there is one to suit almost every occasion: they are perfect for weddings and birthday parties, they round off a meal with a sweet treat or they will give the family a welcome extra to fill up after a rather slim supper.

Small cakes may be baked separately in paper cases or bun tins, or they may be cut from a slab of a larger cake in a variety of decorative shapes. The rich sponge mixture recipe on page 72 is ideal for these cakes and they can be iced in many of the ornamental ways which are given in the chapter beginning on page 88.

Small cakes baked separately and shapes cut from a larger cake with ornamental cutters are iced one by one. If a larger cake is to be cut with a knife to make smaller iced fancies, the larger cake is iced first and then divided afterwards.

This chapter gives you general rules for making small ornamental cakes and some lovely individual recipes.

EQUIPMENT AND ITS PREPARATION

Equipment for making and baking the rich sponge mixture, and then icing it, is described in detail on pages 68-77 and pages 88-103. For small cakes you will also need paper cases, bun or tartlet tins. For some special cakes, dariole tins (sometimes known as castle pudding moulds) are used. If you regularly bake small cakes, individual small cake tins are a necessary investment.

Bun tins should not be confused with tartlet tins, which are used for pastry cases. Bun tins are oblong or square with a number of indentations in them to hold the cake mixture. Bun tins come in various sizes (depending on the number of indentations) which are usually called 'holes'. Tins are sold in combinations of 6-, 9- and 12-hole sizes.

Paper cases are the easiest to use when baking small round cakes as they are ready to use, pre-greased and require no initial outlay on extra baking equipment. They can, of course, be used once only, but they are generally economical to buy and add a professional and attractive touch. Cakes can be baked on a flat baking sheet. Not all paper cases are strong enough to ensure that the cake is a regular shape once baked. A little trick of the trade to ensure they keep their shape is to place the cases very close to each other, or touching. When they are baked each cake supports the adjacent one and this prevents them becoming lopsided or out of shape as the mixture expands.

You can use a paper case in conjunction with bun or tartlet tins, placing one case in each hole. The sides of the case are then kept rigid and upright by the tin.

Dariole moulds (castle pudding moulds) are individual metal tins which resemble miniature buckets, shown on page 108. Although they are mainly employed in the making of puddings, they are used when making traditional madeleines – those delicious sponge cakes coated in jam, sprinkled with coconut and topped with half a glacé cherry.

PREPARING THE TINS

All small cake tins should be brushed lightly with melted fat or oil to ensure that the cake mixture does not stick to the tin during the baking. If large cakes are made for subsequent cutting, prepare the tin as directed on page 9.

When using non-stick tins for the first time, follow the manufacturer's instructions for seasoning the new tin. Otherwise, the tins can be used without any pre-greasing or lining.

SMALL CAKES: QUANTITIES FOR DIFFERENT TINS

Butter margarine	Caster sugar	Medium-sized eggs	Self-raising flour	Tin	Oven temperature	Baking time
50 g [2 oz]	50 g [2 oz]	1	50 g [2 oz]	a 9-hole bun tin or 9 paper cases	200°C [400°F] Gas 6	10-15 minutes
100 g [4 oz]	100 g [4 oz]	2	100 g [4 oz]	18 cm [7 in] square shallow tin or 18 paper cases	200°C [400°F] Gas 6	20 minutes
				or 12 dariole tins	190°C [375°F] Gas 5	20 minutes
175 g [6 oz]	175 g [6 oz]	3	175 g [6 oz]	a 28 × 18 cm [11 × 7 in] Swiss roll tin	180°C [350°F] Gas 4	35-40 minutes

CLEVER CUTTING

If you do not own bun tins and don't have paper cases at hand, there are several interesting ways in which you can cut a larger cake to make several smaller ones. It is important to bake the cake in a shallow tin. Any of the following shapes can be cut from an 18 cm [7 in] square shallow tin or a 28 × 18 cm [11 × 7 in] Swiss roll tin.

The first thing to do is to make and bake the cake. The chart gives you a guide to the quantities you will need for the different types of tin that are suitable for small cakes. Double up for larger quantities. The chart also gives you the different baking times and temperatures you will need.

Make sure that the cake is completely cold before cutting it. It is quite a good idea to use one day-old cake as it cuts better than an absolutely fresh one. Place the cake on a wooden board or work surface and trim the edges of the cake with a long-bladed sharp knife. The reason for this is that the edges tend to be rather more browned and harder than the centre. If these were left on the cake, the harder edges could very well spoil the shape of the cakes.

Round cakes

It is very easy to cut shapes from a round cake; all that is needed is a round pastry cutter and a firm hand. Place the pastry cutter (plain or fluted) on top of the cake and press down in one action so that the resulting cut leaves a clean side. Cut the next shape as close to the first one as possible, planning so there is the minimum of wastage. Use the trimmings for trifles and no-cook puddings.

If you do not have pastry cutters, cut out a small round template from thin card – place on top of the cake and cut around the template. Small round cakes cut from a larger one are always iced after cutting.

Square and rectangular cakes

Square and rectangular cakes can easily be sliced with a sharp knife into a number of different shapes. Since these all have straight sides it is usual to ice the cake first before slicing to save time.

Square cakes: decide on the size of the square cake you want then cut the cake into fingers the width of one side of the cake. Cut each finger of cake at intervals to form a square.

Oblongs and fingers: the first cut is made as for square cakes. Adjust the length of the cutting intervals to make different sized cakes.

Diamonds: these shapes look extremely attractive once decorated and are easier to make than they first appear. Cut the cake into fingers as for the squares. Cut across a finger of cake at intervals, diagonally, thus dividing the cake into diamond shapes.

Triangles: cut the cake into even-sized squares. Cut the squares diagonally, first one way and then the other to form even-sized triangles.

CUTTING SMALL CAKE SHAPES

1 Place the cake on a wooden board or work surface and cut away the baked cake edges.

2 For round cakes, press plain or fluted pastry cutters through the cake with one firm action.

OR place a round template on top of the cake and cut around the template to make circular cakes.

AND using a long-bladed knife, cut across the fingers of sponge to make square shapes.

4 For oblongs or fingers, cut across the fingers at intervals either greater or less than the width.

5 For diamond-shaped cakes, cut across the fingers diagonally at equal intervals.

IDEAS FOR SMALL CAKES

The following ideas are for small cakes all cut from one large cake. A few are iced before cutting: the majority are decorated after cutting.
- Cover the top of a 28 × 18 cm [11 × 7 in] rich sponge cake with lemon-flavoured glacé icing and sprinkle with chopped pistachio nuts. Cut the cake into 4 cm [1½ in] strips, length-ways. Cut each strip into squares, triangles or diamond shapes.
- Cut a 28 × 18 cm [11 × 7 in] chocolate-flavoured sponge into squares. Coat each square with chocolate-flavoured butter-cream icing and coat with chocolate vermicelli. Pipe a small star of chocolate-flavoured butter-cream icing on top of each cake.
- Coat triangles of coffee-flavoured sponge cake with melted apricot jam and coat with toasted desiccated coconut.
- Coat the sides of small round cakes with melted strawberry jam and coat with crushed praline or digestive biscuits. Spread top of each cake generously with strawberry jam and pipe small shells of vanilla-flavoured butter-cream icing around the top outer edge of each cake.

3 For square cakes, cut the cake lengthways into equal-sized fingers, the width of one cake.

6 For triangles, cut the cake into squares. Cut these diagonally one way then the other.

• Cut a selection of fancy shapes from a 28 × 18 cm [11 × 7 in] rich sponge cake. Brush the top of each cake with melted apricot jam. Using the same cutters as you used to cut the cakes, cut out matching shapes from thinly rolled-out marzipan. Place the corresponding marzipan shapes on top of each cake. Cover each one with glacé icing (flavoured and coloured to your taste). Decorate the top of each cake with stars of flavoured and/or coloured butter-cream icing, walnut halves, glacé cherries, chopped nuts, small sugar coated sweets or glacé fruits.
• Coat the sides of small heart-shaped cakes with melted apricot jam and chocolate vermicelli, following the step-by-step instructions on page 98. Cover the top of each cake with peppermint-flavoured glacé icing. Fill a small greaseproof paper piping bag with melted chocolate and on to the top of each cake pipe any of the following: straight lines, 'S' shapes, a trellis design or a continuous figure-of-eight design.
• Coat squares of chocolate and mint-flavoured marble cake with green-coloured peppermint glacé icing. Dip a peppermint cream sweet into melted chocolate to half cover the sweet and place one on top of each cake.
• Using a set of decorative metal cutters, cut a variety of shapes from a 28 × 18 cm [11 × 7 in] plain or flavoured sponge. Place the cakes on a wire rack about 2.5 cm [1 in] apart. Place three small balls of marzipan on top of each cake and coat each cake with plain or coloured glacé icing.
• Coat the sides of small round sponge cakes with chocolate-flavoured butter-cream icing and coat in chocolate vermicelli. Fill a medium-sized piping bag (fitted with a small shell or star nozzle) with vanilla-flavoured butter-cream icing or crème au beurre (see page 252). Pipe lines of icing to cover the top of each cake, then pipe a border of small shells or stars around the top outer edge of each cake. Stand small triangles of chocolate (or chocolate discs) in the icing, so that they radiate from the centre of the cake in a circle.
• Brush the sides of diamond- or triangle-shaped cakes with melted apricot jam and coat with finely chopped nuts. Fill a piping bag fitted with a star nozzle with orange-flavoured crème au beurre or butter-cream icing. Pipe icing in a zig-zag design over the top of each cake and sprinkle with chocolate caraque.
• Cut a 28 × 18 cm [11 × 7 in] sponge cake into strips about 4 cm [1½ in] wide. Cut the strips into 5 cm [2 in] long fingers. Coat half the total amount of fingers with lemon curd and place another finger of sponge on top. Place the cakes on a wire rack and entirely coat each sandwich with melted chocolate or chocolate-flavoured glacé icing. Drain a small can of mandarin oranges and dry each segment. Place about four orange segments lengthways down each finger. Brush the orange segments with melted apricot jam.

ALMOND BUNS

For these small cakes use moulds either with a flat or rounded base; they are sold in trays of 6, 9 and 12 mould sizes.

MAKES 12
100 g [4 oz] self-raising flour
50 g [2 oz] ground almonds
100 g [4 oz] margarine or butter, softened
100 g [4 oz] golden syrup
2-3 drops almond essence
2 medium-sized eggs, lightly beaten
nibbed almonds, to decorate (optional)
caster or icing sugar, for dusting

1 Heat the oven to 190°C [375°F] Gas 5. Grease 12 bun moulds.
2 Sift flour into a bowl, then stir in the ground almonds.
3 In a separate bowl, beat the margarine until very soft and creamy. Add the syrup, a little at a time, beating thoroughly with a wooden spoon after each addition.
4 Beat in the essence, then gradually beat in the eggs. Using a large metal spoon, fold in the flour and almond mixture.
5 Spoon the mixture into the prepared bun moulds, dividing it equally between them, then roughly level each surface. Lightly sprinkle a few nibbed almonds on top, if wished.
6 Bake the buns for 20-25 minutes, until well risen, golden brown and springy to the touch. Cool the buns for 1-2 minutes, then remove from the moulds and place on a wire rack. If any of the buns shows signs of sticking, run a palette knife underneath to loosen them. Sprinkle the buns with caster sugar and leave to cool completely.
7 Serve the buns as soon as they are cold, or store them in an airtight container. The buns will keep fresh for up to 5 days. Do not store them in the same container as biscuits as they will make the biscuits soggy.

Variations
• Vary the topping by substituting chopped walnuts or hazelnuts for the almonds.
• Alternatively, use vanilla essence instead of almond and decorate the cooked buns with glacé icing.

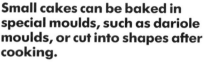

Small cakes can be baked in special moulds, such as dariole moulds, or cut into shapes after cooking.

LEMON TOPS

MAKES 6
six 4.5 cm [1¾ in] sponge rounds
75 g [3 oz] butter-cream (page 14)
2 tablespoons coconut, browned
½ teaspoon lemon juice
a little finely grated lemon zest
2 tablespoons lemon curd

1 Coat the sponge sides with butter-cream and then coconut. Pipe butter-cream round the top edge. Mix the lemon juice and finely grated lemon zest into the lemon curd. Fill the centres of the butter-cream rings on the cakes with the lemon curd.

ICED HEARTS

For cutting out more ambitious shapes, such as hearts, use a template.

MAKES 6
six 5 cm [2 in] long sponge hearts
4 tablespoons apricot jam glaze (see
Caribbean pineapple cakes)
1 teaspoon lemon juice
150 g [5 oz] icing sugar, sifted
few drops of lemon food colouring
40 g [1½ oz] butter-cream icing (page 14)
18 silver balls

1 Coat the sponge sides with glaze. Stir ½ teaspoon lemon juice and 1¼ tablespoons hot water into the icing sugar and ice the cakes.
2 Stir the remaining lemon juice and the lemon colouring into the butter-cream icing.
3 Using a piping bag fitted with a small rose nozzle, pipe a line of butter-cream round the top of each cake, and a rosette in the centre of each. Decorate the tops of the iced hearts with silver balls.

PINEAPPLE OR ORANGE TOPS

MAKES 8
eight 5 cm [2 in] sponge fingers
5 tablespoons apricot jam glaze (see
Caribbean pineapple cakes)
5 tablespoons coconut, coloured yellow or
orange
8 chunks pineapple or mandarin orange
segments, drained

1 Coat cakes all over with glaze and then coconut. Dip fruit segments in glaze and place one on top of each cake, then brush again with apricot glaze to coat.

Simple Almond buns can be prepared and baked in a matter of minutes.

CHERRY AND MARZIPAN BOXES

MAKES 8

275 g [10 oz] marzipan
eight 4 cm [1½ in] sponge squares
100 g [4 oz] butter-cream icing (page 14)
4-8 drops vanilla essence
4 tablespoons icing sugar, sifted
1 teaspoon warm water
few drops of red food colouring
4 glacé cherries, halved
16 almond flakes

1 Roll out the marzipan and cut it into 32 pieces to fit the cake sides. Mix the butter-cream with the essence and coat the sponge sides.
2 Fix the marzipan in place. Mix icing sugar with warm water and a drop of colouring. Fill the tops with icing and decorate with cherries and almonds.

WALNUT TRIANGLES

MAKES 6

six sponge triangles measuring 5 cm [2 in] on matching sides
3 tablespoons apricot jam glaze (see Caribbean pineapple cakes)
½ teaspoon coffee essence
100 g [4 oz] icing sugar, sifted
40 g [1½ oz] butter-cream icing (page 14)
6 walnut pieces

1 Coat the sponge sides with glaze. Stir ¼ teaspoon coffee essence and 1 tablespoon hot water into the icing sugar and ice all the cakes.
2 Stir a few drops of coffee essence in to the butter-cream.
3 Using a piping bag fitted with a small star nozzle, pipe scrolls on the cakes from each corner to the centre. Place a walnut piece in the centre of each cake.

Fancy cakes can be decorated in an endless variety of ways. Left to right: Orange tops, Cherry and marzipan boxes, Lemon tops, Iced hearts, Almond squares, Vanilla squares, Cherry tops, Chocolate rounds, Walnut triangles, Mocha tops, Sweetie tops, Chocolate marzipan fingers.

ICED DIAMONDS

MAKES 6

six 5 cm [2 in] sponge diamonds
3 tablespoons raspberry jam glaze (made
    as for Apricot glaze, see Caribbean
    pineapple cakes)
150 g [5 oz] icing sugar, sifted
few drops of red food colouring
few drops of green food colouring
3 pieces glacé cherry
6 almond pieces

1 Coat the sponge sides with the
glaze. Mix all but 1 teaspoon icing
sugar with 1 tablespoon hot water.
Halve the icing sugar mixture and colour one half pink and the other green.
Ice three cakes pink and three cakes
green. Decorate the pink cakes with
cherry and almond pieces. Mix the
reserved icing sugar with a little water.
Drizzle fine lines over green cakes.

CHOCOLATE MARZIPAN FINGERS

MAKES 6

25 g [1 oz] marzipan
2 tablespoons apricot jam glaze (see
    Caribbean pineapple cakes)
100 g [4 oz] icing sugar, sifted
six 5 cm [2 in] sponge fingers
1 tablespoon cocoa powder, sifted
3 crystallized violets or rose petals.

1 Shape the marzipan into two rolls,
each 15 cm [6 in] long. Dip one side of
each roll in apricot glaze then secure
each roll along the centre of a row of
three sponge fingers. Cut the marzipan
at the edge of each sponge finger. Coat
the sponge sides with glaze. Mix the
icing sugar and cocoa with 1 tablespoon
hot water. Ice the cakes and decorate
tops with crystallized flower petals.

VANILLA SQUARES

MAKES 8

eight 4 cm [1½ in] sponge squares
6 tablespoons raspberry jam glaze (see
    Caribbean pineapple cakes)
6 tablespoons sponge crumbs, browned
100 g [4 oz] butter-cream icing (page 14)
4-6 drops vanilla essence

1 Coat sponge sides with glaze and crumbs. Mix butter-cream with vanilla essence and pipe in lines on top of the squares. Drizzle the jam glaze in lines across the cream.

ALMOND SQUARES

MAKES 8

175 g [6 oz] butter-cream icing (page 14)
4-6 drops almond essence
few drops of green food colouring
eight 4 cm [1½ in] sponge squares
25 g [1 oz] flaked almonds, toasted

1 Mix the butter-cream with almond essence and colouring. To make lids, cut a slice across each sponge square, leaving it attached on one side. Coat the sponge sides and tops with butter-cream and almonds. Carefully lift the lids and pipe a swirl of butter-cream underneath them.

SWEETIE TOPS

MAKES 8

100 g [4 oz] butter-cream icing (page 14)
2 teaspoons cocoa powder, sifted
eight 5 cm [2 in] sponge fingers
5 tablespoons coloured sugar strands
24 coloured chocolate buttons

1 Mix the butter-cream with cocoa and 1½ teaspoons water. Coat sponge sides with butter-cream and sugar strands, swirl butter-cream on top. Dot with chocolate buttons.

MOCHA TOPS

MAKES 6

six 4.5 cm [1¾ in] sponge rounds
3 tablespoons apricot glaze (see
    Caribbean pineapple cakes)
3 tablespoons chocolate sugar strands
50 g [2 oz] butter-cream icing (page 14)
½ teaspoon coffee essence
1 teaspoon warm water
2 tablespoons icing sugar, sifted
6 chocolate dots

1 Coat sponge sides with glaze and chocolate strands. Mix butter-cream with half the coffee essence and pipe round the top edge of sponges. Mix the icing sugar with remaining coffee essence and 1 teaspoon warm water. Spread inside the cream border and place a chocolate dot in the centre.

CHERRY TOPS

MAKES 8

eight 5 cm [2 in] sponge fingers
4 tablespoons raspberry or strawberry jam
    glaze (see Caribbean pineapple cakes)
40 g [1½ oz] walnuts, finely chopped
25 g [1 oz] butter-cream icing (page 14)
few drops of red food colouring
4 glacé cherries, halved

1 Coat the sponge sides with glaze, then walnuts. Add colouring to butter-cream and mix until pink. Pipe a small swirl in the centre of each cake. Put cherry halves in the centre and brush with the glaze.

CHOCOLATE ROUNDS

MAKES 6

100 g [4 oz] butter-cream icing (page 14)
3-4 drops peppermint essence
few drops of green food colouring
six 4.5 cm [1¾ in] sponge rounds
40 g [1½ oz] plain chocolate
angelica leaves, to decorate

1 Mix the butter-cream, peppermint essence and green colouring and coat the sponge cake sides. Melt the chocolate, let it cool and spread it over the top, then pipe rosettes of butter-cream on top. Dot with angelica leaves.

TULIP ROUNDS

MAKES 6

175 g [6 oz] marzipan
175 g [6 oz] butter-cream icing (page 14)
2 teaspoons lemon juice
few drops of yellow food colouring
six 4.5 cm [1¾ in] sponge rounds
16 tiny angelica leaves

1 Roll out the marzipan and cut into 24 rounds, each 4 cm [1½ in] across. Mix butter-cream with lemon juice and colouring. Coat sponge sides with butter-cream and secure four marzipan

rounds to each cake, overlapping the rounds. Pipe rosettes of butter-cream on top and decorate with angelica leaves.

MADELEINES

The cheerful appearance of these cakes makes them popular with children and they are the ones that the 19th century French author Proust remembered so well. Adults will enjoy them too!

MAKES 9 MADELEINES

100 g [4 oz] self-raising flour
2 medium-sized eggs
100 g [4 oz] butter or margarine
100 g [4 oz] caster sugar
175 g [6 oz] red jam
50 g [2 oz] desiccated coconut
halved glacé cherries

1 Brush the insides of nine dariole (castle pudding moulds) tins with melted fat or oil. Stand the tins (moulds) on a baking tray.
2 Heat oven to 190°C [375°F] Gas 5. Sift the flour into a bowl and reserve. Break the eggs into another bowl and lightly whisk together.

3 Place the fat in a mixing bowl and beat until light and creamy. Add the sugar and beat until light in colour and fluffy in texture.
4 Beat in the eggs, a little at a time, beating well after each addition. Fold in the flour, one-third at a time using a metal spoon.
5 Two-thirds fill the prepared tins with the mixture. Bake just above the centre of the oven for 20 minutes, until golden brown.
6 Leave the cakes to cool in tins for 5 minutes, then turn out the cakes on to a wire rack to cool.
7 Using a small sharp knife, cut the 'risen tops' from each cake to form a flat base.
8 Place the jam and 4 tablespoons water into a small saucepan over a low heat until jam has melted. Remove pan from the heat.
9 Sprinkle coconut on to a large sheet of greaseproof paper or foil. Insert a skewer into the cut end of a madeleine and hold the cake over the jam.
10 Brush the entire surface with the jam, then roll the cake in the coconut so that it coats the sides of the cake.
11 Repeat with the remaining cakes. Place a halved glacé cherry, cut side down, on top of each cake.

Madeleines are tiny sponge cakes baked in dariole moulds. They are coated with jam, then covered with desiccated coconut and topped with a cherry.

CARIBBEAN PINEAPPLE CAKES

These unusually decorated individual cakes are suitable for any special occasion and are good enough to create a special occasion just to try them. If you don't own 8.5 cm [3½ in] tartlet tins, bake the same quantity of mixture in a 28 × 18 cm [11 × 7 in] oblong tin and cut out the rounds using a plain 7.5 cm [3 in] round metal cutter.

MAKES 6 CAKES

175 g [6 oz] quantity of rich sponge mixture
   (see chart)

For the decoration:
250 g [8 oz] plain chocolate
6 canned pineapple rings and
   their syrup
3 tablespoons apricot jam
75 ml [3 fl oz] thick cream
6 maraschino or glacé cherries

1 Make sponge mixture as directed on page 72, using quantities given in the chart in this chapter with 175 g [6 oz] flour. Bake the mixture in three tartlet tins or in an oblong tin, following the temperatures in the chart.
2 When the sponge is cold, either cut the individual cakes into two horizontally or, if using an oblong tin, cut out six circles.
3 Melt the chocolate in a bowl placed over a saucepan of gently simmering water. Spread the melted chocolate on to the sides of the cakes.
4 Place the cakes on a wire rack. Drain and reserve the syrup from the canned pineapple. Carefully dry the pineapple rings on kitchen paper.
5 Place 2 tablespoons pineapple syrup in a small saucepan and add the jam. Heat the mixture over a low heat until melted, then sieve.
6 Spoon a little of the remaining pineapple syrup over each cake and top each one with a pineapple ring.
7 Whisk the cream until stiff. Place it in a small nylon piping bag fitted with a star nozzle.
8 Brush the top of each pineapple ring with apricot jam.
9 Pipe a large swirl of cream into the centre of each pineapple ring and place a whole cherry on top of each.

Chocolate box cakes are just the thing to impress. Do not be put off by their complicated look as they are far easier to make than they look. The chocolate squares can even be made in advance, ready for you to stick on the cakes when made.

CHOCOLATE BOX CAKES

MAKES 16 CAKES

450 g [1 lb] plain chocolate
90 g [3½ oz] self-raising flour
15 g [½ oz] cocoa powder
2 medium-sized eggs
100 g [4 oz] butter or margarine
100 g [4 oz] caster sugar
milk
225 g [8 oz] vanilla-flavoured crème au
   beurre (page 252)

1 Break up the chocolate and place in a bowl. Put the bowl over a saucepan of gently simmering water. Stir from time

cover the top of each cake. Then place a chocolate square at an angle on top of each cake, so that the piped crème au beurre shows through.

CAULIFLOWER CAKES

These unusual little cakes resemble miniature cauliflowers – hence the name! Traditionally they are made with green-coloured marzipan. There is no reason why you should not abandon the cauliflower idea and colour the marzipan with whatever colouring you have available, especially if you are serving them by themselves and want an attractive selection.

MAKES 15 CAKES

175 g [6 oz] quantity of rich sponge mixture (see chart)

For the decoration:
225 g [8 oz] marzipan
few drops of green food colouring
175 g [6 oz] apricot jam
3 tablespoons water
275 ml [½ pt] thick cream

1 Make sponge mixture as directed on page 72 using quantities based on 175 g [6 oz] flour used in the chart in this chapter. Bake the mixture in a 28 × 18 cm [11 × 7 in] Swiss roll tin at 180°C [350°F] Gas 4 for 35-40 minutes.
2 Knead the marzipan until soft and pliable. Add a few drops of green food colouring. Knead this into the marzipan until it is evenly coloured a pale green.
3 Roll out the marzipan thinly. Using a 5 cm [2 in] plain round cutter, cut out 90 circles from the marzipan. Reserve.
4 Heat apricot jam in a small saucepan with the water. Sieve melted jam.
5 Whisk the cream until thick and place in a large piping bag fitted with a medium-sized star nozzle.
6 Cut the cooled cake into 15 circles using a 5 cm [2 in] plain round cutter.
7 Brush one side of marzipan circles with apricot jam.
8 Using six circles of marzipan per cake, overlap the marzipan circles around the side of each cake to completely cover.
9 Use the piping bag to pipe stars of whipped cream to cover the top of each cake.

to time until the chocolate has melted.
2 Pour the chocolate on to waxed or silicone paper. Spread it with a palette knife until it is about 6 mm [¼ in] thick and even, then leave it to set.
3 Heat oven to 190°C [375°F] Gas 5. Prepare an 18 cm [7 in] square shallow tin.
4 Make and bake cake as directed on page 72 and in the chart in this chapter.
5 When the cake is completely cold, cut it into four strips, 4.5 cm [1¾ in] wide. Cut each strip of cake into four equal-sized squares to make 16 squares.
6 Spread the sides of all of the cakes with two-thirds of the crème au beurre.
7 Place the last of the crème au beurre in a medium-sized piping bag fitted with a star nozzle and reserve.
8 Using a sharp, long-bladed knife, cut the chocolate into 80 squares each 4.5 × 3 cm [1¾ × 1¼ in].
9 Press a chocolate square against the side of each cake, leaving the top of each cake open.
10 Pipe stars of crème au beurre to

Surprise your guests with these miniature Cauliflower cakes.

NOVELTY PARTY CAKES

Make a birthday or family anniversary into something memorable with a cake that is designed to catch the eye and appeal to the imagination. Novelty cakes come in all shapes and sizes and they are surprisingly simple to make, as this chaper shows.

It is great fun to make a cake that is out of the ordinary, when the occasion demands it. With a bit of imagination you can produce a wonderfully decorative centrepiece for the party table. Do remember that a simple decoration is often the most effective, or there is a danger that the results will be garish instead of entertaining.

This chapter explains how to cut cakes into different shapes, using a cardboard template. They can then be decorated to carry out a theme and various ideas are illustrated, so that you can follow these, then develop your own themes.

Cake boards

Novelty cakes look their most attractive when served on a cake board. These are thick square or round boards covered with a hard wearing silver foil, available from large stationers and department stores. They are sold in a variety of sizes so choose one that matches your cake tin; the board should be about 2.5 cm [1 in] bigger all round than the decorated cake.

Alternative bases for decorated cakes are plain, clean wooden boards covered with silver foil or a cake stand or plate.

CUTTING DECORATIVE SHAPES

A fancy-shaped cake tin will automatically give you a decorative shape – a prettily iced cake, which has been baked in a ring or fluted cake tin is elegant enough to serve as a dinner party dessert. Heart-shaped and numeral tins are available from most large stores. However, if you do not want the expense of a special tin, a knife can easily be used to produce some amazingly decorative cakes starting with a plain square or round shape.

Whichever cake tin you choose, remember that it is essential that it is correctly prepared. If the cake sticks when it is turned out, its appearance will be spoilt. Details on preparation of tins are given on page 9. You must, of course, also use the correct size tin for the amount of cake mix. This is the same as for all-in-one cakes discussed on pages 8-31 and details are given in the guide to cake tins.

Large shaped cakes

Simple designs can be cut from larger cakes baked in deep or sandwich tins. The rich sponge recipe given on page 72 is the most suitable; this may be plain, coloured or flavoured as you wish. Select a suitable size for the number of servings you require.

Choose your design with regard to the cake tins you own. The simplest shape to cut from a round cake is a heart, but a star shape, horseshoe or butterfly is not difficult. The simplest shape to cut from a square is an octagon but you may want to try cutting out a number. First trace your design on to a thin sheet of cardboard. This should correspond exactly with the dimensions of the cake tin, so that the minimum amount of cake is cut away.

The cake must be completely cold before you start. Place it on a wooden board or work surface. You will need a medium-sized and a small sharp knife. If you are working with a cake that has been baked in a deep tin, first cut it into layers. If you are using sandwich cakes place the layers side by side on the work surface or wooden board.

Put the cardboard template on top of each layer of cake and cut around it to form the cake shape. Hold the knife vertically at the side of the template and use a sawing motion to cut as this gives an even neat cake edge. The trimmings need not be wasted as they can be used for trifles and puddings (if they last that long).

IDEAS FOR NOVELTY CAKES

These super novelty cake ideas will make a talking point for a party and make it memorable.

● To make a surprise marshmallow cake, bake a rich sponge cake in a lined 20 cm [8 in] deep cake tin. The moment you take the cake from the oven, cover the entire surface of the cake with pink and white marshmallows, split horizontally, packing them tightly together, cut side down. The heat from the cake melts the sweets and they merge together and stick to the surface of the cake. (The lining paper prevents the marshmallows from slipping off the top before they stick.) Leave the cake to cool in the tin. Turn out and remove lining paper carefully. When cold, cut cake into two layers and sandwich together with vanilla butter-cream icing.

● For a Christmas star, first slice a 23 cm [9 in] deep round cake into three equal layers. Make a star-shaped template from thin cardboard. Place the cake on a wooden board or working surface and using the template, carefully cut round the design. Sandwich each cake layer together with vanilla-flavoured butter-cream icing. Brush the top and sides of the cake with melted apricot jam. Coat cake completely with white glacé icing. When set transfer the cake carefully to a cake board or plate. Pipe shells or stars or vanilla-flavoured butter-cream icing around the top outer edge of the cake. Top each shell or star with a silver ball. Pipe a border of butter-cream icing shells or stars round the base of the cake to finish.

● To make a parcel cake, first cut a 20-23 cm [8-9 in] deep square cake into two layers. Sandwich together with butter-cream icing flavoured to your

taste. Brush the top and sides of the cake with a melted jam to glaze, coat cake with glacé icing. When set, fill a medium-sized nylon piping bag fitted with a plain tube with sufficient butter icing to pipe a name and address on the top of the cake. Next, pipe lines of butter-cream icing to represent the string. Pipe on a stamp, if you like, in the top right hand corner, using your own design.

● To make a festive fruit gateau, first cut a deep round 20 cm [8 in] cake into two layers. Put the layers on a wooden board and cut a circle from the centre of the top layer of cake using a 4 cm [1½ in] cutter and reserve. Sprinkle sherry over the bottom layer of cake to soak in and place on a serving plate. Place the top 'ring' of cake on top of the bottom layer. Brush

Number cakes are a cinch to make – children love them and when you have a coming of age to celebrate the double figures are just as much fun. Make any number you want, following the calculations and diagrams on page 119.

the surface and sides with sieved and melted raspberry jam. Coat cake with pale pink glacé icing, leaving the centre 'hollow' plain. To serve, pipe thick whipped cream which has been flavoured with sherry into the centre hollow and top with fresh raspberries. Sift a little icing sugar over the circle cut from top layer of cake. Place at an angle on top of raspberries.

● For a drum cake, bake two chocolate sandwich cakes in 20 cm [8 in] tins. When cold, sandwich cakes together with chocolate-flavoured butter-cream icing to make a tall drum shape. Check the surface is level and trim any projecting edges. Coat cake completely with white glacé icing. Leave until set. Next, fill a medium-sized piping bag fitted with a plain tube. Half fill with chocolate glacé icing. Pipe diagonal lines of icing from the top to the base of the cake all around the sides. Leave to set, then pipe similar lines, slanting in the opposite direction, to make a diamond pattern around the side of the cake. Pin a narrow band of red paper or satin ribbon around the bottom of the cake. Then pin a second band around the top, so that it stands just above the surface of the cake. For the drumsticks, place two ball-shaped lollipops at angles to each other on top of the 'drum'.

Storing Icing

Butter-cream icing will keep for up to 3 weeks in the refrigerator stored in a covered container. Make up a quantity of plain icing and flavour as required.

To coat small cakes with glacé icing, secure each in turn on a fine skewer and quickly dip in the icing. Place on a wire rack, with a plate underneath to catch any drips, and leave to set.

To thicken up icing, beat in a little sifted icing sugar; to thin icing down, add a few drops of warmed water.

Cakes can be shaped after baking by cutting round a paper template. Use a round or square cake according to your chosen design.

Clever calculations

To find out how much mixture you need to make, measure water into a tin to the depth you want the risen cake to be.

For each 575 ml [1 pt] water use 50 g [2 oz] each of self-raising flour, soft margarine or butter, caster sugar, plus 1 egg. If making an all-in-one cake, add 1 teaspoon baking powder to each 100 g [4 oz] flour used.

Bake creamed mixtures at 180°C [350°F] Gas 4 and all-in-one mixtures at 170°C [325°F] Gas 3. Baking time depends on the depth of the cake. Cover a large cake with greaseproof paper if it starts to overbrown. The cake is cooked when it is golden and springy to the touch.

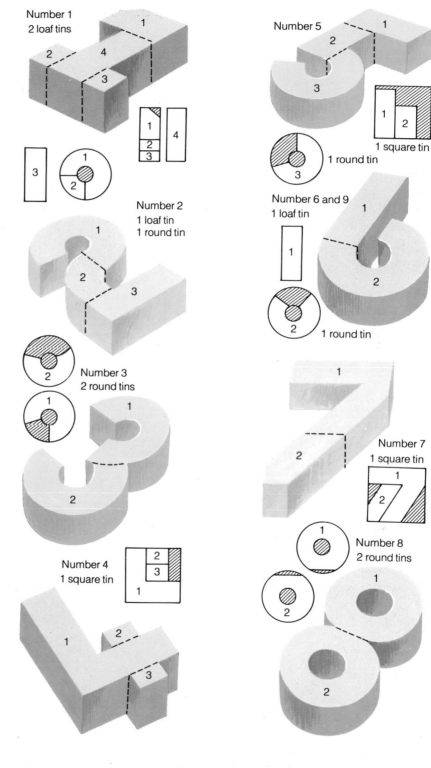

Number 1
2 loaf tins

Number 2
1 loaf tin
1 round tin

Number 3
2 round tins

Number 4
1 square tin

Number 5
1 square tin
1 round tin

Number 6 and 9
1 loaf tin
1 round tin

Number 7
1 square tin

Number 8
2 round tins

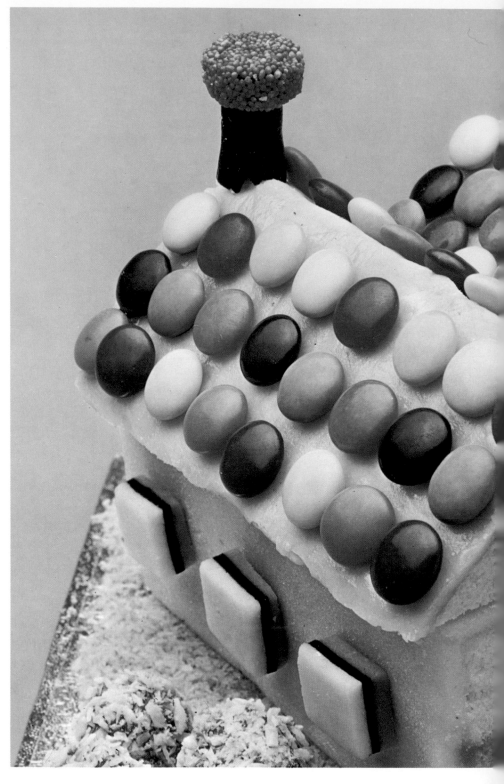

HANDY HINT

When time is short and a special cake is needed for a child's birthday, use ready-made cakes and sweets. This one can be assembled in under an hour. If you have more time on your hands, use homemade Battenburg cakes following the recipe on page 90. You will need a 23 cm (9 in) square silver cake board for this cake.

BATTENBURG VILLA

SERVES 20

25 g [1 oz] desiccated coconut
few drops of green food colouring
4 tablespoons apricot jam
2 tablespoons water
3 Battenburg cakes
3 small tubes sugar-coated sweets
small, mixed liquorice sweets
small packet of coconut mushroom sweets

1 Put the coconut in a small bowl and add a few drops of green food colouring. Mix together with a fork to colour coconut evenly.

2 Put the jam and water in a small saucepan over a low heat. Stir until the jam has melted.

3 Using a pastry brush, coat the cake board with half the melted jam. Sprinkle green coconut over board to represent grass.

4 Brush one side of one Battenburg cake with apricot jam and press a second cake alongside it. Put the two

cakes in the centre of the green coconut on the board.

5 Cut the remaining Battenburg cake into two triangular wedges by cutting from one corner through to the opposite corner.

6 Put the two triangles of cake, cut side down, on a wooden board. Cut a 12 mm [½ in] strip from the long side of each cake triangle, to enable the triangles to fit together neatly.

7 Using half of remaining jam, brush over the top of the two Battenburg cakes on the board. Place the remaining two wedges with the triangle pointing upwards and the cut sides lying together, on top of the whole cakes to represent the roof of the villa.

8 Brush the roof with jam and cover with sugar-coated sweets, to represent 'roof tiles'.

9 Use the remaining jam to stick on the liquorice sweets to represent windows, doors and chimney, as shown in the picture. Position the coconut mushroom sweets in the 'garden' of the house.

Assemble this cake, which will delight any child, using bought cakes and sweets, in less time than it takes to blow up the party balloons.

CLOWN CAKE

*Use the left-over chunks of this jolly
clown cake for the base of a trifle, or
for making a crumble topping.*

SERVES 12

250 g [9 oz] plain flour
3 tablespoons cocoa powder
1 teaspoon bicarbonate of soda
1 teaspoon baking powder
200 g [7 oz] caster sugar
2 tablespoons golden syrup
3 eggs, lightly beaten
150 ml [¼ pt] milk
150 ml [¼ pt] corn oil

**Children will love this colourful
Clown cake with his cheerful
smiling face.**

For the fondant icing:
1 egg white
2 tablespoons liquid glucose

1 teaspoon lemon juice
450 g [1 lb] icing sugar, sifted
few drops of pink food colouring

For the decoration:
250 g [9 oz] chocolate spread
red and blue glossy decorating gel
1 round red lollipop
2 tablespoons apricot jam, for sticking
liquorice sticks and sugar-coated
    chocolate buttons
1 white marshmallow
few drops of red food colouring
250 g [9 oz] marzipan
50 g [2 oz] icing sugar
2 teaspoons water

1 Heat the oven to 170°C [325°F]
Gas 3. Grease a deep 18 cm [7 in]
round cake tin and a deep 18 cm [7 in]
square tin. Line bases of tins with

greaseproof paper. Grease the paper.

2 Sift the flour, cocoa, bicarbonate of soda and baking powder into a large bowl. Make a hollow in the centre and add the sugar, syrup, eggs, milk and corn oil. Using a wooden spoon, gradually draw the flour into the liquid ingredients, then beat for 2-3 minutes.

3 Divide the mixture between the cake tins and level surfaces, then bake for about 45 minutes until firm.

4 Cool the cakes in the tins for 5 minutes, then turn out on to a wire rack and peel off the lining paper. Leave to cool completely.

5 Starting at one corner of the square cake, cut out the sides of the hat. Using the empty round tin as a guide, cut out the curved base of the hat so that it fits closely to the round cake, which will be the face.

6 Slice both the cakes horizontally. Sandwich the cake layers together with the chocolate spread.

7 To make the fondant icing, put the egg white, glucose and lemon juice in a bowl. Beat in the icing sugar, a tablespoon at a time, then knead to a smooth paste, adding more sugar as necessary.

8 Cut the fondant in half and knead pink colouring into one half; cover.

9 Roll out the uncoloured fondant on a surface lightly dusted with icing sugar and cut out a round 5 cm [2 in] larger than the diameter of the round cake. Lift on to the round cake and mould over the top and sides.

10 Roll out the pink fondant and cut out a triangle 5 cm [2 in] larger than the triangular cake. Lift on to the triangular cake and mould over the top and sides to cover, trimming as necessary. Leave to set for 4 hours. Make a bow tie with the remaining fondant and reserve.

11 Draw an exact plan of the clown's face on a piece of greaseproof paper, then, using a pin, prick guide lines through the paper plan on to the top of the round cake.

12 Transfer both cakes to a 40 cm [16 in] round cake board and slot together. Paint on eyes, mouth and cheeks with decorating gel. Press lollipop stick into centre for nose. Use jam to stick liquorice hair in place and sugar-coated buttons for eyes. Stick marshmallow on top of hat and press lines of sugar-coated chocolate buttons down on hat.

13 Knead red food colouring into the marzipan to colour it bright red, then roll out into a 10 cm [4 in] wide strip. Trim and curl around one side of the round cake to make a ruffle collar. Place the fondant bow tie in position.

14 Sift the icing sugar into a bowl, then beat in 2 teaspoons of water until smooth. Spoon into a piping bag fitted with a plain writing nozzle, then pipe two hands and three juggling balls on to the cake board on either side of the cake and fill in coloured balls with gel.

MAKING A CLOWN CAKE

1 Starting at one corner of the square cake, cut out sides of hat. Using the empty round tin as a guide, cut out curved base of the hat so that it fits closely to the round cake.

2 Draw an exact plan of the clown's face on a piece of greaseproof paper, then, using a pin, prick guide lines through the paper plan on to the top of the cake.

This delightful merry-go-round cake is made from three layers of cake, and decorated with animal biscuits and sweets. Make cardboard animal shapes to use as guides when cutting out Animal biscuits.

MERRY-GO-ROUND

SERVES 12

275 g [10 oz] plain flour
6 tablespoons cocoa powder
1 tablespoon instant coffee granules
1 tablespoon baking powder
1½ teaspoons bicarbonate of soda
275 ml [½ pt] milk
juice of ½ lemon
175 g [6 oz] butter, softened
250 g [9 oz] caster sugar
3 large eggs, well beaten
¼ teaspoon vanilla essence
juice of ½ orange

For the chocolate filling:
100 g [4 oz] plain chocolate
50 g [2 oz] unsalted butter
100 g [4 oz] icing sugar, sifted
1 large egg yolk

To finish the cake:
350 g [12 oz] icing sugar
yellow food colouring
9 striped candy sticks, 15 cm [6 in] long
tiny coloured sweets
Animal biscuits (see recipe)
100 g [4 oz] butter-cream icing (page 14),
    coloured orange

1 Brush three 21.5 cm [8½ in] round sandwich tins with melted butter. Cut three circles of greaseproof paper to fit the base of the tins. Line, butter and flour each tin. Heat the oven to 190°C [375°F] Gas 5.

2 Into a bowl, sift together three times the flour, cocoa powder, coffee granules, baking powder and bicarbonate of soda.

3 Put the milk in a bowl and add the lemon juice, stirring until it curdles.

4 In a mixing bowl, combine the butter and caster sugar, beating until fluffy. Beat in 1 tablespoon of the flour mixture.

5 Add the beaten eggs, flour mixture and curdled milk to the creamed mixture, alternately and a little at a time, beating well after each addition. Stop adding milk if the batter becomes too liquid: it should be soft but still hold its shape.

6 Beat in the vanilla essence.

7 Divide three-quarters of the batter between two of the prepared tins and spread evenly. Spread the remaining batter smoothly in the third tin.

8 Bake the cakes until they are well risen and shrink slightly from the sides of the tins. This will take 20 minutes for the thick layers, 15-17 minutes for the thinner one. Leave in the tins for 2-3 minutes, then turn out on to a wire rack and leave to get cold.

9 Meanwhile, make the filling. Break the chocolate into a small bowl and

124

place over a saucepan of hot water until melted. Leave to cool without letting the chocolate harden.

10 In a bowl, beat the butter until creamy. Add the icing sugar gradually, beating vigorously. Beat in the egg yolk until well blended. Gradually add the chocolate, beating until smooth.

11 When the layers are cold, prick the two thick ones all over with a fork. Sprinkle with orange juice. Spread one layer with 7 tablespoons chocolate filling and sandwich with the second layer.

12 Sift the icing sugar into a bowl. Add enough hot water to give a stiff but flowing consistency and tint with a little yellow food colouring. Spread the yellow icing evenly over the top and sides of the sandwiched layers with a palette knife, decorate the sides with rows of sweets then leave to set.

13 To assemble the merry-go-round, place on a board or flat plate. Push the candy sticks firmly into the top of the cake, to resemble poles.

14 Place the remaining layer of cake on a thin 20 cm [8 in] cake board and spread the top and sides smoothly with chocolate filling, using a spatula or palette knife. Decorate with sweets.

15 Carefully place the layer on top of the candy sticks, decorated side up.

16 Stick an animal biscuit to each candy pole with a little dab of chocolate filling. Spoon the butter cream into a piping bag fitted with a star nozzle and pipe round the base of the cake. Decorate the board with more sweets if you wish.

ANIMAL BISCUITS

MAKES 24 BISCUITS
350 g [12 oz] plain flour
50 g [2 oz] icing sugar
50 g [2 oz] caster sugar
225 g [8 oz] butter
flour for rolling

For the icing:
450 g [1 lb] icing sugar
orange blue, yellow and red food
    colouring

1 Heat oven to 375°F [190°C] Gas 5.

2 Sift the flour and icing sugar into a bowl, then stir in the caster sugar.

3 Cut the butter into small pieces. Add to the flour mixture, rubbing in with your fingertips until the mixture has the texture of coarse breadcrumbs. Knead to a smooth, fairly stiff dough.

4 On a lightly floured board, roll out the dough to about 3mm [⅛ in] thick. Alternatively, roll between two sheets of cling film without extra flour. With a sharp knife, using a variety of animal-shaped cardboard cut-outs as guides, cut out 24 animal shapes.

5 Lay the animal shapes on baking sheets and bake for 7-10 minutes, or until crisp.

6 Remove the biscuits from the sheets with a palette knife and lay them on wire racks to cool. Make sure the biscuits do not overlap, or they will bend.

7 Meanwhile, prepare a glacé icing. Sift the icing sugar into a bowl and add enough hot water to give a stiff but flowing consistency. Divide the icing equally between four smaller bowls and tint each with a few drops of different food colouring.

8 Dip six animals into each bowl of icing. Leave to set. To keep the icing flowing, place the bowls in a large pan and pour hot water to come halfway up the sides of the bowls. When the icing on the animals has set, using small piping bags, pipe features in contrasting colours on each animal. Leave to set.

9 Use nine of the biscuits for the cake and serve the rest separately.

Cutting plans

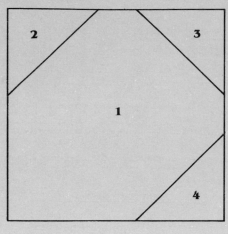

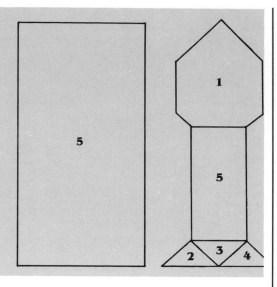

DECORATING THE HICKORY DICKORY DOCK CAKE

HICKORY DICKORY DOCK CAKE

SERVES 20

18 cm [7 in] square sponge cake
900 g [2 lb] rectangular sponge cake
  (made in a loaf tin)
100 g [4 oz] icing sugar
1½ quantities Crème au beurre au sucre
  cuit (pages 252-253)
few drops of food colouring
1 teaspoon cocoa powder
tiny jelly diamonds
sugar mouse (optional)

1 Cut the square cake into four pieces by taking off three corners, following the cutting plan left. (The large piece of cake will form the clock face, the corners make the base.)

2 Trim the edges of the rectangular cake, cutting to make them vertical.

3 On a large cake board or a chopping board covered with foil or pretty, thick paper, assemble the five pieces of cake.

4 To make the clock face, mix the icing sugar with just enough water, to give a thick, flowing consistency.

5 Place a 10 cm [4 in] plain pastry cutter in the centre of the top of the cake and pour the icing into it. Leave to set, then remove the cutter.

6 Make the crème au beurre au sucre cuit and mix 2 tablespoons of it with the cocoa powder and reserve for piping later. Tint the remainder with food colouring.

7 Stick the bits of cake together with a little of the crème au beurre au sucre cuit.

8 Reserve about 10 tablespoons crème au beurre au sucre cuit for decorating at the end. Spread the remainder over the surface of the cake, smoothing over all the cracks to conceal them.

9 Using the reserved cocoa flavoured crème au beurre au sucre cuit, pipe the numbers and hands on the face of the clock – the hands of the clock should point to the age of the birthday child.

10 Pipe a square to neaten the clock face, an outline for the door, and an outline for the base, following the picture opposite.

11 Fill a piping bag, fitted with a small star nozzle, with reserved crème au beurre au sucre cuit. Pipe scrolls and a *fleur-de-lis* above the clock face. Pipe a star in each corner and centre of clock face. Pipe a door knob and a *fleur-de-lis* at the base of the cake.

1 Place a 10 cm [4 in] plain cutter in the centre of the top of the cake and pour the icing into it. Leave to set, then remove cutter.

2 Using cocoa-flavoured crème au beurre, pipe the numbers and hands on the face of the cake – the hands should point to the age of the child.

3 Pipe a square round clock face and an outline for the door and base. Using ordinary crème au beurre, pipe scrolls, then fleur-de-lis above clock face and at base. Pipe stars and a door knob.

4 Pipe a border of shells round the base of the cake on the board. Press jelly diamonds along the two sides and bottom edge of the cake and one on to each diamond fleur-de-lis.

12 Pipe a border of shells all the way round the base of the clock on the cake board.

13 Press the jelly diamonds along the 2 sides and bottom edge of the cake to finish. Then press one on to each diamond *fleur-de-lis*.

14 Place the sugar mouse at the base of the cake. Keep in a cool place until required.

SPORTS SPECIAL

SERVES ABOUT 10
175 g [6 oz] self-raising flour
3 medium-sized eggs
175 g [6 oz] butter or margarine
175 g [6 oz] caster sugar
25 g [1 oz] cocoa powder

For the butter-cream icing:
225 g [8 oz] icing sugar
1½ tablespoons cocoa powder
100 g [4 oz] butter, softened

For the glacé icing:
100 g [4 oz] icing sugar
2 tablespoons warm water

For the decoration:
1 tablespoon apricot jam
3 tablespoons Demerara sugar
two 25 cm [10 in] strips liquorice

50 g [2 oz] marzipan
25 g [1 oz] icing sugar
small box mixed liquorice sweets
4 small plain chocolate-coated biscuits

1 Heat the oven to 180°C [350°F] Gas 4, and grease and line a 20 cm [8 in] round sandwich tin. Grease the paper.
2 Sift the flour into a bowl and reserve. Place the eggs in a small bowl and whisk lightly, then reserve.
3 Place the fat in a mixing bowl and beat until light and creamy. Add the sugar and beat until light and fluffy.
4 Beat in the eggs, a little at a time, beating well after each addition. Fold in the flour using a metal spoon.
5 Place one half of the mixture in a separate bowl. Sift the cocoa powder on to this and fold it in.
6 Place alternate spoonfuls of the cocoa and plain mixtures into the prepared tin.

This car cake will be the pride and joy of any child when birthday time comes around. The cake is made from a rich sponge mixture, marbled inside and uses only one sandwich tin. The art comes in the stylish assembly. You will need a 25 cm [10 in] square silver cake board.

7 Smooth the top of the mixture with a round-bladed knife or palette knife. Bake for 25-30 minutes until cake is cooked.

8 Turn cake on to a tea-towel and then transfer on to a wire rack to cool.

9 Start preparing the icings. To make the butter-cream icing, sift the icing sugar and cocoa powder into a mixing bowl. Beat in the softened butter until light and fluffy.

10 Cover with a damp cloth and reserve.

11 Make the glacé icing as directed on page 16 and cover the bowl with a damp cloth.

12 Make a medium-sized paper piping bag as directed on page 94. Snip off tip from piping bag and slip in a small plain icing tube.

13 To prepare cake board, place the jam in a small saucepan with 1 tablespoon water. Place over a low heat

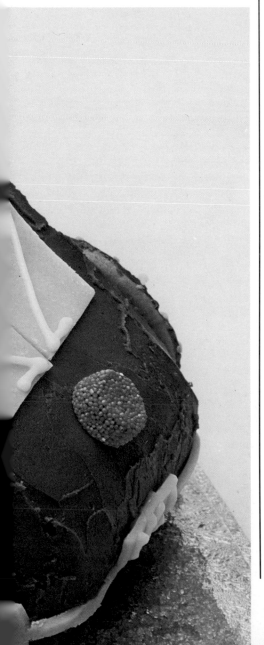

and stir until the jam has melted.

14 Use a palette knife or pastry brush to coat the surface of the cake board with the melted jam.

15 Sprinkle the jam-coated board with Demerara sugar to resemble a road surface. Place two parallel lines of liquorice strips, diagonally on the board to mark the edges of the 'road'.

16 Put the cake on a wooden board and cut it into two equal pieces to make two semicircles.

17 Use 2 tablespoons of chocolate butter-cream icing to sandwich the two cakes together. Stand the semicircles, cut side down, on a board.

18 Cut a small, rounded triangle-shaped wedge from each end of the cake to form the outline of a car. Reserve the wedges.

19 Cut the tip of the triangle from each of the reserved wedges of cake. Space these apart like the front and back axles and place them on the prepared board, so that the 'car' can rest on them. Place the 'car' in position on top.

20 Cover the entire surface of the cake with the reserved butter-cream icing. Smooth the surface.

21 Fill a piping bag with glacé icing. Roll out the marzipan thinly on a board lightly dusted with sifted icing sugar.

22 Use a small blob of glacé icing to stick a round liquorice sweet in the centre of each biscuit. Pipe lines of glacé icing radiating from the sweet in the centre of each biscuit to represent the wheels.

23 Place the 'wheels' in position against the side of the car, sticking them to the wedges under the car with a small blob of glacé icing.

24 Use a sharp knife to cut out 10 small squares from the marzipan for the car 'windows'. Cut out two thin strips for the front and back 'bumpers'.

25 From the remaining marzipan, cut out a small oblong for the 'number plate'.

26 Pipe a number or child's initials on the 'number plate', and reserve.

27 Put two windows on the top front and back of the car. Place three windows along each side of the car. Place a liquorice sweet on the bonnet at the front of the car and two square ones at the back.

28 Place the number plate above the front bumper. Use the remaining glacé icing to outline the windows and to pipe two windscreen wipers (one on each front window).

BUTTERFLY BIRTHDAY CAKE

Very fresh cake is difficult to cut and ice neatly, so it is best to bake the cake a day before decorating. You can assemble and ice the cake on the evening before the party, but not before, otherwise the icing will crack.

MAKES 24 SLICES

225 g [8 oz] self-raising flour
2 teaspoons baking powder
225 g [8 oz] soft margarine
225 g [8 oz] caster sugar
grated zest of 2 oranges
4 large eggs

For the filling and decoration:
225 g [8 oz] apricot jam
25-50 g [1-2 oz] desiccated coconut
225 g [8 oz] icing sugar
2-3 tablespoons water
gravy browning

To finish:
30 cm [12 in] silver cake board
3 chocolate flake bars
candles and candle-holders
3 small packets of sugar-coated chocolate
 buttons
2 liquorice 'pipes'

1 Heat the oven to 170°C [325°F] Gas 3. Grease a deep 23 cm [9 in] square cake tin. Line the sides and base of the tin with greaseproof paper, then grease the paper.

2 Sift the flour and baking powder into a large bowl. Add the margarine, caster sugar, orange zest and eggs. Mix well, then beat with a wooden spoon for 2-3 minutes, or with a hand-held electric whisk for 1 minute, until blended and glossy.

3 Turn the mixture into the prepared tin and level the surface, then make a slight hollow in the centre. Bake for about 65 minutes, until the top of the cake is golden and springy to the touch.

4 Cool the cake in the tin for 5 minutes, then turn out on to a wire rack and peel off the lining paper. Leave the cake upside down to cool.

5 Trim the cake to level it off, if necessary. Slice the cold cake in half horizontally and sandwich together with 5 tablespoons of the apricot jam. Cut the cake in half diagonally to make two triangles, then trim off the triangle tips opposite the cut edge.

6 Sieve all but 1 tablespoon of the remaining jam into a small, heavy-based saucepan and stir over low heat until melted. Brush the sides of the cakes, except the trimmed corners, with some melted jam.

7 Spread a thick layer of coconut on a large plate. Press the jam-coated sides of cake into the coconut one at a time until evenly coated. (Add more coconut to plate if needed.)

8 Brush the trimmed corner of each cake with melted jam. Place the two pieces of cake on the cake board, with the trimmed corners almost touching to make a butterfly shape. Place the chocolate flakes in the gap, one on top of another, then push the 2 'wings' together.

MAKING A BUTTERFLY CAKE

1 Slice cake in half horizontally and sandwich together with 5 tablespoons of the apricot jam. Cut the cake in half diagonally to make two triangles. Trim off triangle tips opposite cut edge.

2 Spread white glacé icing smoothly and evenly over the top of the cake with a knife. Immediately pipe parallel lines of brown icing down the 'wings' before the icing starts to set.

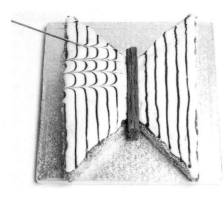

3 Carefully draw a skewer through the brown lines of icing to give a 'feather' effect, working from the inside edge of the butterfly's 'wing' to the outside edge. Repeat on the other 'wing'.

4 Brush a little jam on each sugar-coated chocolate button and stick them round the edges of the cake. Stick in two pieces of liquorice for the 'antennae' and curl them slightly.

9 To make the glacé icing, sift the icing sugar into a bowl, then beat in enough water to give a thick coating consistency, about 2-3 tablespoons.

10 Put 2 tablespoons of the icing into a small bowl. Add several drops of gravy browning, stirring well, to make a fairy dark brown icing. Spoon this icing into a small piping bag fitted with a writing nozzle.

11 Brush the top of the cakes with the remaining melted jam. Spread the white glacé icing smoothly and evenly over the top with a knife. Immediately pipe parallel lines of brown icing down the 'wings'. Speed is essential: the icing must not start to set before you do the 'feather' icing.

12 Carefully draw a skewer through the brown lines to give a 'feather' effect.

13 Neaten the edges, removing any surplus icing, then arrange the candles in their holders on top. Leave to set.

14 Two hours before the party, melt the remaining tablespoon of jam. Brush a little jam on each sugar-coated chocolate button and stick them around the edges of the cake. Stick in two pieces of liquorice for the 'antennae' and curl them around slightly.

This colourful Birthday butterfly cake, decorated with feather icing, makes an impressive party centre-piece.

FLYING SAUCER

This flying saucer will capture the imagination of the young adventurers.

No children's party is complete without an exciting cake as a centrepiece. The trick is to choose a design that looks spectacular, yet is relatively quick and easy to create.

SERVES 12

175 g [6 oz] margarine, softened
175 g [6 oz] caster sugar
3 eggs
175 g [6 oz] self-raising flour, sifted
3 tablespoons jam

For the butter-cream:
75 g [3 oz] butter
175 g [6 oz] icing sugar, sifted
1 tablespoon lemon juice

For the decoration:
5 × 225 g [8 oz] packets vanilla flavour
    fondant icing
few drops of blue food colouring
150 g [5 oz] chewy square sweets
225 g [8 oz] box liquorice allsorts
icing sugar, for dusting

1 Heat the oven to 180°C [350°F] Gas 4. Lightly grease two 23 cm [9 in] pie plates, line the bases with greaseproof paper, then lightly grease the paper. Grease 1 individual bun tin.

2 Beat the margarine and sugar until pale and fluffy. Add the eggs one at a time, beating thoroughly after each addition. Using a large metal spoon, fold in the flour.

3 Spoon 1 tablespoon of the mixture into the bun tin, then divide the remainder between the 2 pie plates and level the surfaces.

4 Bake the large cakes in the oven for 25 minutes, the bun for 15 minutes. Turn them out on to a wire rack, peel off the lining paper and leave until cold.

5 Meanwhile, make the butter-cream, beat the butter, the icing sugar and lemon juice together until pale and fluffy. Cover and set aside.

6 Prepare the decoration, put the fondant icing into a bowl and knead in the blue food colouring for a pale blue effect.

7 To assemble the cake, spread the jam on the top side of one cake and half the butter-cream on the top side of the other cake. Sandwich the two together and spread butter-cream around the edges to fill any gaps. Refrigerate for 1 hour until firm. Cover the remaining butter-cream and refrigerate.

8 Roll 225 g [8 oz] of the fondant into a 12 mm [½ in] thick rope, then place it around the circumference of the cake.

9 Stand the bun upside down and lightly roll out 225 g [8 oz] fondant on a work surface dusted with icing sugar. Place fondant on top of bun. Gently press the fondant down the sides of bun to make top of the flying saucer. Roll a small extra piece of fondant into a ball, flatten and put on top of bun. Set aside to set.

10 Lightly roll out half the remaining fondant. Using an empty pie plate as a guide, cut out a round, 23 cm [9 in] in diameter. Lift fondant onto the cake with a fish slice and mould over cake, pressing gently until the fondant meets the 'rope'. Leave in a cool place for about 1½ hours to set. Wrap remaining fondant in cling film.

11 When the fondant has set, place a 15 cm [6 in] silver board on the top, hold together and invert, so that the cake is standing on the board. Roll out remaining fondant, cut into a 23 cm [9 in] round and place on top of the cake.

ASSEMBLING THE FLYING SAUCER

1 Spread jam on top side of one cake and half the butter-cream on the top side of the other cake. Sandwich together and spread butter-cream around edges to fill any gaps.

2 Roll 225 g [8 oz] of the fondant into a 12 mm [½ in] thick rope, then place it around the circumference of the cake.

3 Stand the bun upside down and lightly roll out 225 g [8 oz] fondant. Place on top of bun, then gently press the fondant down the sides of the bun to make top of the flying saucer. Roll small piece of fondant into a ball, flatten and put on top of bun.

4 Roll out half the remaining fondant, cut into a round and cover the top of the cake. When the fondant has set, turn the cake over, roll out the remaining fondant and cover the other side. Place the bun in the centre and decorate the cake with sweets.

Mould as before. Place the bun in the centre of the cake.

12 Spoon some of the butter-cream into a piping bag fitted with a small plain nozzle, then pipe a little on to the back of the square sweets and stick them round the edge of the flying saucer. Stick the liquorice allsorts on the bun centrepiece with more butter-cream then place candles on top.

13 Leave to set for 2 hours.

Variation

• Colour an extra packet of fondant icing yellow and mould into 4 'stands'. Place under the flying saucer to raise it off the board. Make this variation 2 days in advance to allow stands to harden sufficiently.

SWEETIE HOUSE

SERVES 15-20

550 g [1¼ lb] self-raising flour
2½ teaspoons ground ginger
2½ teaspoons ground mixed spice
225 g [8 oz] caster sugar
275 g [10 oz] block margarine, diced
4 tablespoons black treacle
2 tablespoons golden syrup
1 egg
wrapped sweets

For the royal icing:
3 egg whites
450 g [1 lb] icing sugar
few drops of green food colouring

For the decoration:
5 × 225 g [8 oz] packets vanilla flavour fondant icing
selection of food colourings
icing sugar for dusting

1 Start 2 days before: make templates from thick card for the house walls and roof sections (see diagrams opposite). Heat the oven to 180°C [350°F] Gas 4 and grease two large baking sheets with lard.

2 Sift the flour and spices into a bowl, then stir in the caster sugar. Add the margarine and rub it into the flour until the mixture resembles fine breadcrumbs. Make a well in the centre and spoon in the treacle and syrup, then add egg. Mix to a firm paste.

3 Roll out the paste on a lightly floured surface to a thickness of 3 mm [⅛ in]. Place the templates on the rolled-out dough and cut out two end walls, two side walls and two roof sections. Roll out all the trimmings and, using a 5 cm [2 in] cutter, cut out six windows, an arched door measuring 6 × 3 cm [2¼ × 1¼ in], a step measuring 6 cm × 12 mm [2¼ × ½ in], and an S-shaped path.

4 Using a fish slice, carefully transfer the larger sections to the prepared baking sheets, spacing them well apart to allow for spreading.

5 Bake for 10-12 minutes, cool for 5 minutes on the baking sheets, then loosen them with a fish slice and transfer to a wire rack. If necessary, trim the gingerbread to the original shapes while still hot, using the templates as a guide. Leave until cold.

6 Re-grease one baking sheet and transfer the remaining uncooked sections to the sheet. Bake for 10-12 minutes, then cool in the same way as the large sections.

7 Meanwhile, make the royal icing, in a large bowl whisk the egg whites until frothy. Stir in the sugar, a tablespoon at a time, beating well after each addition. Beat until the icing forms soft peaks, then stir in the food colouring a few drops at a time until the icing is light green. Cover with a damp cloth. Make sure that the royal icing is covered all the time, otherwise it will harden and be impossible to use in a piping bag.

8 Assemble the house, spoon the royal icing into a piping bag fitted with a small plain nozzle, then pipe icing down one edge of a side wall section and stick it to an end wall section. Pipe

ASSEMBLING SWEETIE HOUSE

1 Pipe icing down one edge of a side wall section and stick it to an end wall section. Pipe along bottom edges of walls and stick to cake board. Repeat with other walls.

2 Pipe icing generously along tops of walls and press roof sections in place. Fix gingerbread windows, door, step and path in place with icing. Leave overnight to allow icing to set hard.

3 Colour each packet of fondant, roll out on a surface dusted with icing sugar. Cut out roof tiles, door and window shapes. Make twisted ropes for sides, flowers, door knob, chimney.

4 Fix shapes in position. When sticking tiles in place, start at the top left and, working across, overlap each tile by one third. Spread remaining icing over board and rough up.

along bottom edges of walls and stick to a round 35 cm [14 in] cake board. Hold them in place for a few minutes to allow the joins to set. Repeat with the other side and end walls so that all of the walls are erected and are firmly secured and set to the cake board base.

9 Fix on both sides of the roof: pipe royal icing generously along the tops of the walls and gently press one roof section in place, put the sweets inside house. Fix other side of roof in the same way, then leave for 30 minutes. Pipe a little icing on back of the windows, door, step and path and fix in place. Cover the remaining royal icing with a damp cloth and refrigerate until needed.

10 Leave the house overnight to allow the icing to set hard.

11 The next day, decorate the house, first knead a few drops of food colouring into each packet of fondant icing, using a different colour for each. Wrap each piece in cling film. Lightly dust a work surface with icing sugar, then roll out fondant to a thickness of 5 mm [¼ in]. Using a 4 cm [1½ in] plain round cutter, cut out 16 rounds from each piece of coloured fondant to make the roof tiles. Then cut out a door shape and six window shapes. Gather up the trimmings, keeping the colours separate, then make two twisted ropes for sides, a few flowers, a door knob and chimney.

12 Leave shapes to set for 2 hours.

13 Fix the fondant shapes in position with royal icing – when sticking the tiles in place, start at the top left and, working across, overlap each tile by one third. Spread the remaining royal icing over the board to cover, then rough up with a knife to make 'grass'.

14 Leave the completed cake to set firmly overnight, before serving. To give the children a real surprise, place small, wrapped presents instead of the wrapped sweets inside the gingerbread house before putting on the roof.

TEMPLATES

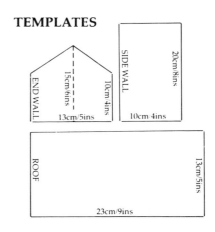

This pretty gingerbread house will appeal to home-lovers and will be especially popular if filled with sweets or little presents.

A Maypole birthday cake is an exceptionally pretty cake which can be made even more tempting perhaps by using longer ribbons with tiny presents on the ends.

MAYPOLE BIRTHDAY CAKE

Straws can be used instead of ribbons, if wished. These have the advantage of being cheap and are light enough not to upset the centre pole. Buy them in varied colours and unravel them, so that they twizzle. Glue or tape them to the central straw.

To adapt the cake to suit an older age group, use crystallized rose petals in place of the sweets.

The cake mixture has more egg yolks than the usual Victoria sponge mixture and is therefore considerably richer.

MAKES 8-10 SLICES
225 g [8 oz] self-raising flour
225 g [8 oz] butter or margarine
225 g [8 oz] caster sugar
3 medium-sized eggs
2 egg yolks
pink food colouring
3 tablespoons raspberry jam

136

For the decoration:
450 g [1 lb] icing sugar
pink food colouring
1 drinking straw
yellow, pink and blue ribbons
jelly babies
sugared jelly sweets

1 Position the shelf above the centre and heat the oven to 180°C [350°F] Gas 4. Grease two 20 cm [8 in] sandwich tins, line bases and grease the paper.

2 Sift the flour and reserve.

3 Put the butter or margarine into a mixing bowl and beat until soft and light. Add the sugar and cream it with a wooden spoon until light in colour and fluffy in texture.

4 Whisk the eggs and egg yolks lightly. Add them to the mixture a little at a time, beating well after each addition. Take care to scrape off any mixture adhering to bowl sides or spoon and beat in.

5 Gently fold in the flour, a little at a time.

6 Place half the mixture in a separate bowl and colour with a few drops of food colouring. Put pink mixture into one tin and plain mixture into the other tin. Level the tops with a palette knife.

7 Bake for about 30 minutes until risen and golden brown. Test by pressing lightly with fingertips. The cakes should be springy but firm. Leave in the tin for 5 minutes to cool.

8 Turn out the cakes on to a tea-towel. Remove paper, then turn cakes the right way up and leave on a wire rack to cool.

9 When cold, place the pink cake on a serving plate or cake board and spread the surface with jam. Sandwich other cake on top. Keep moist by covering with an upturned cake tin or foil until ready to ice.

10 Make the glacé icing following the instructions on page 14. Add the colouring.

11 Pour the icing over the cake and spread over the sides with a palette knife.

12 Leave for about 1 hour, then when the icing is beginning to set, press a straw into the centre of the top, just penetrating the cake beneath, to form the centre maypole.

13 Press jelly babies on to the sides of the cake to form a border as though holding hands.

14 Place the sugared jelly sweets in a circle around the top of the cake and in another ring around the base of the maypole. Leave for a further 1 hour to set.

15 Meanwhile, cut the ribbons to make six equal lengths.

16 When the icing is completely set, poke each ribbon into the top of the maypole. If necessary, secure with glue. Arrange ribbons at even intervals around the cake.

17 Arrange candle-holders containing birthday candles safely out of range of the ribbons.

137

MARZIPAN FESTIVAL CAKE

SERVES 12

350 g [12 oz] self-raising flour
6 medium-sized eggs
350 g [12 oz] butter or margarine
350 g [12 oz] caster sugar
zest and juice of 2 medium-sized lemons

For the decoration:
4 tablespoons apricot jam
2 tablespoons water
about 25 g [1 oz] icing sugar
700 g [1½ lb] marzipan
few drops of orange, green, red, purple
   (or blue) food colourings
angelica
8 whole cloves

1 Grease and line a 23 cm [9 in] deep tin. Make the cake following the instructions for a cake made by the creaming method given on pages 68-87. Bake the cake at 170°C [325°F] Gas 3 for 1 hour 40 minutes.
2 Allow the cake to cool on a wire rack. Place apricot jam and water in a small saucepan; reserve.
3 Lightly sprinkle a board or work surface with sifted icing sugar. Work the marzipan between your hands until soft and malleable.
4 Place 225 g [8 oz] marzipan in a polythene bag and reserve. Roll out 175 g [6 oz] of the remaining marzipan to a 23 cm [9 in] circle.
5 Use a clean piece of string to measure around the circumference of the cake. Cut the string where it meets so you know the exact length of marzipan needed to surround the cake.
6 Measure the depth of the cake with a ruler by placing the ruler vertically against the side of the cake.
7 Roll out the remaining two-thirds of marzipan (about 275 g [10 oz] with the trimmings) to the length of the piece of string and to the depth of the cake. Trim the marzipan if this is necessary.
8 Put saucepan containing the apricot jam over a low heat and stir the jam until it has melted.
9 Brush the side of the cake with apricot jam, reserving enough to coat the top.
10 Hold the top and bottom surfaces of the cake between the palms of your hands and lower the cake on to one end of the long piece of marzipan.
11 Roll the cake along the marzipan strip with a firm but not heavy hand, to secure the marzipan on to the side of the cake. Pat the join to secure it.
12 Place the cake on a 25 cm [10 in] round plate or board. Brush the reserved apricot jam over the top of the cake and cover with reserved circle of marzipan.
13 Press marzipan circle down lightly but securely. Trim any unsightly edges at the top or bottom of the cake if necessary with a very sharp knife so that the edges are even.
14 Remove the reserved marzipan from polythene bag and work this between the hands to soften.
15 To make ears of corn to trim the outside of the cake, first cut a scant quarter of the marzipan (reserving the remainder). Divide this quarter of marzipan into eight equal-sized pieces.
16 Working on one piece at a time, roll each one into a sausage shape, about 5 cm [2 in] long. Use the tip of a sharp knife to cut along each side of

the shape at 6 mm [¼ in] intervals to resemble the ears of the stalk of corn.

17 Repeat with the remaining pieces of marzipan, reserve the ears of corn.

18 Divide the remaining marzipan into five equal portions ready to make different types of fruit.

19 To make oranges, colour one portion with orange food colouring, divide marzipan into four pieces and roll each piece into a ball.

20 Roll each ball lightly against the finest side of a grater so that the ball resembles orange skin. Stick a clove into each ball for the stalk.

21 To make apples, colour one portion of marzipan with green food colouring, divide into four pieces.

22 Roll each piece into a ball shape and stick a clove into each to resemble the stalk. Cut small pieces of angelica to resemble the leaves and stick two leaves by the side of each stalk.

23 To make bananas, divide one portion of marzipan into five pieces.

Roll each piece into a sausage shape about 5 cm [2 in] long.

24 Blend a drop or so each of orange and green food colouring together to make a brown colour. Then use a fine paint brush to paint lines along each banana shape and a little dab at the top end.

25 To make cherries, colour one portion of marzipan with red food colouring.

26 Divide the red marzipan into four pieces. Roll each piece into a ball and stick a 5 cm [2 in] thin piece of angelica into each ball for the stalk.

27 To make grapes, colour the last piece of marzipan with purple food colouring.

28 Divide the purple marzipan into about 24 pieces of varying sizes and roll each piece into a ball. Press balls together to form a bunch of grapes.

29 Arrange 'ears' of corn around top outer edge of cake. Arrange the 'fruit' just off the centre of the cake.

The corn motif makes this splendid cake ideal for a harvest festival tea, but it would do beautifully for many other festive occasions. It tastes every bit as good as it looks. If you are nervous about making the fruit from marzipan, they are available ready made from confectioners and grocers. Buy only 450 g [1 lb] marzipan to cover the cake.

BIRTHDAY BUNNY

MAKES 6 SMALL PORTIONS

50 g [2 oz] plain flour
25 g [1 oz] plus ½ teaspoon butter,
　softened
1 tablespoon icing sugar
1 large egg yolk
few drops of vanilla essence
½ quantity Victoria sandwich sponge
　mixture (page 72)
few drops of red food colouring
350 g [12 oz] butter-cream (page 14)
coloured sugar strands
50 g [2 oz] desiccated coconut
3 pink coated chocolate buttons
1 large white marshmallow
few drops of green food colouring
12 sugar flowers

1 Sift the flour on to a board and make a hollow in the centre. Put the butter, icing sugar, egg yolk and vanilla essence in the centre and, with your fingertips, mix the ingredients until well blended. Gradually draw in the flour, then knead to form a ball.

2 Roll out the pastry and use to line four barquettes (you will only need two for this recipe, the remaining ones can be used for another recipe). Prick the bases and chill for 20 minutes.

3 Meanwhile, heat the oven to 200°C [400°F] Gas 6.

4 Put crumpled foil in each barquette to hold pastry in place. Bake blind for 5 minutes, remove foil and bake for another 5 minutes. Leave to cool completely. Lower the oven temperature to 180°C [350°F] Gas 4.

5 Grease and flour a 19 cm [7½ in] round tin, 4 cm [1½ in] deep. Make the sponge mixture and colour it pink. Turn into the tin and bake for 25 minutes. Let the cake settle for 1-2 minutes then turn onto a wire rack to cool overnight.

6 Make the butter-cream, tinting it pink. Cut the cake in half vertically and sandwich it together with a little butter-cream. Cut a 2.5 cm [1 in] deep wedge one-third of the way round the half circle to make the rabbit's neck and head.

7 Arrange the cake on a small board standing it up on the cut side. Cover the cake completely with butter-cream. Cover the back of the pastry barquettes with butter-cream and put a little inside. Sprinkle sugar strands inside the barquettes.

8 Sprinkle coconut shreds over the entire cake and over the back of the barquettes.

9 Cut a small niche into the rabbit's neck and stick the ears about 12 mm [½ in] into the cake, so they are supported by the back of the rabbit. Pipe pink butter-cream round the ears.

10 Put pink chocolate buttons in place for the eyes and nose and use a little butter-cream to stick the marshmallow in place for the tail.

This sweet little bunny-shaped birthday cake is for tiny children from 2-5 years old, who will prefer the taste of a simple sponge to something more elaborate.

11 Colour the rest of the pink icing with green food colouring and spread it over the cake board. Rough up the icing with a fork to resemble grass. Arrange the sugar flowers in it and serve.

HEDGEHOG

SERVES 8-12

6 large eggs
175 g [6 oz] caster sugar
175 g [6 oz] plain flour, sifted

For the maraschino syrup:
200 g [7 oz] granulated sugar
2 tablespoons syrup from bottle of maraschino cherries

For the praline:
100g [4 oz] granulated sugar
1 teaspoon lemon juice
100 g [4 oz] blanched almonds, toasted

For the filling and decoration:
100 g [4 oz] unsalted butter, softened
75 y [3 oz] caster sugar
2 large egg yolks
175 g [6 oz] bottled maraschino cherries, halved
275 ml [½ pt] thick cream, whipped
100 g [4 oz] blanched almonds, halved and toasted
3 prunes, soaked overnight, drained and stoned

1 Heat the oven to 180°C [350°F] Gas 4. Butter and flour two 1.1 L [2 pt] oval pie dishes.
2 Put the eggs and sugar in a large bowl set over a saucepan of simmering water and whisk continuously until very thick, light and lukewarm.
3 Remove the bowl from the heat, stand it on a cool surface and continue to whisk until the mixture leaves a distinct trail on the surface when the beaters are lifted and the mixture has cooled (5 minutes with an electric mixer at high speed).
4 Sift the flour a little at a time over the egg mixture, folding it in lightly but thoroughly with a large metal spoon.
5 Divide the cake mixture evenly between the prepared pie dishes; level the surfaces. Bake for 25 minutes, or until risen and firm to the touch. Cool the cakes on a wire rack.
6 To make the maraschino syrup, combine the sugar with 275 ml [½ pt] water in a heavy saucepan. Bring to the

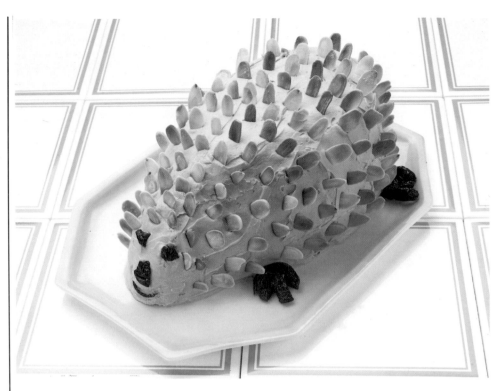

boil, stirring, and simmer for 15 minutes. Cool and flavour with the syrup.
7 To make the praline, dissolve the sugar in a heavy saucepan with the lemon juice and 2 tablespoons water over a gentle heat, then boil to a light caramel. Add the toasted almonds, mix well and pour on to lightly oiled foil on a cold surface. Allow to harden, then break up and pound finely in a mortar or blender.
8 To make the filling, beat the unsalted butter until fluffy and beat in the sugar. Beat in the egg yolks and 8 tablespoons powdered praline until smooth. Fold in the remaining praline and halved cherries.
9 Cut each cake in half horizontally. Cut one layer into strips. Moisten the layers and soak the strips with maraschino syrup.
10 Put the largest layer on an oval plate. Spread with half the whipped cream. Add the next layer and heap the strips in the centre, trimming and patting them to form a hedgehog shape, with the remaining whipped cream. Press on the last layer. Trim one end to a point.
11 Spread the praline butter-cream over the top and sides of the cake. Spike with toasted almonds.
12 Cut up one prune and use pieces for the mouth, nose and eyes. Halve the remaining two prunes for feet. Chill before serving.

This spiky Hedgehog cake will be popular with children of all ages.

141

No party is complete without a gaily decorated colourful cake, and a novelty cake such as this Castle cake is especially exciting.

CASTLE CAKE

MAKES 12-14 SLICES

three quantities all-in-one jam sandwich mixture (see recipe page 19), ½ coloured with green food colouring and ½ coloured with pink food colouring and baked in two deep, 16 cm [6½ in] square tins
6 tablespoons red jam
200 g [7 oz] chocolate hazelnut spread
8 chocolate-covered mini Swiss rolls

To finish:
2 lime jelly tablets
3 chocolate-covered wafer fingers
jelly diamond cake decorations
coloured balls
three 50 g [2 oz] milk chocolate Toblerones
candles and candle holders
toy knights and flags (optional)

1 Trim the cakes, if necessary, and cut each in half horizontally. Sandwich together with jam, then trim off each corner. Place on a 30 cm [12 in] cake board.

2 Use most of the chocolate hazelnut spread to cover the cake. Press 1 mini roll against each of the trimmed corners. Trim one end of the remaining rolls level, if necessary, and spread with a little chocolate spread. Place on top of the first set of rolls to make four turrets. (Fill in any gaps with chocolate hazelnut spread.)

3 Make up the jellies according to the manufacturer's instructions, pour into shallow trays and leave to set.

4 Put chocolate hazelnut spread on the underside and one end of the wafer fingers; place on the cake board, in the centre of the base of the front side of the cake, to represent the drawbridge. Use jelly diamonds to make the portcullis, then use dragées to mark an arched gateway around the portcullis.

5 Make the battlements on the top edges of the cake, between the turrets, using the triangular chocolate bars. Trim the bars to size (use the trimmings on the back edge.)

6 Arrange jelly diamonds around the sides of the cake to represent windows, then stick three more down the front of each turret with chocolate hazelnut spread. Put a little spread on the top of each turret and decorate with a ring of coloured balls. Place candles on cake.

7 Just before serving, break up the jelly with a fork and spoon around the castle to represent the moat. Place the knights and flags in position, if using.

FUN CAKES

MAKES 20

150 g [5 oz] self-raising flour
100 g [4 oz] block margarine, softened
100 g [4 oz] caster sugar
finely grated zest of ½ orange
2 eggs

For the icing and decoration:
450 g [1 lb] icing sugar
2 tablespoons lemon juice
5-6 tablespoons hot water
few drops of pink and green food colouring
100 g [4 oz] vanilla flavour packet fondant
    icing
25 g [1 oz] plain chocolate, broken into
    pieces
marshmallows, liquorice sweets and
    sugar-coated chocolate buttons,
    to finish
little extra icing sugar for dusting

1 Heat the oven to 180°C [350°F] Gas 4 and grease 20 individual bun tins.

2 Sift the flour into a large bowl. In another bowl, beat the margarine and sugar with a wooden spoon or a hand-held electric whisk, until pale and fluffy. Beat in the orange zest, then add the eggs, one at a time, beating thoroughly after each addition. Fold in the flour.

3 Divide the mixture equally between the tins and bake just above the centre of the oven for 15 minutes, until golden and springy.

4 Leave the cakes in their tins for 30 seconds, then turn out on to a wire rack. Leave to cool completely.

5 Meanwhile, to make the icing, sift the icing sugar into a bowl, then stir in the lemon juice and water to give a thick coating consistency.

6 Pour a tablespoon of icing over 10 cakes, to cover completely. Tint the remaining icing pink and use to coat rest of cakes. Leave for 1 hour.

7 To decorate, knead a few drops of pink food colouring into half the fondant icing and a few drops of green food colouring into the other half. Lightly dust a work surface with icing sugar, then roll out the fondant. Cut out hat shapes, hair, ears and faces as in the picture.

8 Put the chocolate in a heatproof bowl. Set the bowl over a saucepan half full of simmering water and leave, stirring occasionally, until the chocolate has melted. Spoon the melted chocolate into a piping bag fitted with a small plain nozzle.

9 Cut 4 marshmallows in half to use as ears for the 'bunny' faces.

10 Fix the fondant shapes and sweets on to the cakes by piping a dot of chocolate on to the back of each. Pipe chocolate details on to the sweets, place each cake in paper cup case cases and leave to set for at least 1 hour.

You will find that these Fun cakes disappear as fast as you can make them.

SPECIAL ICINGS

American icings, or frostings as they are often called, are one of the nicest and simplest ways to give your cakes a luscious topping. These rich toppings can transform the simplest of cakes into rich and delicious tea-time treats.

Every cook must know that sinking feeling when guests drop in at tea-time and the only cake available is a plain sponge, or worse still (especially if the unexpected guest is your mother-in-law), a cake that came from a shop. With the icings given in this chapter, you can do a quick face-lift that will make even the driest cake taste delicious. These icings are different from those given in other chapters because they can be spread thickly and do not need to be smooth – so saving time and effort. They can be used to spread in the centre of the cake too, saving making whipped cream or butter-cream for this purpose.

Here you will find a simpler version of the classic American frosting which is based on cooked meringue, plus several other easier icings.

DOUBLE BOILER OR SIMPLE FROSTING

In this chapter, you will find that simple frosting and several of the other icings given are made in a double boiler. When making these frostings, it is essential that the water in the boiler is just simmering. It is also important that you beat all the ingredients together in the boiler top until they are well blended. With some frostings, you will find that as soon as this point is reached, the frosting must be removed from the heat and then beaten until cold and thick. It is most important that you follow instructions exactly in this case. If you under beat the frosting, it will not stand in stiff peaks and your cake will be spoilt.

INGREDIENTS FOR SEVEN-MINUTE FROSTING

American seven-minute frosting is a unique icing because it does not use icing sugar. Instead, egg whites and caster sugar are cooked over low heat to make a thick meringue.

Egg whites
So that this frosting will set when it is spread on the cake, the proportion of egg white to sugar is quite low. For sufficient icing to coat an 18 cm [7 in] round cake, you will need the white from one large egg. The egg white should be at room temperature, so if stored in the refrigerator, remove one hour before.

Sugar
Caster sugar is always used for American frosting because it dissolves easily in the egg white. For an 18 cm [7 in] round cake, 175 g [6 oz] caster sugar is used.

Stabilizer
In order to stabilize the egg whites and to ensure that the mixture will thicken and hold its shape, a pinch of salt and a pinch of cream of tartar is added to the mixture.

Flavourings
American frosting can be flavoured in several different ways but the flavouring must always be something light – a heavy flavouring, such as chocolate, would break down the mixture. If you want to make a chocolate frosting, it is better to use the recipe for simple frosting given on page 148 and melt the chocolate in the top of the double boiler.
Orange: American seven-minute frosting can be given an orange flavour and colour by adding a few drops of orange essence and colouring to the mixture while it is being beaten and before it thickens. Be very careful when adding the colouring and flavouring as both are very strong and too much will spoil the look and the taste of the frosting.

Lemon: lemon frosting can be made by adding 1 tablespoon lemon juice to the mixture. To give the frosting a delicate lemon colour, add a drop or two of lemon colouring at the same time as the lemon juice, if wished.

Caramel: don't attempt caramel frosting until you have made plain frosting successfully. For caramel frosting, Demerara sugar is used in place of caster sugar. It can be difficult to get the mixture to stiffen, however, because of the larger crystals and the longer time needed for them to dissolve.

Coffee: for the coffee frosting, coffee essence (but never instant coffee powder as this would not dissolve), can be added to the mixture after the other ingredients are lightly whisked together in the top of a double boiler.

MAKING AMERICAN SEVEN-MINUTE FROSTING

This frosting does require concentration to make successfully.

First mixing

Before the frosting is placed over hot water to cook, all the ingredients must be lightly whisked together so that they are just mixed. Whisk until just foamy.

Cooking

The frosting is cooked over hot water in the same way as meringue cuite so that it thickens. The water should be just simmering, not boiling. If the water is too hot, the meringue will over cook and the sugar may begin to caramelize. While the meringue is cooking, it should be whisked

This plain sponge sandwich cake has been transformed into something special with seven-minute frosting.

145

MAKING SEVEN-MINUTE FROSTING

This frosting is slightly more complicated than the simple frosting given in the other step-by-step guide in this chapter. Seven-minute frosting is an easier version of the complicated American or white mountain frosting, which must be made using a sugar thermometer. This is an unusual icing because the ingredients are cooked to make a thick, spreadable meringue which will harden to the consistency of soft glacé icing.

FOR AN 18 CM [7 IN] ROUND CAKE
1 large egg white
175 g [6 oz] caster sugar
pinch of salt
pinch of cream of tartar

1 Prepare a double boiler. Place all the ingredients in the top of the boiler, but do not place over heat.

2 Whisk the ingredients lightly until they are foamy. Place over the double boiler. The water should be just simmering.

3 To make flavoured frosting, add flavouring and colouring before the frosting is stiff.

4 Whisk the mixture using a balloon or electric whisk until it is stiff enought to hold peaks.

5 When the icing is ready (after about 7 minutes), use. Leave the cake to set for 1 hour.

constantly using either a balloon or electric whisk. This process usually takes 7 minutes – hence the name of the frosting.

Adding flavouring
Before the frosting becomes thick enough to hold its shape, add any flavourings. After the flavourings have been added, continue whisking. The frosting is ready when it is stiff enough to hold peaks.

Using the icing
As soon as the frosting is ready, spread it over the cake. Allow to set for about 1 hour before use.

INGREDIENTS FOR SIMPLE FROSTING

Simple frosting is more like a conventional icing than American seven-minute frosting.

Icing sugar
For enough simple frosting to cover an 18 cm [7 in] round cake, you need 225 g [8 oz] icing sugar. This must (as with all icings), be sifted otherwise the lumps will not dissolve and your frosting will have an unpleasantly uneven texture.

Eggs
To bind simple frosting, a whole egg is used. This gives it a rich consistency. For the basic quantities of frosting given in this chapter use a large egg.

Butter
Butter, never margarine, is used in simple frosting to make it taste rich and to give a sheen. For the basic quantity of frosting you will need 25 g [1 oz] butter.

Flavouring
Simple frosting can be flavoured in several different ways.
Chocolate: To make chocolate frosting, use 25 g [1 oz] dark chocolate. Do not use cocoa powder as this will not give such a good flavour or colour.
Coffee: Coffee essence can be used in the same way as for seven-minute frosting. Use 1 teaspoon to flavour the basic quantity.

Other flavourings
Orange or lemon essence and zest or vanilla essence can be used to flavour simple frosting. Be sure to add only a

few drops of these flavourings, otherwise the flavour will be too powerful.

INGREDIENTS FOR OTHER ICINGS

You will find recipes for several other types of icing and frosting, many of which are cooked over a double boiler. The ingredients for these should always be of the best quality to ensure good flavour. Never use margarine in place of butter (unless the recipe says so) and always use fine, sifted icing sugar and good quality cooking chocolate to ensure best results.

MAPLE SATIN FROSTING

This frosting really is as smooth as satin. It is delicious used on a walnut cake. Sometimes, cream is used in satin frosting but in this recipe maple syrup is used instead of cream.

FOR AN 18 CM [7 IN] CAKE
75 g [3 oz] unsalted butter
350 g [12 oz] icing sugar
3 tablespoons maple syrup
few drops of vanilla essence

1 Place the butter in a bowl. Cream until light and creamy.
2 Beat in the icing sugar and maple syrup a little at a time until smoothly blended.
3 When the mixture is smooth, beat in the vanilla essence. Use the frosting immediately.

Variations
● For vanilla satin frosting, use the same quantity of thin cream in place of the maple syrup.
● For lemon satin frosting, use thin cream in place of the maple syrup and replace the vanilla essence with the grated zest of a lemon.
● For coffee satin frosting, use thin cream in place of the maple syrup and add 1 teaspoon coffee essence at the same time as the cream.

Seven minute frosting can be delicately flavoured and coloured to complement the cake it is covering.

MAKING SIMPLE FROSTING

This basic frosting can be flavoured to suit the type of cake you are making. You will find suggestions in the section on flavouring. It is important when making this frosting that the water in the double boiler is just simmering and not boiling.

FOR AN 18 CM [7 IN] ROUND CAKE

225 g [8 oz] icing sugar
1 large egg
½ teaspoon vanilla essence
1 tablespoon lemon juice
25 g [1 oz] unsalted butter

1 Prepare a double boiler and set over low heat. If you are using chocolate as a flavouring, melt it in the boiler.

2 Sift the icing sugar into the double boiler top. Make a well in the centre. Add all the other ingredients.

3 As soon as the butter begins to melt, start beating the mixture with a wooden spoon. Beat until well blended.

4 Beat the frosting until it is thick enough to coat the back of a wooden spoon. Remove from heat.

5 Spread frosting in swirls over a cooled, freshly made sponge cake. Allow to set for 1 hour before cutting.

INSTANT COFFEE FROSTING

Most coffee frostings call for coffee essence. Here is one to use when you have no coffee essence in store – this recipe uses instant coffee. If wished, cocoa powder can be substituted for the coffee to make a chocolate frosting or you can use half cocoa, half instant coffee to make mocha frosting which goes well with a walnut cake.

ENOUGH FOR AN 18 CM [7 IN] CAKE

75 g [3 oz] icing sugar
25 g [1 oz] instant coffee
40 g [1½ oz] butter
1 tablespoon water
50 g [2 oz] caster sugar

1 Sift the icing sugar and the instant coffee into a bowl. Make a hollow in the centre and set aside.
2 Heat the butter, water and sugar in a small heavy-based saucepan.
3 Stir until the sugar and butter have dissolved.
4 Bring to the boil, then remove the pan from the heat.
5 Pour into the icing sugar and coffee mixture. Beat with a wooden spoon.
6 Continue beating until the mixture is stiff and smooth. Allow to cool, stirring from time to time until the mixture is thick enough to coat the back of a wooden spoon.
7 Spread a little of the mixture in the centre of the cake.
8 Pour the remaining mixture over the top of your cake. Spread with a palette knife to coat the cake.
9 Leave for 1-2 hours until firm.

FROSTING A CAKE

1 First slice the cake in half and spread chosen filling in centre.

2 Re-assemble the cake, and spread the frosting over.

3 Using a palette knife swirl the frosting in patterns.

OR rough up the frosting with a knife so that it forms peaks.

CHOCOLATE SOURED CREAM ICING

This icing is too soft for piping. It drips soft and rich over the sides of the cake.

ENOUGH TO FILL AND COVER A 22 CM [8½ IN] CAKE

225 g [8 oz] plain chocolate
150 ml [¼ pt] soured cream
1 tablespoon caster sugar

1 Break the chocolate into pieces and melt it in the top of a double boiler or a bowl set over a saucepan of simmering water. As soon as the chocolate has melted, remove from the heat.

2 Stir in the soured cream and add the sugar if wished.

3 Leave to cool and thicken for 30 minutes. When it becomes as thick as whipped cream, use it to fill the cake and cover the top and sides.

CHOCOLATE COFFEE ICING

FOR A 20 CM [8 IN] CAKE

100 g [4 oz] plain dark dessert chocolate, broken into pieces
50 g [2 oz] butter
225 g [8 oz] icing sugar, sifted
4 tablespoons instant coffee
4 tablespoons hot water
1½ teaspoons vanilla essence

1 Melt the chocolate and butter in a bowl set over a saucepan of simmering water. Remove from the heat and whisk in the icing sugar.

2 Dissolve the coffee in the hot water and whisk into the melted chocolate with the vanilla essence.

3 Use most of the icing to cover the top and sides of the cake. Place the remaining icing in a piping bag fitted with a star nozzle and pipe swirls around the top of the cake.

Instant coffee frosting is easy to make and to use. It goes well with coffee and walnut cake.

LEMON TOPPING

This creamy lemon icing can be used as a topping and a filling for sponge cakes. Decorate the top of the cake with crystallized orange and lemon slices, if wished.

ENOUGH TO FILL AND COVER THE TOP OF A 20 CM [8 IN] CAKE

2 medium-sized eggs
275 g [10 oz] caster sugar
finely grated zest and juice of 2 lemons
50 g [2 oz] plain flour, sifted
575 ml [1 pt] thick cream, whipped

1 In a mixing bowl, whisk together the eggs, sugar and lemon zest until foamy.
2 Measure the lemon juice and make up to 275 ml [½ pt] with water, then beat into the egg and sugar mixture together with the sifted flour.
3 Turn the lemon mixture into a heavy-based saucepan and bring to the boil over a low heat, stirring constantly.
4 Cook the mixture, stirring, for 5-7 minutes until smooth and thick. Remove the pan from the heat and leave the lemon mixture to cool completely.
5 Fold the whipped cream into the cold lemon mixture. Use the creamy lemon mixture to fill and cover the cake.

CHOCOLATE GANACHE

This rich chocolate cream can be used to make a soft icing for the top of a cake or to sandwich two layers together. You must use good quality dessert dark chocolate to make this spread. This icing is best piped.

ENOUGH FOR AN 18 CM [7 IN] CAKE

150 g [5 oz] plain dark chocolate
75 ml [3 fl oz] strong cold black coffee
50 g [2 oz] unsalted butter
2 large egg yolks
2 teaspoons dark rum

1 Set a double boiler over low heat so that the water is just simmering.
2 Break up the chocolate and place in the boiler. Add the coffee.
3 Allow to melt, stirring until chocolate and coffee are blended.
4 Remove from the heat. Cut the butter into small pieces. Beat a piece at a time into the mixture. Be sure each piece has melted and blend before you add the next.
5 Beat in the egg yolks and the rum.
6 Leave the creamy mixture until cold and thick, stirring it from time to time.
7 To use, pipe over the top of a cake, or spread in the centre of a layer cake.

CREAM CHEESE ICING

Cream cheese and icing sugar is a combination often used in the USA to make deliciously creamy toppings for chocolate and plain sponge cakes.

FOR AN 18 CM [7 IN] ROUND CAKE
75 g [3 oz] full-fat cream cheese
1 tablespoon thin cream
100 g [4 oz] icing sugar
2 teaspoons grated lemon zest

1 Place the cream cheese and cream in a bowl. Cream with a wooden spoon or an electric whisk until light and fluffy.
2 Sift the icing sugar a little at a time into the mixture, beating well after each addition.
3 Beat in the lemon zest and use immediately. Allow the icing to set for 1 hour before cutting the cake.

Variation
● For chocolate cream cheese icing, melt 50 g [2 oz] dark chocolate in a double boiler. Beat into cream cheese icing given above, omitting the lemon zest.

CINNAMON ICING

This is a popular choice for fruity gingerbreads and tea-breads.

ENOUGH FOR A 450 G [1 LB] LOAF
6 tablespoons icing sugar
1 teaspoon ground cinnamon

1 Sift the icing sugar into a bowl. Mix in the cinnamon.
2 Make a hollow in the centre. Add 1½ tablespoons hot water.
3 Mix until well blended. Spread over tea-bread and leave to set.

PINEAPPLE AND CHEESE FROSTING

75 g [3 oz] full-fat soft cheese
25 g [1 oz] butter, softened
100 g [4 oz] caster sugar
1 canned pineapple ring, drained
    thoroughly and finely chopped
few drops of vanilla essence

Put the cheese into a large bowl with the butter, sugar, pineapple and vanilla essence. Beat until well blended, then use immediately.

This traditional American frosting gives a lovely moist flavour to plain cakes.

QUICK ORANGE ICING

This quick icing is cooked in the top of a double boiler and, unlike other icings, spreads best if applied to a cake which is still warm. You can give this icing a glossy finish by dipping the palette knife in hot water from time to time when icing the cake. Use natural or frozen orange juice as this has a good colour.

FOR AN 18 CM [7 IN] ROUND CAKE

225 g [8 oz] icing sugar
1 tablespoon melted butter
1 tablespoon grated orange zest
3 tablespoons orange juice
1 tablespoon lemon juice

1 Prepare a double boiler. The water should be just simmering.
2 Place all the ingredients in the boiler top. Beat gently over low heat for 10 minutes until smooth.
3 Remove from heat and beat until cool and of a spreadable consistency.

Variation

● For quick lemon icing, use lemon zest and juice in place of orange juice.

FUDGE TOPPING

This is a favourite topping for chocolate and coffee cakes. It is especially popular with children. Be sure to allow the topping to set for at least 2 hours before you slice and serve the cake.

FOR AN 18 CM [7 IN] ROUND CAKE

225 g [8 oz] icing sugar
2 tablespoons cocoa powder
75 g [3 oz] butter
3 tablespoons milk
75 g [3 oz] caster sugar

1 Sift the icing sugar and cocoa into a large bowl. Place remaining ingredients in a small saucepan over medium heat.
2 Heat, stirring until the sugar has dissolved. Bring to the boil and boil for 1 minute.
3 Make a hollow in the centre of the icing sugar and cocoa mixture. Pour in the butter mixture.
4 Stir until well mixed, then beat until light and fluffy.
5 Use immediately. Spread over your chosen cake, rough up into peaks, then leave for at least 2 hours to set before slicing.

From left to right: Lemon icing, which is a variation of Quick orange icing: Fudge topping: Butterscotch nut icing: Sticky coffee frosting.

BUTTERSCOTCH NUT ICING

This rich icing studded with chopped nuts will make a plain creamed cake into something really special. Because the icing is so rich, use it with a plain Victoria sponge sandwiched together with cream or butter-cream.

FOR AN 18 CM [7 IN] ROUND CAKE

50 g [2 oz] butter
75 g [3 oz] soft brown sugar
75 ml [3 fl oz] evaporated milk
225 g [8 oz] icing sugar
50 g [2 oz] chopped walnuts

1 Place the butter, sugar and evaporated milk in a heavy-based saucepan over low heat.
2 Stir until the butter has melted and the ingredients are well blended.
3 Cool slightly. Sift the icing sugar into the mixture a little at a time, beating well after each addition.
4 Beat until thick and of a spreadable consistency. Beat in the nuts.
5 Spread over the cake, roughing up with a knife so that the icing stands in peaks. Leave until the icing has set before cutting and serving the cake.

STICKY COFFEE FROSTING

This frosting is made deliciously sticky by the use of golden syrup. It can be used as either a coating icing or a frosting. For a coating, pour over the cake as soon as the icing is thick enough to coat the back of a spoon. As a frosting or as a filling, allow the icing to cool and beat with a wooden spoon until it is the consistency of butter-cream.

FOR AN 18 CM [7 IN] ROUND CAKE

175 g [6 oz] icing sugar
25 g [1 oz] golden syrup
40 g [1½ oz] margarine or butter
2 teaspoons coffee essence

1 Sift the icing sugar into a bowl.
2 Place all the remaining ingredients in the top of a double boiler.
3 Stir over low heat until the ingredients are well blended and the mixture is almost boiling.
4 Pour into the sieved icing sugar and mix with a wooden spoon until smooth.
5 To use as frosting, allow to cool and beat until thick and the consistency of butter-cream.

MELTING METHOD CAKES

C ake making by the melting method really is a piece of cake because it requires the minimum of effort. This method is specially designed to cope with extra sweeteners needed to make soft and sticky traditional cakes such as gingerbread and parkin.

Melting-method cakes have a characteristic tacky, sticky texture throughout the cake, and it is this that has made cake like gingerbread so very popular and has given them such a high place in traditional baking. This stickiness is achieved by increasing the proportion of sweetening agents to other ingredients in the cake.

To handle the extra volume of sweetener, a special method is used – one entirely different to the methods covered in previous chapters. With this method the fat is melted with the sweetener before the flour is added. Before cooking the cake mixture has a tacky texture and a consistency similar to a thick batter, rather than the soft dropping consistency of cake mixtures made by the all-in-one or creaming methods.

INGREDIENTS

Proportions
Like all cakes, the amount and the choice of ingredients depend on the method you are using, the flavour and the texture you wish to achieve and/or the recipe you have chosen. Average proportions for cakes made by the melting method are one-third fat to the total amount of flour; one-third sugar to the total amount of flour; and one to two-thirds of sweetener to the total amount of flour. However, these proportions can vary considerably with individual recipes.

One extremely important factor when making cakes by this method is the exact weighing of the ingredients for the individual recipes. As long as there is a correct balance of ingredients to start with, perfect results will follow.

Flour
There are no hard and fast rules about the type of flour to use. As a basic guide, plain flour is best used, because then you can control the amount of raising agent which is important to the mixture. Self-raising flour may be used for certain recipes, but as you have no control over the raising agent you can never be sure whether it is too much or too little for the purpose of making cakes by this method. Certain brown flours can be used depending on your taste. Never use a strong plain flour (the type recommended for bread making), because this will produce a tough and heavy-textured cake. You should never substitute one flour for another in a given recipe, because this could upset the overall balance.

Raising agents
Bicarbonate of soda is the raising agent most often used in this method of cake making as it combines successfully with plain flour. When this chemical raising agent is heated, it gives off a carbon dioxide which produces the rise. Baking powder, another chemical raising agent, is used where self-raising flour is included. The quantities are usually small because of the amounts already in a self-raising flour. Baking powder is added, nevertheless to boost the rising. If you are using a brown flour, you must use baking powder in larger quantities than with self-raising flour. Brown flour is so much heavier than white flour and needs the extra rise that a larger quantity of baking powder will give.

Fat
When making melting-method cakes

These lovely moist Treacle bars get their rich full flavour from a mixture of spices and black treacle.

you can use margarine just as success-fully as butter without fear that the flavour will be less satisfying. With this method, the fat is used purely as a binding medium and usually the flavour from the fat is disguised by the flavourings and sweeteners in the recipe. Butter, hard margarine, lard or a clarified dripping can be used with equal success.

Because the fat is always melted there is no need to bring it to room temperature before use, as is necessary with the other cake methods. If you are using a hard fat, just cut it into small pieces to make it easier to handle.

Sweeteners

There are two kinds of sweeteners that can be used in the melting-method cake: liquid sweeteners, such as treacle, syrup or honey, or sugar.

Liquid sweeteners are the first choice of sweetening agent with this type of cake. This is not only because of their characteristic flavours, but also because the whole melting method has been designed to incorporate and blend them in their liquid form most conveniently. Black treacle alone gives a very handsome colour. Golden syrup will give more of a golden colour and, of course, a very sweet flavour. Other liquid sweeteners, including honey and malt extract may be used.

Sugar: soft brown or a Demerara sugar is generally used if sugar is being included, because of its rich flavour and colour. Caster and granulated sugar are more often used for other types of plainer cakes, but both are suitable for this method.

Combinations: you may also come across a recipe that uses a combination of liquid sweeteners or one that combines liquid and sugar sweeteners.

Eggs

Eggs do not play as important a part in cakes made by this method; they are generally only used in small quantities. The enriching qualities of the cake are amply provided for by the sweetener when liquid sweeteners are used. The egg is not, therefore, included to enrich the cake, as with the creaming-method cakes. In a melting-method cake using sugar rather than all liquid sweetener, an egg does provide richness because it works with the flour in the recipe to form the structure of the cake (usually when there is fruit in the cake).

Liquids

Liquids are added to some, but not all cakes made by the melting method. Before cooking, melting-method cakes must have the consistency of a thick batter (one that is easy to pour, but thick enough to spread slowly). To achieve this consistency, extra liquid is sometimes added to melted ingredients, plus any eggs used. Milk and/or water are most usual additions; milk will give a slightly softer texture than water. However other liquids may be used for additional flavour (see flavourings).

Flavourings

A variety of flavouring ingredients may be used, some for taste and some to give an interesting contrast of textures.

Dry flavourings: spices play a vital role in many melting-method cakes particularly gingerbreads. As well as imparting their own enticing flavour, they play a secondary but important role of disguising the sometimes bitter flavour left when bicarbonate of soda is used.

Ground ginger is, of course, the traditional spice for gingerbreads: but it is best combined with another spice because of its pungency. Combined with ground cinnamon or mixed spice the flavour is detectable but much more subtle. Always sift any spice used with flour to ensure even distribution in the cake.

Citrus zest must always be finely grated. It is an excellent flavouring, as it helps to offset the sweetness.

Nuts chopped or ground, depending on the recipe, add texture and moisture.

Glacé or crystallized fruits and even preserved fruit, make a delicious addition especially to gingerbreads. Finely chop the fruit, unless otherwise directed. When using a preserved fruit, drain the syrup from it and pat it dry before chopping.

Dried fruit may be used successfully. If the fruit is large, chop it to a uniform size.

Liquid flavourings: when these are used, a corresponding reduction must be made of the milk or water used in the recipe. If this is not done, the recipe will be unbalanced and the batter will be too thin. When flavouring extracts are used, however, the amounts are usually so small that they will not disturb the proportions.

● Plain or flavoured yoghurt will give a slightly tangy result.

● Beer, brown ale or stout are ideal and give a rich flavour.

● A little syrup from a jar of preserved fruit is a delicious and economical addition. If using the syrup from preserved ginger, take care not to use too much, as this is particularly strong.

EQUIPMENT

Accurate measuring equipment heads the list of priorities for making cakes by the melting method. In addition you will need a heavy-based saucepan to actually melt the fat and sweetener, and a wooden spoon to amalgamate the melting ingredients.

A sieve and a large mixing bowl are essential for the dry ingredients and a small basin for whisking the eggs. A tablespoon is necessary for blending the melted and dry ingredients together. Be sure to use a metal spoon as the sharp edge of the metal is best for cutting through the ingredients quickly and efficiently.

Preparing the tin

The cake mixture should be baked as soon as it is made, so always choose and prepare your bakeware before you

MAKING A MELTING-METHOD CAKE

1 Position oven shelf in the centre and heat oven. Grease, line and re-grease a baking tin.

2 Place fat and sweetener in a heavy-based saucepan over a low heat. Stir gently, until melted.

3 Remove mixture from heat, when melted. On no account let it boil. Put aside to cool.

4 Sift flour and raising agent into a bowl. Make a well in dry ingredients. Whisk egg lightly.

5 Pour melted mixture into bowl together with egg and any liquid. Stir lightly with a metal spoon.

6 Stir in any additional flavouring ingredients and pour the batter into prepared tin.

7 Bake cake for recommended time. To test, it should feel firm when lightly pressed.

8 Allow cake to cool in the tin for 10 minutes, turn out and remove lining paper, leave to cool.

157

start. Square or rectangular tins are traditionally used for gingerbreads because they are usually served cut into squares. Tea-breads, like bread, are baked in loaf tins so that they can be cut into slices for serving. Provided it is of the right capacity, there is no reason why a round tin cannot be used.

Whatever tin you choose be particularly careful about preparing it correctly. Because you are dealing with a batter there is more chance than usual that the cake will stick during baking. The tin must be completely greased, lined and greased again (see page 35 for lining tins). If using a loaf tin, grease it and only line the base before re-greasing.

THE BASIC METHOD

The melting method is extremely straightforward and practically foolproof. Follow the basic rules and there will be no problems. Measure carefully and accurately, taking particular care over the raising agent. Being over generous with the raising agent will cause the cake to rise too quickly during baking; it could then collapse in the centre.

Melting

When melting the fat and sugar or liquid sweetener, take care that it does not become overheated. Always melt over low heat and never a high one. If the melted ingredients are allowed to boil, the results will be more like toffee and totally unmanageable. If you are interrupted, it is wiser to turn off the heat and remove the pan from the heat to ensure that no mishaps occur.

As soon as the fat and sugar are completely melted remove the saucepan from the heat and allow the mixture to cool slightly.

Dry ingredients and egg

While the melted ingredients are cooling, measure the dry ingredients and whisk the egg. Make a well in the centre of the flour.

Adding the melted ingredients

It is very important that the melted mixture is allowed to cool sufficiently before it is added to the dry ingredients. A good test of whether the melted mixture is ready is if you can comfortably place your hand against the side of the saucepan. Do not use the melted mixture before this point, or the dry ingredients will cook slightly before you have had a chance to combine them. Pour the melted mixture plus 1 egg and liquid (if used) into the centre of the dry ingredients all in one go. Using a metal spoon and a light cutting action, combine the ingredients together until the mixture is smooth and batter-like in consistency.

When the mixture has reached this stage, stir in any flavourings used.

OVEN TEMPERATURE

Once you have the tin prepared, the cake is relatively quick to make. Make sure that the oven shelves are positioned and the correct temperature reached before the cake is prepared.

Because of their high sugar content, melting-method cakes require a lower oven temperature than many other types. As a general guide, 170°C [325°F] Gas 3 is suitable.

Oven times

The cooking time will depend on the size and depth of the cake, as well as the ingredients, so there are no hard and fast rules. As a general guide, a cake made with 225 g [8 oz] flour will require 1¼-1½ hours at a warm temperature. Always follow the time given in the recipe you are using.

MOIST TREACLE BARS

MAKES 10-12
50 g [2 oz] margarine
50 g [2 oz] dark soft brown sugar
125 ml [4 fl oz] black treacle
2 tablespoons natural yoghurt
1 large egg, lightly beaten
100 g [4 oz] plain flour
¼ teaspoon bicarbonate of soda
1½ teaspoons ground mixed spice
1 teaspoon ground allspice
1 teaspoon ground cinnamon

1 Heat the oven to 170°C [325°F] Gas 3. Thoroughly grease a shallow 25 × 15 cm [10 × 6 in] baking tin, line and grease the paper.
2 Place the margarine in a heavy-based saucepan with the sugar and treacle.
3 Place the saucepan over a low heat and heat gently, stirring often, until the

margarine has melted and the brown sugar has dissolved. Remove the pan from the heat and allow to cool for 5 minutes, then add yoghurt and egg and beat with a wooden spoon until well blended.

4 Sift the flour into a large bowl with the soda and spices. Make a hollow in the centre. Pour the treacle mixture into the hollow, then stir with a metal spoon until evenly blended.

5 Pour the mixture into the prepared tin and then level the surface. Bake for 35-40 minutes until risen and springy to the touch, then leave the cake in the tin until it is completely cool.

6 Lift out of the tin, cut cake into bars and store in an airtight container for at least 2 days before serving.

GINGERBREAD

MAKES 16 SQUARES

175 g [6 oz] margarine
200 g [7 oz] golden syrup
150 g [5 oz] black treacle
225 g [8 oz] dark soft brown sugar
450 g [1 lb] plain flour
1 tablespoon ground ginger
1 tablespoon baking powder
1 teaspoon bicarbonate of soda
1 teaspoon salt
1 egg, lightly beaten
275 ml [½ pt] milk

1 Heat the oven to 180°C [350°F] Gas 4. Grease a deep 23 cm [9 in] square cake tin with a loose base. Line the sides and base of the tin with greaseproof paper, then grease again.

2 Place the margarine, syrup, treacle and sugar in a heavy-based saucepan.

3 Place the saucepan over a low heat and heat gently, stirring, until the margarine has just melted. Remove the pan from the heat and allow to cool.

4 Meanwhile, sift the flour, ginger, baking powder, bicarbonate of soda and salt into a large bowl, then make a hollow in the centre.

5 Add the egg, milk and melted mixture to the dry ingredients and mix with a metal spoon until smoothly blended.

5 Pour into the prepared tin and bake for about 1½ hours until just firm to the touch.

6 Cool for 20 minutes, then remove from the tin and peel off the lining paper. Leave on a wire rack to cool completely. Wrap in foil and store in an airtight tin for 1 week before cutting.

Variations

● For a really dark gingerbread, omit the quantity of golden syrup and use all black treacle instead.

● For the reverse, a light gingerbread, omit the black treacle and use all golden syrup instead.

● For a celebration gingerbread, brush the surface of the cake with warmed golden syrup while the cake is still warm, and decorate with pieces of any crystallized fruit.

● Make a gingered gingerbread by adding 50 g [2 oz] chopped crystallized ginger or drained, chopped stem ginger at the end of stage 4.

● With celebrations still in mind, make an almond gingerbread by stirring in 50 g [2 oz] of blanched, chopped almonds at the end of stage 4. When the cake is cooked, but still warm, brush the top of the cake with warmed black treacle and decorate with whole or flaked blanched almonds.

No Scottish clan would call themselves complete without their own particular recipe for making gingerbread. This gives you just some idea how many recipes there are for it. A true Scottish gingerbread should be sticky, rich and above all eaten about a week after it is made. Eating it when it has time to mature means that all those delicious flavours have had time to mingle and develop.

Parkin is a delicious example of a melting method cake. Its distinctive flavour comes from the oatmeal.

PARKIN

The north of England is famous for this special type of gingerbread called parkin. It is very similar to gingerbread except that oatmeal is used in place of a proportion of the flour. Make parkin at least 2 days before eating to allow the flavours to develop and the cake to moisten up. In the north it is traditionally served on Guy Fawkes night around the bonfire.

MAKES 8-12 PIECES

100 g [4 oz] black treacle
100 g [4 oz] soft brown sugar
100 g [4 oz] butter or margarine
100 g [4 oz] plain flour
pinch of salt
1 teaspoon ground ginger
1 teaspoon mixed spice
½ teaspoon bicarbonate of soda
100 g [4 oz] oatmeal
1 medium-sized egg
5 tablespoons milk

1 Heat the oven to 170°C [325°F] Gas 3.
2 Brush a deep 15 cm [6 in] square tin with melted fat or oil, fully line and grease the paper.
3 Place the treacle, sugar and fat in a heavy-based saucepan.
4 Place the saucepan over a low heat and heat gently, stirring from time to time until the fat has melted and the sugar dissolved. Remove the pan from the heat and allow to cool.
5 Sift the flour into a bowl with the salt, spices and bicarbonate of soda. Stir in the oatmeal.
6 Make a hollow in the centre of the dry ingredients. Whisk the egg and milk together lightly.
7 When sufficiently cooled, pour the melted mixture and the egg mixture into the dry ingredients.
8 Using a metal spoon, stir the ingredients together until smoothly blended.
9 Pour the batter into the prepared tin and bake for 1-1¼ hours until the cake is firm to the touch.
10 Leave the cake to cool in the tin for 10 minutes. Turn cake out on to a wire rack and remove lining paper. Leave to cool.

Variations

● For an orange- or lemon-flavoured parkin, omit the spices and use 2 teaspoons grated lemon or orange zest.
● For a lighter cake, use honey or golden syrup instead of treacle.

BROWNIES

This American cake, which is traditionally served cut into squares or bars, has a deliciously chewy texture. Take great care, too, when turning out the cooked cake as it has a soft centre which could crack.

MAKES 12 BARS

50 g [2 oz] plain chocolate
65 g [2½ oz] butter or margarine
175 g [6 oz] caster sugar
65 g [2½ oz] self-raising flour
pinch of salt
2 medium-sized eggs
½ teaspoon vanilla essence
50 g [2 oz] coarsely chopped Brazil nuts or
   walnuts.

1 Heat the oven to 180°C [350°F] Gas 4.
2 Brush a deep 20 cm [8 in] square baking tin with melted fat or oil. Line the tin and grease the paper.
3 Break the chocolate into small pieces in a basin together with the fat.

Place the bowl over a pan of hot but not boiling water. Stir until the ingredients have melted.
4 Remove chocolate mixture from heat and stir in the caster sugar a little at a time. Reserve.
5 Sift the flour and the salt into a bowl.
6 Place eggs in a small bowl and whisk lightly together.
7 Make a well in the centre of the dry ingredients. Add the chocolate mixture to the flour, together with the eggs and vanilla essence. Stir the ingredients together to make a smooth, fairly stiff batter.
8 Stir in the chopped nuts.
9 Pour the mixture into the prepared tin and smooth the surface if necessary. Bake for 35-40 minutes, until the cake is just shrinking from the sides of the tin and the centre feels firm to the touch.
10 Leave the cake in the tin for 10 minutes. Turn out on to a cooling rack and remove the lining paper. Leave cake to cool.
11 Cut cake into 12 bars when cold.

WHOLEMEAL PEANUT LOAF

MAKES A 900 G [2 LB] LOAF

350 g [12 oz] self-raising wholemeal flour
pinch of salt
50 g [2 oz] golden syrup
75 g [3 oz] soft brown sugar
75 g [3 oz] butter or margarine
3 medium-sized eggs
4 tablespoons milk
175 g [6 oz] crunchy peanut butter
25 g [1 oz] chopped salted peanuts

1 Heat the oven to 170°C [325°F] Gas 3.

2 Brush a 900 g [2 lb] loaf tin with melted fat or oil and line the base, then grease the paper.

3 Sift the flour and salt into a bowl. Tip any bran left in the sieve back into the bowl and stir in lightly.

4 Place the syrup, sugar and fat in a heavy-based saucepan.

5 Place the saucepan over a low heat and heat gently, stirring from time to time until the fat has melted and the sugar dissolved.

6 Remove the pan from the heat and allow to cool.

7 Make a hollow in the centre of the dry ingredients. Whisk the eggs and milk together lightly.

8 Pour the melted mixture and the egg mixture into the dry ingredients.

9 Using a metal spoon, stir the ingredients together until evenly blended.

10 Stir in the peanut butter until completely amalgamated.

11 Pour the mixture into the prepared tin and sprinkle the surface of the mixture with the peanuts.

12 Bake for 1½ hours until the cake is risen and golden brown.

13 Leave the cake to cool in the tin for 10 minutes, turn out on to a wire rack and remove lining paper.

14 Leave the cake until completely cold before serving.

Variations

● If wholemeal flour is not available use white self-raising flour. Reduce the milk to 2 tablespoons.

● To make a wholemeal date and walnut loaf, omit the crunchy peanut butter and peanuts. Flavour with a pinch of cinnamon instead of the salt. Stir in 75 g [3 oz] chopped, stoned dates and 75 g [3 oz] chopped walnuts at the end of stage 9.

● For a wholemeal sultana loaf, omit the peanut butter and peanuts. Sift 1 teaspoon mixed spice with the flour. Stir in 175 g [6 oz] sultanas at the end of stage 9.

This is a chewy, protein-packed loaf with an attractive rough surface. Like most of the melted-method cakes, this one is also best eaten a good 24 hours after it is made. Serve cut into slices and thickly buttered or made into sweet sandwiches for an unusual lunchbox filler.

The mix is much stiffer than usual, but do not worry; this is because it has to support the weight of the peanuts which is a heavy addition.

CHOCOLATE APPLE SQUARES

MAKES 16 SQUARES

225 g [8 oz] plain flour
2 teaspoons baking powder
100 g [4 oz] butter or margarine
225 g [8 oz] caster sugar
50 g [2 oz] cocoa powder
2 large eggs, beaten
1 teaspoon vanilla essence
100 g [4 oz] walnuts, chopped
2 apples, peeled, cored and diced
3 tablespoons milk

For the icing:
40 g [1½ oz] butter
3 tablespoons cocoa powder
125 ml [4 fl oz] milk
½ teaspoon vanilla essence
275 g [10 oz] icing sugar

1 Heat the oven to 180°C [350°F] Gas 4. Butter an 18 cm [7 in] square tin, line with greaseproof paper, then butter and flour the paper.
2 Sift the flour and baking powder into a bowl. Place the fat and sugar in a heavy-based saucepan.

3 Place the saucepan over a low heat and heat gently until melted. Stir in the cocoa powder with a wooden spoon and beat to a smooth paste.
4 Remove the pan from the heat, allow to cool slightly, then gradually add the beaten eggs and vanilla essence.
5 Add the sifted flour mixture, chopped walnuts, apple and milk.
6 Pour the mixture into the prepared tin and bake for about 55 minutes, or until set. When a skewer is inserted, it should come out clean. Turn out onto a wire rack and leave to cool completely.
7 To make the icing, in a saucepan, melt the butter, stir in the cocoa and beat until smooth. Pour in the milk and heat, whisking until smooth. Remove from the heat, stir in the vanilla essence and leave to cool.
8 Sift the icing sugar and beat it into the cooled chocolate mixture. Keep beating until the mixture is smooth and glossy, then chill the chocolate icing until thick.
9 Peel the greaseproof paper from the bottom of the cold apple and chocolate square. Using a palette knife, spread the chocolate icing evenly over the whole surface and cut into 16 pieces.

A thick chocolate icing tops these crunchy-textured Chocolate apple squares.

163

WHISKED SPONGE CAKES

This chapter is about true sponges, that is sponges made without fat. The whisking method is used to make this quick and economical cake mixture which can be used for sandwich cakes, Swiss rolls, sponge flans and drops or sponge fingers. A little know-how and a light hand will go a long way towards successful results.

A true sponge contains no fat. It is made by whisking eggs and sugar and folding in flour. The characteristic airy, even texture of the cake depends on the amount of air incorporated during whisking and an even distribution of flour. This means the whisking process must be correctly and thoroughly done; also a light hand is needed when folding in the flour so that the minimum amount of air is lost.

Sponge cakes are meant for eating – not keeping – and are best served the day they are baked. The absence of fat means the cake becomes very dry after 2-3 days.

PREPARATION

When it comes to sponge cakes, being organized is vital for perfect results.
● The ingredients must be at room temperature. Remove eggs from refrigerator well in advance to ensure this.
● Prepare the baking tins before starting the cake.
● Heat the oven to the recommended temperature.
● Equipment and mixing bowls must be clean and free from grease.
● The mixture is delicate and must be baked as soon as it is prepared, or valuable air – and therefore lightness – will be lost.

EQUIPMENT

To make the sponge you will need accurate scales and measuring spoons to ensure that the balance of ingredients is exact. Hit and miss measuring will only produce poor results.

All the whisking is done with the ingredients in a large bowl over a saucepan of hot, but not boiling water. Make sure that the bowl you intend to use will sit on, and not in, the saucepan. Should the bowl touch the hot water it will cause the eggs to 'set' before they have been whisked. Use a large earthenware, china or glass bowl and a large saucepan, half filled with water.

You will need a whisk. A balloon whisk is best as it gives the greatest volume. A rotary or electric whisk can be used if wished and will save time.

Lastly you will need a tablespoon for folding the flour into the mixture.

BAKEWARE

When baking a whisked sponge, there are a few points worth knowing when preparing the baking tins.

Always brush tins with melted fat or oil. For sandwich and flan tins, line with a circle of greaseproof paper, re-grease and then sprinkle with flour. Shake the tin lightly by tapping it against a hard surface to distribute the flour evenly. Tip out any excess flour. This procedure will give the sponge a crisp outer edge and prevents it sticking. When making a Swiss roll, the tin must be lined, as shown in step-by-step to lining a Swiss roll tin on page 170.

INGREDIENTS

A sponge is made with eggs, sugar, flour and flavourings. Compared with other cake mixtures, sponges contain a high proportion of eggs and a small quantity of flour. The average proportions are 25 g [1 oz] each of flour and

caster sugar to each large egg used. The quantity of flour may be varied slightly, depending on how stiff a mix is required and the texture desired. For example, if the flour is slightly decreased, the results will be particularly light, provided the mixture is very carefully handled and baked. On the other hand, if the flour is slightly increased, the mixture will be firmer than usual and can be used to make small individual cakes that are not baked in tins.

A small amount of water is sometimes added to the mixture and a raising agent or self-raising flour can also be used depending on the type of cake required.

Eggs
The lightness in texture that is associated with a whisked sponge, is mainly due to the trapping of air when the eggs are whisked – they act as the raising agent by producing thousands of tiny air bubbles in the mixture. Large eggs are used to give the greatest volume. Ideally, they should be 3 days old and used at room temperature. Always remove the eggs from the refrigerator at least an hour before they are required to allow them to come to room temperature.

Sugar
Always use caster sugar when making a whisked sponge. Its fine sugar crystals dissolve easily which helps to give a smooth, even texture.

Avoid coarse sugars because they do not dissolve readily. Very fine sugars, such as icing sugar, give the cake a hard crusty appearance. Make sure that the sugar is completely dry and free from any lumps.

Flour
A classic whisked sponge uses plain flour as it gives a soft textured cake. However, self-raising flour or the addition of a raising agent to a plain flour is generally acceptable if an extra light texture is required. Using self-raising flour means that the resulting sponge will have to be eaten on the day it is made due to the staling effect induced by the chemical raising agent in the flour.

Use flour at room temperature. Flour straight from a cold larder will make a heavy sponge. The cold flour will chill the egg and some of the trapped air will be released.

Additional ingredients
There is a considerable amount of extra ingredients that can be incorpo-

This Lemon dairy sponge has a filling of cream and lemon curd, giving it a wonderful tangy flavour.

rated into, or used to replace a quantity of, the basic mixture. Each additional ingredient must be added with care and always according to the recipe that you are following so as to avoid upsetting the balance.

Cornflour, arrowroot and rice flour are three ingredients that can be used to replace a proportion of the stated amount of flour. None of these ingredients contain gluten and will therefore have a softening effect giving the cake crumb a more tender texture. When using any of these additional ingredients use them to replace no more than one-third of the stated amount of flour.

Water

If three or more eggs are used, a little water may be added. This thins the mixture slightly and helps give a lighter sponge. As a rule 1 tablespoon water is added to every three eggs used. The water should be warm.

FLAVOURINGS

Because the sponge mixture is a delicate one, heavy ingredients, such as dried fruits and nuts, are never used. The mixture is not stiff enough to hold such ingredients.

Grated lemon or orange zest can both be used. Add to the eggs and stir lightly before they are whisked.

There is a good variety of other ingredients that can be used to introduce different flavours.

Liquid flavourings

Take special care when using a liquid flavouring and always remember to take into consideration the amount of liquid that you are introducing to the mixture. When using a liquid favouring it should be added in place of, and never in addition to, the stated amount of water in a given recipe.

Flavouring should be concentrated in flavour because they are always added in small quantities.
- Rose or orange water will give the sponge a delicate flavour.
- Essences can be used but remember that they should only be added from the tip of a cocktail stick or skewer because of their concentrated flavour. Vanilla, almond and spirit flavours can all be used.
- Liqueurs, such as kirsch or framboise (a strawberry-flavoured liqueur) add

Peaches and cream are a lovely combination – and even nicer with a soft, moist sponge cake. This Peach gâteau is baked in a deep cake tin instead of sandwich tins. So, to bake the cake and prevent the top overbrowning, the oven temperature is reduced during baking.

their own characteristic flavour. Spirits can also be used, rum and brandy give a particularly flavoursome sponge.

● Melted chocolate can be used where a dark chocolate flavour and colour are required.

Powdered flavourings

Whatever powdered flavouring you choose, it must always be sifted with the flour to make sure that it is free of lumps and completely amalgamated with the flour.

● Ground spices are an easy way to add flavour to the basic mixture. When adding them it is not necessary to deduct the amount from the basic quantity of flour as they are only used in very small quantities. Cinnamon, ginger, mixed spice and nutmeg are the four spices most frequently used.

● Powdered chocolate or cocoa can be added to give a rich chocolate flavour and colour. Because they are used in quantitites of over 15 g [½ oz] the corresponding amount of flour must always be deducted to preserve the balance of ingredients.

METHOD

There are several acceptable methods of preparing a whisked sponge and they all have one thing in common. They all rely on incorporating as much air during the whisking process as possible.

The two main methods both use exactly the same principles but they differ in that one is made by whisking the mixture over a saucepan of hot water and the other does not.

The method where the mixture is whisked over hot water is generally accepted as the modern method and is far quicker.

Traditional method

Patience and plenty of time are needed to make a whisked sponge by this method but it definitely has some advantages. The cake will store for at least two days and it will be soft and light in texture.

Sifting the flour

The flour, salt and any powdered flavourings are sifted together. This is done twice to aerate the ingredients as much as possible.

Whisking the eggs

The eggs are placed in a large bowl and

mixed together to amalgamate them. Next the total amount of sugar is added to the egg mixture and they are then whisked together until the mixture is pale and creamy. Using a hand-held electric whisk will mean that the time spent will be around 15 minutes, by hand it will take at least 20 minutes.

The aim is to dissolve the sugar at this stage and to introduce as much air as possible. You will know when the mixture is ready because it will have doubled in volume and a whisk will leave a trail when lifted out of the mixture and dribbled across the surface. The impression should remain for at least 3 seconds. This indicates that the mixture is ready for the flour to be incorporated.

Folding in flour

The sifted flour is folded into the foamy mixture with a figure of eight action. Sprinkle about a quarter of the flour over the surface of the mixture and at the same time, begin to fold the flour in, cutting through the mixture to incorporate the flour completely. Repeat with the remaining flour until it has all been added. Never be tempted to stir the mixture or beat it as this will only result in a loss of the precious air.

The mixture should now be the same, or more or less the same volume as it was before the flour was added. A loss in volume at this stage cannot be corrected. Any liquid flavouring or water is added at this stage by the same folding action. Without wasting time, quickly pour the mixture into the prepared tin and bake immediately.

Modern method

Exactly the same procedure is followed to make a whisked sponge by the modern method with the one major exception – the saucepan of hot water. By placing the eggs and sugar in a bowl over a saucepan of hot water, the heat from the water helps to dissolve the sugar that much quicker and 'set' the air as it is entrapped by the whisking. The modern method will produce a soft, slightly sticky sponge with a light crust to it.

Preparing double boiler

To prevent any delay prepare the pan of hot water before you start whisking the eggs.

Heat the water until it is boiling then transfer to a wooden board with a kitchen cloth on it to prevent the bowl from slipping.

Whisking the mixture

Add the eggs and continue as for the traditional method. The mixture should take between 5 and 15 minutes to reach a mousse-like texture, 5 minutes with a hand-held electric whisk and 15 by hand. As soon as the mixture is ready, remove the mixing bowl from over the hot water. Whisk for another 5 minutes to let the mixture cool. Fold in the flour in stages, as for the traditional method. The mixture will be of a pouring consistency once all the flour, water (if used) or liquid flavourings are added. Using a rubber spatula scrape the mixture into prepared tin.

OVEN TEMPERATURES

A moderate oven is required for most sponge cakes as this allows the air to expand fully before the egg sets (see chart below).

TIN SIZES, BAKING TIMES AND TEMPERATURES

Number of eggs used	Size of cake tin	Oven temperature	Baking time
2	two 18cm [7 in] sandwich	180°C [350°F] Gas 4	20-25 minutes
	one 20 cm [8 in] sandwich	180°C [350°F] Gas 4	25-30 minutes
	one 27 × 18 cm [11 × 7 in] Swiss roll	200°C [400°F] Gas 6	8-10 minutes
	one 20 cm [18 in] flan	180°C [350°F] Gas 4	25-30 minutes
3	three 18 cm [7 in] sandwich	180°C [350°F] Gas 4	20-25 minutes
	two 20 cm [8 in] sandwich	180°C [350°F] Gas 4	25-30 minutes
	one 33 × 23 cm [13 × 9 in] Swiss roll	200°C [400°F] Gas 6	8-10 minutes
	15 cm [6 in] round	180°C [350°F] Gas 4	25 minutes then
		170°C [325°F] Gas 3	40 minutes

MAKING A WHISKED SPONGE

MAKES 8-10 SLICES
75 g [3 oz] plain flour
3 large eggs
75 g [3 oz] caster sugar

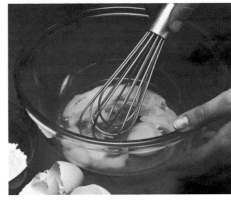

1 Preheat oven (see chart) and prepare baking tin(s). Half fill a large saucepan with water. Bring to the boil and remove from heat.

2 Sift the flour, baking powder, if using, and dry flavourings twice. Place eggs in a large bowl and whisk together.

3 Add sugar to the eggs and place on top of the saucepan of hot water. The bowl must not touch the water.

4 Whisk the eggs and sugar together using either a balloon, rotary or electric whisk until the mixture leaves a trail.

5 Remove the bowl from the saucepan and continue whisking until the mixture cools slightly and is pale in colour.

6 Carefully but quickly fold in the flour, approximately a quarter at a time until it has all been incorporated.

7 Immediately pour the mixture into the prepared tin(s). Bake for the required time.

8 Press the surface of the cake lightly with fingertips. If cooked it should feel firm and leave no impression.

LINING A SWISS ROLL TIN

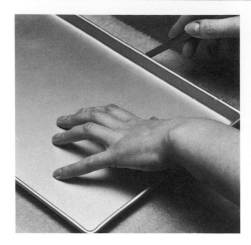

1 Place tin on a large sheet of greaseproof paper and draw around the base of the tin.

2 Cut the greaseproof paper 2.5 cm [1 in] out from drawn line. Crease the paper on line.

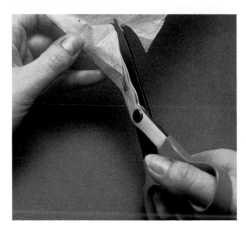

3 Grease the tin and press down the greaseproof paper. Cut and mould the corners.

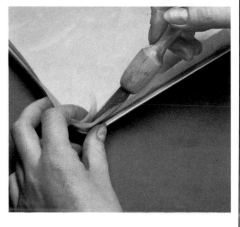

4 Re-grease the tin (this time with the paper in it) and continue as for round tins.

Serving Swiss roll

The quickest way to serve a Swiss roll is to simply dust it with more caster sugar or sift icing sugar over it. Alternatively, the cake can be covered with any of a variety of icings to turn it into something extra special.

Place Swiss roll on a wire cooling rack and cover completely with melted chocolate, sprinkle along top of cake with nuts or chocolate vermicelli while the chocolate is still soft. Allow chocolate to set.

Place Swiss roll on a wire cooling rack and cover completely with glacé icing.

Drizzle the top of a Swiss roll with some plain white glacé icing and allow the icing to dribble down the sides. When the icing is on the point of setting, decorate with a row of glacé fruit and/or chopped nuts.

Swiss rolls require a hotter oven than other cakes as quick baking is essential to keep the cake moist and pliable.

Always heat the oven a good 15 minutes before you intend baking to ensure the temperature is steady and even. Bake at the recommended temperature or the results will be disappointing. If the oven is too hot, the air may rise too quickly, before the structure of the mix can support it and the cake will sink in the centre. On the other hand, the excessive heat may make the egg set before the air has a chance to expand fully and this will result in a close, heavy textured sponge cake.

BAKING

Never allow the mixture to sit in the tin waiting for the oven as the volume that you have worked hard to produce will begin to break down. Place the cake in the heated oven (usually in the centre) and close the door carefully. Slamming the door will cause a sudden jar to the mixture and break down some of the bubbles. Do not be tempted to open the oven door until the recommended baking time is over as this could cause the cake to sink in the centre.

TESTING

To test the cake, when the recommended baking time is over, press the surface of the cake lightly with the fingertips. If the cake is cooked, it should feel firm and leave no impression. The cake should have shrunk from the side of the tin and there should be no sounds of bubbling.

COOLING

As soon as the cake is baked, remove it from the oven and stand the cake (in the tin) on a damp tea-towel for no longer than half a minute. Doing this helps to loosen the cake from the tin. When making a Swiss roll this rule does not apply.

Invert the cake on to a wire cooling rack and carefully peel away lining paper. Carefully invert the cake so that it is now the right way up on a wire cooling rack and leave until the cake is completely cold.

SWISS ROLLS

Swiss rolls and flan cases are made with a whisked sponge mixture because it is so light and soft in texture. It is a mixture that once baked will roll easily, unlike a creamed cake. This is essential in the case of a Swiss roll. Making a Swiss roll is very simple once you know how, but there are a few rules that ensure success.

Preparing the paper

Bake the sponge in the prepared tin and while it is baking place a large sheet of greaseproof paper (at least 2.5 cm [1 in] larger all round than the size of the Swiss roll tin) on a tea-towel. Sprinkle the greaseproof paper heavily with caster sugar and, if using jam as a filling, warm in a small saucepan.

MAKING A SWISS ROLL

1 While the sponge is baking cut a piece of greaseproof paper slightly larger than the Swiss roll.

2 Put greaseproof paper on a tea-towel. Sprinkle paper with 2 table-spoons caster sugar.

3 If using jam for a filling warm 4 tablespoons of jam in a small saucepan.

4 Invert the baked sponge on to the sugared greaseproof paper. Peel away lining.

5 Cut 6 mm [¼ in] from all the edges. This removes the crisp edges and makes rolling easier.

6 Make a cut halfway through the cake, 2.5 cm [1 in] from and parallel to the end to be rolled.

7 Working quickly, spread the jam over the cake to within 2.5 cm [1 in] of the edges.

8 To make a firm start, press the cut end over and hold down with one hand. Grip paper with the other.

9 Working away from you make an even roll. Hold the paper round the roll for a few seconds.

171

Rolling

As soon as the cake is baked, invert it on to the sheet of sugared greaseproof paper. Peel away the lining paper and, using a long-bladed sharp knife, cut away a 6 mm [¼ in] strip of cake from every side. These edges are crisp and if left on they will hamper the rolling process.

Make a cut, half-way through the cake, 2.5 cm [1 in] in from, and parallel to, the end from which the cake is to be rolled. This aids the rolling as it gets it off to an even start.

Working quickly, spread the jam over the cake up to within 2.5 cm [1 in] of the edges.

To make a firm start to the roll, press the half cut end up and over and hold down with one hand. With the other hand, grip the greaseproof paper and, working away from you, roll the sponge firmly to make an even roll.

With the paper still around the roll, hold the cake firmly to set for a second or two. Remove the greaseproof paper and place the roll, seam side down, on a wire cooling rack.

Creamy fillings

For a cream or butter-cream filled Swiss roll, omit the jam and roll the cake, with the greaseproof paper inside. Allow the cake to cool and when completely cold, carefully unroll and spread with required filling, re-roll and discard the greaseproof paper. These fillings would melt if spread on the roll when it is hot.

Mini rolls

To make mini-Swiss rolls, bake the cake as usual, turn out and trim. Then, cut the cake in half lengthways to make two long rectangles. Spread each with jam and roll up, starting at the longer sides to make two long rolls. When the two rolls are completely cool, cut each into even-sized lengths.

SANDWICH AND LAYER CAKES

The traditional sponge is a simply delicious sandwich cake, filled with cream and/or jam, or another soft filling. You can bake the cake in two shallow sandwich tins, or use one deep cake tin and split the cold, baked cake horizontally into two layers.

To make a layer cake you can use three sandwich tins, or you can split one deep cake into three or four rounds. Alternatively you can bake the cake in a shallow rectangular tin. In this case, the baked slab of cake is cut across in equal pieces which are assembled one on top of the other, with a filling between each layer.

Finishing Touches

A simply filled jam or cream sponge looks perfect just dredged with sieved icing or caster sugar.

For a really rich effect, the cake may be lightly soaked in sugar syrup – delicious laced with brandy or rum – and the whole cake smothered with whipped thick cream, then decorated with toasted, flaked almonds. Alternatively, the sides and top of the cake may be decorated in any of the ways suggested for creaming-method cakes (see pages 68-87).

MAKING SPONGE FLANS

Like Swiss roll, sponge flans are usually made with a whisked sponge mixture. The mixture is baked in a ridged tin so that when the cake is baked and inverted, the ridges in the tin form the shape of the flan which will hold a filling and act as a case.

Filling sponge flans

Fillings for sponge flans are numerous but they are always no-cook or pre-cooked and cooled fillings. Any filling should be added as close to serving time as possible to prevent the sponge from becoming soggy if the filling is a 'wet' one. When filling a sponge flan, there is another important point that has to be considered and this is appearance. Whatever the filling, it should be neat, decorative and appealing so always take care when preparing a filling.

Fruit

Fresh fruit makes a mouthwatering treat when arranged decoratively. To prevent the flan from becoming soggy, brush the inside of the flan case with warmed jam before filling with the chosen fruit. Try and choose fruit that is juicy on the inside yet fairly dry on the outside to further guard against ruining the texture.

Once the flan case has been filled, coat the fruit with a little sieved and warmed jam or a jelly glaze. Coating the fruit in this manner will give a shiny appetizing appearance and prevent the sponge from appearing too dry.

• Canned fruit can be used in place of fresh fruit. Just make sure that the fruit is well drained and dried on kitchen paper before arranging in the flan case.

• To add variety, the fruit may be arranged over a layer of thick cream, crème au beurre or a sweetened and creamed soft cheese.

• After the fruit (if used) has been glazed, sprinkle with toasted nuts.

• Fill the flan case with a cheesecake and fruit mixture.

STORING AND FREEZING

Sponges, whatever their form, made by this method are at their best when eaten on the day they are made. If necessary, however, an unfilled or undecorated cake may be stored in an air-tight tin for up to 2 days.

Never attempt to freeze an uncooked sponge mixture as it will be totally inedible. Baked and unfilled, a whisked sponge will store for up to 6 months in the freezer, wrapped tightly in heavy-duty freezer wrap.

To serve, allow to thaw in freezer wrappings at room temperature for 1-2 hours, unwrap and fill as desired.

ZEBRA ROLL

MAKES 8 SLICES

50 g [2 oz] plain flour
25 g [1 oz] cocoa powder
pinch of baking powder
3 large eggs
100 g [4 oz] caster sugar
1 tablespoon hot water
extra caster sugar

For the filling:
275 ml [½ pt] whipping cream
2 tablespoons orange-flavoured liqueur
    (optional)
8 fancy chocolates, to decorate

1 Heat the oven to 200°C [400°F] Gas 6. Grease a 30 × 20 cm [12 × 8 in] Swiss roll tin, line with greaseproof paper, then grease the paper.
2 Sift flour, cocoa and baking powder together.
3 Half fill a saucepan with water, bring to the boil, then remove from heat.
4 Place eggs in a mixing bowl and whisk lightly. Add the sugar.
5 Place the bowl over pan of hot water and whisk the eggs and sugar together

until pale, thick and foamy. When fully whisked, the mixture should hold the trail of the whisk for 3 seconds.
6 Remove bowl from the pan and whisk for a few minutes more, then fold in flour and water. Pour into prepared tin and spread evenly by gently tilting tin. Bake for 12-14 minutes, until well risen.
7 Meanwhile, lay a sheet of greaseproof paper on top of a clean damp tea-towel. Sprinkle paper thickly with caster sugar.
8 Turn baked cake out on to the sugared paper. Peel lining paper off then trim crusty edges with a sharp knife. Make a shallow cut along one short end, about 12 mm [½ in] from the edge. Roll up the cake with paper inside. Place seam-side down on a wire rack and leave to cool for 30 minutes
9 To make the filling, whip cream, with the liqueur if using, until standing in soft peaks. Put one-quarter of cream into a piping bag with large star nozzle and reserve. Whip remaining cream until stiff.
10 Unroll the cake, remove the paper and spread with stiffly whipped cream, then roll up again. Decorate with piped cream and chocolates. Serve the roll on the day of making.

This Zebra roll is filled with a liqueur-flavoured cream. Any dainty chocolates of your choice can be used to decorate the top. Here chocolate mint sticks cut into short lengths have been used.

STRAWBERRY SWISS ROLL

MAKES 6 SLICES
3 large eggs
75 g [3 oz] caster sugar
few drops of almond essence
75 g [3 oz] plain flour

For the filling and decoration:
150 ml [¼ pt] thick cream
few drops of almond essence
1 large egg white
50 g [2 oz] caster sugar
100 g [4 oz] strawberries, hulled and
   crushed
icing sugar for dredging
sliced strawberries, to decorate

1 Heat the oven to 220°C [425°F] Gas 7. Grease a 30 × 23 cm [12 × 9 in] Swiss roll tin, line the tin with greaseproof paper and grease the paper.
2 Half fill a saucepan with water, bring to the boil, then remove from heat.
3 Place eggs in a mixing bowl and whisk lightly. Add the sugar and almond essence.
4 Place the bowl over pan of hot water and whisk until the mixture is thick and foamy and holds the trail of the whisk for 3 seconds.
5 Remove the bowl from the pan and whisk for a few minutes more until the mixture is cool. Sift one-third of the flour over the mixture, then fold it in with a large metal spoon. Add the remaining flour in the same way.

6 Pour the sponge mixture into the prepared tin and spread evenly by gently tilting the tin. Bake the cake for 7-10 minutes until the surface is golden and springy to the touch.
7 While the cake is baking, lay a sheet of greaseproof paper on top of a clean, damp tea-towel. Sift icing sugar thickly over the paper.
8 Turn the baked cake out on to the sugared paper. Carefully peel off the lining paper. Trim the edges of the cake, then make a cut halfway through the cake, 2.5 cm [1 in] from and parallel to the end to be rolled. Roll up the cake, with the sugared paper inside. Place the roll seam-side down on a wire rack and leave until completely cold.
9 To make the filling, whip the cream and almond essence until thick. In a clean bowl and using clean beaters, whisk the egg white until standing in soft peaks. Whisk in the caster sugar, 1 tablespoon at a time, and continue whisking until the meringue is stiff. Fold the meringue into the whipped cream, then fold in the crushed strawberries.
10 Unroll the cake and remove the paper. Spread the filling over the cake, then gently roll it up again. Place on a serving plate, cover and refrigerate for at least 30 minutes.
11 To serve, sift icing sugar thickly over the cake and decorate with sliced strawberries. Serve the cake the day it is made.

CHOCOLATE ARCTIC ROLL

This cake is a delicious combination of textures as well as flavours. Other flavoured ice-cream can be used, but be sure to choose the 'soft-scoop' variety as this will spread easily, without breaking the cake.

MAKES 8 SLICES
65 g [2½ oz] plain flour
small pinch of salt
15 g [½ oz] cocoa powder
3 large eggs
75 g [3 oz] caster sugar

For the filling:
6-8 tablespoons vanilla ice-cream

1 Position the shelf just above centre of the oven and heat to 200°C [400°F]

Vanilla and walnut roll (see Chocolate arctic roll variations).

If fresh strawberries are not in season, use a well-drained 215 g (7¼ oz) can of strawberries for the filling for Strawberry Swiss roll.

Gas 6. Prepare a 33 × 23 cm [13 × 9 in] Swiss roll tin as described in the step-by-step instructions.

2 Half fill a large saucepan with water, bring to the boil, then remove from heat. Meanwhile, sift the flour twice, together with the salt and cocoa.

3 Place the eggs in a mixing bowl and whisk lightly together, using a balloon, rotary whisk or hand-held electric whisk. Add the sugar.

4 Set the mixing bowl over the pan of hot water. Whisk eggs and sugar together until mixture is thick and foamy and will hold the trail of the whisk for 3 seconds.

5 Remove the bowl from the heat and continue whisking for about 5 minutes or until cool.

6 Fold in the flour in gradually.

7 Quickly pour the sponge mixture into the prepared tin. Tilt the tin to spread the mix evenly in the corners. Bake for 8-10 minutes.

8 Meanwhile, prepare equipment for turning out and rolling (see step-by-step instructions given on page 171).

9 Remove the baked sponge from the oven and turn out immediately on to the sugared paper. Peel off lining paper, then trim off crisp edges.

10 Make a cut halfway through the cake, 2.5 cm [1 in] from and parallel to the end to be rolled, then roll up firmly with the sugared paper inside.

11 Hold in position for a few minutes, then transfer to a wire rack and leave until completely cold.

12 Unroll the cold roll very carefully. Spread with ice-cream to within 6 mm [¼ in] of edges. Carefully roll up again, this time with the aid of the paper.

13 Remove greaseproof paper and dredge with caster sugar. Chill in the refrigerator to firm.

Variations

• For a vanilla and walnut roll, omit cocoa and increase the flour content to 75 g [3 oz]. Sprinkle 25-50 g [1-2 oz] finely chopped walnuts over the ice-cream before re-rolling.

• For a honey spiced sponge roll, omit cocoa powder and increase the flour to 75 g [3 oz]. Sift 1½ teaspoons mixed spice with the flour and fold in 1 tablespoon hot water after the flour. Omit the ice-cream and fill the cold roll with the following filling. Cream 100 g [4 oz] butter until very soft, gradually beat in 4 tablespoons honey. When thoroughly blended, add 1 tablespoon water and beat until very smooth.

LEMON AND HONEY ROLL

MAKES 8-10 SLICES
75 g [3 oz] plain flour
pinch of salt
3 large eggs
75 g [3 oz] caster sugar
grated zest of 1 lemon
extra caster sugar

For the filling:
175 g [6 oz] full-fat soft cheese
4 teaspoons clear honey
icing sugar, for dredging

1 Heat the oven to 200°C [400°F] Gas 6. Grease a 33 × 23 cm [13 × 9 in] Swiss roll tin; line the tin with greaseproof paper and grease the lining paper.

2 Sift the flour with the salt.

3 Half fill a saucepan with water, bring to the boil, then remove from heat.

4 Place eggs in a mixing bowl and whisk lightly. Add the sugar and lemon zest.

5 Place the bowl over the pan of hot water and whisk the mixture until thick and foamy. Continue until the mixture is thick enough to hold the trail of the whisk for 3 seconds.

6 Remove the bowl from the pan, whisk for a few minutes more until the mixture is cool, then gradually fold in the sifted flour.

7 Pour the mixture into the prepared tin and spread it evenly by gently tilting the tin. Bake the cake for 8-10 minutes until the surface is golden and springs back when lightly pressed.

8 While the cake is baking, lay a sheet of greaseproof paper on top of a clean, damp tea-towel. Sprinkle the paper generously and evenly with caster sugar.

9 Turn the baked cake out on to the sugared paper. Trim off the crisp edges with a sharp knife. Make a cut halfway through the cake, 2.5 cm [1 in] from and parallel to the end to be rolled, then roll up with the paper inside.

10 Hold in position for a few minutes, then transfer to a wire rack and leave until completely cold.

11 To make the filling, beat the cheese with the honey until soft and smoothly blended. Unroll the cake and remove the paper. Spread the cake with the filling, then gently roll it up again. Sift icing sugar over the top.

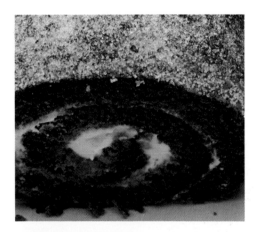

Chocolate arctic roll

Honey spiced roll

CHERRY CHOCOLATE ROLL

MAKES 8-10 SLICES

3 large eggs
75 g [3 oz] caster sugar
1 teaspoon vanilla essence
50 g [2 oz] plain flour
pinch of salt
25 g [1 oz] cocoa powder

For the filling:
125 g [4 oz] glacé cherries
3 tablespoons kirsch
150 ml [5 oz] thick cream, whipped

For the decoration:
1 large orange
2 tablespoons icing sugar

1 Marinate the glacé cherries for the filling in the kirsch overnight.
2 The next day, pare the zest from the orange with a potato peeler and cut into 2.5 cm [1 in] lengths, then into very fine julienne strips. Blanch for 5 minutes in simmering water. Drain, refresh under cold running water and drain again.
3 Heat the oven to 200°C [400°F] Gas 6. Line a Swiss roll tin with greaseproof paper and grease the paper.
4 Half fill a saucepan with water, bring to the boil, then remove from heat.
5 Place eggs in a mixing bowl and whisk lightly. Add the sugar and vanilla essence.
6 Place the bowl over the pan of hot water and whisk the mixture until thick and foamy. Continue until the mixture is thick enough to hold the trail of the whisk for 3 seconds.
7 Remove the bowl from the saucepan and whisk for another 5 minutes or until cold.
8 Sift the flour, salt and cocoa powder over the egg and sugar mixture and fold in with a large metal spoon. Pour into the tin and level the surface. Bake for 12-15 minutes or until the sponge shrinks slightly from the sides of the tin and the surface springs back when touched.
9 Lay a large piece of greaseproof paper on a flat surface. Carefully turn the sponge out onto the paper and peel off the lining paper.
10 Trim the edges with a sharp knife. Lay another piece of greaseproof paper on top. Carefully roll up the Swiss roll with the paper inside. Leave to become cold on a wire rack.
11 Unroll the Swiss roll carefully, discarding the paper. Spread with the whipped cream. Drain the marinated cherries and spread them over the cream. Re-roll the Swiss roll and sift over the icing sugar. Sprinkle with the orange julienne and serve.

PEACH GATEAU

MAKES 8-10 SLICES

75 g [3 oz] plain flour
3 large eggs
75 g [3 oz] caster sugar

For the filling:
425 g [15 oz] canned peaches
275 ml [½ pt] thick cream
50-75 g [2-3 oz] toasted flaked almonds

1 Position oven shelf in the centre of the oven. Heat the oven to 180°C [350°F] Gas 4.
2 Brush a deep 15 cm [6 in] round cake tin with melted fat or oil. Line tin fully with greaseproof paper and grease the paper. Sprinkle with flour, shake and tip out excess flour.
3 Half fill a saucepan with water, bring to the boil, then remove from heat. Sift the flour twice.
4 Place eggs in a mixing bowl and whisk lightly. Add the sugar.
5 Place the bowl over pan of hot water and whisk the eggs and sugar together until pale, thick and foamy. When fully whisked, the mixture should hold the trail of the whisk for 3 seconds.
6 Remove the bowl from the heat and continue whisking for about 5 minutes until cool.
7 Add a quarter of the sifted flour and lightly fold it in. Repeat with remaining flour. When the flour is incorporated, lightly fold in 1 tablespoon warm water.
8 Quickly turn the sponge mixture into the prepared tin and bake for 25 minutes.
9 Reduce the oven temperature to 170°C [325°F] Gas 3 and bake for a further 40 minutes, until the surface of the sponge feels firm in the centre.
10 Remove cake from the oven and stand the tin on a damp tea-towel for 30 seconds. Then turn out on to a wire rack and leave until completely cold.
11 Drain the peach slices and pat dry on kitchen paper. Reserve a few of the

With its marinated cherry filling and pretty decoration of orange julienne, Cherry chocolate roll is a special occasion Swiss roll.

best slices for decoration, chop the remainder. Whip the cream until thick.

12 Slice the cold cake horizontally into three even layers. Spread the bottom layer with about 3 tablespoons whipped cream, then sprinkle over half the chopped peaches.

13 Place the centre layer of sponge on top and spread with another 3 tablespoons cream. Sprinkle over the remaining chopped peaches. Top with the final layer of sponge.

14 Coat the top and sides of the cake with all but 2-3 tablespoons cream. Then press the almonds around the sides of the cake, a few at a time, with a palette knife.

15 Put the remaining cream in a piping bag fitted with a star nozzle and pipe stars of cream around top outer edge of cake. Decorate with reserved peach slices.

WALNUT CAKE

MAKES 8 SLICES

6 large eggs
225 g [8 oz] caster sugar
225 g [8 oz] walnuts, ground
225 g [8 oz] plain flour, sifted
1 tablespoon instant coffee granules
    dissolved in 2 teaspoons boiling water
few drops of vanilla essence
walnut halves, to decorate

For the icing:
50 g [2 oz] icing sugar
100 g [4 oz] butter, softened
few drops of vanilla essence
1 tablespoon instant coffee granules
    dissolved in 2 teaspoons boiling water
25 g [1 oz] walnuts, ground

1 Heat the oven to 180°C [350°F] Gas 4. Grease a 23 cm [9 in] round cake tin. Line with greaseproof paper and grease the paper.

2 Put the eggs and sugar into a large bowl and whisk together until pale and fluffy and doubled in volume.

3 Gradually fold in the ground walnuts and flour alternately, then thoroughly stir in the dissolved coffee and vanilla.

4 Spoon the mixture into the tin and level surface. Bake in oven for 1 hour 10 minutes until a warmed fine skewer inserted into the centre comes out clean.

5 Cool the cake for 5 minutes, then remove from the tin and peel off the lining paper. Place the right way up on a wire rack. Leave the cake to cool.

6 Meanwhile, make the icing, sift the icing sugar into a bowl, then add the butter. Beat until smooth and creamy. Beat in the vanilla essence and dissolved coffee and ground walnuts.

7 Place the cake on a serving plate and swirl the icing over the top. Decorate with walnut halves.

This Walnut cake is made by the traditional method, rather than whisking the mixture over hot water. The result is a cake that will keep slightly longer than other whisked sponges.

A glamorous Orange cream sponge is a real treat for any tea-time.

ORANGE CREAM SPONGE

MAKES 6-8 SLICES

3 large eggs
75 g [3 oz] caster sugar
75 g [3 oz] plain flour

For the filling and decoration:
150 ml [¼ pt] thick cream
1 tablespoon milk
5 tablespoons orange curd
6-8 orange twists

1 Heat the oven to 190°C [375°F] Gas 5. Lightly grease two 18 cm [7 in] sandwich tins, line their bases with greaseproof paper, then grease the paper.
2 Half fill a saucepan with water, bring to the boil, then remove from heat.
3 Place eggs in a mixing bowl and whisk lightly. Add the sugar.
4 Place the bowl over pan of hot water and whisk the eggs and sugar together until pale, thick and foamy, and thick enough to hold the trail of the whisk for 3 seconds.
5 Remove the bowl from the pan and whisk for a few minutes more, until the mixture is cool. Sift one-third of the flour over the mixture, then fold it in

with a large metal spoon. Add the remaining flour in the same way.
6 Divide the mixture equally between the prepared tins and spread it evenly by gently tilting the tins. Bake for 15 minutes until the cakes are golden and spring to the touch.
7 Cool for 1-2 seconds, then turn out of the tins on to a wire rack. Peel off the lining paper and leave to cool completely.
8 To serve, whip the cream with the milk until standing in soft peaks, then fold in the orange curd. Place one cake on a serving plate and spread with some of the orange cream. Place the other cake on top. Spread the remaining orange cream over the top and sides of the cake, covering it completely. Decorate with orange twists and serve as soon as possible.

MANDARIN FLAN

SERVES 6

50 g [2 oz] plain flour
2 large eggs
50 g [2 oz] caster sugar

For the filling:
75 g [3 oz] unsalted butter
25 g [1 oz] icing sugar
1 medium-sized egg yolk
1 tablespoon orange flavoured liqueur or
    ½ teaspoon vanilla essence
312 g [11 oz] canned mandarin oranges
2 tablespoons apricot jam

1 Position the shelf in the centre of the oven and heat the oven to 180°C [350°F] Gas 4. Prepare a 20 cm [8 in] sponge flan tin and line the base with a circle of greaseproof paper. Grease the lining paper.
2 Half fill a saucepan with water, bring to the boil, then remove from heat. Sift the flour twice and set aside.
3 Place the eggs in a mixing bowl and whisk lightly together, using a balloon or rotary whisk. Beat in the sugar.
4 Set the bowl over the pan of hot water – it should sit comfortably, without touching the water. Whisk the eggs and sugar together until pale, thick and foamy and the mix holds the trail of the whisk for 3 seconds.
5 Remove the bowl from the pan and continue whisking for about 5 minutes until the mix is cool.
6 Fold in the flour gradually, then turn into the prepared tin and bake for 25-30 minutes.

7 Remove the baked sponge from the oven and stand the tin on a damp cloth for 30 seconds. Then turn out on to a wire rack. Leave until completely cold.

8 To make the crème au berre ménagère, place the soft butter in a bowl and beat until creamy. Sieve icing sugar and add to the butter. Beat the egg yolk lightly. Add egg yolk and flavouring to butter. Beat together until smooth.

9 Spread the butter-cream evenly in the cold flan case. Drain the mandarin segments and pat dry on kitchen paper. Arrange decoratively over the butter-cream, closely overlappping.

10 Warm the jam, together with 1 tablespoon water, and use to glaze the surface of the fruit.

Variations

● Pineapple sponge flan: use drained, canned pineapple pieces instead of mandarin orange segments. Flavour the butter-cream with kirsch instead of an orange liqueur.

● For raspberry sponge flan, use fresh raspberries instead of canned mandarin oranges. Flavour the butter-cream with framboise and glaze the fruit with redcurrant jelly. Pipe a border of whipped cream.

PINEAPPLE SPONGE

MAKES 6-8 SLICES

75 g [3 oz] plain flour
½ teaspoon ground mixed spice
¼ teaspoon ground ginger
3 large eggs
75 g [3 oz] caster sugar

For the filling and topping:
375 g [13 oz] can crushed pineapple,
    drained with syrup reserved
25 g [1 oz] custard powder
2 teaspoons lemon juice
150 ml [¼ pt] whipping cream

1 Heat oven to 190°C [375°F] Gas 5. Lightly grease two 18 cm [7 in] sandwich tins, line the base of each with greaseproof paper, then grease the paper.

2 Sift the flour with the spices.

3 Place eggs in a mixing bowl and whisk lightly. Add the sugar.

4 Place the bowl over pan of hot water and whisk the eggs and sugar together until pale, thick and foamy, and thick enough to hold the trail of the whisk for 3 seconds.

5 Remove the bowl from the pan and whisk for a few minutes more until the mixture is cool. Using a large metal spoon, fold in the flour one-third at a time.

6 Divide the mixture between the prepared tins and spread evenly by tilting the tins. Bake for 15 minutes until golden and springy to the touch.

7 Leave to stand for 2-3 seconds, then turn out on to a wire rack. Peel off the lining paper, turn the cakes the right way up and leave until cold.

8 Meanwhile, make the filling. Make up the reserved pineapple syrup to 275 ml [½ pt] with water.

9 In a bowl, blend the custard powder with some of the pineapple liquid. In a pan, bring the remaining liquid to the boil, then stir into the custard. Return mixture to pan and simmer, stirring, for 1-2 minutes until thickened.

10 Remove from the heat and stir in the crushed pineapple and lemon juice. Leave to cool completely.

11 To assemble the cake, spread one sponge with two-thirds of the pineapple mixture. Place the remaining sponge on top and spread with the rest of the pineapple mixture to within 12 mm [½ in] of the edges. Whip the cream until standing in soft peaks, then pipe round the edge. Serve as soon as possible.

This layered Pineapple sponge has an unusual pineapple custard-based filling and topping.

RICH FRUIT CAKES

When you want a cake for a special occasion the traditional choice is a rich fruit cake. Packed with dried fruit, spices and other good things, these cakes keep well, taste good and are the perfect base for Christmas, Easter and birthday decorations.

Making your own wedding or Christmas cake or a cake for a special celebration might seem rather daunting but once you can make the basic rich fruit cake on which all these are based, you will find the rest easy. In this chapter learn how to make the basic cake. Pages 194-209 show you how to make almond paste to cover the cake, how to make traditional royal icing and how to design, assemble and ice a variety of cakes for those special days.

Rich fruit cakes are all based on the creaming method (see pages 68-87). These cakes are high in butter, sugar and eggs and are made extra delicious by the addition of dried fruit, chopped peel, nuts and spices. They have excellent keeping qualities and if stored correctly will remain moist for several months. Some cakes (notably Christmas and wedding cakes which have spirit added at intervals after baking) actually improve with keeping.

It is true that rich fruit cakes can crack or sink but this only happens if you fail to line the tin correctly, use the wrong size tin or bake at the wrong temperature. The guides to quantities and temperatures that you will find here will ensure your success.

INGREDIENTS

It is the quantity of fat and sugar in

This Fruity pudding cake keeps well for several weeks and mellows with age. To store it, wrap in foil or cling film and keep covered in an airtight container in a cool place.

relation to flour which determines the richness of a cake. It is not, as is often thought, the amount of fruit used. The proportions of fat to sugar for rich fruit cake are basically the same as for creaming cakes (see page 68) but more of each is used. In some recipes, proportions may vary slightly. If there is more fat than sugar, the cake will be richer than if equal quantities were used. If there is more sugar, the cake will have a spongy texture. In this chapter you will find a chart giving amounts of ingredients for making rich fruit cakes of varying sizes. For fruity cakes, a little more flour than fat or sugar is used because of the high fruit and egg content.

Flour

Usually plain white flour is used for rich fruit cakes. The amount of flour used is almost always the same as the amount of butter or fat and sugar, except for very rich traditional cakes (see chart on pages 186-7).

Raising agent

To help the cake rise, a raising agent is sometimes but not always added with the flour. For a very rich fruit cake with a dense texture, such as a wedding or Christmas cake, a raising agent is often omitted entirely.

The usual raising agent is bicarbonate of soda for a dark cake or baking powder for a light cake. Quantities depend on the amount of other ingredients in the cake.

Fat

There is no doubt that butter gives the finest flavour to rich cakes and it is well worth using if the cake is for something like a wedding or christening. A combination of butter and hard margarine gives good results or you can use hard margarine alone. The amount of fat is usually the same as the amount of flour, except in very fruity cakes where it is about 25-100 g [1-4 oz] less.

Have the fat soft but not oily when you come to use it. This makes creaming easier and gives lighter results.

Sugar

Caster or soft brown sugar are the sweet choices for rich fruit cakes. Soft brown sugar gives darker results. Treacle, golden syrup or marmalade may be used in place of some of the sugar but it is best to find a recipe and follow carefully if you want to do this. The quantity of sugar is always the same as the quantity of butter or fat and flour, except in very rich cakes where quantities are as given in the chart on pages 186-187.

Eggs

Eggs add moisture, flavour and colour to the cake and also help to give a good, soft texture. They also help the cake to rise. Large eggs are usually used for rich cakes.

Liquids

Sometimes a little extra liquid is added both to give flavour and to produce the steam which helps the cake to rise. For very rich traditional cakes, brandy, rum or sherry are used. The amount depends on the individual recipe. Cakes with spirits added in this way keep extremely well. Other liquids which can be added to fruit cakes are milk, orange juice, cold strained tea or beer.

Fruit

Fruit adds colour, flavour, texture and sweetness to rich cakes. It also contributes to their keeping qualities. Only dried and crystallized or glacé fruits are used to make rich fruit cakes. Canned or fresh fruit is too soft and contains too much liquid to make a satisfactory cake.

As a guide, you can add between 225 g and 1.4 kg [8 oz-3 lb] fruit to every 450 g [1 lb] flour. The richer the cake, the higher the proportion of fruit.

You can use just one kind of fruit or several different kinds. Currants, raisins, sultanas, candied peel and glacé cherries, the traditional cake fruit, are all good choices. Prunes and dates are excellent in dark cakes. Less usual, but well worth trying in light fruit cakes are dried pears, apricots and peaches.

Always use good quality fruit. It should look plump and juicy. Most cake fruit is ready washed these days so there is no need to go to all the trouble of washing and drying. Avoiding washing is a good thing because wet fruit tends to sink. All dried fruit should be tossed in a little of the flour used for making the cake to prevent it sinking during baking.

Most dried fruit is sold stoned but you may still find some large raisins sold unstoned. Remove the stones by rolling each fruit between your fingers until the stone pops out.

Glacé fruit must, of course, be washed and well dried before being included in rich cakes. The sugar which coats glacé fruit can make the fruit sink to the bottom and spoil the cake. Glacé cherries, pineapple, apricots and greengages are all good, particularly in light fruit cakes. Candied peel can be bought ready-shredded in packets, but for superior flavour it is best if you can buy peel in what old fashioned grocers call 'caps'. These are large pieces of peel (often half the fruit from which the peel was taken) which are filled with sugar in the centre. Before using, scoop out the sugar, then mince or shred the peel to roughly the same size as the ready-cut kind.

Angelica can be used in light fruit cakes. It should be soaked in warm water to remove the sugar, patted dry, then chopped into small pieces. Crystallized ginger, although not a fruit, can be included in the fruit content for rich cakes. Treat in the same way as angelica.

Use dried fruit and lemon and orange zest to add colour, flavour and texture to rich cakes as well as helping them to keep well.

Nuts

Chopped nuts are often used in fruit cakes or can be used whole on top of traditional cakes such as Dundee cake.

Almonds, hazelnuts and walnuts are the usual choice. The nuts should always be of the skinned variety as the skin can taste rather bitter in a cake. Like fruit, nuts should be tossed in flour.

Spices

Spices are an essential ingredient in dark rich cakes, both to give flavour and to aid in preserving the cake. The spices should always be ground. Nutmeg, cinnamon, ginger, mixed spice and allspice are best for cakes. Always follow recipe instructions carefully when adding spice as too much can overpower the cake.

Fruit zest

Grated orange or lemon zest are favourites to include in light and some dark fruit cakes.

MAKING THE CAKE

Making a rich fruit cake demands a fair degree of organisation from the cook. It goes without saying that with so many ingredients, everything should be measured out first and be ready to use before you start mixing the cake. Follow the plan given here and all will go smoothly.

Preparing the tin

Fruit cakes are baked in deep round, square or 'novelty' tins. These must be fully lined and greased, as shown on page 35. It is advisable to put a double layer of greaseproof paper on the bottom of the cake with grease between the layers.

Large rich fruit cakes which need long slow baking must have extra protection to prevent the edges burning before the middle is cooked. This can be given by tying a double thickness of strong brown paper around the outside of the tin. The tin is then baked sitting on several layers of brown paper or newspaper so that the bottom is protected.

Heating the oven

As with all cakes, the oven must be heated well in advance so it is at exactly the right temperature when you put the cake in. Usually the larger and richer the cake, the lower the oven heat needs to be. This means that some wedding cakes may need several hours baking. Always follow the temperatures given in recipes.

Preparing the fruit and nuts

Next prepare the dried fruit and chop the nuts. Ordinary cake fruit will need no preparation, but glacé cherries must be washed, dried and halved. Other glacé fruit should be treated in a similar way. Full details are given in the section on fruit (see left). Toss fruit and nuts in a little of the flour used for the cake. When you have measured out all your ingredients, you can start on the cake.

Creaming

The making of a rich fruit cake starts with creaming the fat and sugar together, as described on page 74.

Adding eggs and flour

It is when the eggs and flour are added that the making of rich fruit cakes differs from the making of creamed cakes. The eggs are beaten with any other liquid (such as spirits) and added alternately with the sieved flour, spices and any raising agent used. As there are usually quite a lot of eggs in a rich fruit cake, this reduces the risk of curdling.

Adding the fruit

The dried fruit is beaten into the mixture after all the eggs, liquid and flour have been incorporated. Mix to distribute it throughout the mixture.

Filling the tin

The mixture should be of a soft dropping consistency when turned into the tin. Level the top in the usual way. Hollow the centre slightly to prevent peaking. If the cake contains a high proportion of fruit and is to be iced, make the hollow deeper than usual to ensure a good level surface. If you are making a cake requiring prolonged baking, it is a good idea to wet your fingers and smooth the top. The film of moisture prevents the cake drying out during cooking.

Dundee cake is one of the most popular of all the rich fruit cakes.

BAKING

Bake the cake as directed in the recipe. When the top begins to colour, protect the surface with a piece of kitchen foil or greaseproof paper. Foil is easier to manage because it can be moulded to the edge of the tin. The foil can be removed just before the end of cooking to complete browning the top of the cake.

Always test that the cake really is cooked at the end of the cooking time recommended. Ovens can vary in temperature according to the variances of the power supply, so it isn't always safe to think that the time for baking a cake in a recipe is guaranteed. There are a couple of simple tests that you can do to check that cakes of this type are cooked.

Testing

To test the cake, gently insert a skewer into the centre. If the skewer comes out clean, the cake is cooked. A second test is to remove the cake from the oven and hold it to your ear. If the cake is still making a 'singing' noise, then it is not completely cooked.

Cooling

When the cake is cooked, remove from the oven and leave to cool in the tin. This helps to keep the crust soft and avoids the danger of the cake cracking or breaking when turned out. When the cake is cool enough to handle easily (after about 30 minutes), turn out on to a wire rack and leave until it is completely cold before wrapping the cake in foil and storing it.

STORING

Light fruit cakes can be eaten the day after they are made, but very rich cakes such as a wedding cake, need time to allow the flavour to mature. These are best kept for 2-3 months. To store these cakes, leave the lining paper attached and allow the cake to become completely cold. Wrap the cake in kitchen foil and store in an airtight tin or snap-top container.

A good way to enrich the cake during this time is to add alcohol. To do this, prick the surface of the cake with a cocktail stick or very fine skewer and, using a pastry brush, brush the top of the cake with a little brandy, rum of sherry every week until the cake is needed for icing.

Toppings

Fruit cakes which are not required for icing can have fruit or nut toppings added before baking. These are applied to the cake after you have put it in the tin, levelled the surface and made the anti-peak hollow in the middle.

For traditional Dundee cake, arrange blanched almonds in concentric circles on top of the cake.

For crunchy-topped cake, scatter the surface of the cake with flaked almonds.

For a caramel topping, roughly crush sugar cubes and scatter over the top of the cake.

For fruit and nut topping, sprinkle the cake with chopped glacé fruit and roughly chopped Brazil nuts.

Dundee cake is one of the most famous of all rich cakes and provides a good example of how these cakes are made. This mixture is rich enough to use for a wedding cake or christening cake.

MAKES 8-10 SLICES

50 g [2 oz] candied peel
50 g [2 oz] glacé cherries
100g [4 oz] blanched almonds
100 g [4 oz] currants
100 g [4 oz] raisins
100 g [4 oz] sultanas
275 g [10 oz] plain flour
275 g [10 oz] butter or margarine
275 g [10 oz] soft brown sugar
1 teaspoon of mixed spice
grated zest of 1 lemon
4 large eggs

4 Chop half of the almonds. Split the other half lengthwise and set aside. Toss fruit and nuts in a little flour.

8 Transfer the mixture to the prepared tin. Level the top. Make a hollow in the centre to prevent peaking during cooking.

MAKING A DUNDEE CAKE

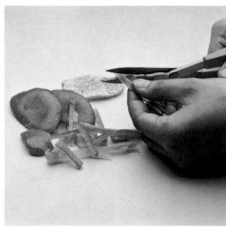

1 Line a 20 cm [8 in] round or 18 cm [7 in] square cake tin with greaseproof paper. Tie brown paper round the tin.

2 Heat the oven to 170°C [325°F] Gas 3. Scrape sugar from candied peel caps and chop the peel roughly.

3 Wash syrup from glacé cherries using warm water. Dry well. Halve the cherries using a sharp knife. Set aside.

5 Put fat and sugar into a large bowl and cream with a wooden spoon or an electric whisk until light and fluffy.

6 Sift the flour and spice. Add lemon zest. Beat eggs. Add a little of the egg to the creamed mixture.

7 Continue adding egg and flour alternately until it has been used. Beat in all the fruit and chopped nuts.

9 Arrange the halved nuts in concentric circles. Put a thick piece of newspaper on a baking tray and put the cake tin on it.

10 Bake for 2½-3 hours. When the cake is coloured, cover with foil. At the end of cooking time test with a fine warmed skewer.

11 Cool the cake in the tin until it can be handled, then turn on to wire cooling rack. Leave to cool completely before storing.

QUANTITIES OF INGREDIENTS AND CORRESPONDING SIZED TINS FOR RICH FRUIT CAKES
(Suitable for a cake to be covered in almond paste and royal icing)

Size of tin	15 cm [6 in] round	15 cm [6 in] square 18 cm [7 in] round	18 cm [7 in] square 20 cm [8 in] round	20 cm [8 in] square 23 cm [9 in] round
Currants	225 g [8 oz]	350 g [12 oz]	450 g [1 lb]	625 g [1 lb 6 oz]
Sultanas	90 g [3½ oz]	140 g [4½ oz]	200 g [7 oz]	225g [8 oz]
Raisins	90 g [3½ oz]	140 g [4½ oz]	200 g [7 oz]	225 g [8 oz]
Glacé cherries	50 g [2 oz]	75 g [3 oz]	150 g [5 oz]	175 g [6 oz]
Chopped candied mixed peel	25 g [1 oz]	50 g [2 oz]	75 g [3 oz]	100 g [4 oz]
Chopped blanched almonds	25g [1 oz]	50 g [2 oz]	75 g [3 oz]	100 g [4 oz]
Plain flour	175 g [6 oz]	215 g [7½ oz]	350 g [12 oz]	400 g [14 oz]
Salt	pinch	pinch	pinch	pinch
Mixed spice	¼ teaspoon	½ teaspoon	½ teaspoon	1 teaspoon
Cinnamon	¼ teaspoon	½ teaspoon	½ teaspoon	1 teaspoon
Fat (butter or margarine)	150 g [5 oz]	175 g [6 oz]	275 g [10 oz]	350 g [12 oz]
Soft brown sugar	150 g [5 oz]	175 g [6 oz]	275 g [10 oz]	350 g [12 oz]
Eggs	2½ large	3 large	5 large	6 large
Brandy or rum	1 tablespoon	1 tablespoon	1-2 tablespoons	2 tablespoons
Oven temperature*	150°C [300°F] Gas 2	150°C [300°F] Gas 2	150°C [300°F] Gas 2	150°C [300°F] Gas 2
Approximate cooking time	2½-3 hours	3 hours	3½ hours	4 hours
Weight of cooked cake	1.15 kg [2½ lb]	1.45 kg [3¼ lb]	2.2 kg [4¾ lb]	2.7 kg [6 lb]

Grated lemon or orange zest is often included, see recipes, or use according to taste.

*For cakes 25 cm [10 in] and over, reduce oven temperature to 130°C [250°F] Gas ½ after two-thirds of cooking time.

23 cm [9 in] square* 25 cm [10 in] round*	25 cm [10 in] square* 28 cm [11 in] round*	28 cm [11 in] square* 30 cm [12 in] round*	30 cm [12 in] square*
800 g [1¾ lb]	1.15 g [2½ lb]	1.5 kg [3 lb 2 oz]	1.7 kg [3¾ lb]
375 g [13 oz]	400 g [14 oz]	525 g [1 lb 3 oz]	625 g [1 lb 6 oz]
375 g [13 oz]	400 g [14 oz]	525 g [1 lb 3 oz]	625 g [1 lb 6 oz]
250g [9 oz]	275 g [10 oz]	350 g [12 oz]	425 g [15 oz]
150 g [5 oz]	200 g [7 oz]	250 g [9 oz]	275 g [10 oz]
150 g [5 oz]	200 g [7 oz]	250 g [9 oz]	275 g [10 oz]
600 g [1 lb 5 oz]	700 g [1½ lb]	825 g [1 lb 13 oz]	1 kg [2 lb 3 oz]
pinch	pinch	pinch	pinch
1 teaspoon	2 teaspoons	2½ teaspoons	2½ teaspoons
1 teaspoon	2 teaspoons	2½ teaspoons	2½ teaspoons
500 g [1 lb 2 oz]	600 g [1 lb 5 oz]	800 g [1¾ lb]	950 g [2 lb 2 oz]
500 g [1 lb 2 oz]	600 g [1 lb 5 oz]	800 g [1¾ lb]	950 g [2 lb 2 oz]
9 large	11 large	14 large	17 large
2-3 tablespoons	3 tablespoons	4 tablespoons	6 tablespoons
150°C [300°F] Gas 2	150°C [300°F] Gas 2	150°C [300°F] Gas 2	150°C [300°F] Gas 2
6 hours	7 hours	8 hours	8½ hours
4 kg [9 lb]	5.2 kg [11½ lb]	6.7 kg [14¾ lb]	7.7 kg [17 lb]

Rich fruit cake needs to be stored for at least a month to allow the flavours to mature before it is used.

RICH FRUIT CAKE

MAKES 12-16 SLICES

225 g [8 oz] sultanas
225 g [8 oz] seedless raisins
225 g [8 oz] currants
150 g [5 oz] glacé cherries, washed, dried and quartered
150 g [5 oz] cut mixed peel
200 ml [7 fl oz] brandy or rum
300 g [11 oz] plain flour
1 teaspoon ground cinnamon
1 teaspoon freshly grated nutmeg
150 g [5 oz] blanched almonds, chopped
4 large eggs
1 tablespoon golden syrup
grated zest of 1 lemon
225 g [8 oz] slightly salted butter, softened
225 g [8 oz] dark soft brown sugar
½ teaspoon bicarbonate of soda
1 tablespoon milk

1 Put the dried fruits, cherries and peel into a bowl. Pour over the brandy, mix well, cover and leave to soak for 1 hour.
2 Heat the oven to 150°C [300°F] Gas 2. Line a deep, 20 cm [8 in] round cake tin with greaseproof paper. Tie a double thickness of brown paper round the tin.
3 Sift the flour with the spices. Drain the fruit mixture, reserving all the brandy. Sprinkle 3-4 tablespoons of the sifted flour over the fruit mixture and stir lightly, then stir in the chopped

almonds. Set aside until required.
4 Using a fork, lightly beat the eggs with the syrup and lemon zest.
5 In a large bowl, cream the butter and sugar together with a hand-held electric whisk or wooden spoon until pale and fluffy. Beat in the egg mixture, a little at a time.
6 Using a large metal spoon, stir in one-quarter of the remaining sifted flour, then one-quarter of the fruit and nut mixture, followed by one-quarter of the reserved brandy. Continue in this way until all the flour, fruit and brandy are incorporated. Dissolve the bicarbonate of soda in the milk and stir into the mixture.
7 Turn the mixture into the prepared tin and level the surface, then make a hollow in the centre.
8 Stand the tin on several layers of brown paper on a baking tray. Bake for 1½ hours, then lower the heat to 140°C [275°F] Gas 1 and bake for a further 3-3½ hours until the cake is cooked. When the cake is coloured, cover with kitchen foil. At the end of the cooking time test with a skewer.
9 Stand the tin on a wire rack and leave the cake to cool for about 30 minutes. Remove the cake from the tin and leave to cool on a wire rack, then peel off the lining papers. Wrap the cake in kitchen foil or cling film, put into an airtight container and store to allow the flavour to mellow.

CRYSTALLIZED FRUIT CAKE

MAKES 10 SLICES

100 g [4 oz] sultanas
100 g [4 oz] seedless raisins
100 g [4 oz] currants
100 g [4 oz] glacé cherries, washed, dried
    and quartered
225 g [8 oz] plain flour
½ teaspoon ground mixed spice
½ teaspoon ground cinnamon
175 g [6 oz] butter or margarine
175 g [6 oz] caster sugar
3 eggs
1 tablespoon milk

To decorate and glaze:
40 g [1½ oz] crystallized pineapple, cut
    into small chunks
40 g [1½ oz] glacé cherries, halved
25 g [1 oz] split almonds
3 tablespoons apricot jam
1 tablespoon water
½ teaspoon lemon juice

1 Heat the oven to 170°C [325°F] Gas 3. Line a deep 15 cm [6 in] square cake tin with greaseproof paper. Tie a double thickness of brown paper round the tin.

2 Toss the fruit in a little of the flour. Sift the remaining flour and spices into a bowl and set aside until required.

3 In a large bowl, cream butter and sugar together with a hand-held electric whisk or wooden spoon until pale and fluffy. Beat in the eggs one at a time until evenly incorporated.

4 Fold flour and fruit alternately into egg mixture. Fold in the milk. Turn the mixture into the prepared tin and level the surface. Make a hollow in the centre to prevent peaking during cooking. Arrange pineapple, glacé cherries and almonds over the top of the cake.

5 Stand the tin on several layers of brown paper on a baking tray. Bake for 1 hour, then lower the temperature to 150°C [300°F] Gas 2 and bake for a further 1½-2 hours.

6 Cool the cake in the tin for 30 minutes, then turn out of the tin on to a wire rack and peel off paper. Turn the right way up, then leave to cool completely.

7 To make the glaze, put jam and water in a pan and boil for 2 minutes. Stir in lemon juice, then sieve, return to pan and heat gently. Brush over fruit on top of cake. Leave the glaze to cool and set before serving. This cake freezes very successfully, but must be frozen unglazed. Wrap in a polythene bag, then seal, label and freeze for up to 6 months. To serve, defrost the cake at room temperature for 4-5 hours, then glaze.

Crystallized fruit cake has a chunky topping of crystallized pineapple, glacé cherries and split almonds.

SIMNEL CAKE

MAKES 12-16 SLICES

225 g [8 oz] glacé cherries
225 g [8 oz] chopped mixed peel
700 g [1½ lb] plain flour
large pinch of salt
2 teaspoons mixed spice
2 teaspoons cinnamon
700 g [1½ lb] butter
700 g [1½ lb] soft brown sugar
11 large eggs
3 tablespoons black treacle
finely grated zest and juice of 2 lemons
    and 2 oranges
1.1 kg [2½ lb] currants
450 g [1 lb] sultanas
450 g [1 lb] raisins
225 g [8 oz] almonds, blanched and
    chopped
3 tablespoons brandy or rum
800 g [1¾ lb] marzipan
2-3 tablespoons sieved apricot jam
beaten egg white
caster sugar

1 Heat the oven to 130°C [250°F] Gas ½. Grease a 25 cm [10 in] square or 28 cm [11 in] round tin. Line the base and sides with greaseproof paper; grease the paper. Wash and dry the cherries. Cut them into quarters. Wash and dry peel. Put them into a bowl. Stir in a little of the flour and stir until fruit and peel is coated. Sift remaining flour, salt and spices into another bowl and set aside until required.

2 Cream the butter and sugar together until the mixture is light and fluffy. In a bowl beat together the eggs, black treacle and fruit juices. Gradually beat the egg mixture into the creamed mixture. Add a little flour with the last additions of egg.

3 With a metal spoon, fold in the remaining flour, fruit zests, dried fruits and nuts, then add the brandy or rum. Fold in until mixture has a dropping consistency.

4 Reserve 100 g [4 oz] marzipan. Divide the remaining marzipan in half and roll one piece to a 25 cm [10 in] square or 28 cm [11 in] round.

5 Place half the prepared cake mixture in the lined and greased tin. Smooth the surface then put the rolled-out marzipan on top and cover with the remaining cake mixture. Smooth the surface and bake for 5 hours until the cake is cooked. When the cake is coloured, cover with kitchen foil. At the end of the cooking time test with a skewer.

6 Leave the cake to cool in the tin for 30 minutes. Turn out and leave to cool completely on a wire rack. When the cake is cold, roll out another marzipan 25 cm [10 in] square or 28 cm [11 in] round. Brush the top of the cake with warm, sieved apricot jam and place the rolled-out marzipan on top. With a sharp knife cut the edge into a series of v-shapes.

7 Make 11 small balls from the reserved marzipan. Place them around the edge of the cake pushing down slightly to anchor them. Brush the surface and the balls with well beaten egg white, sprinkle with caster sugar

Traditionally Simnel cake was made for Mothering Sunday (the 4th Sunday in Lent) when girls who were in service were allowed to visit their mothers! Nowadays, it is associated with Easter, and the marzipan balls represent the faithful Apostles.

and heat under a hot grill until golden brown, watching carefully to make sure it does not burn.

8 Leave to cool and spread a little glacé icing in the centre. Tie a ribbon around the cake and place fluffy chicks on top.

FRUIT AND NUT CAKE

MAKES 8 SLICES

100 g [4 oz] stoned dates, coarsely chopped
150 g [5 oz] glacé cherries, halved
4 tablespoons chopped mixed peel
4 tablespoons sultanas
4 tablespoons seedless raisins
100 g [4 oz] blanched whole almonds
100 g [4 oz] shelled walnut halves
100 g [4 oz] shelled whole Brazil nuts
75 g [3 oz] plain flour
pinch of salt
6 tablespoons caster sugar
2 large eggs, beaten
finely grated zest of 1 orange
3 tablespoons brandy
3 tablespoons dark rum
1 teaspoon vanilla essence

1 Heat the oven to 150°C [300°F] Gas 2. Grease a 1.7L [3 pt] loaf tin. Line it with greaseproof paper and grease the paper lightly.
2 In a large bowl, combine the coarsely chopped dates, halved glacé cherries, chopped mixed peel, sultanas, seedless raisins, whole almonds, walnut halves and half the Brazil nuts. Stir in a little of the flour and stir until fruit and nuts are coated.
3 Sift the remaining flour, salt and caster sugar over the fruit and nuts and mix very thoroughly.
4 Whisk together the eggs, finely grated orange zest, brandy, rum and vanilla essence until blended. Stir the whisked mixture into the fruit and nut mixture with a wooden spoon until well blended. The mixture should be stiff.
5 Spoon the mixture into the prepared tin, smooth the top with a palette knife and decorate with the remaining Brazil nuts. Bake for 2½ hours.
6 Remove the cake from the oven and leave to cool in the tin for 10 minutes. Turn it out on to a wire rack to cool completely, removing the paper.
7 When the cake is cold cut into slices to serve.

FRUITY PUDDING CAKE

MAKES 8 SLICES

175 g [6 oz] sultanas
175 g [6 oz] currants
75 g [3 oz] cut mixed peel
75 g [3 oz] glacé cherries, quartered, rinsed and dried
175 g [6 oz] plain flour
50 g [2 oz] ground almonds (optional)
175 g [6 oz] margarine or butter, softened
175 g [6 oz] soft brown sugar
grated zest of 1 orange
3 eggs, beaten
25 g [1 oz] blanched almonds

1 Heat the oven to 140°C [275°F] Gas 1. Grease and line a deep, 15 cm [6 in] round tin. Grease the paper.
2 Combine the sultanas, currants, mixed peel and cherries in a bowl. Sift in 2-3 tablespoons of the flour and stir until the fruit and peel are evenly coated. Sift the remaining flour into another bowl and stir in the ground almonds, if using.
3 In a third bowl, beat the margarine, sugar and orange zest together until pale and fluffy. Add the eggs, a little at a time, beating thoroughly after each addition. Fold in the flour, then fold in the fruit and peel.
4 Turn the mixture into the prepared tin and level the surface, then make a shallow hollow in the centre. Arrange the blanched almonds on the top. Bake for 2½ hours, until a skewer inserted in the centre comes out clean.
5 Cool the cake in the tin for 30 minutes, then turn it out on to a wire rack and remove the lining paper. Turn the cake the right way up and leave to cool completely. Store for 24 hours before cutting.

This delicious Fruit and nut cake is unlike other rich fruit cakes in that it contains no fat. It has a much higher proportion of fruit and nuts than the other cakes, and is made in a slightly different way. It is delicious served with coffee.

To store it, wrap in foil and keep in an airtight tin. In very hot weather it is best if the cake is kept in the refrigerator.

BLACK BUN

Black bun, also known as Scotch Bun, is a dark, highly-spiced fruit cake in a pastry crust. Traditionally served in Scotland with glasses of whisky as the clock chimes herald in the New Year, it is ideal for greeting a large number of 'first footers' in the early hours. The fruit mixture for a Black Bun differs from other rich fruit cakes in that it is made without butter and uses much less sugar. Although expensive to make, a little goes a long way, and it can be stored for up to a year.

The shape of a Black bun, and the exact ingredients, vary from region to region, but all the recipes feature the pastry crust. This keeps the cake moist and preserves the aroma of the spices and spirit until the cake is cut. The maturing process is vital to the taste, and Black bun should always be made well in advance.

PREPARING BLACK BUN FOR BAKING

1 Roll the pastry over the rolling pin and carefully lift it into the cake tin.

2 Lift edges of pastry circle and ease into shape of tin. Trim.

3 Spoon in fruit filling, pressing it down firmly with the back of a spoon, then fold the edges of the pastry over the filling.

4 Roll out remaining pastry into a circle 20 cm [8 in] in diameter, brush the edges with cold water. Press firmly into position.

MAKES 20-30 SLICES

For the pastry:
275 g [10 oz] plain flour
pinch of salt
150 g [5 oz] butter, diced
3-4 tablespoons cold water
beaten egg or egg yolk, to glaze

For the fruit filling:
225 g [8 oz] plain flour
pinch of salt
1 teaspoon bicarbonate of soda
1 teaspoon cream of tartar
1 teaspoon ground cinnamon
1 teaspoon ground ginger
1 teaspoon ground allspice
¼ teaspoon freshly ground black
   pepper
100 g [4 oz] dark soft brown sugar
100 g [4 oz] candied peel, chopped
350 g [12 oz] seedless raisins
850 g [1¾ lb] currants
100 g [4 oz] almonds, chopped or
   shredded
1 egg
6-8 tablespoons brandy or whisky
3 tablespoons treacle
2-3 tablespoons milk (optional)

1 Brush a 20 cm [8 in] round loose-based cake tin 7.5 cm [3 in] deep with vegetable oil.

2 To make the pastry, sift the flour and salt into a bowl, add the butter and rub it in with your fingertips until the mixture resembles very fine bread-crumbs. Add enough water to mix to a firm but soft dough. Wrap in cling film and refrigerate while you prepare the filling.

3 Heat the oven to 170°C [325°F] Gas 3.

4 For the filling, sift the flour, salt, raising agents and spices into a large bowl. Stir in the sugar, candied peel, raisins, currants and almonds. Mix together thoroughly.

5 In a bowl, beat the egg with the brandy, stir in the treacle, then add to the fruit mixture and stir well. If necessary, add 2-3 tablespoons of milk to bind the mixture together.

6 Roll out two-thirds of the pastry into a circle about 35 cm [14 in] in diameter, then roll the pastry over the rolling pin and carefully lift it into the cake tin.

7 Lift the edges of the pastry circle and ease it into the shape of the tin. Gently press it over the base and sides of the tin. Trim.

8 Spoon in the fruit filling, pressing it down firmly with the back of a spoon,

then fold the edges of the pastry over it.

9 Roll out remaining pastry into a circle 20 cm [8 in] in diameter, brush the edges with cold water. Press firmly into position, pressing round the top with your thumb to make indentations.

10 Brush the top with beaten egg and prick it all over with a fork, then use a skewer to make 5 or 6 holes right down to the bottom of the tin.

11 Bake for 3-3½ hours, placing a piece of foil over the top after 1 hour or when the pastry is golden brown. The filling is cooked when no sizzling or hissing sounds emerge.

12 Remove from the tin very carefully. Place on a wire rack to cool. When removing the cake from the tin, you must be careful not to break the pastry. Remember, too, that it will be very heavy, so for cooling use a sturdy rack which will not collapse.

13 When completely cold, wrap closely in foil and store in an airtight tin in a cool place for at least 1 week for the flavour to mature.

14 To serve, unwrap, place on a serving platter. Cut out a wedge, then slice this to make several small portions.

15 Repeat to make a total of 20-30 slices. Black bun, decorated with pastry trimmings, makes an impressive centrepiece for a party. Serve with whisky and other spirits, or with spicy mulled wine. Serve Black bun with Champagne or other wine as an alternative to iced rich fruit cake on a festive occasion such as a christening.

Black bun is a rich fruit cake encased in pastry. It still needs time to mature like other fruit cakes.

HANDY HINTS

Ingredients for Black bun

For the best colour and flavour, use dark, unrefined sugar such as muscovado or molasses.

Buy whole candied peel in preference to cut peel and chop it finely and, if possible, choose unblanched almonds and include the skins when chopping or shredding them.

SIMPLE CELEBRATION CAKES

The focal point of any wedding reception, christening or engagement party, or Christmas tea, is inevitably the cake. Packed with luscious fruit and beautifully decorated, a home-made celebration cake is a real tribute to your skills as a cook. In this chapter a rich fruit cake can be beautifully, yet simply, iced to grace any party table.

Traditional iced fruit cakes have always been an important part of any family celebration. Unfortunately, although most cooks can manage the baking of the cake without too much difficulty, they fall down when it comes to the icing. Icing traditional cakes is nothing to be afraid of, if you follow the advice given in this chapter and learn to walk with the simpler forms of decoration before you go off at a headlong gallop with elaborate piping and intricate designs.

Celebration cakes are always based on a rich fruit cake mixture. Full details on making a variety of suitable cakes is given on pages 180-193. To turn a fruit cake into something special, you must first coat it with almond paste and then cover it with white royal icing – a special stiff icing that sets very hard and gives a good, glossy finish.

BASIC EQUIPMENT

Although you can improvise, if you are making a very special cake, it is well worth having the right equipment for the job.

A turntable is essential for really smooth flat icing as it enables you to move the cake around evenly as you work.

A cake board is traditional and necessary for royal iced cakes as they are awkward to transfer to a serving plate after icing. Cake boards can be bought or you can cover a board with silver paper or foil.

A palette knife is essential to spread the icing evenly.

Plain edged scraper: a piece of card or plastic will do for this. The scraper is simply a straight edge which can be used to smooth the sides of the cake.

An icing ruler helps to keep the top of the cake smooth and if you buy a good one, can be useful if many other ways. Good icing rulers have letter and shape stencils for run out designs and are marked in centimetres or inches so you can plan the spacing of your design.

ALMOND PASTE

The first thing to do towards decorating your celebration cake is to prepare the almond paste.

Ingredients
The quantity of ingredients depends on the size you want your cake to be. Quantities of almond paste for completely covering cakes of various sizes are given in the chart. The weight of paste made is twice the weight of ground almonds used.

Almonds
The most obvious ingredient of almond paste is, of course, ground almonds. It is the flavour of these almonds which makes the paste contrast so pleasantly

with the sweet icing. When making almond paste, the quantity of almonds is the same as the quantity of sugar. The quantity of almonds is also always half the amount of the weight of paste you are making. Therefore if a recipe calls for 450 g [1 lb] of almond paste, it would be made with 225 g [8 oz] ground almonds.

Sugar

For really smooth paste, always use equal quantities of caster and icing sugar.

Flavourings

To give the paste a good flavour, a little lemon juice and almond essence are always added to the paste. For 450 g [1 lb] paste, add 1 teaspoon lemon juice and a few drops of almond essence.

Eggs

To bind the almonds and sugar together and make a smooth, workable paste, beaten egg is used. Generally speaking, you will need one medium-sized egg for each 225 g [8 oz] ground almonds and 225 g [8 oz] mixed caster sugar and icing sugar, but add it gradually – you may not need the whole egg.

MAKING THE PASTE

Making almond paste is a fairly simple business. It should not be made too far in advance of the time that it is to be used, otherwise the surface may dry

Once you have learned how to flat ice a cake, it is a simple step to producing professional results like these.

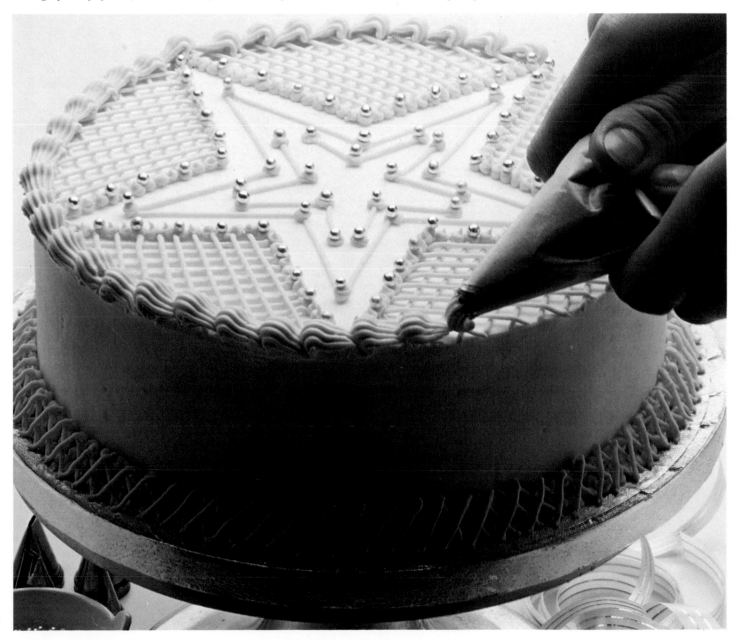

out and crack. Follow these principles for a smooth paste which is easy to use.

Sifting almonds and sugar

Sift the ground almonds and sugar together to ensure that they are evenly mixed and that no coarse particles get into the mixture, as these would spoil the smooth appearance of the paste. Make a hollow in the centre.

Adding the liquid

Beat the egg and all the liquid together. This will ensure that the flavourings are evenly distributed throughout the mixture. Add the liquid to the almonds and mix well.

Kneading

To make the almond paste smooth and free from cracks, it must be kneaded. To do this, turn the paste on to a board which you have scattered with a little sifted icing sugar. This will prevent the paste sticking to the board and as the icing sugar is smooth it will not add coarse granules. Knead the paste by hand for about 3 minutes until is it smooth and free from cracks.

USING THE PASTE

Before you can apply almond paste to a cake, you must prepare the cake and make an apricot glaze to stick the paste on to the cake.

Preparing the cake

Needless to say, you must have a level surface to which you apply the almond paste. If the top of the cake has peaked slightly, cut it level and then turn the cake over so that the flat bottom becomes the top to which you apply the almond paste. Applying almond paste to a cut, crumby surface can be rather difficult. By turning the cake over, you play safe.

Preparing the glaze

Almond paste will not stick to your cake by magic. To make it stick, a glaze made from melted apricot jam is used. You do not need very much glaze – about 3 tablespoons is usually sufficient. If more is needed, you can always sieve in a little more jam and re-heat. If less is needed, the unused glaze can be left to set and poured back into the jam jar.

To make the glaze, sieve the jam into a small, heavy-based pan. Add a squeeze of lemon juice and melt over low heat. Other jams can be used but apricot is the traditional choice.

Measuring the paste

Applying almond paste to a cake defeats many cooks because they do not measure the paste properly. It is most important that you measure the paste to fit the cake, following the simple method shown in the step-by-step instructions.

If the cake is to be iced, the almond paste must be allowed to dry out, otherwise the almond oil will discolour

BASIC ALMOND PASTE

MAKES 450 G [1 LB]
100 g [4 oz] icing sugar
100 g [4 oz] caster sugar
225 g [8 oz] ground almonds
1 teaspoon lemon juice
few drops of almond essence
1 medium-sized egg, beaten

1 Sift the sugars and the ground almonds into a bowl. Make a hollow in the centre.

2 Add the lemon juice, almond essence and some of the egg. Mix well. If there is not enough liquid, add more egg.

3 Mix to a smooth paste. Turn out on to a board sprinkled lightly with icing sugar. Knead for 3 minutes until smooth and free from cracks.

the icing. Keep the cake uncovered in a cool, airy place for about a week before icing.

Decorations

If you do not want to royal ice a cake, quite effective decorations can be made using coloured almond paste. The paste is coloured using edible food colourings.

Before you colour the paste, draw out the design you want to use for the cake on a piece of paper. Mark in the colours you will be using.

To colour the paste, divide the paste into appropriate amounts and colour, by adding a little food colouring and working in with your fingers.

ROYAL ICING

For traditional celebration cakes, royal icing is always used to cover the almond paste and to decorate the cake. Royal icing sets very hard so it will hold quite a complicated decoration.

Ingredients for icing

Royal icing is simply made from icing sugar and egg whites. A little lemon juice is added for flavour and glycerine is included to give the icing a sheen. The proportions for royal icing are 225 g [8 oz] icing sugar to every egg white and 1 tablespoon lemon juice plus 2 teaspoons glycerine to every four egg whites. In this way, you will be able to make an icing which is stiff, glossy and easy to work with. The chart on page 199 shows how much icing is needed for cakes of various sizes. The weight of icing given in the chart is based on the weight of icing sugar used in the recipe.

Making the icing

Making the icing is quite simple, but it does involve a lot of beating. If wished, an electric whisk can be used for this.

Sift the icing sugar then whisk the egg whites until they are just frothy – not until they are approaching the consistency of meringue. This makes the whites easy to mix with the icing sugar. To make good royal icing, the icing sugar must be beaten into the egg whites a little at a time. Ideally, you should beat in only 1 tablespoon at a time until half the icing sugar has been used. At this point, you can add the lemon juice. The remaining icing sugar is incorporated in same way then the glycerine may be added.

MAKING ALMOND PASTE DECORATIONS

1 To colour almond paste, work edible food colouring into it. Deep colours look best.

2 For holly leaves, draw a leaf on to card. Use as a template to cut shapes. Mark veins with a knife.

OR cut out small rounds, using a plain cutter. Cut away the edges with a smaller cutter.

3 For holly berries, roll small balls of almond paste coloured red with food colouring.

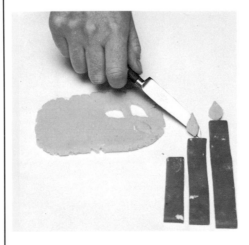

4 For candles, colour paste red. Cut one large candle shape or smaller ones. Use yellow almond paste for flames.

5 For bells, draw bell shapes on to card. Assemble small bells in bunches. Large bells can be used alone.

USING ALMOND PASTE

1 Using string, measure edge. With another piece, measure depth.

2 Cut the top of the cake level if necessary. Turn it over.

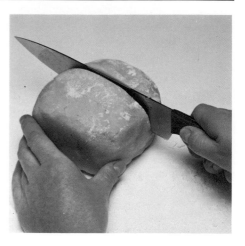

3 Cut off two-thirds of the paste.

4 Roll to half length of string and twice depth of cake. Halve lengthways.

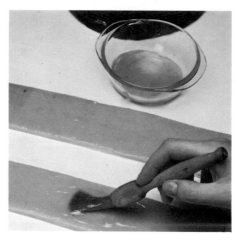

5 Brush each strip with sieved, melted apricot jam.

6 Roll the cake on the strips so that sides are covered. Neaten joints.

7 Roll out remaining third of the paste to fit the top of the cake. Brush cake top with melted jam.

8 Brush a rolling pin with icing sugar. Roll gently over the paste on top of the cake.

9 Run a straight-sided jar around the edges. It will help the paste to adhere. Store for a week before icing.

QUANTITIES OF ALMOND PASTE AND ROYAL ICING

Tin size:

round	15 cm [6 in]	18 cm [7 in]	20 cm [8 in]	23 cm [9 in]	25 cm [10 in]	28 cm [11 in]	30 cm [12 in]	—
square	–	15 cm [6 in]	18 cm [7 in]	20 cm [8 in]	23 cm [9 in]	25 cm [10 in]	28 cm [11 in]	30 cm [12 in]
Almond paste	350 g [12 oz]	450 g [1 lb]	550 g [1¼ lb]	800 g [1¾ lb]	900 g [2 lb]	1 kg [2¼ lb]	1.1 kg [2½ lb]	1.4 kg [3 lb]
Royal icing	450 g [1 lb]	550 g [1¼ lb]	700 g [1½ lb]	900 g [2 lb]	1 kg [2¼ lb]	1.1 kg [2½ lb]	1.4 kg [3 lb]	1.6 kg [3½ lb]

Storing

Royal icing must be kept for 24 hours before it can be used. This allows it to stiffen to the correct texture for icing the cake. Store the icing in a covered container.

USING ROYAL ICING

Royal icing can be used for intricate piping but it is best to wait until you are used to working with it before you attempt this. In this chapter, you will see how to rough ice a cake, how to flat ice it and how to do simple piping.

Preparing to ice

Before you ice any cake, it is important to anchor it to your cake board. To do this, put a blob of icing on the centre of the board and place the cake on it.

For flat icing, it is rather more important to have a turntable as it is difficult to achieve a good, smooth finish without one. You must start icing the cake at least 2 weeks before it is required as the icing must be allowed to set firmly between coats and must be rock hard on the day you start piping. The piping itself should set too, so the further in advance you start, the better.

Rough icing

The easiest point at which to begin working with royal icing is to rough ice a cake. This method involves covering the cake in icing, then roughing it up so that it stands in peaks. This idea is good for Christmas cakes as it gives a frosty effect.

Spreading the icing

Put all the icing on top of the cake. Do not worry that this looks like an awful lot, it spreads over quite thinly. Using a palette knife or an icing ruler, spread the icing over the cake, working backwards and forwards. This will burst any air bubbles in the icing which could spoil the appearance of the cake. When the bubbles have broken, spread the icing to the edges of the top of the cake and then spread it around the sides. It does not matter if the icing is not perfectly smooth as you will be roughing up the surface.

Roughing

When you have spread the icing and the top and sides of the cake are all covered, use the blade of a round-bladed knife to rough up the icing in peaks. Leave to set for at least a week before cutting the cake.

Flat icing

Flat icing provides a smooth foundation for intricately piped designs. It is quite difficult to do but must be mastered if you are determined to become a good cake icer.

Starting to ice

During the process of flat icing a cake, keep the bowl of icing covered. This is important if it is your first attempt at flat icing as the icing can harden while you are painstakingly trying to get the surface flat.

It is wiser to apply the top and sides of the cake on separate days as there is less danger of spoiling one while you are trying to get the other flat.

Starting with the top is easiest. Put your cake board on the icing turntable, then put about half of the total quantity of icing on top of the cake. Using a palette knife or icing ruler, spread icing over the surface, working backwards and forwards. This will get

MAKING ROYAL ICING

MAKES 900 G [2 LB] ROYAL ICING
900 g [2 lb] icing sugar
4 large egg whites
1 tablespoon lemon juice
2 teaspoons glycerine

1 Sift the icing sugar twice to ensure the icing is free from lumps.

2 Place the egg whites in a large bowl. Whisk until frothy but not until stiff.

3 Beat the icing sugar into the egg whites gradually, about 1 tablespoon at a time.

4 When half the sugar has been added, beat in the lemon juice. Add remaining sugar as before.

5 Beat in the glycerine. Cover with a damp cloth and leave the icing to stand for 24 hours.

ROUGH ICING A CAKE

1 Put a blob of icing in the centre of your cake board and place the cake on top of this.

2 Put all icing on cake. Work back and forth to remove bubbles, then spread over the top and sides.

3 Using the blade of a knife or the handle of a teaspoon, rough up the icing in peaks.

FLAT ICING A CAKE

1 Put a blob of icing on a cake board. Place the cake on this and then put board on a turntable.

2 Put half the icing on top of the cake. Keep the rest covered. Work icing over the cake.

3 Using an icing ruler and working towards you, pull smoothly across the top of the cake.

4 Remove any excess icing from the sides of the cake. Add a little more to top and smooth again.

5 Leave the top of the cake to set for at least 24 hours before starting on the sides.

6 To ice the sides, spread icing around the cake. Hold a flat scraper or palette knife against the cake.

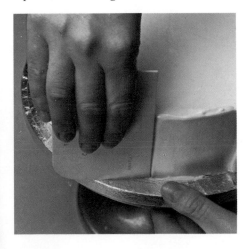

7 Revolve the turntable so the scraper smooths the icing. Lift off just before end.

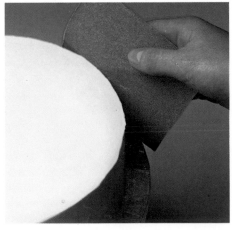

8 Leave the sides to set for 24 hours. Smooth rough edges with emery board or sandpaper.

9 If wished, cover the cake again in the same way using thinned down royal icing.

rid of any air bubbles trapped in the icing. Scrape away any surplus icing that has run down the sides.

Now with the icing ruler at an angle of 30 degrees draw it steadily towards you so that it scrapes across the icing and leaves a smooth, ridge-free surface. Repeat this operation if the cake is not perfectly smooth first time, turning the cake through 90 degrees and adding a little more icing if necessary.

You will find that some surplus icing has run down the sides of the cake. You must remove this before the top of the cake sets or it will harden on the sides and be impossible to remove later. To remove this icing, simply scrape gently away with the blade of a palette knife, taking care not to break into the side of the cake and get crumbs in it. Return the surplus icing to the bowl. Leave the top of the cake overnight to dry before flat icing the sides of the cake.

Coating the sides

Coating the sides of the cake with flat icing is quite a tricky operation but is made much simpler if you have a turntable. First cover the sides of the cake with icing as described for the top, working it back and forth. When the air bubbles·have gone hold a plain-edged scraper or a palette knife in one hand to the edge of the cake. With the other hand, revolve the turntable just a little more than a complete revolution. Lift the scraper away so that the minimum mark is left behind. Surplus icing can be gently removed with a palette knife.

Second coat

To give your cake a really smooth professional finish, follow the pâtissiers and give a second coat of thin icing. This should be applied about 48 hours after the first coating.

First of all, remove any rough icing at the top edge of the cake by sanding down with an emery board. This will

Equipment for royal icing
To pipe with royal icing, you will need an icing bag (bought or home-made see page 94) and a selection of nozzles. Nozzles for royal icing are small and nearly always made of metal to give a clean edge.

Initially, the list of nozzles suggested here is quite adequate. The illustration shows you what kind of nozzles are available and the designs they will produce.

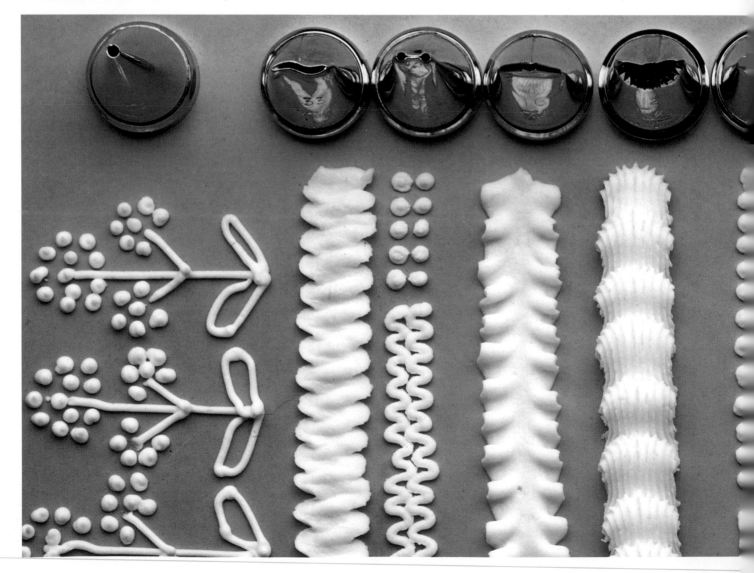

give a really smooth edge. Make up royal icing in the usual way but add an extra egg white to the quantity for the cake you are making so that you have a thin icing. Apply to the top and sides of the cake as before. Wipe any surplus icing away from the edges of the cake board and leave the cake to set for 48 hours.

PIPING

Piping with royal icing may seem rather daunting but with practice, you will find that it is quite easy.

How to pipe

See page 95 for how to fill and hold the piping bag.

Lines can be used straight – to decorate one half of a cake while the other half is left plain, or can be used to make a trellis. They can also be made wavy or squiggly if wished. Lines are usually used on top of the cake, not on the sides. See page 96 for details of piping lines.

For wavy lines, move the nozzle to and fro.

For squiggles, to fill up an area of cake with a different colour, for instance, wave the nozzle about so that you get 'worm tracks'.

Writing names needs practice and it is best to try them out on a piece of greaseproof paper first. Before you start to pipe a name, work it out on a piece of greaseproof paper the same size as the top of the cake so that you know it will fit. Prick the design through on to the cake as described for planning a design. Using a plain or writing nozzle, carefully follow the pin pricks.

Stars

Stars can be used to make a border around the top of the cake and where it joins the cake board. They can also be used to pipe patterns such as stars

Plain or writing nozzles are useful for piping lines, plain dots and for writing names. They come in various sizes – it is best to have a couple of these nozzles, one to produce thin lines and writing, one for thicker lines.

Star nozzles will make rosettes, zig-zags and ropes.

Shell nozzles produce shell borders for the top and bottom edges of your cake. You only need one of these initially.

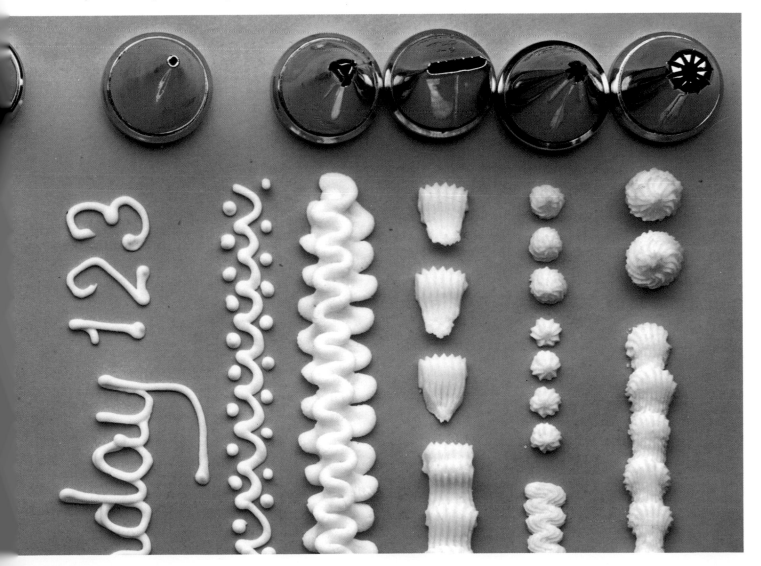

SIMPLE PIPING

1 Prepare cake with almond paste. Cover with royal icing and leave to set until hard before piping.

2 Plan your design on greaseproof paper. Put the paper on the cake. Prick design through with a pin.

6 For squiggles, mark off the area of cake you want to fill. Use a plain pipe as above, but move around with a squiggling motion.

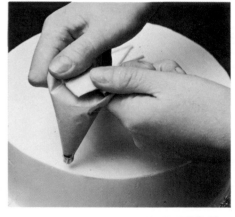

7 For stars, use a star nozzle. Hold the nozzle almost upright to the cake. Pipe out a little icing. Push nozzle down, then pull up.

Planning the design

Before you start icing a cake, it is wise to plan a design. Draw the design out on a piece of greaseproof paper the same size as the top of the cake. Lay it over the cake and, using a pin, prick through the paper into the icing so that you can see exactly where the design will fall on the cake.

If you are having a design in more than one colour, you will need more than one bag for the icing. Divide the icing up before you start and colour it using edible food colourings. Generally speaking, pastel colours look best.

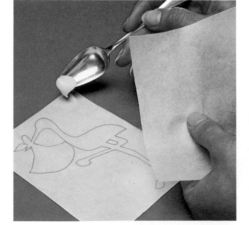

11 For run out designs, first draw simple design on card. Cover with non stick paper. Secure with dots of icing.

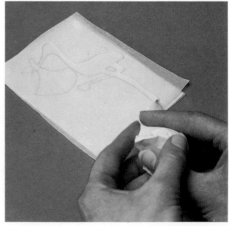

12 Pipe the outline of the design using a writing nozzle. Thin the icing with egg white so it will flow.

3 To pipe lines, use a writing or plain nozzle. Squeeze out just enough icing to stick to the cake. Raise the nozzle.

4 Direct the sagging line of icing in the direction you want it to go. Keep the pressure even.

5 For writing, prick out the name using a pin. Follow the letters as directed for piping a line.

8 For a star border, pipe a series of stars in this way. The tops can be decorated with silver cake balls if wished.

9 For shells, use a shell nozzle. Hold at an angle of 45 degrees to the cake. With the nozzle almost on the cake, pipe out a head of icing.

10 Gradually release the pressure. Pull away the nozzle so that the icing curves in a shell shape. Use for borders.

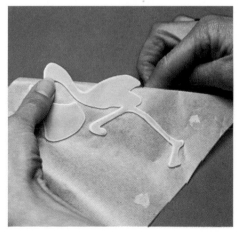

13 Put the icing into a greaseproof paper forcing bag. Cut off the tip. Flood outline of design with icing.

14 Leave the design to dry for several days. Gently lift off the card. Very carefully, peel away the paper.

15 Stick the run out to the cake using thin royal icing. Thick icing raises it from the cake too much.

on the top of the cake. See page 99 for details of piping stars.

Shells

Shells are good for borders around the top of the cake and where it meets the cake board at the bottom. See page 99 for details of piping shells.

Run out design

Run out designs are piped on to card and then transferred on to the cake when dry. They are a good idea for Christmas cakes as you can make bells, candles and holly leaves.

To pipe a run out, first draw a simple shape on card. Cut a piece of non-stick paper to cover the card and glue in place with a spot of icing at each corner. Using a writing nozzle, trace the outline of the design. Thin the icing down with beaten egg white so that it will flow rather than being stiff as royal icing usually is. Pour the icing into a small paper forcing bag without a nozzle (see page 95). Cut the tip off the bag and floor the icing into the outline. It will run smoothly into place.

Leave the shape to set for at least 3 days, then carefully remove the silicone paper from the card. Peel the paper off the back of the shape and stick it to the top of the cake with icing.

Run out designs can be piped straight on to the cake but this is something which requires great skill as mistakes cannot be rectified very easily once they are on the cake.

ICING IDEAS

Given here are some simple ideas for celebration cakes.
● For a simple christening cake, flat ice the cake. Pipe a shell border around the bottom where it joins the board. Using pale colours, pipe straight lines across half of the cake. Using the same colour, pipe the name of the baby on the other half. Using a small writing nozzle, pipe some dots in the shape of rosettes and then pipe large dots all round the edge of the cake to neaten the top and the ends of the straight lines. Add a bought christening cake decoration if there is room and tie a lace ribbon around the cake.
● For a poinsettia cake for Christmas, cover cake with almond paste. Colour equal quantities of almond paste red and green. Using a seed catalogue or

an actual plant as a guide, draw a poinsettia flower and a few leaves and use as a template. Mark the leaves with veins using a sharp knife. Stick on the cake.
● For a merry Christmas cake, cover with almond paste. Make a template for the words 'Merry Christmas', cut out in coloured almond paste and stick on the cake.
● For Christmas star cake, flat ice your cake. Pipe a star border in a different colour around the top and bottom edges. Top the stars with silver cake balls on the bottom edge. Make a template of a star. The points should reach the edge of the cake. Pipe out the edges using the same colour as for the star borders. Fill in the middle of the star with piped stars.
● For a very easy Christmas cake, flat ice the top and rough ice the sides. Pipe a shell border around the top edge. Decorate the middle with a large ribbon.

FLOWER FRUIT CAKE

MAKES 20-24 SLICES
20 cm (8 in) round rich fruit cake
3 tablespoons apricot jam
550 g (1¼ lb) almond paste
700 g (1½ lb) royal icing
yellow food colouring
piped sugar flowers, pages 214-215

1 Cover the cake with the almond paste following the instructions on page 198. Leave to dry before icing the cake.
2 Make up the royal icing following the instructions on page 200. Tint the icing with a few drops of food colouring, then swirl the icing over the cake. Leave to set until hard before sticking on the decorations.
3 Decorate the cake with the piped sugar flowers.

FRUIT-TOPPED CELEBRATION CAKE

MAKES 20-24 SLICES
20 cm (8 in) round rich fruit cake
3 tablespoons apricot jam
550 g (1¼ lb) almond paste
marzipan fruits, pages 138 and 139

1 Cover the cake with the almond paste following the instructions on page 198, then crimp the edges of the almond paste all the way round the top of the cake, forming a raised border. Leave to dry.

2 Heat the grill to moderate. Toast the almond paste topping under the grill until topping and border are lightly browned.

3 Using the point of a sharp knife score the top of the cake diagonally first one way and then the other to make a diamond pattern on the surface of the almond paste, making the diamonds quite large.

4 Decorate the cake with the fruits, arranging them in little groups in the diamond shapes and around the base of the cake on the cake board, if liked.

ROUGH-ICED CHRISTMAS CAKE

MAKES 20-24 SLICES
20 cm (8 in) round rich fruit cake
3 tablespoons apricot jam
550 g (1¼ lb) almond paste
700 g (1½ lb) royal icing
gold and green decorations

1 To cover the cake with almond paste, heat the jam in a small saucepan, sieve, then brush the cake with the jam. Cover with almond paste following the instructions on page 198.

2 Rough ice the cake with the royal icing following the instructions on page 200. Decorate with gold balls and a star and cake decoration green leaves.

CHRISTMAS CAKE

With this rich fruit cake, the egg yolks and whites are added to the mixture separately.

MAKES 24-26 SLICES

250 g [9 oz] butter at room temperature
250 g [9 oz] Barbados sugar
6 medium-sized eggs, separated
grated zest and juice of 1 orange
4 tablespoons molasses or black treacle
350 g [12 oz] plain flour
1 teaspoon mixed spice
½ teaspoon ground cinnamon
½ teaspoon ground ginger
pinch of grated nutmeg
½ teaspoon salt
1 teaspoon bicarbonate of soda
350 g [12 oz] currants
225 g [8 oz] seedless raisins
225 [8 oz] sultanas
100 g [4 oz] glacé pineapple, chopped
100 g [4 oz] mixed candied peel, chopped
275 ml [10 fl oz] milk
5 tablespoons brandy

The simplest designs are often the most effective. Here a flat iced Christmas cake is decorated with a border of shells round the top and base, and simple coloured fondant decorations.

For the decoration:
3 tablespoons apricot jam
900 g [2 lb] almond paste
900 g [2 lb] royal icing
green and red food colouring

1 Grease a 23 cm [9 in] round, deep cake tin and line the base and sides with a double thickness of greased, greaseproof paper. Tie a double thickness of brown paper round the tin. Heat the oven to 140°C [275°F] Gas 1.

2 Beat the butter and sugar together until the mixture is light and fluffy. Beat in the egg yolks, one at a time, then the orange zest, orange juice and molasses or treacle.

3 In a large bowl, sift half the flour with the spices and salt. In another bowl, mix the remaining flour with the bicarbonate of soda and the dried fruits and peel. Mix together the milk and brandy.

4 Gradually stir the spiced flour into the egg mixture and stir well. Stir in the floured fruit, alternately with the milk mixture. When all the ingredients have been incorporated, beat well.

5 Whisk the egg whites until stiff peaks form and fold them into the mixture.

6 Turn the mixture into the tin and level the top, making a shallow depression in the centre so the cake rises evenly.

7 Bake for 2½-3 hours, until a skewer inserted in the centre comes out clean. Cool and store as described on page 184.

8 To decorate the cake, melt the jam in a small pan over low heat, then sieve.

9 Cover the cake with 800 g [1¾ lb] almond paste, as described on page 198.

10 Flat ice cake as shown on page 201. Spoon remaining icing into a piping bag fitted with a small shell nozzle, then pipe shells around base and top edge.

11 Colour three-quarters of the remaining almond paste three shades of green and use to make holly leaves as described on page 197. Colour half the remaining paste red for holly berries and leave the rest uncoloured for mistletoe berries (see picture). Using icing, stick the decorations on to the cake.

12 Finish by tying a coloured ribbon around the cake. Secure in position with a pin.

VALENTINE CAKE

MAKES 8-10 SLICES

50 g [2 oz] candied peel
50 g [2 oz] glacé cherries
50 g [2 oz] blanched almonds
100 g [4 oz] currants
100 g [4 oz] raisins
100 g [4 oz] sultanas
275 g [10 oz] plain flour
275 g [10 oz] butter or margarine
275 g [10 oz] soft brown sugar
1 teaspoon mixed spice
grated zest of 1 lemon
4 large eggs

For the decoration:
3 tablespoons apricot jam
sqeeze of lemon juice
800 g [1¾ lb] almond paste
700 g [1½ lb] royal icing
red food colouring
silver cake balls (dragées)

1 Make up the cake according to the instructions on pages 184-185, without decorating the top with nuts. (Chop all the almonds at stage 4).
2 Cool the cake in the tin. Turn out on to a wire rack. Store for at least 2 months before decorating.
3 To decorate the cake, sieve the jam into a small pan. Add the lemon juice and melt over low heat, stirring.
4 Cover the cake with 550 g [1¼ lb] almond paste, as described on page 198. Leave to dry.
5 Colour the royal icing pale pink and flat ice the top of the cake as shown on page 201. Leave to dry. Flat ice the sides and leave to dry. Flat ice the top again to give a good finish and allow to dry.
6 Spoon the remaining icing into a piping bag fitted with a small star nozzle. Pipe vertical lines all around the cake, then pipe stars around base and top edge. Leave to dry.
7 To make the almond paste hearts, cut three heart-shaped templates from thick card: 2 cm [¾ in] wide, 4 cm [1½ in] wide and 6 cm [2⅜ in] wide.
8 Colour the remaining almond paste pale pink with the food colouring, then cut off enough paste to make four large and eight medium-sized hearts.
9 Add more food colouring to the remaining almond paste to tint it a stronger pink colour.
10 Roll out the darker almond paste thinly and cut out 12 large hearts and four small hearts. Roll out the lighter paste and cut out four large and eight medium-sized hearts.
11 Press silver balls into the points of the small hearts. Brush all the hearts very lightly with water and leave them to dry overnight on a wire rack.
12 Using icing, stick the four large pale pink hearts, four of the dark pink and the four small dark pink hearts on to the top of the cake (see picture). Add the silver balls.
13 Stick the eight medium-sized light pink hearts on to the centre of the remaining eight large dark pink hearts, then stick to the side of the cake.

This delightful Valentine celebration cake is surprisingly easy to create, although you will need to allow time for the decorations to set.

ELABORATE CELEBRATION CAKES

Making a shaped cake or an elaborately iced cake for a christening or birthday is something almost every cook would like to try. Once you know the basics of icing the cake, these more advanced skills are easy.

Simple icing and piping is explained in detail on pages 194-205. Making almond paste and flat icing is also covered there. This chapter explains how to make shaped fruit cakes without special tins, how to do elaborate designs in royal icing and how to pipe flowers.

MAKING SPECIAL SHAPES

Heart shapes, keys and so on are always popular. Special tins can be bought for these but as with numbers this is rather unnecessary expense as the cake can be nicely shaped using a template or by putting two cakes together, as explained in the recipe for the key cake on page 219.

SIZE OF CAKE

The size of cake depends on the number of people you plan to serve. As people only have small fingers of these rich celebration cakes, bakers reckon that each 450 g [1 lb] cooked cake will provide eight pieces (see chart pages 186-187). You will also need to allow extra weight for those who could not come to the celebration and will receive cake by post. As some of the cake in a shaped cake is cut away, allow about 450 g [1 lb] extra. This errs on the generous side as you are unlikely to cut away quite this much.

Making the template
You can cut a heart, horseshoe, star or bell from either a round or a square cake, using a template as a guide.

(Freehand cutting is much too risky.)

To make a template, draw the required shape on a thin sheet of cardboard – it should correspond with the dimensions of the cake. Then cut the shape out.

Trim the top of the cake level if necessary or turn upside down – the surface must be flat. Anchor your cardboard template to the cake top with a little royal icing.

Use a serrated knife for cutting. Hold the knife vertically and, using a sawing action, cut around the template.

Coating the cakes with almond paste follows the same principle as described for plain round and square cakes except that the paste must be moulded to the curved edges of the cake. Roll out a third of the paste, lay it on top of the shape and then trim it to the shape of the cake. Combine the trimmings with the remaining paste and roll them out to an oblong. Cut a strip the depth of the cake and use this to cover the sides, rerolling the trimmings as necessary.

MAKING NUMBER CAKES

For a special birthday – such as an 18th or 21st, depending on how you view coming of age – a number cake marks the occasion in a way that everyone will remember. Alternatively you could make a key cake. A heart-shaped cake makes a pretty engagement cake. You can buy special tins for numbers or hearts and this of course makes the whole thing very

simple but as you are likely to only ever make a couple of these cakes, it is quite an extravagance. The answer is to shape the number(s) yourself.

The chart overleaf gives the number and shape of the cake(s) required to make different numerals. Where both a round and a square cake are used, the round cake should be 4 cm [1½ in] larger in diameter than the width of the square cake. Otherwise, the pieces will not be in proportion.

Cutting and assembling

Cutting and assembling numbers is the same as for novelty sponge cakes illustrated on page 119. Cut the cake(s) as indicated by the dotted lines. Use a circular cardboard template to cut the centre from round cakes. The shaded areas indicate pieces that are not needed (reserve these for another use). Arrange the remaining pieces of cake on a cake board as shown, then stick them together using apricot jam glaze.

To make a number '0', simply cut the centre from a round cake. The surplus cake can be cut up and used for family tea.

Decorating a celebration cake is simple once you know the basic rules of icing.

THE DESIGN

It is not true that the more elaborate the design on a special cake, the better it looks. Very fancy designs become overpowering while something very simple can look quite stunning.

You should decide on the design for your cake and equip yourself with the necessary piping equipment well in advance. Draw out your design on greaseproof paper as described on page 204 and then it will be ready to prick through on to the flat iced cake when the icing is dry.

Before you can pipe your cake however, you need to know how to make the traditional flowers, leaves etc. that are added to iced cakes and how to make lace, trellises, initials, bows and all the other features usually found on celebration cakes.

CAKES REQUIRED FOR MAKING NUMERALS

Number	Square cake	Round cake
0		One
1	One	
2	One loaf	One
3		Two
4	One large	
5	One large	One
6	One loaf	One
7	One large	
8		Two
9	One loaf	One

If necessary, trim the top and sides of each cake to straighten out.

NOZZLES AND THEIR USES

Nozzle	Sizes	Uses
Writing nozzle	00,0,1,3	Lines, writing, lace, piped on flowers and other designs.
Petal	Small, medium	For making flowers to stick on the cake later.
Leaf	Small, medium	For leaf shapes, curved lines.
Star	Small, medium, large	For borders, star shapes.
Half shell	Small, medium, large	For shell edgings.
Basket weave	Nos. 22,23	Basketwork effect for sides of cakes.

EQUIPMENT

As well as the icing nozzles suggested on pages 202-203 for simple piped cakes it is wise to equip yourself with smaller sizes of each of these for delicate work, a couple of fine writing nozzles to make lace and trellis work, and various-sized petal nozzles for piping flowers. If you have all the nozzles listed below, you will be equipped to pipe any cake.

All of these tubes and nozzles are best used in conjunction with paper or plastic forcing bags and are easier to control if screw collars are used.

You will also need a turntable (as described on page 194) and an icing ruler for use when flat icing. It is also wise to equip yourself with a good quantity of greaseproof paper as this is used when piping flowers, planning designs etc.

Icing nail

As icing nail is a nail with a little platform on top. It is used when flowers are piped. Stick a small piece of greaseproof paper on to the nail with a little icing. As you pipe each petal on to the paper you turn the nail. Icing nails can be bought but it is easy to improvise by sticking a small square of Formica or wood to the head of a large nail or screw.

PIPING

The designs for the side must be planned very carefully so that scallops etc are all the same size and bunches of flowers, initials or whatever fall at regular intervals. To do this, cut a strip of greaseproof paper the length of the sides of each cake. Draw the design on this, scaling down for the smaller cakes and prick through to the icing with a pin.

Before you start piping on to the cake, decorations to be stuck on such as flowers or run out designs (see page 204) must be made. These must be made about 2 weeks before required so that they will dry out.

Making flowers

Flowers to be stuck on the sides of a cake are usually piped. Flowers to decorate the top and/or the corners of a cake are moulded by hand.

Piped flowers

Roses, daisies, apple blossoms and

little sprays of flowers for the sides of a cake are fairly easy to make. To make them, you will need petal tubes and an icing nail. If you want coloured flowers, colour the icing first, sticking to pastel colours.

Finishing touches

Bought artificial flowers, silver horse-shoes, and so on, for silver weddings or other big occasion cakes should be planned into your design when piping. Do not however attach them until the last minute. Good places to put the decorations are at intervals around the base of the cake and at points where the lines of scallops meet.

Positioning the pillars

Before you put your cake pillars in place, check that the bases are level. If they are not, the cake will topple. The best way to check this is with a spirit level. If the little bubble appears in the centre of the marked off division in the glass tube, then the pillars are level. If not, rub down the pillars with emery or fine wet-and-dry sandpaper until they are level.

Smear the bottom of the pillars with icing and position in the places you decided when you planned your design. Very gently lower the second tier on to the pillars. Don't thump it down or the bottom layer of pillars will go right through the bottom cake. It is advisable to put the cake on the pillars in the place where it will be served. It is impossible to move safely otherwise.

OTHER SPECIAL CAKES

The techniques in this chapter can be used for christening, special birthday and other anniversary cakes. Once you can pipe and flat ice, designing and decorating the cake is easy.

Design ideas

To make the cakes for these suggestions and for quantities of icing and almond paste required, see chart on page 199.

● For the golden wedding cake shown on page 211, cover a round cake with almond paste and flat ice with royal icing. Make a run out 50 and leave to dry. Mark eight scallops around the top and sides of the cake. Outline with double lines of white and yellow on top, single lines on the sides. Fill in with white lace. Pipe a large white dot where the scallops meet at the edge of the cake. Top with a yellow dot. Pipe a line of four yellow dots as shown. *(Continued on page 218).*

This elegant white Christmas cake has a Bethlehem star piped on the top and a shell border round the top and base.

PIPING FLOWERS

1 Cut one small square of greaseproof paper for each flower you wish to make. Set aside.

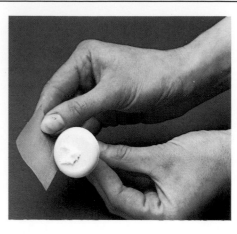

2 Fit a forcing bag with petal nozzle and fill with royal icing. Stick a piece of paper on your icing nail with icing.

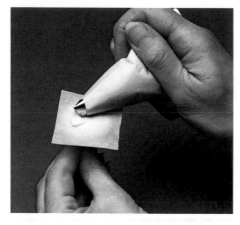

6 For roses, with wide end of petal nozzle touching the paper and holding bag at an angle, squeeze out icing.

7 Turn the nail as you squeeze to make a tight coil. This is the centre of your rosebud.

11 Slightly overlapping, pipe four more petals in the same way. Remove paper from nail and leave to harden.

12 For apple blossom, use pink icing. Use a petal nozzle. Hold nozzle on centre of nail at a slight angle.

HANDY HINT

Layered shaped cakes
If making a layered, shaped cake, cut the shape from each separate layer in turn. Then fill and assemble before icing.

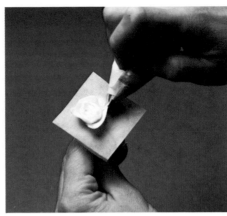

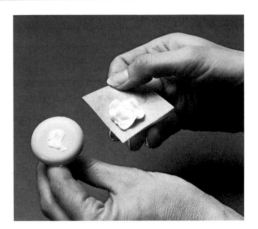

3 Holding the nozzle in a vertical position, squeeze out a little icing to make the first petal.

4 Turn the nail slightly and pipe another petal. Continue until you have made a flower.

5 Remove paper from the icing nail and leave the flower to dry until required for the cake.

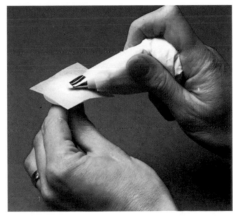

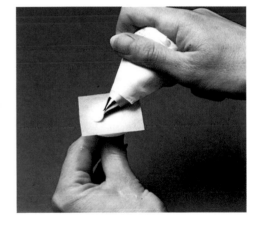

8 For the petals, hold the nozzle in a horizontal position. Twist the bag, so the nozzle turns over, turing the nail.

9 For primroses, use a petal nozzle. Hold the bag with the nozzle touching the paper and parallel with the surface.

10 Sqeeze out a little icing. Turn outer point of nozzle a quarter turn, keeping inner point down.

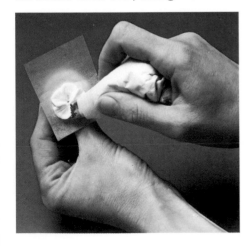

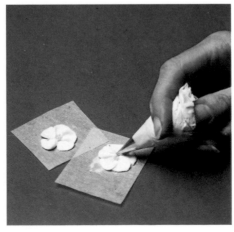

13 Turn anti-clockwise, squeezing the bag at the same time to make a small, flat petal. Make five petals like this.

14 Using a fine writing nozzle and yellow icing, pipe in little dots for the stamens of the flower.

15 When the flowers have completely dried, they can be peeled off the greaseproof paper.

PIPING SIDE DESIGNS

1 Eyelet embroidery is simple to do. First draw out a design on greaseproof paper.

2 Using a knitting needle or other implement, make the eyelets in the cake. The cake should show through.

3 Tilt cake towards you. Using a fine writing nozzle, pipe a ring around the hole. Pipe petals to make a flower.

7 Position a daisy on the end of each piped stem. Finish with a dot of icing or with a silver ball.

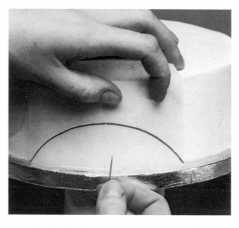

8 For scallops at the bottom of a cake, first work out the width of each on greaseproof paper.

9 Using a writing nozzle, pipe a single curve. Join the curves at the bottom of the cake.

13 Now pipe lines the other way to fill up the space in the centre of the scallop.

14 To pipe ferns on the side of a cake, use a fine nozzle to pipe a straight line 2.5 cm [1 in] long.

15 Pipe two curving lines from the top to make an arrow shape. Pipe two more below it.

4 To make a spray of flowers, use a fine writing nozzle. Pipe fine lines for the stems.

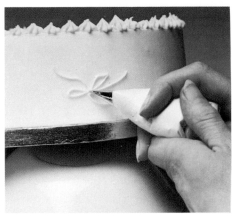

5 Using the same nozzle, pipe the leaves, tilting the cake towards you and holding the nozzle at 45°.

6 Peel previously piped daisies off greaseproof paper. Dot a little icing on the back.

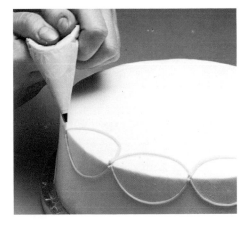

10 Scallops at the top edge are made in the same way but a corresponding scallop is piped on the top of the cake.

11 Lace can be used to fill in the scallop. Use a fine writing nozzle and pipe squiggly lines to fill the space.

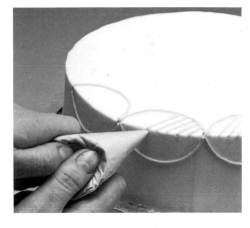

12 Trellis work can also be used to fill scallops. Using a writing nozzle, pipe sloping diagonal lines.

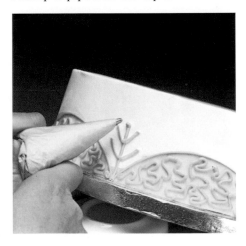

16 Finish the top of the fern with a dot of icing, again using a plain writing pipe. Add a silver ball if wished.

17 Graduated dots look attractive. Pipe one large one at the bottom then two smaller ones above it.

18 Finish the top dot with a silver cake ball. Lines of dots can be used around the bottom of the cake.

Decorate around base with a line of large white dots topped by small yellow dots. Attach the 50 and pipe white dots around the edges. Trim with yellow ribbon.

● For a baby boots christening cake, cover a round or square cake with almond paste and flat ice with royal icing. Roll two pieces of almond paste into balls about the size of golf balls. Make an indentation in each ball with your thumb then, working carefully, model the balls to the shape of a pair of baby shoes. Set aside to dry then coat the shoes with royal icing. To do this, impale each shoe on a skewer and dip into the icing. Let the excess icing drip off and then leave to dry.

Rub down any rough icing edges with emery paper or fine wet-and-dry paper. Using a writing nozzle, pipe a bow of blue or pink ribbon on each boot, depending on whether the child is a boy or girl. Cover each shoe with tiny dots. Allow the shoes to dry, then stick to one side of the top of the cake with royal icing.

Decorate the sides and top edge of the cake with scallops using the same colour icing as for the boots. Make a row of dots around the bottom where the cake meets the board. Write the child's name on top of the cake if wished, following the instructions given on page 203.

● For a daisy chain christening cake, flat ice the top and sides of the cake. Make about 18 blue or pink daisies, depending on the sex of the child. Cut a circle of greaseproof paper the size of the top of the cake. Fold into 12 sections. Using the marked sections as a guide, prick scallop shapes on top edge and side of the cake so that they run alternately with one scallop on top, one at the side. Pipe out marked lines using a writing pipe or a small shell nozzle. Attach the daisies where the scallop lines touch the rim of the cake. Pipe a dot of white icing in the centre of each daisy. Pipe the baby's name on top of the cake if wished. Finish off where the cake meets the board with a shell border.

This coming-of-age cake is made from three cakes which are iced with green royal icing and decorated with green and white icing.

• For a wedding bell cake, flat ice a square cake. Make bell-shaped run out designs in a pastel colour. Attach two to each side of the cake, tilting at an angle to each other so that they form a triangular shape. Attach two to each corner of the cake in the same way. Using a writing nozzle and same colour icing as the bells, pipe in the striker and a bow at the top and bottom edge of the cake and top each one with a silver cake ball. This design can be used for a tiered cake but remember that you must make the bells correspondingly smaller to keep the proportions correct on the second and third tiers.

• For an initial wedding cake, flat ice round cakes. Divide the sides with lines spaced equally. The lines can be carried on to the top of the cake in a scallop. The lines divide the cake up into sections.

Fill each alternate section with eyelet hole embroidery, as shown in the step-by-step guide on page 216. If wished, the flowers for the embroidery can be piped in a contrasting colour.

In the sections not filled with embroidery, pipe the first initials of the couple, intertwining if possible. It is best to work this out carefully on greaseproof paper first and then follow the pricked through design exactly. Fill the alternate scallops with eyelet hole embroidery. Leave the remaining scallops plain.

• For a coming-of-age cake, shape numbers from three cakes: cut a '1' from an 18 cm [7 in] square cake, and an '8' from 15 cm [6 in] and 18 cm [7 in] round cakes (see page 117 for cutting information and diagrams). Assemble the cut cakes on a cake board and stick together with apricot

jam glaze to make '18'. Flat ice the cakes with pale green royal icing. Make white icing flowers and stick on to the top of the cakes. Pipe on leaves and stems with dark green icing, then make dots of dark green icing around the edges of the cakes.

• For a key cake, make a cake in an 18 cm [7 in] round tin, and one in a loaf tin about 23 cm [9 in] long and 12.5 cm [5 in] wide. Cut an oblong, 9 cm [3½ in] wide from the loaf cake. Cut a slice off one side of the round cake the same width as the end of the oblong (see diagram). Brush the cut face of the round cake and the end of the oblong with apricot glaze. Stick the cakes together.

Cut two pieces from the remaining strip of loaf cake and then stick these to the end of the oblong to form the shank.

Cover the cakes with almond paste. Flat ice the top and sides of the cake with royal icing. Leave to set.

Using a saucer as a guide, prick out a circle on the round part of the cake. There should be about 5 cm [2 in] of cake around the outside of the circle. Using a writing nozzle and pale pink royal icing, pipe a scalloped line of dots, following the line of the pricked out circle.

Using an icing ruler as a guide, prick two parallel lines of dots down the shank of the key. There should be about 7.5 cm [3 in] space between the lines. Pipe dotted scallops down the lines to match those on the round part of the key. Pipe a name down the centre of the key, spacing the letters equally. Decorate the round part of the cake with a bought cake ornament. Pipe a shell border around the base of the cake.

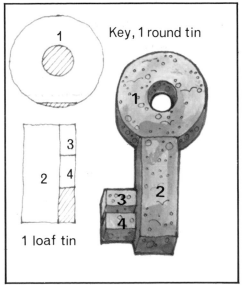

Made from one round cake and one loaf-shaped cake, this key cake is easier to make and decorate than it might appear.

ENGAGEMENT CAKE

The icing used for this attractive cake is a quick fondant, which is particularly good for moulding over shaped cakes and making simple decorations. This icing can be used as soon as it is made.

MAKES 20 SLICES

150 g [5 oz] glacé cherries
450 g [1 lb] raisins
175 g [6 oz] currants
2 tablespoons mixed peel
1 tablespoon angelica chopped
100 g [4 oz] walnuts, chopped
225 g [8 oz] plus 2 tablespoons
    self-raising flour
225 g [8 oz] butter
225 g [8 oz] brown sugar
6 large eggs
1½ teaspoons ground allspice
1 teaspoon salt
2 tablespoons sherry
700 g [1½ lb] almond paste
3 tablespoons apricot jam glaze

The icing for this Engagement cake is very simple; it is the added decorations that make it extra special.

For the quick fondant icing:
900 g [2 lb] icing sugar
2 egg whites
4 tablespoons liquid glucose
red food colouring
egg white or water to soften.

1 Heat oven to 150°C [300°F] Gas 2. Line a heart-shaped cake tin, about 3.4 L [6 pt] capacity, width at widest point 20 cm [8 in], length 18 cm [7 in] with a double thickness of greaseproof paper and grease the paper.
2 Chop the cherries, combine all the fruit and nuts and toss them lightly in 2 tablespoons flour.
3 Cream the butter and sugar in a bowl until light and fluffy. Lightly beat the eggs, then add to the creamed mixture a little at a time.
4 Sift the flour, spice and salt, then fold into the mixture with the fruit. Stir in the sherry.
5 Turn the mixture into the cake tin. Make a dip in the centre. Bake for 2½-3 hours until a skewer inserted into the centre of the cake comes out clean.
6 Allow the cake to go cold in the tin before turning out.
7 Cover the cake with almond paste following the instructions on page 198. Press the paste on to the sides of the cake, rather than rolling the cake on the paste.
8 To make the fondant icing, sift 800 g [1¾ lb] icing sugar into a basin. Make a well in the centre.
9 Pour egg whites and liquid glucose into the centre and work together to form a firm paste. If necessary, work in a little more icing sugar. Reserve 225 g [8 oz] and colour the remaining icing pink. Set aside a small piece of each icing for decoration.
10 Dredge a little icing sugar on to a working surface. Roll out the icing so it is 5 cm [2 in] larger all round than the top of the cake.
11 Place the icing on top of the cake and roll and shape it over the heart.
12 Soften the reserved icing to a pipeable consistency with extra egg white or water and spoon into a piping bag fitted with a small star nozzle. Pipe stars or shells around the bottom edge of the cake. Use the reserved small pieces of fondant to make two hearts for the top of the cake.
13 For an extra special touch, add a posy of fresh rose buds tied with ribbon and scatter rose petals around the base of the cake. Tie a lacy ribbon round the cake.

CELEBRATION CAKE

MAKES 35-40 SLICES

1.5 kg [3lb 4 oz] mixed dried fruit
100 g [4 oz] glacé cherries, halved
100 g [4 oz] shelled walnuts, chopped
450 g [1 lb] plain flour
1 tablespoon ground mixed spice
a pinch of salt
350 g [12 oz] margarine or butter
350 g [12 oz] light soft brown sugar
7 eggs
grated zest and juice of 1 lemon
grated zest and juice of 1 orange
3 tablespoons brandy
750 g [1½ lb] almond paste
4 tablespoons apricot jam

For the icing:
½ quantity of quick fondant icing (see
   recipe for Engagement cake)
few drops of yellow food colouring
extra icing sugar and a little cornflour, for
   dusting

For the decorative icing:
1 egg white
225 g [8 oz] icing sugar, sifted
few drops of yellow food colouring

This elegant celebration cake is suitable for a wedding, christening or anniversary.

1 Heat the oven to 170°C [325°F] Gas 3. Grease and line the sides and base of a 23 cm [9 in] square cake tin with a double thickness of greaseproof paper. Grease the paper. Tie a double thickness of brown paper round the tin.

2 Mix the dried fruit, glacé cherries and walnuts in a bowl. Sift the flour with the spice and salt into a separate bowl, then add half the flour to the fruit and mix well.

3 Cream margarine and sugar until pale. Gradually beat in eggs adding a little flour with each. Fold in remaining flour.

4 Stir in fruits, citrus zest and juice and brandy. Turn into tin, level and make shallow hollow in centre.

5 Bake for 3½-4 hours or until a warmed fine skewer inserted in centre comes out clean. Leave to cool for 30 minutes. Prick top and spoon on brandy. Leave until cold.

6 Turn out, peel off the greaseproof paper, wrap in foil and store in an airtight tin for at least 2 months.

7 Cover the cake with almond paste following the instructions on page 198.

8 The day before the cake is required, make the fondant icing, working in the yellow food colouring when the fondant is a smooth paste.

9 Sift a little icing sugar over a work surface and roll out icing to a 30 cm [12 in] square. Place on the cake and, using hands dusted with cornflour, ease down the sides.

10 While the icing is still soft, mark a line 12 mm [½ in] in from the edge all the way round the top. Mark another line along the sides 12 mm [½ in] down from the edge, and another line 12 mm [½ in] up from the base. Set aside.

11 To make the decorative icing, beat the egg white until frothy, then stir in the icing sugar, 1 tablespoon at a time. Beat until the icing forms soft peaks. Stir in food colouring.

12 Spoon the icing into a piping bag fitted with a small plain nozzle. Using the marked lines as a guide, pipe lines vertically over the edge of each side and more lines down to the base and out on to the board.

13 Pipe a dot on both ends of each line. Squeeze a dot of icing on to the back of the cake decorations of your choice and fit on to each corner and in centre, then pipe two lines at right angles in each corner. Decorate with more dots on top of cake and on board. Dry overnight, then tie the ribbon round the cake.

MAKING A WEDDING CAKE

A beautifully decorated, tiered wedding cake is a real work of art. While many cooks feel confident about the baking, they shy away from the decorating, often preferring to hand this over to an expert. This chapter shows you how the decorating is done. The satisfaction you will feel will be surpassed only by the delight of the happy couple and the admiration of your guests.

Traditionally wedding cakes are rich fruit cakes covered with almond paste, then finished with royal icing. For a truly memorable cake worthy of the big day, make the cake with the richest mixture, use 'real' almond paste and decorate with beautifully piped royal icing.

Making, baking and storing rich fruit cakes are fully covered on pages 180-187; making almond paste on page 196 and applying the paste to the cake in the step-by-step pictures and instructions on page 198. Making royal icing and using it to flat-ice cakes is described on pages 197-201. Various piping techniques are given on pages 202-203. This chapter gives you some new, more advanced piping techniques and shows you how to plan and assemble a beautiful, three-tiered, round wedding cake.

SIZE AND SHAPE

The size of the cake depends upon the number of portions you want to cut. As a good rule-of-thumb guide, you can expect to cut eight fingers from each 450 g [1 lb] of cake (cooked weight, before icing). So, if you are catering for 24 guests and want to send another 24 'postings' (making 48 portions in all) you will need at least 2.7 kg [6 lb] of cake. The cooked weight of different sized cakes is given in the chart on pages 186-187.

If you want to follow tradition and save the top tier intact for another red letter day (such as the first wedding anniversary or the christening) you must not, of course, include the weight of the top tier in your calculations. If you do want to keep the top tier for longer than 2 months, strip off the paste and icing and decorate nearer the day – otherwise mould might form between the paste and the cake. Also, the icing will be impossibly hard to eat.

The question of round or square is really a matter of personal preference. Either way, do not attempt the larger sizes unless you have, or can borrow, an oven big enough to allow 2.5 cm [1 in] gap between the sides of the cake tin and your oven.

Proportion of the tiers

Highly elaborate cakes can have as many as six tiers. However, one layer is quite acceptable, although two or three are more usual – and look more sumptuous than a single layer.

The tiers must be in proportion to each other otherwise the cake will look unbalanced (see the chart). The bottom tier should be proportionately deeper than the others, otherwise the cake will look top-heavy. If, after baking, the cake is not the correct depth either trim or build up with almond paste as necessary.

COLOUR SCHEMES

A wedding cake is often an all-white affair, but there is no reason why you should not use another suitable colour. For a particularly impressive result, use two colours – one for the basic covering icing and another for piped decoration. If you do use a coloured icing for wedding cakes, pastel shades generally look best. Remember, always

match your ribbons and flowers accordingly.

The cake we have chosen is a beautifully decorated, three tiered round cake. The first layer (bottom tier) measures 30 cm [12 in] in diameter; the second layer (middle tier) is 20 cm [8 in] in diameter, the third layer (top tier) is 15 cm [6 in]. The basic coating icing is tinted a delicate apricot to offset the elegant white piped decoration. Finishing touches are provided by ribbons and flowers chosen to match the overall colour scheme.

You can, of course, make the same cake all in white or use another delicate colour for the covering icing.

How to colour royal icing

Making royal icing is described on page 200. The golden rule is to colour all the necessary amount of icing at once. Colouring small quantities of icing in batches will result in uneven colouring which will make the cake look unattractive.

Have ready the total amount of royal icing you require. Place the bottle of edible food colouring on a saucer as a precaution against drips or spillage (which will stain). If colouring small amounts of icing, dip the tip of a skewer into the colouring, then shake it gently over the icing so that a few drops will fall into the icing. If colouring large quantities of icing, pour some of the food colouring into a teaspoon and shake over the icing. Beat until the icing is evenly coloured and there are no streaks or concentrations of colour.

Continue adding the food colouring little by little until the colour you want is reached. Never, ever, pour the colouring straight from the bottle – it only takes a slip of the hand to ruin the whole batch of icing.

When using coloured royal icing for flat icing, sandpaper the surface of the first coat only. Sanding the second and top coats gives an unattractive, streaky effect. So, take care when applying these coats to make them as smooth and as even as possible.

TIMING

Making a tiered cake is an ambitious project and you simply cannot afford any last-minute errors. The whole operation is completed in successive stages and you must work out just how far in advance you need to start. To do this, calculate how much time you have to allow for each stage and then work backwards from the date of the reception.

Our countdown timetable has been worked out so that everything, bar the final finishing touches and assembly, is completed two full weeks before the big day. This allows time for the piped decoration to dry – it also leaves you free to cope with other preparations for the wedding.

Making and baking

This is the first stage. The method for rich fruit cakes and the quantities of ingredients required for different-sized cakes is given on pages 180-187.

As you will be dealing with large quantities and different baking temperatures, the best plan is to make and bake the largest cake one day, then make the smaller cakes the next day.

Bake your cakes 2-3 months in advance. This gives time for the flavour to mature and allows for the decorating. Store as described on page 184.

Almond paste

The second stage is to cover the cakes with almond paste so they are ready for flat icing. Instructions for making 'real' almond paste are given on page 194.

For our cake you will need 2.3 kg [5 lb] paste (made weight). Cover each cake as shown in the step-by-step pictures and instructions on page 198. Then place the cakes on a large board and leave, uncovered, in a dry place for 4-5 days before flat icing. This is important: if the cake is iced before the paste has dried out, oil from the paste

---

Spare egg yolks

Royal icing will leave you with a lot of spare egg yolks. Beat them two at a time with salt, allowing 1 teaspoon to every two yolks. Then freeze them, two to a container, ready to make 275 ml [½ pt] each of mayonnaise for the wedding. They will freeze for 6 months. Allow them to defrost for 2-3 hours before making the mayonnaise.

SIZES FOR TWO-TIER ROUND OR SQUARE CAKES

1st tier	Depth	2nd tier	Depth
30 cm [12 in]	7.5 cm [3 in]	20 cm [8 in]	6.5 cm [2½ in]
25 cm [10 in]	7.5 cm [3 in]	15 cm [6 in]	6.5 cm [2½ in]

SIZES FOR THREE-TIER ROUND OR SQUARE CAKES

1st tier	Depth	2nd tier	Depth	3rd tier	Depth
30 cm [12 in]	7.5 cm [3 in]	20 cm [8 in]	7 cm [2¾ in]	15 cm [6 in]	5 cm [2 in]
28 cm [11 in]	7.5 cm [3 in]	18 cm [7 in]	6.5 cm [2½ in]	12.5 cm [5 in]	5 cm [2 in]

will seep into and discolour the icing. Furthermore, there is no remedy – the icing would have to be stripped off and the cake iced afresh.

Royal icing

It is impossible to give the exact quantity of icing required with none left over: there must be enough to cover the cakes and then scrape off, leaving a good smooth surface. For safety, therefore, estimates are on the generous side. However, the excess need not be wasted – correctly stored royal icing will keep for weeks in the refrigerator so any left over from flat icing can be used for further decoration.

The chart on page 199 gives a guide to quantities for different sized cakes. For our cake you will need about 2.3 kg [5 lb] royal icing. This provides enough for flat icing and for the board run outs.

For this you'll need 2.3 kg [5 lb] icing sugar, 10 egg whites, 37.5 ml [2½ tablespoons] lemon juice and 25 ml [5 teaspoons] glycerine. Make up the whole batch (using an electric whisk for ease) exactly as described on page 197. If following our colour scheme, beat in enough pink and yellow edible food colouring to tint the icing apricot.

Storing royal icing

Always make the amount of icing you need the day before required and rebeat before use to the right consistency. If the icing becomes a little too thick during storage, thin down with a little lightly beaten egg white.

Royal icing dries out when exposed to air and must be stored in an airtight container. When using royal icing, keep the bowl containing the icing covered with a clean damp cloth.

Flat icing

This is the third stage. Read the background notes on page 199 and flat-ice the cakes as described in the step-by-step instructions and pictures on page 201.

For very special cakes, such as wedding cakes, it is best to give three coats of icing. Each gives a smoother, finer finish and, therefore, a more beautiful appearance. Take care that the coats are very thin: the finished thickness should be no more than 6 mm [¼ in], otherwise the icing will be unpleasantly hard to eat.

The icing must be quite dry and firm

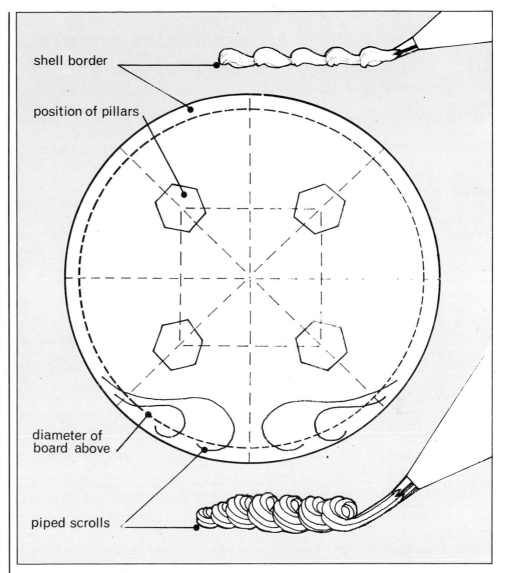

shell border

position of pillars

diameter of board above

piped scrolls

before any piped decoration is added. (Should any mistakes occur, it is much easier to remove fresh icing from a hard surface than from a soft one.) Leave the cakes in a warm dry place for one week to dry – an airing cupboard is ideal – then wrap in foil until required for decorating.

DECORATING THE CAKE

This is perhaps the most creative – and certainly the most demanding – stage. There are no shortcuts to success – for professional results you just have to practise until perfect. It is well worth making a practice board. To do this, simply cover the underside of a thick, silver cake-board with some plain self-adhesive plastic. (This way the silver side can still be used as a cake-board.) Make up a batch of royal icing and use the board to experiment with designs and to practise icing techniques.

THE WEDDING CAKE DESIGN
The diagram above shows the design for the cake tops. Remember, you must plan the position of the pillars at the same time as the design. A border of shells runs along the edge to the start of the scroll design.

The design for sides and base can be seen in the picture on page 223. The shell border at the base of each cake is finished with a star. Graduated dots (see page 217) are piped on either side of the ribbon to decorate the sides. Dots are used to pick out (and neaten) the edge of the board run outs. They are used again, in the same fashion, around the base of each pillar and the ornamental vase.

225

COUNTDOWN FOR THE CAKE

2-3 months before the day

Buy ingredients for the cake. Make and bake cakes. When cold, wrap in foil and store in airtight tins for at least 1 month or until required for icing. Plan design and make greaseproof paper templates.

30 days before

Make 2.3 kg [5 lb] almond paste. Prepare cakes, trimming tops level if necessary. Cover with almond paste. Store uncovered in a cool airy place for 4-5 days to allow the paste to dry out.

29-27 days before

Make greaseproof templates for board run outs. Practise piping. Organize equipment and ingredients for flat icing.

26 days before

Make 2.3 kg [5 lb] apricot coloured royal icing. Store for 24 hours.

25 days before

Flat-ice the top of each cake.

24 days before

Flat-ice the sides of each cake.

23 days before

Smooth any rough edges with emery board, then give the top of each cake a second thin coat of flat icing.

22 days before

Give the sides of each cake a second thin coating of flat icing.

21 days before

Give the top of each cake a final thin coating of icing.

20 days before

Give the sides of each cake a final thin coat of icing. Store remaining icing in an airtight container in the refrigerator (to use for board run outs).

19 days before

Organize all equipment and ingredients for piped decoration. Buy 3.3 m [3¾ yd] ribbon 12 mm [½ in] wide and an ornamental vase.

18 days before

Make board run outs. Leave for 1-2 days to dry.

17 days before

Make 900 g [2 lb] white royal icing for piped decorations. Store in a covered container for 24 hours.

16 days before

Decorate cake tops, bases and board run outs. Reserve rest of icing.

15 days before

Secure ribbon round cakes with a dot of icing. Decorate sides of cakes. Store cakes in suitable containers for 2 weeks to dry out.

The day before

Check the pillars stand level. Fix pillars in position. Secure silver vase in centre of top tier with a dab of icing.

On the day

Arrange flowers in vase and assemble the tiers on site.

EQUIPMENT

Make a checklist of all the things you need. Never start decorating the cake before you are organized, with all your equipment to hand and the cakes and icing ready and waiting.

Best results need a steady hand. So work at a comfortable level and, before you begin, make sure you are not interrupted. Take the telephone off the hook, lock the kitchen door and warn the family that you are not to be disturbed.

Cake boards: these are the first item on the agenda. To preserve the balance, the boards should be proportionately larger than their respective cakes. For our cake you will need three boards of the following sizes: 40 cm [16 in] in diameter; 28 cm [11 in] in diameter and 20 cm [8 in] in diameter.

Do not be tempted to economize and make the boards yourself. A tiered cake is heavy and the boards must be strong enough to take the weight.

A turntable: this is essential for decorating.

Piping bags and nozzles: you can use icing pumps or icing bags for piping.

However, icing bags do have the edge when it comes to tackling advanced work, particularly if using two different colours. If you are, it is worth making several greaseproof bags (see page 94) for each cake. Check that you have the right nozzles and that they fit the bags – if necessary invest in two nozzles of the same type and size. This way you will not have to stop to change the nozzle to another bag, or start refilling bags.

For our cake you will need the following: one plain writing tube (no. 3 size) plus one small and one large star nozzle.

Design equipment: you will also need a pencil, a sharp pair of scissors, plenty of greaseproof paper, a sheet of thin cardboard and some pins. These are for making the template (for the board run out) and for transferring the design to the cake.

Cake pillars: to assemble the tiers you will need cake pillars. These come in various sizes and can be round or square, depending on the shape of the cake. You will need four pillars for each tier and each set should be proportional in size. For our cake, choose 7.5 cm [3 in] tall pillars for the bottom tier and 5 cm [2 in] tall pillars for the top tier.

Ornaments and ribbons: the top of the cake is usually decorated with an ornament. This can be a small silver vase filled with fresh flowers, a silver horseshoe or artificial flowers. For extra glamour a ribbon is often tied around each cake. For our cake you will need approximately 3.3 m [3¾ yd] ribbon 12 mm [½ in] wide. (The ribbon used was oyster coloured.) In addition, you will need a silver vase.

Containers for storing: you will also need containers for storing the piped cakes. (Do not use foil as this could damage the decoration.) Remember the containers must be large enough to accommodate the boards as well. If you cannot lay your hands on suitably large tins, use large, foil-covered cardboard boxes and line the insides with tissue or kitchen paper.

The design

Simple designs are often the most effective. The design we have chosen is illustrated in the diagram. If making your own design, be sure to plan this well in advance. Remember to leave the centre of the cake tops clear to allow for the pillars.

The sides of a tiered cake usually have fairly elaborate decoration as this is the part on show. Work out the design very carefully to ensure all decoration is the correct size.

Always decorate the top of the cakes before the sides: draw the design on a sheet of greaseproof paper the same size as the cake top and prick out the key points on to the icing as described on pages 230 and 231. When the tops are piped, leave for 24 hours to dry.

If using ribbons, secure in place (at the back) with a dab of icing before decorating the sides.

NEW TECHNIQUES

The design we have chosen combines various piping techniques covered in other courses with some new, more advanced work.

Board run outs

These add interest to the board and give the cake a sophisticated appearance.

Board run outs are very similar to ordinary run outs. The difference is that the design, instead of being made separately and then attached, is applied directly and left to harden on the board.

Fifteen days left to go – time to decorate the sides of the cakes. Follow the countdown opposite and all will run smoothly.

MAKING A TEMPLATE FOR A BOARD RUN OUT [ROUND CAKE]

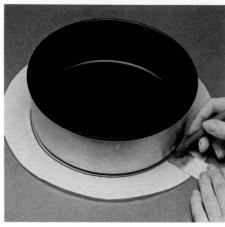

1 Place the cake board on a sheet of greaseproof paper and draw the outline. Then carefully cut out the circle.

2 Measure diameter of iced cake. Place cake tin or plate of equivalent size in centre of greaseproof circle. Draw round outline.

3 Fold the circle of greaseproof paper in half, then into three to make a triangle with a rounded base.

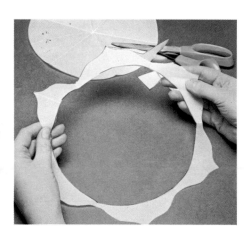

4 Draw the design using the full depth of space from the outer edge of circle to the inner pencil line.

5 Cut out the design, then cut along the inner pencil line. Reserve paper centre to use for top of cake.

6 Unfold greaseproof pattern and smooth out. The template is now ready to use for the board run out.

Simple decoration is often most effective. This diagram shows the design chosen for the template for the board run outs.

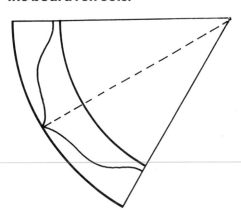

Template

This provides a guide and so helps eliminate error. The same design is used on each board but because they are different sizes, you must make a separate template for each one.

A template for a square cake is made in the same way as for a round cake (as shown in the step-by-step pictures and instructions) but you will, of course, be using square boards and tins etc.

Relief piping and flooding

You will need stiff royal icing for piping

the outline of the design and some thin icing for flooding the run out. There should be sufficient left over from flat icing.

When you are ready to make the run outs, place some of the royal icing in a bag fitted with a no. 1 writing tube. Thin the remainder with lightly beaten egg white. Place in a greaseproof piping bag, but do not cut the tip.

Make the board run outs one at a time. Snip the template at one point, so that you can ease it round the cake, then pin on its respective board. Draw round the edge with a pen. Remove the

MAKING BOARD RUN OUTS

 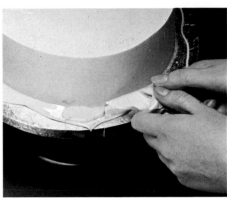 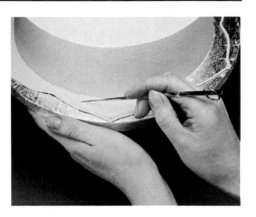

1 Pin template on cake board. 'Draw' round outline. Remove template, then pipe the outline in royal icing using a no. 1 plain writing tube.

2 Flood run out with thinned icing. Start from back of cake and work anticlockwise. Work back and forth from outline to cake base.

3 Using a skewer, draw the edges of the icing to close any gaps. When run out is flooded, prick out air bubbles. Leave 1-2 days to dry.

PIPING SPIRAL SCROLLS

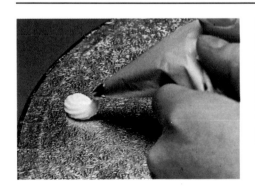  

1 Using a medium star nozzle, hold bag at an angle of 60° to surface. Press out icing, moving bag to make spiral.

2 Without stopping, repeat the movement, slightly overlapping the next spiral with the first. Continue.

3 Increase pressure towards the middle of the scroll to make larger spirals; decrease towards end.

template, then pipe the outline in stiff royal icing, using the marked line as your guide.

Next, cut the tip of the greaseproof icing bag and flood the run out with the thin icing. Start from the back of the cake (use the 'take off' mark from flat icing as a guide) and work anticlockwise. This way the join where the icing meets will not be visible. Use a 'paddling' motion and work from inside the piped line to the base of the cake, then out again.

Close any gaps carefully drawing the edges of the icing together with a skewer. When the run out is completely flooded, prick out any air bubbles that have formed. Make remaining run outs, then leave for 1-2 days to dry.

PIPING SPIRAL SCROLLS

This is a new, more advanced technique – not easy, but very decorative. The action you have to perfect can be likened to that of twirling a skipping rope – but in an anti-clockwise direction.

Practise the method as shown in the step-by-step pictures and instructions until you can confidently produce a single line of slightly over lapping spirals in one continuous, flowing movement.

For our design, start at the outer edge of the cake top, where the border of shells ends. Increase pressure as you work towards the centre of the scroll, then decrease pressure right at the end to make the curved 'tail'. This way the scroll will be thicker in the centre and will be tapered at either end.

When you have completed all piped decoration, store the cakes in air-tight containers for at least 2 weeks to dry out. (Do not use foil for wrapping as this could damage the decoration.)

DECORATING AND ASSEMBLING A THREE-TIERED WEDDING CAKE

1 rich fruit cake 15 cm [6 in] in diameter
1 rich fruit cake 20 cm [8 in] in diameter
1 rich fruit cake 30 cm [12 in] in diameter
2.3 kg [5 lb] almond paste
2.3 kg [5 lb] royal icing
pink and yellow food colouring
lightly beaten egg white

To decorate:
900 g [2 lb] royal icing
3.3 m [3¾ yd] ribbon, 12 mm [½ in]wide
4 cake pillars, 7.5 cm [3 in] high
4 cake pillars, 5 cm [2 in] high
1 ornamental silver vase
rosebuds

Assembling the cake

The day before the reception, fix the pillars and attach bought decorations (such as artificial flowers, silver horseshoes or a tiny vase). Then do a 'test run' of the assembling.

Always check the pillars stand level on each tier before fixing in position. (Otherwise the cake will topple.) Use a spirit level to do this – the little bubble should register in the centre of the marked off division in the glass tube. If it does not, rub down the pillars with fine emery board until they stand level.

If using a cake-stand, place the bottom tier on the stand. Then smear the base of each of the first four pillars with a little royal icing. Fix these in the positions you decided when planning the design. Next, fix remaining pillars in place, then gently and carefully lower the middle tier on to the pillars. Never push it down or the bottom pillars will sink into the cake. Assemble the top tier.

When you have checked all is well, carefully dismantle the tiers, leaving the pillars fixed in place.

Leave the final assembly to the last moment practicable on the big day. Assemble the cake in the place where it will be served, as it is impossible to transport safely.

Cutting The Cake

Wedding cakes are cut into flat slices – not into triangular wedges. When the bride and groom have ceremonially 'cut the cake', it is removed 'behind scenes' for the job to be finished. Dismantle the tiers and slice the bottom layer first. Cut the cake in half, then cut each half across into long slices, about 2 cm [¾ in] thick. Cut each slice into pieces about 7.5 cm [3 in] long. Cut the middle layer of cake next, in exactly the same way. The top tier may be sliced or kept intact for a future celebration.

You can expect about 118 small portions from the bottom layer of our cake; 38 portions from the middle layer and 20 portions from the top layer.

1 Cover cakes with almond paste, leave for 4-5 days to dry. Make 2.3 kg [5 lb] royal icing; colour apricot with some pink and yellow food colouring. Store 24 hours.

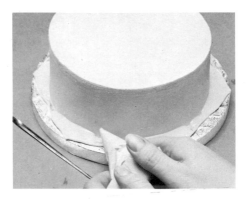

5 Pipe outline of run outs, using the drawn line as a guide. Then cut tip of greaseproof bag and flood run outs with the thinned icing. Leave for 1-2 days to dry.

6 Make 900 g [2 lb] royal icing; store for 24 hours. Prick out design of spiral scrolls on cake tops, using respective greaseproof templates.

10 Using a no. 3 plain writing tube, pipe pyramids of graduated dots on either side of the ribbon on each cake. Store for 2 weeks.

11 Carefully prick out position of pillars. Place bottom tier on cake-stand. Check each pillar stands level with a spirit level.

230

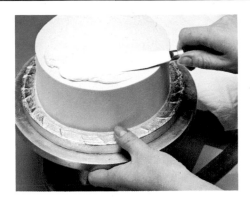

2 Give each cake three coats flat icing. Allow each coat to dry for 24 hours before adding the next. (Reserve and store remaining icing.) Leave cakes to dry for 1 week.

3 Begin board run outs. Pin template on board and lightly draw round outline. Repeat for other two boards, using their respective templates.

4 Place 6 tablespoons reserved icing in a bag fitted with a no. 3 writing tube. Thin remaining icing with egg white and place in a greaseproof icing bag.

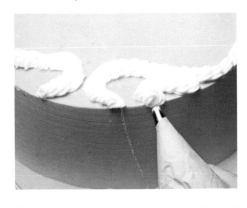

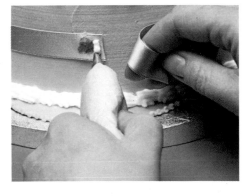

7 Pipe shell border around edge of cake tops to start of scroll design. Pipe scrolls. Use a small star nozzle for top and middle tiers; large star nozzle for bottom cake.

8 Pipe shell border around cake bases, using appropriate nozzles. Finish with a star at front of each cake. Pipe dots along edge of run outs with a no. 3 writing tube.

9 Prick out design for the sides. Next, secure ribbon around the centre of top and middle tiers with a little icing. Secure two ribbons around bottom tier.

12 Smear bases of tallest pillars with icing and place in planned positions. Next, pipe dots around the base of each pillar to decorate and neaten.

13 Fix remaining pillars on middle tier in the same way and pipe dots around the bases. Lower middle tier on to the bottom pillars.

14 Fill vase with a spray of flowers, then secure in centre of top tier with icing. Pipe dots around base. Carefully place top tier on middle pillars.

SPECIAL GÉNOISE CAKES

Génoise cakes are made for those special occasions which call for a gâteau rather than just a cake. Deliciously light and buttery, they are rightly famed as the queen of sponges!

Génoise, the French butter cake is the classic of sponge cakes and the most versatile cake of all. It can be used for petits fours, French madeleines, cheesecakes and many other unforgettably delicious gâteaux and desserts. Its special qualities of richness and lightness are made by adding melted butter to a whisked sponge mixture, described on pages 164-179. Génoise needs a slightly longer baking time than fatless sponges and will keep better because of the amount of fat included in the mixture.

There are two basic génoise recipes: génoise fine and génoise commune. As the name suggests, the fine is richer than the commune. They are both made with the same quantities of eggs and sugar, but génoise commune uses half the quantity of butter and more flour to compensate. The methods for making both types are exactly the same.

A third member of the génoise family is called biscuit fin au beurre. This is made by a slightly different method. Whereas in a génoise fine or commune, whole eggs and sugar are whisked together over hot water, in biscuit fin au beurre, the yolks of the eggs are whisked with the sugar in a warm bowl and then the eggs whites are folded in with the flour before the butter is added. This cuts down the overall beating time by about half. When baked, the cake has a less fluffy texture then génoise fine or commune. It is used mostly for gâteaux that are to be iced, because it gives a firmer surface on which to spread an icing or frosting.

INGREDIENTS

Génoise contains eggs, sugar, flour and butter.

Eggs
These should always be medium-sized and used whole. The light texture that is associated with a génoise sponge is achieved by the raising properties of the whisked eggs. The eggs also give a good golden colour to the sponge.

Always use eggs at room temperature. Remove them from the refrigerator or larder at least one hour before they are required. If time is short and does not permit an hour's wait, then break the eggs into a basin and place the basin in a bowl of lukewarm water for 15 minutes.

Sugar
Only caster sugar is suitable; granulated sugar will not dissolve quickly enough and would result in a coarse, heavy texture.

Flour
A fine cake flour is the perfect choice but as this is not usually available use standard fine white plain flour. In the absence of fine cake flour add a little cornflour to the plain flour to produce a finer textured sponge. Use approximately 1 tablespoon per 75 g [3 oz] flour. Self-raising is unsuitable as all the necessary 'rise' comes from the whisked eggs.

Butter
Butter is the only suitable fat for a génoise. Do not be tempted to use

margarine; it has neither the fine flavour of butter, nor a suitable make up. It contains too much water which evaporates on melting, causing loss of volume and a heavy textured cake.

Always use unsalted butter. Melt it carefully so that it does not overheat or separate. Use when liquid but cool.

FLAVOURINGS

A basic génoise has a delicate buttery flavour that does not need any additional flavouring. There is no reason, however, why you should not experiment!

The traditional flavouring for a génoise is orange water. It is used in very small quantities, usually 1 teaspoon per four eggs, to impart only a slight hint of flavour. An alternative is finely grated orange or lemon zest, again in very small quantities, no more than 1 teaspoon per four eggs. Any more will result in a sticky cake.

A rather unusual, though traditional, method of flavouring is to place two small sweet rose or lemon verbena leaves on the base of the prepared cake tin before the cake mixture is poured in. This method adds just the correct amount of subtle flavouring to a plain génoise cake.

Chocolate: melted chocolate can be

Light génoise sponge makes a perfect special occasion gâteau decorated with peaches and almonds.

added to give a rich chocolate flavour. Use up to 75 g [3 oz] for the quantity of génoise given in the step-by-step recipe. Add it alternately with the butter and take special care to do this slowly to avoid any lumps of chocolate.

Alternatively use cocoa powder, substituting 15 g [½ oz] cocoa powder for the same weight of flour. Sift it with the flour before folding it in.

Nuts: ground nuts, up to 50 g [2 oz] for one basic quantity of génoise can be added for a rich texture. Ground almonds and hazelnuts are two of the most popular nuts for a génoise because they complement the buttery flavour of the sponge.

Spices: use only in very small quantities to complement the buttery flavour rather than override it. Never use more than ½ teaspoon of any of the following: ground cinnamon, mixed spice, nutmeg, cloves or ginger.

EQUIPMENT

Apart from cake tins, there is no special equipment for génoise sponges. The traditional tin to use has a rather unusual name – moule à manqué – which can be loosely translated as 'a foolproof mould'. This tin is round with sides slightly sloping outwards toward the rim; it is approximately 5 cm [2 in] deep. The cake when turned out has slightly sloping sides down which the icing runs quickly and easily. This makes for rather an unusual and attractive shape, particularly effective when iced.

Deep cake tins are seldom used because a génoise is a very light cake which could not support itself in a deep tin. Sandwich tins or alternatively the larger versions now being imported from France with a diameter of 25 cm [10 in] or more can be used as well as fancy moulds, individual cake tins and patty tins.

Small cakes called madeleines are a classic of the génoise type. These are baked in shallow, shell-shaped moulds which form a set in a single tin. They are available in a variety of sizes. When baked these resemble shells and are served upside-down to show off the shape. They are really the French equivalent of English sponge fingers.

Preparing cake tins

Brush the inside of the tin very lightly with melted butter and put aside until the butter is just on the point of setting and a cloudy film is visible.

Using a flour dredger or sieve, sift in a little flour. Shake the tin to make sure that a fine film of flour covers the tin and shake out any excess flour. Do take care not to overflour the tin or a hard crust will form on the outside of the cake which will cause the delicate sponge to crack when cut.

A whole selection of gâteaux can be made using génoise as the base.

GETTING ORGANIZED

Génoise mixtures must be prepared and baked immediately if they are to be light and buttery. Get organized before you start. Remove the eggs from the refrigerator to allow them to come to room temperature.

Heat the oven, allowing 10-15 minutes for it to reach the right temperature. Check that the oven shelf is positioned in the centre of the oven, unless of course you are using a fan-assisted oven.

Next check that you have all the necessary equipment to hand so that you do not have to stop halfway through to find essential equipment. Prepare the cake tins and have all the ingredients ready before you start.

MAKING GÉNOISE SPONGE

It is careful attention that is the secret of successful génoise. You need a light hand in the whisking and folding. The method for both génoise fine and génoise commune is identical.

Melting the butter

Dice the butter and put it in a small bowl over hot but not boiling water until it has just melted. Do not let it overheat. Turn off the heat – the warmth of the bowl will stop the butter resolidifying.

Sifting the flour

Sift together the flour and cornflour. This both ensures even distribution of the cornflour and introduces extra air, which helps the cake to rise.

Whisking

Place the eggs – usually in quantities of 4 medium-sized eggs to every 140 g [4½ oz] caster sugar – in a mixing bowl. Place the bowl over a saucepan of hot, but not boiling, water. A low heat under the saucepan provides just the right temperature, Whisk the eggs and sugar together so that they become completely amalgamated. If using a hand-held electric whisk this first mixing together can be done on a low speed.

Once the mixture is combined, continue whisking at a higher speed. The mixture gradually turns from a rich golden egg colour to a pale yellow. Continue whisking until it has doubled in size and resembles whipped thick cream and will just hold its own shape when the whisk is lifted.

If any mixture gathers around the side of the bowl, scrape this down with a spatula or it will set with the heat from the water and be unusable.

Cooling

As soon as the mixture has reached this stage it should be removed from the top of the saucepan and placed on

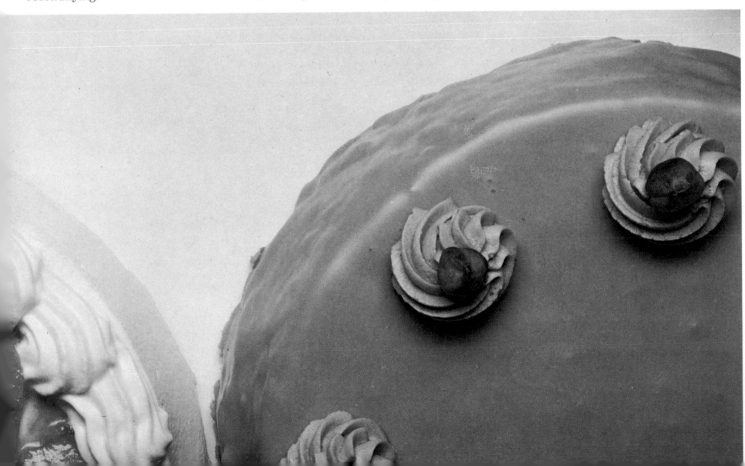

a steady surface to cool. A wooden board is ideal.

By now whisking will have introduced thousands of tiny air bubbles into the eggs and sugar. To save these bubbles and to help the mixture cool quickly, continue to whisk until the side of the bowl is no longer warm to the touch. This will take approximately 3 minutes.

Folding

The next step is to distribute the flour evenly into the whisked mixture. Sprinkle a little of the sifted flours over the surface of the mixture. Then, using a figure-of-eight action, cut the flour down into the bowl so that the flour slips gently off the side of the spoon.

Continue, adding a little flour at a time until all the flour has been added and there is no visible 'floury' look on the surface of the mix. Never be tempted to hurry this process along by beating, or stirring the flour in, because either of these will break down the precious air bubbles, so reducing the overall volume of the cake.

Adding the butter

Because the butter is added in a liquid rather than a solid form, extra care must be taken to make sure that it is completely mixed in. Add a spoonful of butter at a time and again use the folding figure-of-eight action. Take the spoon right to the base of the bowl before turning it, so that all the butter moves through the mixture. Never add more than a spoonful at a time and only add more when you are sure the previous spoonful has been completely mixed in.

If the mixture is over worked at this crucial stage it will liquefy and turn a greenish colour. The only thing to be done then is to throw it away and start again.

As soon as the flour and butter are safely folded in, pour the mixture straight into the cake tin. If a trace of butter appears on top of the mixture in the tin, it may be pressed in with a single stroke of a spoon. Bake at once.

BISCUIT FIN AU BEURRE

The method for baking biscuit fin au beurre is slightly different from the other two génoise sponges – and considerably quicker. The eggs are separated at the outset and the yolks are whisked with the sugar, in a warm bowl but not over heat, until they are thick and pale.

The volume and lightness comes from the egg whites, which are whisked separately until they form soft peaks. These are then folded into the sugar mixture, sifting in the flours at the same time, with the same important folding action used before. The butter is then quickly added at the end, in the same manner as before. The mixture must be baked at once.

BAKING TIMES

These vary according to the type of tin that is used but a génoise will usually take 25-30 minutes to bake. Bake in the centre of the oven unless the recipe states otherwise. Never be tempted to open the oven door once the cake is inside as a sudden rush of air into the hot oven can make the cake sink in the centre.

The génoise will be cooked to perfection when it is evenly risen, soft but firm to the touch and a rich golden brown colour. To test, insert a very fine skewer into the centre. When it is lifted out, it should be clean with no uncooked cake adhering to it. If the cake is not cooked, return to the oven and bake for another three minutes at a time until the cake is cooked.

BISCUIT FIN AU BEURRE

This type of génoise sponge is simpler to make than génoise fine or commune. Its firm surface makes it specially suitable for icing.

MAKES 20 CM [8 IN] CAKE
50 g [2 oz] unsalted butter
75 g [3 oz] plain flour
1 tablespoon cornflour
4 medium-sized eggs
140 g [4½ oz] caster sugar
pinch of salt

1 Heat the oven to 190° C [375° F] Gas 5. Prepare the cake tin by greasing, then sifting over flour.
2 Dice the butter and place in small bowl over a pan of hot water, until melted. Remove from heat.
3 Sift together the flours. Separate the eggs and put the yolks and sugar into a warm bowl. Whisk until thick.
4 Whisk the egg whites with a pinch of

MAKING A GÉNOISE SPONGE

There are two basic recipes for génoise sponge. The ingredients listed here are for génoise fine.

Génoise commune is made with less butter and so has a firmer surface. It is used mostly for gâteaux that are to be iced.

To make a génoise commune, use the quantities of eggs, cornflour and sugar listed here, but use 100g [4 oz] plain flour and only 50 g [2 oz] butter.

MAKES 20 CM [8 IN] CAKE
90 g [3½ oz] unsalted butter
75 g [3 oz] plain flour
1 tablespoon cornflour
4 medium-sized eggs
140 g [4½ oz] caster sugar

1 Heat the oven to 190° C [375° F] Gas 5. Prepare the moule à manqué by greasing, then flouring.

2 Dice the butter and place in a small bowl over a pan of hot water, until melted. Remove from heat.

3 Sift flours together. Place eggs and sugar in a bowl over a saucepan of hot but not boiling water.

4 Whisk eggs and sugar together until amalgamated. Use low speed if using an electric whisk.

5 Increase speed until mixture doubles in size and turns pale. Take off heat. Whisk until cool.

6 Sprinkle on a little flour. Fold in with a figure-of-eight action. Fold in all flour, in spoonfuls.

7 Fold in the butter a spoonful at a time, with the same action, until it is all incorporated.

8 Pour the mixture straight into the tin and bake in the centre of the oven for 25-30 minutes.

salt until they will form soft peaks.

5 Add a spoonful of egg white to the yolks, sift over a little flour and fold in.

6 Continue folding in egg white and flours together until all is used.

7 Quickly add the butter, a little at a time and fold it in. Pour into the tin and bake for 25-30 minutes.

IDEAS FOR SMALL CAKES

A génoise provides the perfect base for a selection of small tea-time cakes that any good cook would be proud of. Any of the three basic recipes for sponge given in this chapter can be used.

Make the sponge and bake in a Swiss roll tin. See pages 106-107 for instructions on cutting a large cake into individual cakes.

Because a génoise is a little special, then the decorations for a selection of small cakes also need to be special to be worthy of the sponge.

● Cut the cake into rounds and split each round of sponge in half, horizontally. Sandwich the cakes together with a circle of almond paste (page 196), cut to fit each cake exactly. Cover each cake entirely with coffee-flavoured butter icing (pages 14-16). Sprinkle toasted, nibbed (that is, blanched and chopped) almonds over the top and sides of each cake – press on gently with a palette knife if necessary. Sift icing sugar and cocoa together over each cake, then finish off with a large piped swirl of cream in the centre of each cake.

● Cut the cake into rounds, then cut each round into three layers. Sandwich the cakes back together again with chocolate-flavoured crème au beurre (pages 252-253) to which crushed ratafias or macaroon biscuits have been added. Spread a thin layer of chocolate crème au beurre to entirely cover the cakes. Lay plain chocolate curls in one direction over the top of each cake. Place a finger just above the cake and sift icing sugar on to the top of each cake. Remove your finger and a strip of the chocolate curls will remain plain.

● Cut the cake into squares and prick each cake with a fork. Drizzle over a little sweet sherry and allow it to soak into the cake. Cover each cake entirely with delicately piped swirls of cream, then sprinkle the cake with a few chopped pistachio nuts.

● Cut a large cake into diamond shapes and cut each diamond into two

Génoise sponge can be used for
all kinds of small fancy cakes and
decorated however you like.

layers. Sandwich each cake together again with vanilla-flavoured butter-cream icing (pages 14-16). Spread the sides of each cake with butter-cream and dip into grated chocolate to coat. Place two cubes of crystallized pineapple and a cherry on the top of each cake and cover with white glacé icing (page 14).

● Home-made sponge fingers are excellent for lining charlotte moulds, making the base for a trifle or for serving with ice-creams and sorbets. To make sponge fingers (or biscuits à cuiller as they are called), make up the basic quantity of biscuit fin au beurre and heat the oven. Using a plain piping nozzle, pipe the sponge on to a baking sheet as you would for éclairs. Bake for 20-25 minutes until firm.

GÉNOISE MADELEINES

These traditional little French cakes are baked in special tins that resemble oval shells with fluted tops to them. The mixture is a particularly buttery génoise fine. Serve them upside down so that the flutes are shown to their best advantage.

MAKES 12 CAKES
2 medium-sized eggs
50 g [2 oz] caster sugar
50 g [2 oz] plain flour
50 g [2 oz] butter, melted
icing sugar

1 Heat the oven to 190° C [375° F] Gas 5. Make the cake mixture following the step-by-step instructions for génoise sponge.
2 Divide the mixture between a 12-hole madeleine tin and bake for 10 minutes or until well risen and golden brown.
3 Leave the cakes to cool in tin for 2 minutes and invert on to a wire rack to cool.
4 Dredge cakes with sieved icing sugar and place on a serving plate.

Variations
● Omit dredging the cakes in icing sugar and instead dip the narrow end of each cake into melted plain chocolate and then quickly into toasted chopped nuts. Place cakes on a wire cooling rack until the chocolate has set.
● Carefully split the cakes horizontally and

sandwich together with whipped thick cream and halved strawberries.

● Carefully split the cakes horizontally and spread the bottom cake with strawberry preserve and the top layer with vanilla-flavoured crème au beurre (pages 252-253). Sandwich the two cakes together and dredge with icing sugar.

● Brush the top of each cake with sieved apricot jam and carefully dip in toasted shredded coconut.

MOUSSELINE AUX NOISETTES

This delicious nut cake is a variation on biscuit fin au beurre, but ground nuts are added before the egg white. It is finished with crème au beurre of the same flavour.

This cake is particularly suitable for serving with morning coffee.

MAKES 23 CM [9 IN] CAKE
40 g [1½ oz] unsalted butter
65 g [2½ oz] plain flour
75 g [3 oz] toasted hazelnuts
4 medium-sized eggs
140 g [4½ oz] caster sugar
pinch of salt

For the decoration:
275 ml [½ pt] vanilla-flavoured crème au beurre ménagère (pages 252-253)
25 g [1 oz] toasted hazelnuts

For special glacè icing:
100 g [4 oz] icing sugar
few drops of vanilla essence

1 Heat the oven to 190° C [375° F] Gas 5. Prepare a 23 cm [9 in] cake tin by greasing and sifting over flour.
2 Melt the butter in a small bowl over a pan of hot water and set aside. Sift the flour. Grind the 75 g [3 oz] nuts.
3 Separate the eggs and put the yolks and sugar into a warm bowl. Whisk until thick. Fold in half the ground nuts.
4 Whisk the egg whites with a pinch of salt until they form soft peaks.
5 Fold the egg whites and flour alternately by spoonfuls into the egg yolks.
6 Fold in the melted butter quickly and turn into the prepared tin.
7 Bake for 25-30 minutes until done. Leave in the tin for 3 minutes, then invert on to a wire rack to cool.
8 Make the crème au beurre ménagère as instructed on pages 252-

253 and stir in the remaining ground nuts.
9 Sandwich the cold cake together using one third of crème au beurre. Put one third into a piping bag with a star nozzle.
10 Make the special glacè icing by sifting the icing sugar into a bowl and adding 1 tablespoon warm water. Stand the bowl on a trivet in a pan one-third full of hot water. Stir the icing for several minutes until it becomes smooth and glossy, like thick cream. Flavour with a few drops of vanilla essence. Use it immediately.
11 Pour the glacè icing into the middle of the cake to cover just the top. Leave to set.
12 Use the remaining crème au beurre to coat the sides of the cake. Chop nuts for decoration and press into the sides of the cake. Pipe a shell border round the top of the cake.

TEA-TIME SPONGE

A simple sponge sandwiched together with jam and butter cream, with a sprinkle of icing sugar is a classic, ideal for Sunday tea.

MAKES 20 CM [8 IN] CAKE
3 medium-sized eggs
100 g [4 oz] caster sugar
75 g [3 oz] plain flour
1 tablespoon cornflour
75 g [3 oz] unsalted butter, melted
few drops of vanilla essence
275 ml [½ pt] vanilla-flavoured crème au beurre ménagère (see pages 252-253)
50 g [2 oz] strawberry jam
icing sugar

1 Heat the oven and make the cake following the step-by-step instructions for génoise sponge. Pour the cake mixture into a 20 cm [8 in] round cake tin and bake for about 25-30 minutes until well risen and golden brown.
2 Leave cake to cool in tin for 3 minutes, then invert on to a wire rack to cool.
3 Make crème au beurre ménagère while the cake is cooling, and chill it. Cut the cake into two, horizontally, and spread the crème over the bottom half.
4 Spread the strawberry jam on to the cut side of the top layer of sponge and sandwich the two cakes together.
5 Sift a little icing sugar on to the top of the cake to serve.

ALMOND MOCHA GATEAU

This almond and coffee cake makes a perfect accompaniment to mid-morning coffee. It should be baked in a 20 cm [8 in] moule à manqué tin.

Make the cake and the crème au beurre à l'anglaise the day before you intend to serve it because the cake will improve in texture and be easier to cut. Making this crème au beurre can be time-consuming so it is best prepared in advance ready for the final assembly. Store, covered, in the refrigerator.

MAKES 20 CM [8 IN] CAKE

4 medium-sized eggs
140 g [4½ oz] caster sugar
75 g [3 oz] plain flour
1 tablespoon cornflour
90 g [3 oz] unsalted butter

For the crème anglaise:
275 ml [½ pt] milk
2 egg yolks
25 g [1 oz] caster sugar
2-3 drops vanilla essence

For the filling and decorations:
75 g [3 oz] blanched almonds, split and
    shredded
225 g [8 oz] unsalted butter
2 tablespoons strong, black coffee
about 25 g [1 oz] icing sugar

1 Heat the oven to 190° C [375° F] Gas 5 and prepare a 20 cm [8 in] moule à manqué tin and make and bake the cake, following the step-by-step instructions for génoise sponge.
2 Leave cake to cool in tin for 3 minutes, then invert on to a wire cooling rack.
3 Spread almonds for the decoration on to a baking tray and toast under a moderate grill until golden. Cool.
4 To make crème anglaise, heat the milk until the edge of the milk bubbles. Remove from heat.
5 Put the yolks and sugar into a large bowl and beat until thick and creamy. Pour the hot milk in a thin stream on to the egg mixture, stirring with a wooden spoon. Stir in the vanilla essence.
6 Strain through a sieve into the top of a double boiler and cook over hot water, stirring constantly, for about 15 minutes until thick.
7 Make crème au beurre à l'anglaise

following the instructions on page 252. Add the coffee at step 3. Chill crème until ready to use.
8 Cut the cake into two horizontally and place the bottom half on a serving plate.
9 Spread a quarter of the crème over the bottom layer, then top with the remaining layer.
10 Put 4 tablespoons crème in a small paper piping bag fitted with a medium star tube and reserve.
11 Use the remaining crème au beurre to entirely cover the sides and top of the cake.
12 Sprinkle the shredded almonds over the cake to cover the top and sides. Sift enough icing sugar over the cake to cover it lightly.
13 Pipe eight swirls of crème au beurre around the outer edge of the cake and serve.

CHOCOLATE GÂTEAU

MAKES 6-8 SLICES

For the chocolate genoise:
75 g [3 oz] plain flour
15 g [½ oz] cocoa powder
15 g [½ oz] cornflour
3 large eggs
75 g [3 oz] caster sugar
50 g [2 oz] butter, melted

For the chocolate filling:
3 large eggs, separated
25 g [1 oz] caster sugar
175 g [6 oz] bitter chocolate
25 g [1 oz] butter
1 tablespoon grated orange zest
salt

To assemble the cake:
2 tablespoons cointreau
1 tablespoon grated orange zest
275 ml [10 fl oz] thick cream, whipped
50 g [2 oz] chocolate vermicelli

1 Heat the oven to 180°C [350°F] Gas 4. Brush a loose-bottomed 20 cm [8 in] cake tin with melted butter. Line the base with greaseproof paper and brush with more butter. Lightly coat the tin with flour.
2 To make the chocolate genoise sponge, sift the flour, cocoa powder and cornflour together three times.
3 In another bowl, combine the eggs and sugar. Set the bowl over a pan of simmering water and whisk until thick,

light and lukewarm (about 10 minutes).

4 Remove the bowl from the heat and continue whisking until the mixture has cooled and leaves a trail when the beaters are lifted. Resift the flour mixture over the surface. Fold in with a large metal spoon.

5 Cool the melted butter and fold it in quickly. Pour the mixture into the tin. Bake for 25-30 minutes. When cooked, turn on to a wire rack. Peel off the lining paper and leave to cool.

6 Meanwhile, make the chocolate filling, in a bowl beat the egg yolks with the caster sugar until creamy and lemon-coloured.

7 Melt the chocolate with the butter in a bowl over hot water.

8 Add the melted chocolate and finely grated orange zest to the beaten egg yolk mixture. Fold in with a metal spoon until it is smoothly blended. The next step must be done quickly or the chocolate will set too hard to work.

9 Add a pinch of salt to the egg whites and whisk until stiff but not dry. Fold the egg whites into the chocolate mixture thoroughly. Spoon the mixture into a 575 ml [1 pt] dish, chill and set.

10 Cut the cake into two layers. Sprinkle the insides of the layers with cointreau and spread the bottom layer with the chilled chocolate filling. Replace the top layer. Fold the grated orange zest into the whipped cream and cover the entire cake with a thin layer, leaving enough cream mixture to decorate the top. Coat the sides of the cake with chocolate vermicelli. Using a star nozzle, pipe a cream border around the top outer edge of the cake.

This Chocolate gâteau is glamorous enough for a dinner-party dessert or a celebration tea-time.

PEACH AND BRANDY GÂTEAU

The basis of this gâteau is a génoise sponge made from flour with a little cornflour added to give lightness and a firm texture. Try to make the sponge cakes the day you will eat them as this type of cake gets stale quickly.

MAKES 6-8 SLICES
3 medium-sized eggs
100 g [4 oz] caster sugar
75 g [3 oz] plain flour
15 g [½ oz] cornflour
40 g [1½ oz] melted butter

For the topping:
825 g [1lb 13 oz] canned white peach halves
6 tablespoons brandy
250 ml [9 fl oz] thick cream
1 teaspoon arrowroot
25-50 g [1-2 oz] flaked almonds, toasted

1 Line the base of two 18 cm [7 in] sandwich tins with a circle of greaseproof paper and brush with melted butter. Dust the tins with a little flour. Heat the oven to 190°C [375°F] Gas 5.
2 Put the eggs and sugar into a fairly large bowl, or the bowl of an electric mixer, and whisk vigorously until the mixture is very thick and light. If you are doing this by hand it is helpful to stand the bowl over a saucepan half-filled with very hot water. Whisk for 5 minutes with an electric whisk, 10-15 minutes by hand.
3 Sift the flour and cornflour into the egg mixture. Use a metal spoon to fold the flour in with an over and under, figure-of-eight movement, being careful not to beat the mixture too much. Add the melted butter in the same way, folding until blended.
4 Pour the mixture into the prepared tins, gently levelling the tops. Bake for 20 minutes, until the sponges are well risen and firm to a light touch. Remove from the oven, cool slightly in the tins, then turn out on to wire racks and leave until cold.
5 About an hour before serving drain the peaches, reserving 150 ml [¼ pt] of the juice. Reserve seven perfect peach halves and chop the rest. Whisk the cream with 2 tablespoons of the brandy until it will stand in soft peaks. Sprinkle the remaining brandy over the sponge circles.

6 Put one sponge on to a serving dish and spread with a quarter of the cream and the chopped peaches. Spread with another quarter of the cream, then top with the second sponge. Arrange the peach halves over the cake.
7 Mix together the arrowroot and reserved juice in a small saucepan. Heat gently, stirring all the time, until the mixture thickens. Glaze the peaches, then cool.
8 Spread a little of the remaining cream round the sides of the cake and press the almonds into the cream, using a palette knife. Put the remaining cream into a piping bag fitted with a large star nozzle and pipe rosettes of cream on top of the gâteau. Decorate each one with almonds.
9 Keep the gâteau in the refrigerator or a cool place until ready to serve.

CELESTINES

These elegant little petit fours are traditionally made in barquette moulds but if you do not have these, round tins are equally suitable.

Use the candied peel that comes in caps for the decoration as this is much juicier than the ready chopped kind. If you are unable to obtain this, use flaked almonds.

MAKES 18
100 g [4 oz] plain flour
pinch of salt
50 g [2 oz] butter
50 g [2 oz] caster sugar
2 medium-sized egg yolks
2 drops vanilla essence
6 tablespoons apricot jam
basic quantity of biscuit fin au beurre

For the icing:
100 g [4 oz] icing sugar
juice of 1 orange
1 tablespoon water
1 cap candied orange peel

1 Sift flour and salt onto a working surface. Make a well in centre.
2 Cut the butter into dice. Put the butter, sugar, yolks and vanilla in the well.
3 First work the ingredients in centre together, then pull in the flour to make a dough. Chill for 1 hour.
4 Heat the oven to 190° C [375° F] Gas 5. Roll out the pastry and use to line 18 small barquette moulds.
5 Put a little apricot jam in the bot-

tom of each mould. Fill each mould with the sponge mixture and smooth the top.

6 Bake in the centre of the oven for 25 minutes, until the sponge is firm and well-risen. Turn out on to a wire rack and cool.

7 Sieve the remaining apricot jam into a small heavy-based pan. Melt over low heat to make the glaze.

8 Sieve the icing sugar into a small heavy-based pan. Add the orange juice and 1 tablespoon cold water.

9 Stir the mixture over low heat until the liquid is absorbed and the icing is smooth and glossy. Remove from heat.

10 Scoop out the sugar from the candied peel cap and reserve for another use. Chop peel roughly.

11 Brush the top of each little cake with apricot glaze. Spread a little orange icing over and scatter with candied orange peel.

ROSE WEDDING CAKE

A deep tin is used for this cake as a double quantity is being cooked. Bought fondant can be used for the decoration if wished.

MAKES 24-28 SLICES

3 quantities génoise commune (page 237)
225g [8 oz] fondant (page 101)
few drops of pink and yellow food
    colouring
300 g [10 oz] granulated sugar
700 g [1½ lb] unsalted butter
1.4 kg [3 lb] icing sugar, sifted
4 medium-sized egg yolks
about ½ teaspoon lemon essence
225 g [8 oz] apricot jam
ribbon and lace ribbon
34 bought silver leaves

1 Up to 5 days before the wedding, heat the oven to 170°C [325°F] Gas 3. Grease a 23 cm [9 in] deep square tin, line with greaseproof paper and grease again. Dust with flour and shake out the excess. Make up a double quantity of sponge mixture and pour into the tin. Bake for 1½ hours. Cool 15 minutes, then turn out onto a wire rack and remove the paper. Increase the heat to 180°C [350°F] Gas 4.

2 Prepare an 18 cm [7 in] deep square tin. Make up a single quantity of sponge and bake for 45 minutes. Let both cakes get cold, then keep for 24 hours in an airtight container to set.

3 Tint the fondant pale pink, then divide in three. Using pink and yellow, tint one batch a little darker and the

This American-style Rose wedding cake is made from génoise sponge rather than the traditional rich fruit cake. Iced with butter-cream, it can be completed within a week.

other darker still. Make eight medium-sized and two small pale roses; two large, four medium and 10 small roses in the middle shade; and eight medium and 20 small dark roses. Leave to dry.

4 To make the butter-cream, gently dissolve the sugar in 150 ml [5 fl oz] water in a saucepan, then boil until the syrup reaches 108°C [220°F] on a sugar thermometer.

5 In a large bowl, beat the butter until light and fluffy. Gradually beat in half the icing sugar, a little at a time, then add the egg yolks, one at a time. Beat in the remaining icing sugar alternating with the syrup to give a smooth spreading consistency.

6 Add 2 drops of pink colouring, plus lemon essence to taste.

7 Split cakes horizontally and sandwich together using about one-third of the butter-cream. (Reserve the rest, covered.) Centre the larger cake, bottom upwards, on a silver cake board 30 cm [12 in] square.

8 Place the smaller cake, bottom upwards, on a thin cake card 15-18 cm [6-7 in] square (or cut a cardboard template to fit).

9 Sieve the apricot jam into a small pan, add 4 tablespoons water and bring to the boil. Cool slightly, then brush glaze over both cakes. Leave the cakes to settle for 30-60 minutes.

10 Coat both cakes quickly with butter-cream, smoothing with a palette knife dipped in hot water. Leave to set for 2-6 hours.

11 Tint the remaining butter-cream to match the middle-shaded roses with pink and yellow colouring. Place the butter-cream in a piping bag fitted with a medium-sized star nozzle.

12 Centre the small cake (with its board) on top of the large cake.

13 Pipe a neat row of shells as shown. Arrange the ribbons, flowers and leaves as shown. The cake will keep for 2-3 days in a cool, dry place.

BLACK FOREST CHERRY CAKE

To make the chocolate caraque for the top and sides of this cake, melt 100 g [4 oz] chocolate, then pour in a thin layer on to a cold work surface. Leave to set. Holding a large knife with both hands, push the blade across the surface to shave off long chocolate curls.

MAKES 23 CM [9 IN] CAKE
8 medium-sized eggs
275 g [10 oz] caster sugar
25 g [1 oz] cocoa powder
175 g [6 oz] plain flour
200 g [7 oz] butter, melted

For the filling and decoration:
850 g [1 lb 14 oz] canned black cherries, stoned
2 teaspoons arrowroot
850 ml [1 ½ pt] thick cream
6 tablespoons kirsch
100g [4 oz] chocolate caraque curls

Black Forest cherry cake is the most famous chocolate cake in the world. It comes from the Black Forest area of Bavaria in southern Germany. Flavoured with kirsch and decorated with whipped cream and black cherries, it makes a glorious centrepiece, suitable for any special celebration. For children use orange juice instead of liqueur.

1 Heat the oven to 180° C [350° F] Gas 4. Make two cakes following the step-by-step instructions, substituting cocoa powder for cornflour.

2 Bake the cakes for 25-30 minutes until well risen. Leave in tins for 3 minutes, then invert on to wire racks to cool.

3 Drain syrup from cherries. Reserve 12 well-shaped cherries and 150 ml [¼ pt] syrup. Halve the remaining cherries.

4 Blend arrowroot with 2 tablespoons reserved syrup. Boil with rest of reserved syrup. Stir until clear. Add cherries. Cool.

5 Cut each cake in two horizontally. Put base on serving dish. Drizzle 1 tablespoon kirsch over each of the four layers.

6 Whisk cream to form soft peaks. Stir in 2 tablespoons kirsch. Put a little cream in a piping bag with a big star nozzle. Reserve.

7 Spread base and two layers of cake with half the cream. Add a third of the halved cherries and syrup to each of the layers.

8 Place the undecorated layer on top. Spread remaining cream over the top and sides of the cake to cover completely.

9 Pipe rosettes with the reserved cream. Decorate with the whole cherries. Stick caraque on sides and centre of cake.

GLAMOROUS GÂTEAUX

Gâteaux are the aristocrats of all cakes. This chapter describes how to make a series of sensational creations, worthy of any Viennese patissier's trolley.

Gâteaux are cakes for special occasions, made with the best and freshest of ingredients and decorated with the utmost care. The word gâteau comes from the French 'gasteau' which means a delicate food. In Austria, Hungary and Poland, they are called 'torte'.

Over the centuries almost every European country has evolved its own special gâteau – Germany the Black Forest cherry cake (pages 246-247), Hungary the doboz torte (pages 250-251), Austria the famous Sachertorte (pages 258-259), and France too many delicious gâteaux to mention individually.

Many gâteaux have a sponge base, but there are types with rich pastry cases, like gâteau de St-Honoré. There are also the splendid creations made from meringue, such as the almond and apricot meringue cake on page 254.

The name 'torte' comes from the Latin 'torta', which means a round. Tortes can be made from pastry or sponge, generally of many layers rather than the two-layered sponge of the Victorian sandwich. They have little resemblance to 'tarts' though the names have the same origin.

Not all layered cakes are made by slicing one or two layers of cake horizontally; many are made from a whisked sponge mixture which is spread and baked on several baking sheets for assembly later.

Making gâteaux or torten at home requires first and foremost, time, and secondly patience. However, by planning carefully, and preparing fillings, toppings and decorations in advance, you can enjoy making a stunning and impressive cake in easy stages.

FILLINGS AND DECORATIONS

Fresh Chantilly cream (page 254) or the different types of crème au beurre (pages 252-253) are the traditional fillings for gâteaux. These fillings are usually flavoured to complement the base and decoration. Fruit and preserves are often added too.

Doboz torte is a bit special; the topping is made from a sheet of caramel. This has be to scored while still warm, otherwise it would be impossible to slice and the attempt to cut it would produce a squashy disaster, because the inside layers would collapse under the pressure of the knife.

Well thought out decorations and care when matching flavours of sponges to fillings and toppings, are especially important when considerable time and expense are involved. These are cakes which really show off what you can do in the baking line.

GETTING ORGANIZED

Many gâteaux are made from sponge bases. You can use either the whisked sponge (pages 164-173) or the creamed sponge (pages 68-77) or the sophisticated gènoise (pages 232-240).

Whatever the gâteau, begin by reading through the recipe thoroughly. Make sure that you have every ingredient and piece of equipment gathered before you start.

Some gâteaux are made from as many as six layers of sponge. These require additional baking equipment if they are baked simultaneously (assuming your oven is large enough). Either borrow the extra equipment required or bake in relays. These sponge torte rounds do not require

baking tins, as the whisked sponge is spread carefully on to baking sheets covered with non-stick silicone paper. These will be either 19 or 20 cm [7½ or 8 in] in diameter.

SWISS CHOCOLATE CREAM CAKE

It is a very common sight any afternoon to see people sitting in the Swiss cafés enjoying slices of rich, creamy chocolate cake, and drinking cups of coffee topped with cream.

MAKES 6–8 SLICES

100 g [4 oz] dark chocolate
175 ml [6 fl oz] milk
75 g [3 oz] butter
100 g [4 oz] caster sugar
1 medium-sized egg yolk
275 ml [10 fl oz] whipping cream
24 sponge fingers

For the decoration:
150 ml [5 fl oz] thick cream, whipped
    (optional)
chopped nuts or grated chocolate

1 Line an oblong cake tin, 20 × 10 cm [8 × 4 in] or a 1.5 L [3 pt] loaf tin with foil or thick greaseproof paper, leaving a good border each side to lift out the cake.

2 Grate the chocolate coarsely. Melt the chocolate in half the milk in a saucepan over low heat, removing it as soon as the chocolate is melted. Stir in the remainder of the milk and reserve.

3 Cream the butter and sugar together until they are light and creamy, beat in the egg yolk and then the chocolate mixture, and continue beating until the mixture is smooth. Whip the cream until it is thick.

4 Pour one-third of the chocolate mixture into the lined tin, cover with a layer of sponge fingers, then a third of the whipped cream. Repeat with the rest of the layers, finishing with whipped cream. Chill overnight.

5 When ready to serve, turn the cake out on to an oblong serving plate, cover the sides with the remainder of the whipped cream and decorate with some chopped nuts or grated chocolate. If wished, you can pipe a border of whipped cream around the edge of the cake.

Swiss chocolate cream cake

249

MAKING SIX CAKE LAYERS FOR A TORTE

1 Position the shelves in the centre and just above the centre of the oven. Heat the oven to 190° C [375° F] Gas 5. Assemble ingredients.

2 Grease and fully line three baking sheets with non-stick silicone paper. Mark 19 or 20 cm [7½ or 8 in] circles on to the paper.

3 Make the whisked sponge mixture. Spoon on to the centre of each marked circle, then spread out first batch with the spoon.

4 Bake, in two batches, for 8-10 minutes, until set and golden. Leave to cool on sheets for 2 minutes then transfer to wire racks. Trim.

5 When sponge layers are cold, divide the measured quantity of cream or crème au beurre equally between five discs, reserving the top.

6 Carefully pile up the layers. For a doboz torte, coat the top layer with caramel. Decorate top and sides of cake following individual recipe.

DOBOZ TORTE

This many layered drum gâteau from Hungary is sandwiched together with rich chocolate filling and it is characterized by a shiny caramel top. It is sandwiched together with crème au beurre meringuée, a light butter-cream using meringue cuite. Allow yourself plenty of time when making this cake as it takes time and patience to make, but the results are more than worth the effort.

SERVES 8-10
150 g [5 oz] plain flour
4 large eggs
175 g [6 oz] caster sugar
few drops of vanilla essence

For the caramel topping:
175 g [6 oz] caster sugar

For the crème au beurre meringuée:
125 g [4 oz] plain chocolate
175 g [6 oz] icing sugar
3 medium-sized egg whites
pinch of salt
225 g [8 oz] butter, softened

For the decoration:
75 g [3 oz] chocolate vermicelli

1 Position the oven shelves, heat the oven and prepare equipment following

MAKING CARAMEL TOPPING

1 Place 175 g [6 oz] caster sugar in a small heavy-based saucepan over a low heat until it has dissolved.

steps 1 and 2 of the step-by-step instructions on the left.

2 To make the sponge, first sift the flour. Place the 4 large eggs, 175 g [6 oz] caster sugar and the vanilla essence in a mixing bowl. Place the bowl over a saucepan of hot but not boiling water.

3 Whisk the eggs and sugar together until the mixture has doubled in size, is thick and foamy and leaves a trail when the whisk is lifted.

4 Remove the bowl from the saucepan and place on a wooden board. Whisk until the mixture cools. Fold the flour into the egg mixture, a little at a time until it has all been incorporated.

5 Spread out the mixture on the prepared baking sheets, and bake, following steps 3 and 4 of the step-by-step instructions. Cool and select the best round for the top.

6 Make the caramel, coat the top layer, mark and leave to cool as shown in step-by-steps below.

7 To make the crème au beurre meringuée, first break the chocolate into small pieces and put it in a bowl over a saucepan of hot but not boiling water. Reserve when melted.

8 Make the meringue cuite, using the quantities given in the recipe and the method given on page 254.

9 Place the softened butter in a bowl and beat well with a wooden spoon. Add the meringue mixture a little at a

The glamorous Hungarian gâteau Doboz torte

time, beating well after each addition. Stir in the melted chocolate. Allow to go cold.

10 Spread a generous half of crème over five rounds as shown in steps 5 and 6. Place the caramel-covered layer on top.

11 Place 2 tablespoons of crème in a small piping bag fitted with a star tube and reserve.

12 Spread the sides of the cake with the rest of the crème. Coat the sides of the cake with the chocolate vermicelli by patting them on with a palette knife.

13 Pipe a swirl of the crème in the centre of the caramel, where the sections meet.

2 Without stirring, bring to the boil slowly and boil steadily until the mixture turns a rich brown colour.

3 Stand a cake layer on a greased wire rack. Pour the caramel over. Spread quickly with an oiled knife.

4 With the knife, mark the top of the caramel into eight sections before it has set. Trim and leave to cool.

MAKING CRÈME AU BEURRE A L'ANGLAISE

MAKES ABOUT 575ML [1PT]
225 g [8 oz] unsalted butter
275 ml [½ pt] crème anglaise (see page 242), tepid
2 tablespoons liqueur or strong, black coffee or 50 g [2 oz] melted chocolate

1 Place softened butter in a bowl and beat with a wooden spoon until it is smooth in texture.

175 g [6 oz] unsalted butter
50 g [2 oz] icing sugar
2 medium-sized egg yolks
2 tablespoon liqueur or 1 teaspoon vanilla essence

2 Add the tepid custard to the butter, a little at a time, beating well with a wooden spoon or a hand-held electric whisk.

3 Add required flavouring (liqueur, coffee or chocolate) by beating it into the mixture until it has all been incorporated.

MAKES ABOUT 575 ML [1 PT]
225 g [8 oz] unsalted butter
1 medium-sized egg plus 3 egg yolks or 5 egg yolks
125g [4 oz] granulated sugar
2 tablespoons black coffee or liqueur

4 Using a wooden spoon, beat the mixture for 3 minutes, until thick and creamy. Chill in the refrigerator until ready to use.

OR if using hand-held electric whisk, beat for 1-2 minutes. Chill in the refrigerator until ready to use.

4 Pour the syrup into the egg mixture in a steady stream, beating continually by hand or hand-held electric whisk.

MAKING CREME AU BEURRE MÉNAGÈRE

1 Place soft butter in a warm bowl and beat with a wooden spoon or a hand-held electric whisk until the butter is smooth.

2 Sift the icing sugar and add to the butter and lightly beaten egg yolks and flavouring (liqueur or vanilla essence).

3 Beat all the ingredients together for 2 minutes using a hand-held electric whisk or beat 5 minutes with a wooden spoon. Chill.

MAKING CRÈME AU BEURRE AU SUCRE CUIT

1 Place the butter in a warmed bowl and beat until smooth. Place the eggs in another bowl and beat together.

2 Place the sugar in a heavy-based saucepan with 3 tablespoons water and bring to the boil.

3 Boil the sugar syrup until the soft ball stage is reached, 110-116°C [230-240°F]. Remove the pan from heat.

5 Place the syrup and egg mixture in the top of a double boiler. Beat for 4-5 minutes until doubled in volume.

6 Place the top of the double boiler in a bowl of cold water and beat the mixture until tepid.

7 Beat the egg mixture, a spoonful at a time in to the creamed butter. Finally beat in the flavouring.

MAKING MERINGUE CUITE

250 g [9 oz] icing sugar
4 egg whites
pinch of salt
3 drops vanilla essence

1 Sift the icing sugar. Select a pan into which the bowl will fit, without touching tepid water at the bottom.

2 Place egg whites in the bowl. Add a pinch of salt and stir. Whisk until foamy but not until stiff and standing in peaks.

3 Whisk in the icing sugar 1 teaspoon at a time. Whisk in the vanilla essence. Place the pan over low heat and position bowl.

4 Whisk the meringue mixture over heat until it thickens. This will take about 8 minutes. When ready, it will leave a thick trail.

CARAMEL CHIPS

Quick to make, these coloured sugar chips make an attractive decoration for an exotic cake, such as the splendid gâteau Valencia on page 258. The sugar is cooked to the caramel stage. After cooking it is smashed into chips. These will keep in a completely dry, airtight jar but eventually become sticky, so use them up quickly.

Sprinkle chips over gâteaux immediately before serving, otherwise the caramel will melt in the juices.

DECORATES 1 GATEAU
100 g [4 oz] caster sugar
3 tablespoons water

1 Put the sugar and water in a small heavy-based saucepan over a low heat. Dissolve, stirring all the time.

2 With a dampened pastry brush, brush down sides of pan to prevent crystals forming.
3 Boil until the sugar turns a golden brown and reaches the 'caramel' stage, 150-180°C [302-356°F].
4 Meanwhile line a baking tray with foil and grease it well.
5 Pour the caramel on to the baking tray in a thin layer. Allow it to become completely cold.
6 Remove the foil from the tray and break the caramel in half. Remove one piece of caramel, fold half the foil over the caramel and thump it with a rolling pin to break the caramel into chips. Continue in this way until all the caramel is broken up.

CHANTILLY CREAM

This sweet cream, faintly flavoured with vanilla, is a French classic. It can be soft whipped and served as an accompaniment to dessert cakes, or whipped to the second stage of thickness for filling cakes and piping.

MAKES 275 ML [½ pt]
275 ml [½ pt] thick cream
25 g [1 oz] caster sugar
¼ teaspoon vanilla essence

1 Pour the cream into a cool mixing bowl. Whip the cream slowly until it takes on a matt finish and is slightly thickened.
2 To serve as an accompaniment to a dessert, fold in sugar and vanilla essence and turn the cream into a small bowl.
3 For piping or for use as a filling, whip the cream more slowly, until it is just thick enough to leave a trail and will slowly drop off the whisk.
4 Carefully spoon cream into a piping bag until half full and use for piping on to cakes.

ALMOND AND APRICOT MERINGUE CAKE

This almond-flavoured cake is filled with apricot-flavoured cream and served with an apricot sauce. Dried apricots are used and they are soaked overnight in strained tea for extra flavour.

SERVES 6

100 g [4 oz] dried apricots
400 ml [¾ pt] lukewarm strained tea
pinch of salt
4 egg whites
250 g [9 oz] caster sugar
1 teaspoon malt vinegar
2-3 drops vanilla essence
75 g [3 oz] ground almonds
50 g [2 oz] granulated sugar
150 ml [¼ pt] water
2 teaspoons lemon juice
400 ml [¾ pt] whipped cream
25 g [1 oz] plain, dark chocolate

1 Soak the apricots in the strained tea for 8 hours or overnight. Set aside when soaked. Prepare two 20 cm [8 in] loose-bottomed cake tins or two baking sheets. Heat the oven to 140°C [275°F] Gas 1.

2 Add salt to the egg whites, stir and whisk until they will stand in stiff peaks.

3 Add the caster sugar to the egg whites 1 teaspoon at a time, making sure all the sugar is dissolved before adding more.

4 Whisk the vinegar and vanilla essence into the meringue mixture. With a figure-of-eight movement, lightly fold in the almonds.

5 Divide the mixture equally between the baking tins or spread into two 20 cm [8 in] rounds on the baking sheets. Cook for 50 minutes.

6 Meanwhile, turn the apricots and their soaking liquid into a heavy-based pan and simmer gently for 15 minutes.

7 While the apricots are cooking, place the granulated sugar in a heavy-based pan. Add the water and the lemon juice. Stir, bring to the boil and boil for 2 minutes. Remove from heat.

8 Purée the apricots in a liquidizer or by pushing through a sieve.

9 Mix one-third of the apricot purée with two-thirds of the whipped cream. Set aside. Stir remaining apricot purée into cold lemon syrup to make a sauce.

10 When the meringue cakes are cooked, gently peel away the paper from the base and cool.

11 Sandwich the cakes with apricot-flavoured cream. Pipe remaining cream on the top. Grate the chocolate and sprinkle a little on the cream whirls. Serve apricot sauce separately.

Almond and apricot meringue cake

GÂTEAU MEXICAIN

A must for chocolate lovers in the family, this gâteau has a hint of coffee which points up the rich chocolate flavour. The cake is characterized by the delicate cobweb pattern. Make the royal icing 24 hours ahead.

SERVES 8-10

65 g [2½ oz] plain flour
15 g [½ oz] cocoa powder
1 tablespoon cornflour
75 g [3 oz] butter
1 teaspoon instant coffee powder
3 medium-sized eggs
125 g [4 oz] caster sugar
75 g [3 oz] apricot jam
1 teaspoon lemon juice

For the filling:
275 ml [½ pt] chocolate ganache
  (see page 150)

For the chocolate icing:
50 g [2 oz] caster sugar
150 ml [¼ pt] water
175 g [6 oz] plain chocolate

For the royal icing:
225 g [8 oz] icing sugar
1 large egg white
1 teaspoon lemon juice
½ teaspoon glycerine

1 Twenty-four hours before needed, make the royal icing with the quantities given in the recipe, and using the method on page 200.
2 Position shelf in centre of oven and heat oven to 190°C [375°F] Gas 5.
3 Brush two 18 cm [7 in] sandwich tins with melted fat or oil and line the bases with circles of greaseproof paper. Grease the paper.
4 Sift the plain flour, cocoa powder and cornflour together and reserve. Place the butter in a small saucepan over low heat until it has melted. Stir the coffee powder into the butter.
5 Place the eggs and caster sugar in a mixing bowl and place the bowl over a saucepan of hot, but not boiling water. Whisk until the mixture has doubled in size, is thick and foamy and leaves a trail when the whisk is lifted.
6 Remove the bowl from the saucepan and place on a steady surface. Gently fold in the flour mixture, a little at a time, until it is completely incorporated.
7 Using a metal spoon, fold in the melted butter and coffee.

8 Divide the mixture between the two prepared tins and bake in the centre of the oven for 35-40 minutes until well risen and springy to the touch.
9 Invert the cakes on to a wire rack, remove the greaseproof paper and leave to cool.
10 Sieve the apricot jam into a small saucepan and stir in the lemon juice. Stir over a moderate heat until the jam has melted. Reserve.
11 Split each cake into two horizontally as shown on page 13. Divide the chocolate ganache between three layers, spreading it out evenly, then pile up the layers.
12 Brush the top and sides of the cake with apricot glaze and leave to set.
13 To make the chocolate icing; dissolve the sugar in the water and bring to the boil. Boil for 2 minutes without stirring.
14 Meanwhile, melt the chocolate over hot water. Add the sugar syrup and stir in. Use the icing to coat the top and sides of the cake. Leave to set hard.
15 Put the royal icing into a piping bag fitted with a plain writing nozzle.
16 Pipe parallel lines across the cake about 2.5 cm [1 in] apart. Pipe a line round the rim of the cake and pipe vertical lines down the sides. Now draw the blade of a knife through the lines, first in one direction, then in the other, to make a feather decoration, as shown on page 96. Leave to set.

Variations

• Make a gâteau forestière – a chocolate cake covered with woodland 'mushrooms'. Make a chocolate sponge cake as described. For the filling and cake coating make a mocha crème au beurre à l'anglaise, using 275 ml [½ pt] crème anglaise (page 242), 225 g [8 oz] unsalted butter and flavouring it with 2 tablespoons strong coffee; follow the instructions on page 252. Use the crème to sandwich together the cake and to cover top and sides entirely. Reserve 4 tablespoons for sticking together the champignons.

To make meringue champignons, make meringue cuite, using 50 g [2 oz] icing sugar and 1 egg white and following the instructions on page 254. Put in an icing bag with plain tube. Line a baking sheet with oiled greaseproof paper, then pipe on 12 rounds, 2 cm [¾ in] across, for the mushroom tops. Pipe 12 much smaller rounds for the stalks, pulling the tube and working upwards. Bake in an oven heated

to 110°C [225°F] Gas ¼ for 1-2 hours. Peel away the paper and cool.

Stick the meringues together in pairs to make mushrooms. Use the reserved cream and trim the bottom stalks where necessary to fit. Dust cocoa powder lightly over the tops. Arrange the mushrooms at equal intervals round the cake and group the remaining mushrooms in the middle. Use 50 g [2 oz] chocolate to make caraque. Scatter a few scrolls between the mushrooms to resemble leaves etc on the forest floor. Stick the rest round the sides.

• For a gâteau Suchard, make a chocolate sponge as described. Sandwich the two layers together with one-third of the mocha crème au beurre à l'anglaise described in the recipe for gâteau forestière. Put 4 tablespoons into a piping bag with a fine writing tube. Use the rest to cover the top and sides of the cake. Put the cake in the freezer for 1 hour to firm the crème au beurre. Make double the quantity of chocolate marquise given on page 260 and put the cake on a wire rack over a tray. Coat the cake several times, until covered. Pipe a series of the letter S across the top and sides.

• For a gâteau Valencia, make the sponge using 75 g [3 oz] plain flour and substituting the zest of one orange for the coffee and cocoa powders.

When cold, split each cake in half horizontally. Drizzle 2 tablespoons Grand Marnier over the middle two layers. Make an apricot purée: cook 125 g [4 oz] dried apricots in 75 ml [3 fl oz] water and 2 teaspoons lemon juice. Purée in a blender, then stir in 2 tablespoons coarse marmalade. Spread over one of the soaked layers.

Whip 575 ml [1 pt] thick cream. Put one-third of the cream in a bowl and add 1 tablespoon caster sugar and 2 drops of vanilla essence. Stir in gently, then spread half of this over one firm layer of cake. Top with the purée-covered layer and then put on the second soaked layer. Spread over the other half of the vanilla-flavoured cream and put on the cake top.

Reserve just over half the remaining cream in a piping bag with a medium-sized star nozzle. Use the rest of the cream to cover the sides of the cake. Carefully roll the sides in 100 g [4 oz] nibbed almonds.

Melt 5 tablespoons orange jelly marmalade with 1 tablespoon lemon juice. Paint a thick layer over the top of the cake. Allow to set.

Pipe a lattice of cream over the top of the cake and then a border of shells round the top. To finish, scatter fine caramel chips (page 254) over the lattice.

SACHERTORTE

Created over 150 years ago in Vienna by Franz Sacher, a pastry cook to the statesman Prince Metternich, sachertorte soon became the centre of a storm of controversy. When another Viennese baker called Demel, made a similar cake, Sacher began a lawsuit. Both bakers claimed that their gâteau was the original. The difference between the two was that Sacher's cake had a layer of apricot jam through the centre of the cake as well as on the top. Demel's cake had only an outer coating of apricot jam. The court settled the matter by saying that the cakes were equally good and both rated the name of Sachertorte.

SERVES 10
75 g [3 oz] plain flour
100 g [4 oz] butter
175 g [6 oz] caster sugar
6 egg yolks
175 g [6 oz] plain chocolate
few drops of vanilla essence
8 egg whites
pinch of salt

For the glaze:
175 g [6 oz] apricot jam
2 teaspoons lemon juice

For the icing and decoration:
100 g [4 oz] caster sugar
3 tablespoons cocoa powder
few drops of vanilla essence
75 g [3 oz] butter
50 g [2 oz] milk chocolate

1 Position shelf in centre of oven and heat oven to 180°C [350°F] Gas 4.
2 Grease and fully line a 23 cm [9 in] deep, round cake tin and grease again. Sift the flour.
3 Beat the butter in a mixing bowl until soft and light.
4 Add the sugar to the butter and cream together until light and fluffy. Scrape down the spoon and sides of the bowl with a spatula.
5 Add the egg yolks one at a time, beating well after each addition.
6 Break the chocolate into pieces and place in a bowl over a saucepan of hot, but not boiling, water. Stir until melted. Cool slightly.
7 Add the melted chocolate to the creamed mixture, beating well. Beat in the vanilla.
8 Fold in the sifted flour until it is completely incorporated.

9 Place the egg whites in a large, clean, grease-free bowl and whisk them with a pinch of salt until stiff. Fold into the creamed mixture using a metal spoon.

10 Put the mixture into the prepared tin and smooth over the surface with a palette knife. Bake for 1 hour until it is evenly risen and springs back when pressed lightly.

11 Allow the cake to cool in the tin for 5 minutes before turning out on to a wire rack. Leave to cool completely.

12 Cut the cake horizontally into two equal layers, as shown on page 13, then place the bottom layer on a wire rack.

13 Sieve the apricot jam into a small saucepan and stir in the lemon juice. Melt the jam over a low heat, then allow to cool slightly.

14 Spread half the jam over the bottom layer of cake, then put the remaining layer on top. Brush the top and sides of the cake with the remaining jam.

15 To make the icing, put the sugar, cocoa and 2 tablespoons water into a saucepan. Blend well, then bring to the boil. Boil for 1 minute, stirring all the time.

16 Off the heat, beat in the vanilla essence. Add the butter in small pieces and beat in. Allow to cool slightly.

17 Coat the top and sides of the cake with icing; leave to set.

18 Melt the milk chocolate. Put in a piping bag with a fine writing nozzle.

19 Pipe 'Sacher' across the top of the cake. Do not cut the cake before it is set.

Gâteau Suchard has a hidden inner layer of mocha cream beneath the rich chocolate icing that coats the cake.

CHOCOLATE MARQUISE

This special chocolate icing will elevate an ordinary chocolate cake into something special. This icing must be used as soon as it is ready otherwise it will spoil – stir in the rum and vanilla essence and use to ice and fill the cake immediately. Give the icing time to set before serving.

Gâteau forestiere is topped with mushrooms made from meringue.

ICES A 20 CM [8 IN] CAKE

100 g [4 oz] plain dark dessert chocolate
3 tablespoons cold coffee
15 g [½ oz] unsalted butter
1 teaspoon dark rum or brandy
few drops of vanilla essence

1 Melt the chocolate in a bowl over hot water. Stir in the coffee. Cube the butter. Add to chocolate; stir until melted. Remove from heat.
2 Stir in the rum and vanilla.

CHOCOLATE ALMOND GÂTEAU

MAKES 8 SLICES

100 g [4 oz] plain flour
25 g [1 oz] cocoa powder
4 medium-sized eggs
175 g [6 oz] caster sugar
100 g [4 oz] apricot jam
1 tablespoon water
75 g [3 oz] nibbed almonds
75 g [3 oz] plain dessert chocolate,
    coarsely grated

For the mocha filling:
175 g [6 oz] margarine or butter
350 g [12 oz] icing sugar
4 teaspoons cocoa powder
4 teaspoons coffee and chicory essence
1 teaspoon dark rum

1 Heat the oven to 190°C [375°F] Gas 5. Grease a deep 20 cm [8 in] round cake tin, then line the base with greaseproof paper. Grease the paper.
2 Sift the flour and cocoa powder into a bowl and set it aside.
3 Put the eggs and sugar into a large heatproof bowl. Set the bowl over a saucepan half-full of gently simmering water. Using a rotary whisk or hand-held electric whisk, beat until the mixture is thick enough to hold the trail of the whisk for about 3 seconds.

4 Remove the bowl from the pan and beat the mixture for a few minutes more until it is cool. Using a large metal spoon, fold in the sifted flour, one-third at a time.
5 Pour mixture into the prepared tin and spread evenly by gently tilting the tin. Bake immediately for 35-45 minutes until the surface is golden in colour and springy to the touch. Leave to stand in the tin for 1-2 seconds, then turn out on to a wire rack to cool.
6 Meanwhile, make the filling, beat the margarine until creamy, then gradually beat in the icing sugar. Dissolve the cocoa in the coffee and chicory essence, then beat into the filling with the rum.
7 Heat the apricot jam with the water until runny, then pass through a sieve. Return to the pan and boil until it thickens to a coating consistency, then allow it to cool.
8 Using a long serrated knife, cut the cooled cake horizontally into three layers. Use half the filling to sandwich the layers together.
9 Brush the apricot jam around sides of cake, then press almonds on to the sides using a palette knife. Transfer to a serving plate.
10 Put the remaining filling in a piping bag fitted with 12 mm [½ in] star nozzle and pipe a border around the top edge. Sprinkle chocolate over the top of the cake.

This impressive Chocolate almond gâteau has a covering of almonds and grated chocolate.

GÂTEAU AUX PETITS CORNETS

This most sophisticated cake is flavoured with Brazil nuts and decorated with little cornets.

SERVES 8
150 g [5 oz] plain flour
4 large eggs
175 g [6 oz] caster sugar
few drops of vanilla essence
50 g [2 oz] Brazil nuts, ground

For the cornets:
40 g [1½ oz] butter, melted
1 large egg white
50 g [2 oz] caster sugar
25 g [1 oz] plain flour
1 drop vanilla essence

For the crème au beurre ménagère:
500 g [1 lb 2 oz] unsalted butter
175 g [6 oz] icing sugar
6 medium-sized egg yolks
4 tablespoons Grand Marnier
zest of 1 large orange

For the decoration:
100 g [4 oz] granulated sugar
125 ml [4 fl oz] water
100 g [4 oz] Brazil nuts

1 Make the decoration: heat the sugar and water in a small, heavy-based pan over low heat until sugar has melted. Increase heat to high and cook for about 4 minutes until deep golden caramel. Add the nuts and pour on to an oiled baking sheet. Leave until cold.
2 Position shelves in centre and just above centre of oven and heat oven to 190°C [375°F] Gas 5.
3 Grease and fully-line three baking sheets with non-stick silicone paper. Mark two 19 cm [7½ in] circles on each prepared baking sheet.
4 Sift the flour and reserve. Place the eggs, caster sugar and vanilla in a bowl over a pan of hot water.
5 Whisk the eggs, sugar and vanilla together until the mixture has doubled in size and is foamy.
6 Remove the bowl from the saucepan and place on a steady surface. Whisk until the mixture is cool.
7 Mix flour with the ground nuts and

Valencia cake hides an orange flavour under a cream lattice; Gâteau aux petits cornets is made with Brazil nuts.

fold into the egg mixture until they have both been thoroughly incorporated into the mixture.

8 Divide the mixture between the prepared baking sheets, spreading the mixture evenly to fill the 19 cm [7½ in] marked circles. Bake for 8-10 minutes or until golden brown.

9 Leave to cool on baking sheets for 2 minutes then carefully transfer to wire racks to cool. Lower oven temperature to 180°C [350°F] Gas 4.

10 For the cornets, brush a baking sheet with one third of the butter.

11 Place the egg white in a bowl, add the sugar and, using a balloon whisk, beat until smooth. Sift the flour.

12 Gradually add the flour and remaining butter, beating well after each addition. Beat in the vanilla essence.

13 On the prepared baking sheet, spacing them well apart, make two circles. Use 2 teaspoons mixture for each and spread it out. Bake 7-8 minutes, until golden brown round the edges.

14 Leave the cooked circles on the tray for a few seconds, then remove with a palette knife. Mould the biscuits in turn round the end of a kitchen knife into little horn shapes; the closed ends should be quite tight, the open ends about 2.5 cm [1 in] across.

15 Use the rest of the mixture to make more horns; you need eight perfect horns.

16 Make the crème au beurre ménagère, following the instructions on pages 252-253. Chill until firm.

17 Put 4 tablespoons crème au beurre ménagère in a piping bag with a medium-sized star nozzle and reserve.

18 Use half of the crème au beurre ménagère to cover five cake layers, then sandwich the cake together. Use the remaining crème to cover the top and sides of the cake entirely.

19 Chop the caramel-coated Brazil nuts and cover the sides of the cake with the chopped nuts and caramel, flicking the nuts up.

20 Lay the cornets on the cake with the narrow end almost touching the centre. Sprinkle chopped nuts on the cream between the cornets.

21 With the reserved crème, pipe a star in the mouth of each cornet and one in the centre of the cake.

HANDY HINT

Making gâteaux aux petits cornets

Gâteau aux petits cornets is quite a complicated cake to make, so it is a good idea to coat the Brazil nuts the day before. You can make the crème au beurre too, but do not put in the liqueur. Beat the crème au beurre well before using; it may separate if made beforehand.

BÛCHE DE NOËL

Bûche de Noël is the traditional cake with which the French celebrate Christmas.

MAKES 10 SLICES

65 g [2½ oz] plain flour
40 g [1½ oz] cocoa powder
1 teaspoon instant coffee powder
4 medium-sized eggs
100 g [4 oz] caster sugar
1-2 drops vanilla essence
100 g [4 oz] unsalted butter, melted
caster sugar, for dredging

For the filling:
2 egg yolks
50 g [2 oz] icing sugar, sifted
150 g [5 oz] unsalted butter, softened
100 g [4 oz] canned sweetened chestnut
    purée, drained
1 tablespoon dark rum

For the frosting:
50 g [2 oz] dark chocolate
50 g [2 oz] unsalted butter
350 g [12 oz] icing sugar, sifted
pinch of salt
1 tablespoon instant coffee
    powder
3 tablespoons single cream

The chocolate sponge may be filled with plain whipped cream, or chestnut or chocolate cream. Glaze the sponge if liked with warm, sieved apricot jam, to help the frosting adhere more firmly. The French like to serve the *bûche* decorated with little meringue mushrooms, but you may of course use your favourite Christmas cake decorations, or serve the cake plain, with a little icing sugar sprinkled over the frosting.

1 Heat the oven to 230°C [450°F] Gas 8.

2 Lightly grease a 36 × 25 [14 × 10 in] Swiss roll tin. Cut out greaseproof paper 4 cm [1½ in] larger than tin; line tin. Brush with a little of the melted butter.

3 Sift the flour, cocoa and coffee powders together two or three times on to a plate and set aside.

4 Put the eggs and sugar in a bowl that will fit snugly over a large saucepan one-quarter filled with barely simmering water. (The bowl must not touch the water in the pan or the mixture will cook and overheat.) Using a balloon whisk or hand-held electric beater, whisk the mixture over very gentle heat until pale and creamy and increased in volume.

5 Hold up the whisk and let a little mixture drop back into the bowl. When it forms a ribbon trail that will hold on the surface for 5 seconds, remove from heat. Continue whisking until the mixture has cooled and increased in volume two or three times. Beat in the vanilla essence.

6 Sift about one-third of the flour and cocoa mixture across the surface of the egg mixture then, using a large metal spoon, fold it in lightly in a figure-of-eight motion. Never stir when folding in: cut down with the edge of the spoon held at right angles to the surface. Lift the spoon high into the air between each figure-of-eight movement, to incorporate air. Rotate the bowl as you work to make sure all the mixture is evenly incorporated. Gently pour over one-third of the cooled melted butter and fold it in. Repeat twice more with the remaining flour and cocoa mixture and melted butter.

7 Pour the mixture into the prepared Swiss roll tin and with a rubber spatula very lightly ease the mixture into the corners; lightly smooth the surface. Rap the tin sharply on the work surface once, to break any air bubbles.

8 Place the tin on a baking sheet. (Chocolate cakes burn very easily: the baking sheet gives extra protection, but watch the cake carefully towards end of specified baking time.) Bake for about 10 minutes until cake is well risen and browned, and springy to the touch.

9 Meanwhile, lay a clean tea-towel on the work surface and cover with a large sheet of greasproof paper. Dredge the paper with caster sugar.

10 Turn the baked sponge on to the

DECORATING THE LOG

1 Trim one end of the log straight and cut the other at an angle.

2 Pipe uneven lines of frosting down the log to look like bark.

paper and carefully peel off the baking paper.

11 Trim the edges of the sponge neatly with a sharp knife and make a shallow cut along one short side, 12 mm [½ in] from the edge. Carefully roll the sponge up from this short side. The cake crisps as it cools: it must be rolled while still hot. Place the roll on a wire rack, join side down, and cover with a slightly damp clean tea-towel. Leave to cool for 30 minutes.

12 Meanwhile, make the filling, put all the filling ingredients, except the rum, in a bowl, and beat with a wooden spoon or hand-held electric beater until smooth. Add rum, cover and chill in the refrigerator until the cake is ready for filling.

13 To make the frosting, heat the chocolate and butter in a saucepan over very gentle heat until just melted; remove the pan from the heat, add half the icing sugar, the salt and the coffee and beat until smooth with a wooden spoon or hand-held electric beater. Fold in the remaining sugar and the cream.

14 Unroll the chocolate sponge and spread the chestnut filling evenly over the surface, taking it right up to the edges. Re-roll firmly. Trim one end straight and cut the other at an angle, to look like a log (see Steps).

15 Fill a piping bag fitted with a star nozzle with the frosting, and pipe uneven lines of frosting, close together down the length of the cake. Pipe small irregularities in two or three places to look like bark (see Steps). Smooth or pipe the frosting over each end of the log to finish.

This clever concoction of cake and cream is sure to impress; it's time consuming to make but well worth the effort.

STRAWBERRY BASKET

Piping cream in a novel way produces the basket look for this sensational fruit gâteau.

SERVES 8-10

4 large eggs
175 g [6 oz] caster sugar
1 teaspoon almond essence
150 g [5 oz] plain flour
50 g [2 oz] ground almonds

For the filling and decoration:
125 g [4 oz] white chocolate
25 g [1 oz] butter
50 g [2 oz] plain chocolate
450 g [1 lb] strawberries, hulled
65 ml [2½ fl oz] sweet sherry
25 g [1 oz] caster sugar
575 ml [1 pt] thick cream
575 ml [1 pt] crème au beurre au sucre cuite (pages 252-253) flavoured with ½ teaspoon vanilla essence

1 Position oven shelves to centre and just above centre and heat oven to 190°C [375°F] Gas 5.
2 Grease and fully line three baking sheets with non-stick silicone paper. Mark two 19 cm [7½ in] circles on each prepared baking sheet.
3 Place the eggs, sugar and almond essence in a mixing bowl. Place the bowl over a saucepan of hot, but not boiling, water. Whisk together until the mixture has doubled in size, is thick

circle of cake. When the chocolate is just on the verge of setting, cut the circle in half to make two semi-circles. Reserve these to make the basket lid.

9 Melt the plain chocolate, then pour into a piping bag with a plain tube. Pipe the chocolate on to a sheet of greaseproof paper in the outline of a leaf, as shown in the steps on pages 204-205. Pipe a delicate lattice of chocolate in the centre of each leaf outline and leave to set.

10 Reserve half the strawberries and cut the remainder into quarters. Sprinkle the cut strawberries with the sherry and caster sugar, toss to coat them.

11 Whip the thick cream until stiff. Then stir in the cut strawberries. Divide the strawberry cream mixture equally between the five layers and pile up the layers.

12 Use a little of the crème au beurre to coat the sides of the cake to make a flattish surface.

13 Prepare two greaseproof piping bags. Put a plain writing nozzle into the bottom of one and a ribbon nozzle into the second.

14 Prepare a third nylon bag with a star nozzle. Put into it 8 tablespoons of crème; reserve.

15 Put a little crème into the bag with the plain nozzle. Pipe straight lines across the half circles to form the lid; pipe at right angles to the cut and 2 cm [¾ in] apart.

16 Put a little crème into the bag with the ribbon nozzle. Starting at one vertical line, pipe over the next vertical and stop at the one beyond. Repeat along the row. In the succeeding line, shift along one vertical, so that the exposed vertical in one row is covered in the next (see picture).

17 Refill both bags as necessary and pipe the crème in the same basket design on the sides of the cake.

18 Using reserved bag with a star tube, pipe a shell design around the outer edge of the top.

19 Place the reserved strawberries on the cream-covered top layer working from the outer line of shells towards the centre. Leave a column in the centre bare.

20 Place the basket lids on the cake tilted like wings so the straight edges touch the cake centre, and pipe a line of shells down the central join. Chill the gâteau.

21 Carefully ease each chocolate leaf from its base and use to decorate cake.

and foamy and leaves a trail when the whisk is lifted.

4 Remove the bowl from the saucepan and whisk until cool. Sift the flour and fold into the egg mixture a little at a time. Fold in almonds.

5 Divide the mixture between the prepared baking sheets, spreading the mixture to fill marked circles. Bake for 8-10 minutes.

6 Leave to cool on baking sheets for 2 minutes then carefully transfer to a wire rack to cool.

7 Break up the white chocolate. Place with butter in a bowl over a saucepan of hot water.

8 Place the best circle of cake on a wooden board and pour over the melted chocolate. Spread with a palette knife to completely cover the

FRENCH MERINGUE GÂTEAU

SERVES 6

6 large eggs, separated
175 g [6 oz] granulated sugar
2 tablespoons water
grated zest of 1 lemon
75 g [3 oz] plain flour
2 tablespoons cornflour
pinch of salt
440 g 15½ oz] canned halved apricots, drained

For the filling:
440 g [15½ oz] canned halved apricots, drained
4 tablespoons marmalade

For the meringue:
4 large egg whites
8 tablespoons caster sugar

1 Heat the oven to 180°C [350°F] Gas 4. Grease two 23 cm [9 in] sandwich tins with butter. Line the bases with buttered greaseproof paper and dust with flour, shaking out the excess.
2 Choose a large bowl which will fit over a saucepan. Put the egg yolks and sugar, water and the lemon zest in the bowl. Set it over barely simmering water and whisk with a hand-held electric mixer until pale, light and fluffy. The mixture should leave a trail when the beaters are lifted.

3 Off the heat sift the flour, cornflour and salt over the whisked mixture. Fold in with a large metal spoon.
4 Whisk the egg whites until stiff but not dry and fold gently into the cake mixture. Divide the mixture between the two tins and bake for 30-35 minutes or until golden. When pressed lightly with a finger, the cake should spring back. Turn out the cakes on to wire racks to cool. Cover with a clean cloth and leave for 1 day.
5 Heat the oven to 220°C [425°F] Gas 7. For the filling, blend the well drained apricots until smooth or purée with a vegetable mill. Pour into a bowl, add the marmalade and mix well.
6 Cut each cake horizontally into two layers. Sandwich three layers with apricot mixture and put the plain layer on top. Cover a baking sheet with foil, oil it lightly and place the cake on it.
7 In a bowl, whisk the egg whites until stiff. Add the sugar gradually and continue to whisk until the meringue stands in stiff peaks. Mask the cake with the meringue, using a palette knife to spread it evenly. Bake for 10-15 minutes or until the meringue is lightly golden and set.
8 To decorate, slice the remaining canned apricots thinly. Arrange an overlapping circle of slices round the top edge of the cake. Serve immediately, while the meringue is still warm.

This French meringue-covered gâteau should be served as soon as it is decorated while the meringue is still warm.

STRAWBERRY AND ALMOND GÂTEAU

MAKES 8-10 SLICES

4 large egg whites
250 g [9 oz] caster sugar
½ teaspoon vanilla essence
1 teaspoon malt vinegar
100 g [4 oz] ground almonds

For the filling and icing:
150 ml [¼ pt] whipping cream
3-4 drops vanilla essence
250 g [9 oz] strawberries
100 g [4 oz] icing sugar
1½ teaspoons instant coffee powder
4-5 teaspoons warm water
25 g [1 oz] ground almonds, toasted

1 Heat the oven to 180°C [350°F] Gas 4. Grease two 4 cm [1½ in] deep, 20 cm [8 in] round sandwich tins and line bases with foil or non-stick vegetable parchment paper.

2 In a clean, dry large bowl, whisk egg whites until standing in stiff peaks. Whisk in sugar, 1 tablespoon at a time, then whisk in vanilla essence and vinegar. Fold in the almonds.

3 Divide mixture equally between prepared tins and level each surface. Bake for 15 minutes, then lower heat to 170°C [325°F] Gas 3 and bake for 25 minutes more.

4 Cool the meringues for 2-3 minutes, then run a palette knife around the sides to loosen and carefully turn out of tins. Peel off the lining paper then leave meringues on a wire rack to cool completely.

5 To make filling, whip cream and vanilla until standing in soft peaks. Put half the cream into a piping bag fitted with a large star nozzle and reserve. Spread remaining cream over one meringue. Reserve a few strawberries; hull and slice the rest and arrange over cream. Place remaining meringue on top.

6 Sift icing sugar and coffee powder into a bowl, then stir in enough water to give a coating consistency. Pour icing over gâteau and allow to run down the sides. Sprinkle ground almonds around top edge, then decorate with piped cream and reserved berries.

Variation

Use sliced bananas, sprinkled with lemon juice, instead of strawberries.

ITALIAN WALNUT GATEAU

A beautiful fluffy coating of American frosting gives this walnut cake a party air.

SERVES 8

4 medium-sized eggs
140 g [4½ oz] caster sugar
65 g [2½ oz] plain flour
1 tablespoon cornflour
90 g [3½ oz] butter
50 g [2 oz] walnuts, finely chopped.

For the filling and topping:
275 ml [½ pt] crème au beurre ménagère (pages 252-253)
25 g [1 oz] walnuts, chopped
2 tablespoons strong black coffee
450 g [1 lb] granulated sugar
8 tablespoons water
2 medium-sized egg whites

pinch of cream of tartar
2 drops vanilla essence
8 walnut halves

1 Heat the oven to 190°C [375°F] Gas 5. Line and grease two 20 cm [8 in] cake tins. Grease the paper.

2 Make the cake following the step-by-step to génoise on page 237, folding in the nuts with the flour in step 6. Bake as directed; cool in the tins for 3 minutes then invert on to a wire rack to cool.

3 Meanwhile mix the crème au beurre with the nuts and coffee.

4 Split each cake layer into two. Spread three layers with crème and pile up. Top with the plain layer.

5 Make the American frosting with the quantities given in the recipe and following the steps on pages 286-287.

6 Quickly pile the frosting on to the top of the cake, then spread over the sides of the cake to cover. Decorate with walnut halves and leave to set for 30 minutes.

Layers of meringue sandwiched together with cream and fresh strawberries bring a touch of summer to any meal.

BLACK AND WHITE CHOCOLATE GÂTEAU

Chocoholics will drool over this mouthwatering creation – it's deliciously different and makes a perfect special occasion dessert.

Red wine is the secret ingredient in these moist, rich chocolate cake layers and they are sandwiched with jam and cream round a melt-in-the-mouth meringue centre. It is then smothered in more cream, decorated with pretty dark and white chocolate curls and dusted with icing sugar.

SERVES 8-10

For the meringue layer:
2 large egg whites
pinch of salt
100 g [4 oz] caster sugar
½ teaspoon cornflour
½ teaspoon white vinegar

For the chocolate layer:
100 g [4 oz] butter, softened
250 g [9 oz] caster sugar
2 medium-sized egg yolks
1 large egg
225 g [8 oz] plain flour
1 teaspoon bicarbonate of soda
50 g [2 oz] cocoa powder
200 ml [8 fl oz] red wine

For filling and decorating:
225 g [8 oz] plain chocolate
225 g [8 oz] white chocolate
6 tablespoons raspberry jam
575 ml [1 pt] thick cream
icing sugar and cocoa powder

1 Heat the oven to 100°C [200°F] Gas ¼. Line a baking sheet with non-stick baking paper marked with a 23 cm [9 in] circle, and grease the paper lightly.

2 Using a hand held whisk, whisk the egg whites and salt until stiff. Reserve 1 tablespoon sugar and whisk the remaining sugar, a tablespoon at a time, into the egg whites, whisking well between each addition, until the meringue is stiff and glossy.

3 Add the cornflour to the reserved 1 tablespoon sugar and whisk into the meringue, then stir in the vinegar. The mixture should now stand in very stiff peaks, when the whisk is lifted.

4 Spread the meringue mixture on to the marked circle on the baking sheet, using the back of a large spoon to level the surface.

5 Bake the meringue for about 4 hours until completely dried out and crisp. Leave to cool, peel off the paper, then store in an air-tight tin until required. If left in a warm kitchen for any time the meringue will become 'tacky' and lose its crispness.

6 Heat the oven to 180°C [350°F] Gas 4. Brush the bases of two 24 cm [9½ in] sandwich tins with oil, line with greaseproof paper, then oil again.

7 To make the chocolate cake, cream the fat and half the sugar together in a mixing bowl until light and fluffy. Add the remaining sugar and beat well again. If you have a food processor, fit it with a metal blade, add the fat and sugar and process briefly until mixed. Add the eggs and dry ingredients and process for 30 seconds. Add the wine

and process for 15 seconds. Do not over-mix or it will become too soft.

8 If you are not using a processor, add the eggs to the mixing bowl, one at a time, beating well after each addition until thoroughly combined.

9 Sift together the flour, bicarbonate of soda and cocoa powder. Using a metal spoon or spatula, lightly fold the sifted flour mixture into the mixing bowl, alternately with the red wine, beginning and ending with flour.

10 Divide the mixture evenly between the tins and level the surfaces. Bake for about 25 minutes until the cakes feel just firm to the touch. Leave to cool slightly then turn out on to wire racks and leave until cold.

11 Meanwhile, make chocolate caraque for decorating. Break the plain dessert chocolate into pieces and melt in a bowl over simmering water (do not stir). Line a baking sheet with foil, grease it and pour the melted chocolate on to it. Using a metal palette knife, spread the chocolate out thinly and evenly until it is about 3 mm [⅛ in] thick and leave until completely set. Holding a long sharp knife at a slight angle, shave the chocolate into long curls.

12 Make white chocolate curls, use a swivel-type potato peeler and peel the white chocolate to form curls. Alternatively, scrape the reverse side of the chocolate bar using a small round-bladed knife to form curls. Chill until required.

13 To assemble the gâteau, split the two cakes in half horizontally and spread the base of each with raspberry jam. Sandwich each cake together again. Whip the cream stiffly (take care not to over-whip or the cream will become grainy looking). Place one chocolate cake on a serving plate. Spread with about a quarter of the whipped cream and top with the meringue layer. Spread meringue with another quarter of the cream and top with the second chocolate cake. If necessary, trim the edges of the meringue with a sharp knife level with the edges of the cakes.

14 Spread the remaining cream over the top and sides of the assembled gâteau. Lightly press the dark chocolate caraque on to the sides of the gâteau using a palette knife.

15 Arrange the white chocolate curls on the top of the cake and sprinkle with sieved icing sugar and cocoa powder. Chill until required.

HANDY HINTS

The meringue layer can be prepared in advance and stored in an airtight tin or container for up to 1 week.

Freeze the chocolate cake layers for up to 3 months. Defrost at room temperature for 2-3 hours before assembling.

RASBERRY ICE CREAM GÂTEAU

This delicious ice cream gâteau is made with a génoise sponge cut into three layers.

MAKES 8 SLICES

4 medium-sized eggs
140 g (4¼ oz) caster sugar
75 g (3 oz) plain flour
1 tablespoon cornflour
90 g (3¼ oz) unsalted butter, melted
75 g (3 oz) plain chocolate, melted
6 tablespoons sweet sherry
1 L (1¾ pt) vanilla flavour soft scoop ice cream
350 g (12 oz) raspberries
275 ml (½ pt) thick cream
25 g (1 oz) plain chocolate polka dots

1 Heat the oven to 190°C [375°F] Gas 5. Prepare a 20 cm [8 in] moule à manque by greasing, then flouring. Make and bake the cake following the instructions for génoise sponge on page 237, adding the melted chocolate with the butter.

2 Leave the cake to cool in the tin for 3 minutes, then invert the cake on to a wire cooling rack. When cold, cut the cake into three horizontally.

3 Lightly oil and line the sides of a 20 cm [8 in] loose-bottomed, deep cake tin.

4 Place one of the sponge layers inside the tin, trimming if necessary to fit. Sprinkle with 2 tablespoons sherry. Quickly spoon half the ice cream over and smooth the surface.

5 Reserve eight raspberries for decoration. Spread half the remaining raspberries over the ice cream and press in. Position the second layer of sponge on top; sprinkle with 2 tablespoons sherry and add a second layer of ice cream. Press in the remaining raspberries. Position the third sponge layer and sprinkle with the remaining sherry.

6 Cover with cling film and freeze for 1 hour.

7 To decorate the gâteau, whisk the cream until it forms soft peaks. Take the cake out of the freezer and slide it out of the tin. Remove the lining paper.

8 Spread two-thirds of the cream over the sides and top of the gâteau. Pipe the remaining cream around the top and decorate with the chocolate polka dots and reserved raspberries.

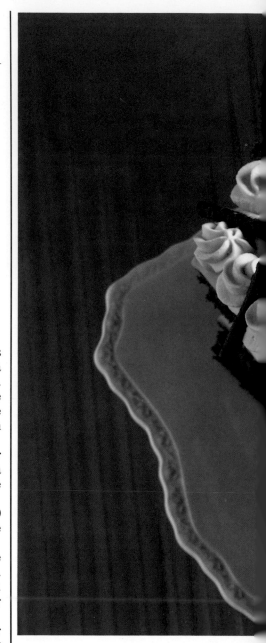

MOCHA GÂTEAU

MAKES 8-10 SLICES

200 g [7 oz] self-raising flour
25 g [1 oz] cocoa powder
2 teaspoons baking powder
225 g [8 oz] soft margarine
225 g [8 oz] dark soft brown sugar
4 large eggs, lightly beaten

For the filling and topping:
175 g [6 oz] icing sugar, plus 1 teaspoon
2½ teaspoons coffee and chicory essence
4-5 teaspoons warm water
150 ml [¼ pt] whipping or thick cream
chocolate buttons or coffee-flavoured chocolate 'matchsticks', to decorate (optional)

272

1 Heat the oven to 170°C [325°F] Gas 3. Grease two shallow 18 cm [7 in] square tins, line bases with greaseproof paper, then grease paper.

2 Sift the flour, cocoa and baking powder into a large bowl. Add the margarine, sugar and eggs and beat with a wooden spoon for 2-3 minutes, until evenly blended.

3 Divide the mixture equally between the prepared tins, level each surface, then make a shallow hollow in the centre. Bake for 25-30 minutes, or until the cakes are springy to the touch.

4 Cool the cakes for 5 minutes, then turn out of the tins on to a wire rack and peel off the lining papers. Turn the cakes the right way up and leave to cool completely.

5 To assemble the gâteau, sift 175 g [6 oz] icing sugar into a bowl, add 1½ teaspoons coffee and chicory essence, then stir in enough water to give a smooth icing that just coats the back of the spoon. Spread half the icing over top of each cake.

6 Whip the cream until thickened. Add the remaining essence and 1 teaspoon icing sugar, and continue beating until soft peaks form.

7 Spread one-quarter of the coffee cream over one iced cake, then place the other cake on top. Lift the cake gently as the icing cracks easily.

8 Pipe or spoon the remaining coffee cream around the top edge of the gâteau, then decorate with chocolate buttons or matchsticks, if liked.

Chocolate sponge is sandwiched together and topped with coffee cream.

273

Austrian chestnut gâteau

AUSTRIAN CHESTNUT GÂTEAU

This is a most impressive gâteau, which makes a marvellous dinner party dessert.

SERVES 12

6 medium-sized egg yolks
175 g [6 oz] caster sugar
700 g [1½ lb] canned unsweetened
   chestnut purée
75 g [3 oz] finely ground almonds
1½ tablespoons dry breadcrumbs
2 teaspoons vanilla essence
8 medium-sized egg whites
250 ml [9 fl oz] thick cream
2 tablespoons brandy
12 glacé chestnuts (marrons glacés)

1 Heat the oven to 180°C [350°F] Gas 4 and butter a 23 cm [9 in] cake tin.
2 In a large mixing bowl, beat the egg yolks with a wire whisk or rotary beater until light and fluffy. Add the sugar and beat thoroughly.
3 Add the chestnut purée to the egg yolk mixture, mixing well. Stir then beat in the ground almonds, breadcrumbs and vanilla essence.
4 Whisk the egg whites until they form stiff peaks. Using a large metal spoon, carefully fold the egg whites into the chestnut mixture.
5 Spoon the mixture into the prepared cake tin, smoothing the surface with the back of a spoon. Bake for 1½ hours, or until the skewer inserted into the centre of the cake comes out clean.
6 Leave the cake to cool in the tin for 15 minutes. Then remove it from the tin and place it on a wire rack to cool.
7 In a medium-sized mixing bowl, whisk the thick cream until stiff. Fold in the brandy to taste.
8 Not more than 1 hour before serving, place the cake on a serving plate. Spread the cream over the top of the cake, making 12 decorative swirls with a flat-bladed knife. Alternatively pipe the swirls using a small piping bag fitted with a 6 mm [¼ in] star nozzle. Arrange a glacé chestnut in each swirl. Serve as soon as possible.

GRAPE GÂTEAU

MAKES 6-8 SLICES
75 g [3 oz] plain flour
pinch of salt
pinch of baking powder
3 large eggs
150 g [5 oz] caster sugar

For the filling and decoration:
275 ml [½ pt] thick or whipping cream
3 tablespoons kirsch
2 teaspoons icing sugar, sifted
250 g [9 oz] seedless grapes, halved, or
    black grapes, halved and seeded
10 ratafia biscuits, crushed
extra ratafias (optional)

1 Heat the oven to 190°C [375°F] Gas 5. Grease a 33 × 23 cm [13 × 9 in] Swiss roll tin; line tin with greaseproof paper and grease paper.
2 Sift the flour with the salt and baking powder and set aside.
3 Put the eggs and sugar into a large heatproof bowl. Set the bowl over a pan half full of gently simmering water. Using a rotary or hand-held electric whisk, beat the mixture until thick and foamy. Continue beating until the mixture is thick enough to hold the trail of the whisk for about 3 seconds when beaters are lifted.
4 Remove the bowl from the pan and beat for a few minutes more until the mixture is cool. Using a large metal spoon, fold in the sifted flour, one-third at a time.
5 Pour mixture into the prepared baking tin and spread evenly by gently tilting the tin. Bake the cake immediately for 15-20 minutes until the surface is golden and springy to the touch. Leave to stand in the tin for 1-2 seconds, then turn out on to a wire rack. Peel off the lining paper and leave to cool completely.
6 To make filling, whip cream in a bowl with the kirsch and sugar until standing in soft peaks. Spoon half the whipped cream into another bowl and fold in three-quarters of the prepared grapes.
7 To assemble the gâteau, cut sponge across into three equal rectangles, then sandwich them together with the grape cream in between. Spread three-quarters of the remaining whipped cream over the top and sides. Transfer to a serving plate.
8 Using a palette knife, press the crushed ratafias over the sides of the gâteau. Put the remaining cream into a piping bag fitted with a large star nozzle and pipe a border around the top edge. Decorate with the remaining grapes and the ratafias, if liked. Keep in a cool place and serve within 2 hours.

This Grape gâteau is made from a whisked sponge baked as one cake and then cut into three pieces.

CHOCOLATE PEPPERMINT GÂTEAU

MAKES 20 SLICES

100 g [4 oz] plain chocolate
275 ml [½ pt] milk
225 g [8 oz] light soft brown sugar
100 g [4 oz] soft margarine
2 eggs, separated
225 g [8 oz] plain flour
1 teaspoon bicarbonate of soda

For the icing and decoration:
100 g [4 oz] butter or margarine, softened
225 g [8 oz] icing sugar, sifted
few drops of green food colouring
few drops of peppermint flavouring
2-3 tablespoons water
75 g [3 oz] chocolate vermicelli
4 wafer-thin peppermint chocolates, cut
    diagonally in half
25 g [1 oz] plain chocolate, grated

Children and adults alike will love this delicately coloured gâteau with its peppermint icing.

1 Heat the oven to 170°C [325°F] Gas 3. Grease a deep 20 cm [8 in] square cake tin, line with greaseproof paper and grease the paper.

2 Break the chocolate into a small bowl set over a pan of simmering water. Add half the milk and half the sugar. When the chocolate has melted, remove from the heat and gently stir in the remaining milk and mix well.

3 Beat the fat and remaining sugar in a bowl with the egg yolks. Beat in the chocolate mixture, then sift in the flour and bicarbonate of soda. Mix until well blended, then beat for 1 minute.

4 In a clean dry bowl, whisk the egg whites until standing in stiff peaks. Then, using a metal spoon, carefully fold 1 tablespoon into the mixture, then fold in the rest of the egg white.

5 Turn mixture into prepared tin and smooth the top with a palette knife. Bake for 1-1¼ hours, until the cake springs back when lightly pressed. Turn on to a wire rack, remove the lining paper, turn the cake the right way up and leave to cool.

6 Meanwhile, to make peppermint icing, beat butter until it is soft and creamy. Gradually beat in the icing sugar, green colouring, peppermint flavouring and enough water to give a smooth butter-cream which will hold its shape.

7 Spread one-third of the icing round

the sides of the cake. Spread the vermicelli out on a piece of greaseproof paper then, holding the cake firmly in both hands, dip it in the vermicelli until the sides are completely coated.

8 Put the cake on a serving plate. Spread half the remaining icing over the top of the cake then, using a piping bag with a large rosette nozzle, pipe the rest in a border around the edge of the cake. Arrange the peppermint chocolate halves in the piped icing and then sprinkle the grated plain chocolate over the centre of the cake, for an attractive decoration.

STRAWBERRY TORTE

SERVES 4-8

32 trifle sponge fingers
700 [1½ lb] strawberries, hulled
575 ml [1 pt] thick cream
1 teaspoon vanilla essence

For the glaze and decoration:
800 g [1¾ lb] strawberries
3 tablespoons granulated sugar
1½ teaspoons cornflour
2 tablespoons water
1 teaspoon lemon juice
275 ml [½ pt] thick cream, whipped
100 g [4 oz] flaked almonds, toasted to a golden brown

1 Cut the sponge fingers into three horizontally. Grease a 22 cm [8½ in] spring-release, loose-bottomed cake tin and line the bottom and sides with half of the sponge pieces, cut sides against the tin.

2 Purée 225 g [8 oz] strawberries in a blender then sieve to remove the seeds. Slice 450g [1 lb] strawberries. Whip the cream in a large bowl until stiff and fold in the purée, vanilla and sliced strawberries.

3 Spoon half the cream mixture into the sponge-lined tin, smoothing the surface. Using half of the remaining sponge pieces, cover the strawberry cream. Repeat with the remaining strawberry cream and sponge pieces. Cover the surface with greaseproof paper, then a plate which fits inside the tin exactly and place a weight on top. Chill overnight.

4 Meanwhile to make the glaze, purée 175 g [6 oz] of the ripest strawberries in a blender then sieve. In a small saucepan mix the sugar and cornflour in the water. Stir in the strawberry purée. Simmer, stirring, over a gentle heat for 1-2 minutes or until thickened. Stir in the lemon juice and cool.

5 Turn the strawberry torte out on to a flat serving platter. Coat the sides of the torte with half the whipped cream. Press toasted flaked almonds around the sides, using a clean palette knife.

6 Arrange the remaining whole strawberries on the top of the torte. Spoon the cooled glaze over the fruit and chill.

7 To serve, pipe the remaining cream around the top of the torte.

This Strawberry torte takes very little time to make as it uses trifle sponge fingers as the base.

ANGEL FOOD CAKE

I magine a cake with the melting texture of meringue combined with the softness of sponge – that is angel cake. Add a sweet, marshmallowy frosting and you have an American classic. This chapter shows you how it is done.

Angel food cake is perhaps the most impressive of the true American cakes, a real special occasion treat. Snowy white, and light and airy – it contains no fat – it is not unlike soufflé, or a meringue with a little flour folded in. Like soufflés and meringues, angel food cake requires time and patience, but the spectacular result is the well-earned reward.

A well-made angel cake truly lives up to its name. Feathery light, it has a texture so soft and sweet that it really does melt in the mouth.

Although classed as a whisking method cake, since only the whites of the eggs are used, angel cake is not made in quite the same way as a whisked sponge. The method is a cross between that used for meringues and the method used for whisked sponges as described on page 164.

An added bonus of this famous cake is versatility. You can serve it in the classic manner – completely plain, accompanied with a light pouring sauce or a bowl of sugared, soft, fresh fruit – as a refreshing summer treat. You can fill and cover it with whipped cream for a richly satisfying dessert. Light and easy to digest, an angel cake is ideal for children's parties too. Try it

the American way, with frosting, then watch how fast it disappears!

INGREDIENTS

Angel cakes are made basically from egg whites, sugar, flour and flavouring. Compared with most other cake mixtures, the proportion of flour is very low. Average proportions are: 5 egg whites and 100 g [4 oz] sugar to every 50 g [2 oz] flour used. Because only whites of eggs are used, an angel cake contains no fat whatsoever.

Flour

American cooks use a specially ground flour, called cake flour, for making angel cakes. Very soft and starchy, this gives an excellent tender texture, and a colour as white as paper. Unfortunately, since cake flour is not widely available outside the USA, it is practically impossible to make a 100% authentic US angel cake in other countries. However, you can make your own soft flour at home by sieving and thoroughly mixing one part cornflour with three parts of plain flour. The

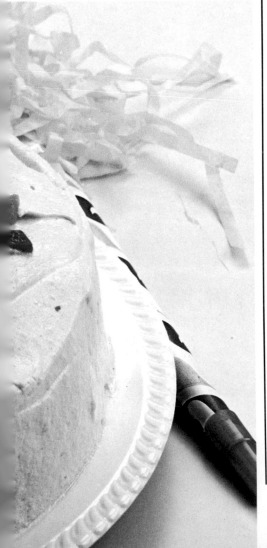

softer and finer the flour the better. Self-raising flour is unnecessary because volume and lightness are provided by the whisked egg whites.

Salt

A pinch of salt is added to help bring out the flavour of other ingredients. Always sieve the salt with the flour to ensure even distribution.

Sugar

Caster sugar is always used, because its fine crystals dissolve easily. Granulated sugar is unsuitable. The coarse crystals would break down the stretched albumen of the egg whites, causing loss of air and, therefore, lightness.

The sugar is added in two stages. Approximately one quarter is sieved with the flour as this helps keep the flour evenly distributed when it is folded into the mix. The remaining sugar is whisked into the egg whites.

The sugar is always sieved first to ensure it is quite free of lumps and to introduce air.

Eggs

Only the whites of eggs are used. These are whisked to give a traditional light texture to the mixture. If you use whites of eggs that are 2-4 days old and at room temperature, you will find that they whisk quicker and to a greater volume.

Cream of tartar

To help the egg whites hold their shape, a little cream of tartar is added during whisking. The cream of tartar also helps to produce a whiter cake.

Liquid

Where a large number of whites are used (such as 10), liquid is added to help give a lighter cake. This may be all water, but a combination of water and lemon juice is best. Lemon juice also produces a whiter cake.

FLAVOURINGS

The most suitable flavourings are those which are concentrated and can be used in small amounts. Heavy ingredients (such as dried or crystallized fruit) must be avoided: the mix is too delicate and they would simply sink.

Dry flavourings

Ground spices are excellent – only a small quantity is needed for a good

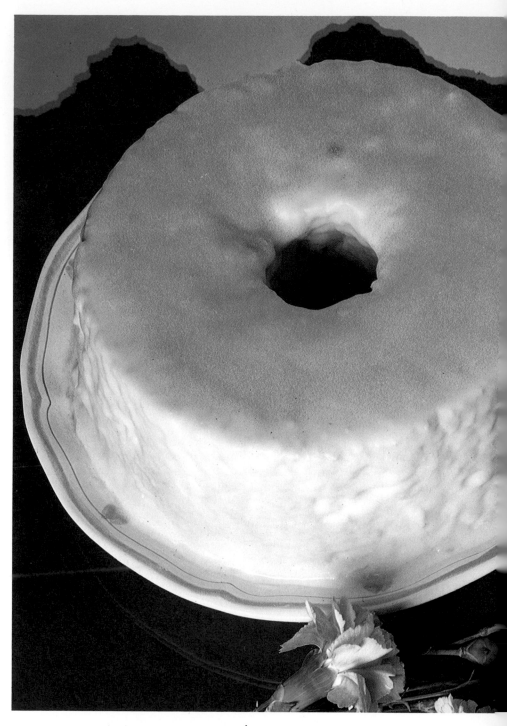

flavour. Cinnamon, cloves, mixed spice and nutmeg are all popular. Always sieve the spices with the flour.

Where a rich chocolate flavour and colour is desired, cocoa powder is used instead of one quarter of the flour. Cocoa must be sieved with the flour to ensure it is evenly blended.

Finely grated citrus zest offers a subtle flavour and a tang which helps offset the sweetness of the cake. It is beaten into the whisked egg whites (rather than being sieved with the flour) as this help release its flavour.

Liquid flavourings
Essences are ideal – their flavour is concentrated so only a little is used. There is a wide range to choose from, including peppermint and raspberry as well as the usual almond and vanilla.

Beat essences into the whisked egg whites until thoroughly distributed.

GETTING ORGANIZED

The mix is very delicate – any delay between making and baking leads to loss of volume and, consequently, of

lightness. Like a good girl guide, you must 'be prepared'. Always heat the oven and organize all your equipment before you so much as crack an egg.

Oven temperature

The baking of angel cakes has been the subject of endless research. Experiments have included starting with a very cool oven and ending with a hot one. However, it is generally agreed that, at home, best results are obtained if the cake is baked at a moderate temperature throughout – 180°C [350°F] Gas 4 on a shelf just below the centre of the oven. This way, air and steam contained in the beaten egg whites can expand fully before the cake has set, giving it its characteristic light texture.

EQUIPMENT

To bake the cake you should really have a special tin called an angel cake or tube tin. This is a deep, round metal tin, about 20 cm [8 in] across with 10 cm [4 in] sloping sides and a funnel or

Party angel cake can be served with fruit, or covered with a delicately coloured glacé icing.

tube in the centre attached to a flat base which lifts out. The shape of the tin gives a very pleasing-looking cake. It also serves a practical purpose: the funnel provides additional support for the delicate mix, so helping it to hold its shape.

Unfortunately the genuine tin is difficult to obtain. A spring release tin with a detachable tube base is also suitable. One 23 cm [9 in] in diameter will have a capacity of 2.3 L [4 pt]. You may also find angel tins which look like kugelhopf moulds, with an ornamental base and a central funnel.

A 23 cm [9 in] savarin mould can also be used, though this does not have very high sides. Check the capacity of yours: they vary widely. The chart on page 284 gives a guide to the quantity of mixture needed for different-sized tins.

Preparation is quite different from the usual greasing and lining. Be sure that the tin is spotlessly clean, dry and quite free of grease.

Angel cakes can also be made in small paper cases. For about 10 cup cakes, halve the quantities given in the first column of the chart. Be careful to smooth over the top, or they will peak. Fill the cases only two thirds full if you want to frost the cakes with American frosting.

As for other equipment, you will need the usual weighing and measuring equipment, plus a fine sieve and three bowls for sieving the flour and sugar.

To whisk the egg whites you need the same equipment required for making meringues: a large copper, pottery or glass bowl and a suitable whisk. A balloon whisk is best. Although hard work, it gives the greatest volume. You can use an electric whisk instead, but in that case note that a slightly different method of mixing is required.

Never try to whisk more than five egg whites in the same bowl. The volume gets so big that it is difficult to handle! instead whisk two separate bowlfuls and then combine them.

Use a large metal spoon or plastic spatula for folding in the sieved flour.

MAKING AND BAKING

When you have heated the oven, checked the tin and organized your equipment, measure your ingredients and separate the eggs. The next step is to make the cake itself.

This feather-like cake mixture is not a sponge, though it is made by a similar method to a whisked sponge. If you use a hand whisk, omit the sugar from step 5 (see Adding the sugar).

SERVES 10-12
10 medium-sized eggs
75 g [3 oz] plain flour
25 g [1 oz] cornflour
large pinch of salt
225 g [8 oz] caster sugar
1 tablespoon lemon juice
1 tablespoon hot water
1 teaspoon cream of tartar
1 teaspoon vanilla essence

4 Place half the egg whites in a large bowl. Add half the lemon juice and water and whisk together lightly.

8 When all the flour mixture is incorporated, turn the mixture into the tin. Smooth the surface with a palette knife.

MAKING AN ANGEL CAKE

1 Position shelf just below centre of oven. Heat oven to 180°C [350°F] Gas 4. Have ready a 23 cm [9 in] clean tin. Separate the eggs.

2 Sift the flours alone, then sift again, together with salt and any powdered flavourings you intend to use.

3 Sift caster sugar. Add about one quarter of the sugar to the flour and sift together three times. Set flour mixture aside.

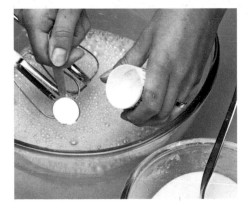

5 When foamy add half the cream of tartar and a little sugar. Whisk to stiff peak stage. Repeat with remaining whites. Combine.

6 Whisk in the remaining caster sugar, about 1 tablespoon at a time. Beat in any grated zest or flavouring essences (if used).

7 Sift the flour mixture over the surface of the egg whites, 2 tablespoons at a time, and fold in lightly but thoroughly.

9 Draw the knife through the mixture to release any large pockets of air. Bake immediately for 45 minutes.

10 To test if the cake is cooked, press the surface lightly – it should feel firm, no impression of your fingertips should remain.

11 Stand the tin upside down on a wire rack. Leave about 1½ hours until cold and set. Then ease away from sides and turn out.

MAKING A SURPRISE FILLING

1 Using toothpicks as a guide, slice a 2.5 cm [1 in] layer from top of cake with a sharp serrated knife. Reserve layer to use as the lid.

2 Next, cut right around the inside of the cake, 2.5 cm [1 in] from the inner edge, and to within 2.5 cm [1 in] of the base.

3 Repeat, this time 2.5 cm [1 in] from the outer edge. Scoop out the crumb from the channel with a teaspoon.

4 Spoon prepared filling into hollowed channel. Replace the lid. Mask with whipped cream and decorate. Chill.

Sifting

To make a really light angel cake, sifting is vital. It aerates the ingredients and ensures that they are evenly blended. Do not be tempted to skip the sifting process, even though the flour is sifted six times in all!

Sift both the flours into the measuring tray for weighing, then sift again with the salt and any powdered flavourings into a bowl. Do not use your largest mixing bowl for this, because you will need this to contain the beaten egg whites.

Sift the caster sugar into a second bowl. Add about one-quarter of the sugar to the flour and sift the flour mixture three more times. It is convenient to do this to and from between the tray of the scales and the bowl.

Whisking the egg whites

Place half the egg whites in a mixing bowl together with half the water and lemon juice specified in the recipe. Begin whisking, slowly at first and tilting the bowl to allow maximum incorporation of air.

When the whites turn foamy, it is time to add half the cream of tartar, then continue whisking. Increase speed, until whites are stiff enough to stand in peaks. Repeat with the remaining egg whites, water, lemon juice and cream of tartar, and then combine the two (this only applies when using more than five eggs).

Once you have whisked the egg whites, carry on with the remaining stages of the recipe without delay. If you leave the whites to stand, they will soon flatten.

QUANTITIES OF ANGEL CAKE MIXTURE

Mould size	850 ml [1½ pt] ring mould or 18 cm [7 in] savarin tin or about 20 paper cases	1.7 L [3 pt] ring mould 23 cm [9 in] savarin mould	2.3 L [4 pt] ring mould or 23 cm [9 in] spring release ring or 20 cm [8 in] angel cake tin
Quantity of ingredients	35 g [1½ oz] plain flour 15 g [½ oz] cornflour pinch of salt 100 g [4 oz] caster sugar 4 medium-sized egg whites ½ teaspoon cream of tartar	50 g [2 oz] plain flour 20 g [¾ oz] cornflour pinch of salt 150 g [5 oz] caster sugar 7 medium-sized egg whites ½ tablespoon lemon juice 1 teaspoon hot water ½ teaspoon cream of tartar	25 g [1 oz] cornflour 75 g [3 oz] plain flour large pinch of salt 225 g [8 oz] caster sugar 10 medium-sized egg whites 1 tablespoon lemon juice 1 teaspoon vanilla essence 1 teaspoon cream of tartar
Cooking time	For a ring cake 25 minutes, for small cakes on a lower shelf 15-20 minutes	35 minutes	45 minutes

Adding the sugar

Gradually whisk the sifted sugar into the egg whites, about 1 tablespoon at a time. Make sure each addition is dissolved before the next is made. If the sugar is added too quickly, the meringue will collapse.

If you are using an electric whisk you should begin adding the first spoonfuls of sugar immediately after you have added the cream of tartar, as a precaution against overbeating the egg whites.

When the sugar has been smoothly incorporated, whisk in any citrus zest or liquid flavouring.

Folding in the flour

The last stage is crucial. The flour mixture is sifted over the egg whites a little at a time, then quickly folded in, with a cutting, figure-of-eight action.

Remember that the aim is to blend the ingredients with as little loss of air

as possible. A light hand is essential, but the flour must be evenly blended. Never, ever, beat or stir at this stage or you will end up with a sad cake.

Baking

Turn the cake mixture into the spotlessly clean, ungreased tin and smooth the surface level with a palette knife. Next, draw the blade of the knife through the batter to release any pocket of air. Bake immediately, in a moderate oven – 180°C [350°F] Gas 4 – on a shelf just below the centre of the oven.

Do not open the oven door during baking or the cake is liable to sink. After 45 minutes test whether the cake is done by pressing the surface lightly – it should feel firm and spring back. If any impression of your fingertips remains on the surface of the cake, return the cake to the oven for a few more minutes, then test again.

A surprise filling hidden under the coating of frosting makes an angel cake twice as enjoyable.

MAKING AMERICAN FROSTING

This icing must be used the moment it is made, so have everything prepared – and the cake cold and ready – before you start whisking. This is the most difficult frosting to make, and you should have a sugar thermometer to attempt it. If you are willing to risk disaster, you could try it using the soft ball test: drop a little syrup into cold water. Remove and roll with your fingers: it should form a soft ball.

FOR A 20 CM [8 IN] CAKE
225 g [8 oz] granulated sugar
4 tablespoons water
pinch of cream of tartar
1 medium-sized egg white
small pinch of salt (optional)

1 Put sugar and water in a heavy-based pan. Heat gently, stirring continuously, until sugar is dissolved. Stir in cream of tartar.

2 Bring to the boil and cook without stirring, to 116°C [240°F]. Brush down sides of pan to prevent crystals forming. Use a wet brush.

4 Pour the hot (but not boiling) syrup immediately on to the whisked egg white, beating at a high speed all the time.

5 Add essences or flavourings. Whisk at high speed until frosting thickens, turns opaque, will coat a spoon and is almost cold.

6 Additions such as citrus zest, chopped nuts or raisins should be made at the last moment, before spreading.

MAKING SYRUP FROSTING

This is a very soft, light frosting. It is much easier to make than American frosting, as no sugar boiling is involved.

MAKES 225 G [8 OZ] FROSTING
2 medium-sized egg whites
2 tablespoons golden syrup

1 Prepare a double boiler. Place the egg whites and syrup in the top.

2 Whisk them together, then place over the water just simmering.

3 Meanwhile, whisk egg white together with salt (if used) until stiff. Remove syrup from heat and allow bubbles to subside.

7 Working quickly, pour on to the cake and spread evenly with a wet warm palette knife. Add any decoration before the frosting sets.

3 Whisk the mixture until it thickens, then pour it over the cake.

Cooling

Remove the baked cake from the oven and stand the tin, upside-down, on a wire cooling rack. Leave the cake in the tin until completely cold and set. This takes 1¼-1½ hours, depending on size. Then shake the cake gently out of the tin on to the rack or a serving dish. It should come out easily. Do not try and persuade an angel cake to leave its tin prematurely – it will stick and be spoilt!

SERVING SUGGESTIONS

The naturally decorative shape of the cake – baked in the correct tin – lends itself to a number of different serving suggestions.

Classic accompaniments

The classic way to serve an angel cake is the simplest and easiest of all. Place the cake on a pretty serving dish and serve separately a bowl of light pouring sauce made from fruit purée or jam. Alternatively, serve it with sugared, soft fresh fruit.

Fruit and cream filling

A quick, but effective, trick is simply to fill the centre cavity with fruit. Soft fresh fruit makes a mouthwatering and refreshing filling, but well-drained poached or canned fruit can be used instead.

Surprise filling

The third method is the most elaborate. Here, the cake is given a surprise filling, so called because the filling is hidden until the cake is cut. Although more time-consuming, it is well worth the extra trouble (see right).

AMERICAN FROSTING

An American speciality, sometimes called white mountain icing, this is one of the more advanced icings – and one of the most attractive. Although tricky to make, it is well worth the challenge! It spreads and swirls very easily, and at the same time has a marshmallowy texture.

The method is based on a principle known as Italian meringue, which involves cooking egg whites by whisking into them a hot (but not boiling) sugar syrup. Success depends on careful cooking of the syrup and on recognizing when the icing has reached the right consistency.

Angel cake fillings

To prepare fruit fillings, clean and hull the fruit and chop any large fruit into bite-sized pieces. Spoon the fruit into the hollow cavity in the centre of the cake. Alternatively, the fruit can be combined with whipped cream and finely chopped nuts for extra interest. Do not add this mixture until just before serving, as the dampness might make the cake collapse. The filling may be heaped in the centre, or cut off the top of the cake for a lid and sandwich with the filling.

To prepare surprise fillings, first slice off the top of the cake to make a lid. Unless you are blessed with a very steady hand – and loads of confidence – it is best to mark the cutting lines with toothpicks. Place your free hand on the top of the cake to hold it steady and cut along the line with a sawing action.

Next, cut a circular channel from the inside of the cake and scoop out the crumb. (The crumb can either be mixed with the filling or saved for use in puddings and other sweets.) Take care when making the channel to leave a wall of cake 2.5 cm (1 in) thick on either side, otherwise the cake may collapse. To guard against cutting through the base, mark a line 2.5 cm (1 in) from the base with toothpicks.

Spoon the prepared filling into the hollow channel, replace the lid and press lightly to secure. It is a good idea to chill the cake before serving: this helps set the shape and makes it easier to cut into wedges.

Whipped cream is the most popular filling. It is thick and firm, but soft enough to cut easily. The cream can be combined with soft fresh fruit or well-drained canned fruit. Dried or crystallized fruit, nuts, desiccated coconut or finely crushed caramel can be mixed in with the cream for added flavour.

When re-assembled, the cake can be masked with whipped cream and decorated with piped cream, if wished.

Equipment

You will need all the usual equipment for making the sugar syrup. Do not leave things to chance – it is essential to use a sugar boiling thermometer. The syrup must be boiled precisely to the soft ball stage: this can be tested by dropping a little syrup into water and then rolling into a ball, but a thermometer is more accurate. Undercooked frosting will be too thin. On the other hand, if it is over-cooked the frosting will harden too quickly. If you do not possess, or cannot borrow, a sugar thermometer, then it is better to make the softer, but easier, seven-minute frosting described on page 146.

You will also need a suitable bowl and a beater for whisking the egg whites. An electric mixer is a great help here, as the egg whites must be continually beaten while the hot syrup is poured on to them. If you have to, use a rotary whisk instead, but do get someone to help you, as you need three hands! The bowl and whisk must, of course, be clean and free of grease.

A palette knife dipped in warm water is the best tool to use for easy spreading.

Ingredients

The recipe for basic American frosting, given in the step-by-step instructions, makes 225 g [8 oz] frosting – enough to cover the top and sides of an angel cake made with 10 egg whites, baked in 20 cm [8 in] angel cake tin.

The proportions of the basic ingredients are 225 g [8 oz] sugar plus 4 tablespoons water to each medium-sized egg white used. A pinch of cream of tartar is added to prevent the syrup sugaring and becoming gritty. Granulated sugar is generally used as it is the least expensive. However, caster sugar or loaf sugar are also suitable. Alternatively, if you want a caramel tinge, use Demerara sugar instead of white. You can also add a small pinch of salt to encourage the egg white to whip quickly to the stiff peak stage.

Flavourings

You can easily make different flavoured frostings. The flavourings suggested below should be added at stage 5 in the step-by-step instructions, that is during beating, before the frosting thickens. Quantities given are for 225 g [8 oz] frosting.
● For vanilla frosting, add ½ teaspoon vanilla essence.
● For orange frosting, use a few drops of orange essence plus a little orange colouring.
● For coffee frosting, add 1 teaspoon coffee and chicory essence.

Alternatively, try adding a handful of stoned, chopped raisins or chopped nuts. (These are particularly good if the frosting is to be used as a filling.) They should be added at the last possible moment – just before spreading, as they contain oils which would otherwise thin the icing. The same rule applies if using grated citrus zest – here acid is the culprit.

An angel cake covered with American frosting is irresistible.

Making American frosting

The frosting must be used the moment it is thick enough for spreading. So always have your cake ready and waiting before you make the frosting itself. Also have to hand a small quantity of boiling water or a little lemon juice to add as a softener in case the icing hardens too soon.

The time the frosting takes to thicken once the syrup has been incorporated into the egg whites is roughly 6-9 minutes using an electric whisk or 12-15 minutes if beating by hand. But do not rely on this as a precise guide – experience is really the best way to learn just when the right consistency has been reached. The signs to watch for are changes in texture and appearance. When ready, the frosting should have thickened enough to coat the back of a spoon and should look duller and opaque.

Use the frosting immediately and work quickly – speed is essential as the frosting very quickly becomes too hard for spreading. Do not use the icing from around the sides of the bowl as this will be hard.

Rectifying mistakes

If things go wrong, you could be faced with a frosting that refuses to thicken. (This would be because the syrup was under-cooked.) Do not give up – place the frosting in a heat-resistant bowl over a pan of hot water and beat hard until it is thick enough for spreading.

On the other hand, you may be confronted by the opposite problem – the frosting is much too hard. (This is caused by over-boiling the syrup.) In this case, thin the icing by beating in 1-3 teaspoons boiling water or a few drops of lemon juice.

Storing frosted cakes

Frosted cakes are best eaten within 3-4 days; after this time the icing develops a sugary crust.

Angel food cake can be decorated in various ways. Here the cake is covered with plain frosting and decorated with mimosa balls and angelica diamonds.

289

CHOCOLATE ANGEL CAKE

This is a special treat for everyone aged 5 to 105! Serve this deliciously light cake with a light pouring sauce or a jug of thin cream. A sauce made with puréed raspberries would be a good accompaniment.

SERVES 10-12

50 g [2 oz] plain flour
20 g [¾ oz] cornflour
large pinch of salt
25 g [1 oz] cocoa powder
225 g [8 oz] caster sugar
10 medium-sized egg whites
1 tablespoon lemon juice
1 tablespoon hot water
1 teaspoon cream of tartar
1 teaspoon vanilla essence

Serve Chocolate angel cake filled with raspberries accompanied by a pouring sauce.

1 Position the shelf just below the centre of the oven and heat the oven to 180°C [350°F] Gas 4.

2 Sift flours alone then together with the salt and cocoa powder. Next, sift the caster sugar separately.

3 Make the cake following the step-by-step guide, steps 3-11.

Variations

● For a layered chocolate angel cake, split the cold, baked cake horizontally into two equal layers. Whip 425 ml [¾ pt] thick cream until stiff. Use some of the cream to sandwich the cake layers together, then mask the cake with most of the remainder. Press toasted flaked almonds around the sides of the cake and decorate the top with whirls of cream.

● For a silver wedding cake, omit the cocoa powder and increase the plain flour to 75 g [3 oz] and the cornflour to 25 g [1 oz]. Make and bake as usual. Ice the cold, baked cake with 350 g [12 oz] vanilla-flavoured American frosting and decorate with silvered sugar balls.

SPICED ANGEL CAKE WITH COFFEE FROSTING

This angel cake is smaller than most. Bake in an 18 cm [7 in] savarin mould or a 450 g [1 lb] loaf tin.

SERVES 6-8

40 g [1½ oz] plain flour
15 g [½ oz] cornflour
½ teaspoon mixed spice
½ teaspoon ground cinnamon
pinch of ground cloves
100 g [4 oz] caster sugar
4 medium-sized egg whites
½ teaspoon cream of tartar

For the decoration:
225 g [8 oz] coffee-flavoured American
    frosting
walnut halves (optional)

1 Make the cake, following the step-by-step instructions for angel cake and bake for 25 minutes. Cool.
2 Put the cold cake upright on a wire rack before you begin the icing.
3 Make the American frosting following the step-by-step method. Beat in 1 teaspoon coffee and chicory extract at step 5.
4 Spread the frosting quickly over the top and sides of the cake with a warm, wet palette knife. Stud the surface with the walnuts if used.

Variation

● For frosted orange cake, omit the spices and flavour and mix with 1 teaspoon finely grated orange zest. Ice with orange instead of coffee-flavoured frosting. Decorate with slices of crystallized orange.

PARTY ANGEL CAKE

One of the best descriptions of Angel food cake was given many years ago by a judge in a cake-baking contest at a County Fair in Colorado. He said: 'This cake must be as high as the Rockies, as white as our mountain snow, as delicate as a mother's kiss, and as light as a feather from an angel's wing.'

MAKES 6-8 SLICES

50 g [2 oz] plain flour
1½ tablespoons cornflour
200 g [7 oz] caster sugar

¼ teaspoon salt
8 large egg whites
¾ teaspoon cream of tartar
¼ teaspoon vanilla essence
¼ teaspoon almond essence

For the decoration:
icing sugar
225 g [8 oz] strawberries

1 Make the cake following the step-by-step instructions for angel cake and bake for about 40 minutes. Leave upside down in the tin to cool.
2 When cool, remove from the tin and sift icing sugar over the cake. Fill the centre with strawberries.

Variation

● For a tea-time treat cover the cake with pink glacé icing.

SURPRISE ANGEL CAKE

This cake has a filling revealed when the cake is cut. Chill the finished cake for at least 2 hours before serving. This will help set the filling and make slicing easier.

SERVES 10-12

angel cake mixture made with 10 egg
    whites

For the filling:
275 ml [½ pt] Chantilly cream
    (see page 254).

1 Make the cake following the step-by-step instructions for angel cake.
2 Slice the cake and take out the crumb following the step-by-step instructions for surprise angel cake.
3 Fill with Chantilly cream and replace the top of the cake and press lightly.

Variations

● For a chocolate filling, fold 75-100 g [3-4 oz] melted chocolate into the cream with the sugar and vanilla essence.
● To make coffee filling, use 1 teaspoon coffee and chicory extract in place of vanilla. Fold 50-75 g [2-3 oz] finely crushed caramel into the whipped cream.
● For an almond filling, use almond essence in place of vanilla essence. Fold 50-75 g [2-3 oz] chopped, blanched almonds into the whipped cream.

Make individual cup cakes in paper cases and decorate them with frosting, cream or fruit.

HANDY HINTS

Cutting angel cake

When cutting an angel cake, be sure not to press down too hard, as this will flatten its delicate texture. Insert the point of a thin, sharp knife into the centre of the cake, keeping the point down and the handle up. Then slice carefully, pulling the knife gently towards you with a short, sawing motion.

Alternatively you can gently pull apart the cake by using two forks — this is the traditional way.

MICROWAVED CAKES

All kinds of cakes can be cooked in minutes in the microwave. In this chapter you can discover how to microwave everything from simple all-in-one sponges to rich fruit cakes suitable for weddings or christenings.

There are a few simple techniques to learn when you start cooking cakes in the microwave.

EQUIPMENT

Conventional metal baking tins cannot be used in the microwave as metal reflects microwaves, preventing the microwaves reaching the food so it does not cook. Metal can also cause sparking inside the cooker which can damage the microwave. For these reasons, microwave cakes are cooked in cake 'dishes'.

Microwave cookware

There is a wide choice of special microwave cookware available and this is particularly good for cooking cakes.

Ring moulds are especially good as they ensure even cooking right through the cake. If you do not have a ring mould, you can place a tumbler in the centre of a round dish and pour the cake mixture around it (see step-by-step instructions for Chocolate ice cream cake, page 308).

Glass and china

Conventional heatproof glass and china dishes, such as soufflé dishes or pudding basins can also be used for cakes. The more regular the shape of the container, the more evenly the cake will cook. Well rounded corners and concave undersides, allowing even food distribution, are very important for efficient microwave cooking. Choose dishes large enough to hold the mixture and allow plenty of room for the cake to rise.

ARRANGING

Small cakes should be arranged in a circle, preferably about 5 cm [2 in] apart, for microwave cooking. Do not put a cake in the centre of the circle. If you cannot arrange them in a circle, then rearrange them once or twice during the cooking time.

COVERING

Covering food during microwave cooking keeps food moist, but this is not usually required for cakes. Do not cover a cake for cooking in the microwave unless specified in the recipe.

ROTATING

With microwave cooking, foods need to be stirred whenever possible so the food from the centre of the dish is brought to the edge of the dish and vice versa. As cakes cannot be stirred, the dish must be rotated instead. Rotating instructions are given for individual recipes.

It is a good idea to rotate the dish at least once during cooking even if your microwave has a turntable. Many microwaves have a hot or cold spot and rotating the dish means that the food changes its position and does not remain in one of these spots for the whole of the cooking time.

Converting cake dish sizes

Round	Square	Oblong
18 cm [7 in]	15 cm [6 in]	–
20 cm [8 in]	18 cm [7 in]	–
23 cm [9 in]	20 cm [8 in]	25 × 15 cm [10 × 6 in]
25 cm [10 in]	23 cm [9 in]	28 × 18 cm [11 × 7 in]

COOKING

All the recipes in this chapter have been tested on a 650/700 watt machine, but can be cooked in 500 or 600 watt machines. To adjust the recipes for a 600 watt machine, add 20 seconds per minute to the cooking time unless otherwise instructed.

With a 500 watt machine, 100% [High] is roughly equivalent to 50-70% [Medium-High] on a 650/700 watt machine. Recipes specifying microwaving at 100% [High] will need extra time – this can be anything up to 40 seconds per minute for dense mixtures. Recipes specifying microwaving at 50% [Medium] need to be cooked in a 500 watt machine at 100% [High] for slightly less than the times given in the recipes.

Undercook cakes rather than overcook them – they can always be returned to the microwave for another minute or two, but an overcooked cake will be ruined.

Cakes are tested for doneness either by inserting a skewer to see if it comes out clean, or by pressing lightly on the top to see if it springs back. Other cakes have to be removed from the cooker while they are still slightly moist on the top so they can finish cooking during the standing time. Follow the instructions for the individual recipes.

STANDING TIME

When food is removed from the microwave cooker, it continues to cook because of the heat generated within itself. Standing time is therefore an important part of the process.

Most cakes need to stand in the dish for anything from 5-15 minutes depending on the type and density of the cake.

Chocolate cakes are always popular especially when they are as deliciously light-textured as this Chocolate tipsy cake.
A boilable pudding basin is used, instead of a baking dish. This does not need lining and enables you to turn out the cake with ease. Covering the basin with absorbent paper while the mixture cooks holds in heat but allows steam to escape. This way the cake does not taste like a steamed pudding. When done, the cake shrinks slightly from the sides of the basin. Serve this versatile treat at tea-time or as an elegant dessert.

MAKING CHOCOLATE TIPSY CAKE

CHOCOLATE TIPSY CAKE

This rich cake-cum-pudding is excellent served as a dessert with fresh fruit or at tea-time.

MAKES 6-8 SLICES

75 g [3 oz] self-raising flour
4 tablespoons cocoa powder
100 g [4 oz] butter or margarine, softened
100 g [4 oz] soft brown sugar
4 tablespoons ground almonds
few drops of vanilla essence
3 medium-sized eggs, lightly beaten
2 tablespoons hot water

For the syrup:
1 tablespoon instant coffee granules
4 tablespoons caster sugar
150 ml [¼ pt] water
2 tablespoons brandy

For the decoration:
150 ml [¼ pt] whipping cream
caster sugar to taste
½ teaspoon drinking chocolate
few blackberries
crystallized violets
slices kiwi fruit

1 Sift the flour and cocoa powder into a bowl, add the fat, soft brown sugar, almonds, vanilla essence, eggs and hot water. Beat for 1 minute until blended.

2 Spoon the mixture into a 1.1 L [2 pt] basin and smooth level. Rest a sheet of kitchen paper over top of basin. Stand in the microwave on an upturned saucer.

3 Microwave at 100% [High] for 4-5 minutes, turning after 2 minutes. To test, pierce centre of cake with cocktail stick; it should come out clean. Leave the cake to cool.

4 Stir coffee and caster sugar into the water in a measuring jug. Microwave at 100% [High] for 2 minutes, stirring after 1 minute. Cool, then stir in the brandy.

5 Pour the coffee syrup over the cake in the basin. Refrigerate, covered, for at least 1 hour. Turn out cake (loosening with a knife if necessary) on to a serving plate.

6 Whip the cream and sweeten to taste. Spread over the cake and, if liked, pipe rosettes. Dust with drinking chocolate and decorate with blackberries, violets and sliced kiwi fruit.

1 Sift the flour and cocoa powder into a bowl. Add the fat, brown sugar, almonds, vanilla essence, eggs and hot water. Beat for 1 minute.
2 Spoon mixture into a 1.1 L [2 pt] pudding basin and smooth top.
3 Rest a sheet of kitchen paper over top of basin. Stand in the microwave on an upturned saucer.
4 Microwave at 100% [High] for 4-5 minutes, turning after 2 minutes. To test, pierce centre of cake with a cocktail stick; it should come out clean. Leave the cake to cool.
5 To make the syrup, stir the coffee and caster sugar into the water in a jug. Microwave at 100% [High] for 2 minutes, stirring after 1 minute. Leave to cool, then stir in the brandy.
6 Pour the coffee syrup over the cake in the basin. Refrigerate, covered, for at least 1 hour. Turn out the cake on to a serving plate.
7 To decorate, whip the cream and sweeten to taste. Spread over the cake and, if liked, pipe rosettes on the top. Dust with drinking chocolate and decorate with blackberries, violets and kiwi fruit.

APRICOT RING

SERVES 9-10

75 g [3 oz] digestive or plain sweet biscuits, crushed
100 g [4 oz] plain flour, sifted
150 g [5 oz] sugar
1¼ teaspoons baking powder
pinch of salt
½ teaspoon vanilla essence
65 g [2½ oz] butter or margarine, softened
2 medium-sized eggs
4 tablespoons milk
grated zest of 1 orange

To serve:
100 g [4 oz] apricot jam
1 tablespoon lemon juice
fresh fruit tossed in lemon juice
150 ml [¼ pt] whipping cream

1 Grease a 1.4 L [2½ pt] ring mould, or a 1.7 L [3 pt] straight-sided dish. Coat the base and sides with three-quarters of the biscuit crumbs. (If using the large, straight-sided dish, use only half; grease the sides of a 575 ml [1 pt] heatproof tumbler and use a quarter of the crumbs to coat the outside, then stand in the centre of the prepared dish to improvize a ring mould.)

2 Place the flour, sugar, baking powder, salt, vanilla essence, butter or margarine, eggs, milk and orange zest, in a bowl and beat until smooth. Either use an electric whisk for 1 minute, or beat by hand for 2 minutes. Spoon the mixture into the prepared dish.

3 Microwave at 50% [Medium] for 6 minutes, giving the dish a quarter turn after 3 minutes. Increase the power to 100% [High] and microwave for 1-3 minutes, checking every 30 seconds to see if it is cooked. The cake is done when the top springs back when pressed.

4 Sprinkle the top with the remaining crumbs and leave to stand for 5 minutes. Loosen the edges of the cake with a palette knife and turn out on to a serving dish.

5 While the cake is standing, microwave the jam and lemon juice at 100% [High] for 15-30 seconds, until bubbling. Mix and spread over the cake. Leave until cold.

6 To serve, decorate with fruit and cream.

A simple sponge mixture is an ideal base for many different dessert cakes. Apricot ring is cooked in a ring mould, glazed with jam and lemon juice and then the top and centre filled with fresh fruit of your choice.

Top: **Marble cake**
Bottom: **Spice cake**

2 Cream together the butter or margarine and sugar until light and fluffy. Add the eggs gradually, beating well after each addition.
3 Sift the flour, then fold into the creamed mixture with a large metal spoon. Divide the mixture equally between three bowls.
4 Mix the cocoa powder and water into one bowl of mixture. Add a few drops of red colouring to the second, and the vanilla essence to the third.
5 Alternating the colours, place spoonfuls of the three mixtures in the prepared dish. Lightly cut through the mixture with a knife.
6 Microwave at 100% [High] for about 7 minutes. Stand for 10-15 minutes. Cool on a wire rack.
7 To make the icing for the decoration: place the butter in a large bowl, cover and microwave at 20-30% [Defrost] for 15 seconds, until soft but not melted.
8 Gradually mix in the icing sugar until thick and creamy. Stir in lemon juice and colouring.
9 Spread the icing over the whole cake, lifting it into rough peaks. Decorate with the fresh or crystallized rose petals.

LEMON CARROT CAKE

MAKES 10-12 SLICES

225 g [8 oz] butter or margarine
225 g [8 oz] caster sugar
4 large eggs
275 g [10 oz] self-raising flour, sifted
grated zest and juice of 2 lemons
½ teaspoon almond essence
225 g [8 oz] carrots, peeled and finely grated

For the lemon cheese cream:
100 g [4 oz] butter or margarine
175 g [6 oz] icing sugar, sifted
2 teaspoons milk
75 g [3 oz] cream cheese
½ teaspoon grated lemon zest

For the decoration:
angelica leaves
mimosa balls

1 Lightly oil a 2.3 L [4 pt] ring mould. Place butter or margarine in a bowl and microwave at 100% [High] for 15 seconds to soften.

MARBLE CAKE

SERVES 8

175 g [6 oz] butter or margarine, softened
175 g [6 oz] caster sugar
3 medium-sized eggs, beaten
225 g [8 oz] self-raising flour
1 tablespoon cocoa powder, mixed with a little water
few drops of red food colouring
½ teaspoon vanilla essence

For the decoration:
100 g [4 oz] butter
225 g [8 oz] icing sugar, sifted
2 teaspoons lemon juice
few drops of red food colouring
rose petals or crystallized petals

1 Lightly grease a 20 cm [8 in] round cake dish and line the base with a circle of greaseproof paper.

2 Beat in the sugar, eggs and flour with a wooden spoon or in a blender or food processor, mixing to a soft, smooth texture; do not overbeat. Mix in the lemon zest and juice, almond essence and grated carrot.

3 Spread the mixture in the prepared ring mould. Microwave at 50% [Medium] for 11-12 minutes, turning three times to make sure the cake cooks evenly.

4 Test the cake by pressing the top lightly with your fingers. The cake should be springy to the touch and almost dry on top. Any small damp patches on the surface will dry during standing.

5 Meanwhile, make lemon cheese cream. Place butter or margarine in a bowl and microwave at 100% [High] for 10-15 seconds to soften.

6 Add the icing sugar and milk and beat until smooth. Beat in the cream cheese and zest.

7 Place the cold cake on a serving plate. Swirl the lemon cheese all over the cake, then arrange angelica leaves and mimosa balls attractively in groups on the top.

Variations

● For a lemon sponge, omit the carrots, almond essence and lemon juice, but add the grated zest.

● For an ordinary butter-cream icing, omit the cream cheese.

MICROWAVING LEMON CARROT CAKE

1 Spread the lemon sponge mixture evenly in the microwave ring mould. Microwave at 50% [Medium] for 11-12 minutes, turning three times to make sure the cake cooks evenly.

2 Test for doneness by pressing the top lightly with your finger. The cake should be springy to the touch and almost dry on top. Any small damp patches will dry during standing.

3 Place cold cake on a serving plate. Decorate by swirling the lemon cheese cream all over, then arrange angelica leaves and mimosa attractively in groups on top.

SPICE CAKE

MAKES 8-10 SLICES

200 g [7 oz] plain flour
100 g [4 oz] soft brown sugar
1 teaspoon baking powder
1 teaspoon ground cinnamon
½ teaspoon bicarbonate of soda
pinch of salt
¼ teaspoon grated nutmeg
¼ teaspoon ground cloves
175 ml [6 fl oz] milk
75g [3 oz] margarine, softened
1 medium-sized egg, beaten

For the topping:
25 g [1 oz] butter or margarine
4 tablespoons soft brown sugar
2 tablespoons plain flour
75 g [3 oz] chopped nuts

1 Place all the ingredients except those for the topping in a large bowl. Beat together using an electric mixer at low speed for 1-2 minutes until blended.
2 Spread in a greased 23 cm [9 in] round or 20 cm [8 in] square dish.
3 Place the butter or margarine in a small bowl. Cover and microwave at 100% [High] for 15-30 seconds until melted.
4 Place all the other topping ingredients in a bowl and stir in the melted butter. Mix well until crumbly.
5 Spread the topping over the cake.
6 Place the dish on an inverted plate in the cooker and microwave at 50% [Medium] for 6 minutes, giving the dish a quarter turn every 2 minutes.
7 Increase the power to 100% [High] and microwave for 4-8 minutes, rotating after 4 minutes.
8 Test for doneness after 4 minutes by pushing a cocktail stick into the centre. The cake is cooked when it comes out clean. The top will be springy to the touch. If the dish is glass, there should be just a little uncooked mixture visible through the base.
9 Leave to stand for 10 minutes to complete the cooking process. Turn out on to a wire rack to cool.

POPPY SEED CAKE

Cakes and pastries made with poppy seeds are popular throughout Eastern Europe. They have a nutty flavour and texture.

MAKES 8-10 SLICES

75 g [3 oz] black poppy seeds
125 ml [4 fl oz] boiling water
100 g [4 oz] self-raising flour
2 teaspoons baking powder
100 g [4 oz] ground almonds
300 g [11 oz] soft brown sugar
4 medium-sized eggs
2 tablespoons vegetable oil
275 ml [½ pt] double cream, whipped
50 g [2 oz] toasted flaked almonds

1 Place the poppy seeds in a 575 ml [1 pt] jug, pour over the water and cover. Microwave at 100% [High] for 2 minutes until some water is absorbed.
2 Sift the flour and baking powder into a large bowl, add the ground almonds, sugar, eggs and oil and stir. Stir in the poppy seeds.
3 Grease and base line a deep 20 cm [8 in] round cake dish. Pour in the cake mixture and microwave at 100% [High] for 7-9 minutes or until well risen and springy to the touch, giving the dish half a turn two or three times during cooking. Stand for 5 minutes.
4 Turn the cake out on to a wire rack and leave to cool completely.
5 Split the cake into three horizontally and sandwich back together with two-thirds of the whipped cream. Spread the remaining cream on top and sprinkle with the toasted almonds. Chill if wished, but serve same day.

COCONUT AND SYRUP CAKE

MAKES 8 SLICES

100 g [4 oz] butter or margarine
100 g [4 oz] caster sugar
2 large eggs
100 g [4 oz] self-raising flour, sifted
2 teaspoons vanilla essence
1 tablespoon golden syrup

For the base:

50 g [2 oz] butter or margarine
5 tablespoons golden syrup
100 [4 oz] desiccated or part-shredded coconut

1 Line a 20 cm [8 in] diameter container that is 7.5 cm [3 in] deep with greaseproof paper.
2 To make the base, put the butter or margarine into a bowl. Microwave, covered at 100% [High] for 45-60 seconds until melted and bubbly. Stir in the syrup and coconut and

microwave at 100% [High] for 1 minute. Spread evenly in the container.

3 Make up the sponge mixture as for Lemon carrot cake, page 296 including the essence and syrup. Spread evenly over the coconut and microwave at 50% [Medium] for 7-8 minutes turning three times. The cake should spring back when pressed.

4 Stand for 15 minutes. Turn out on to a wire rack to cool.

AUSTRIAN RING CAKE

This ring cake can be stored in a covered container in the refrigerator for up to 3 days if necessary.

MAKES 10-12 SLICES

100 g [4 oz] butter or margarine
100 g [4 oz] caster sugar
2 large eggs
100 g [4 oz] self-raising flour
2 teaspoons instant coffee granules
    dissolved in 1 teaspoon boiling water
1 tablespoon warm water

For the syrup:
1 tablespoon instant coffee granules
75 g [3 oz] caster sugar
175 ml [6 fl oz] boiling water
6 tablespoons brandy, rum or Tia Maria

For the decoration:
150 ml [¼ pt] whipping or double cream
few drops of coffee essence
coffee or cocoa powder for sprinkling

1 Lightly oil a 1.7 L [3 pt] fluted ring mould.

2 Place butter or margarine in a bowl and microwave at 100% [High] for 10-15 seconds to soften.

3 Beat in the sugar, eggs and flour with a wooden spoon, blender or food processor, mixing to a soft smooth texture; do not overbeat. Beat in the dissolved instant coffee and the warm water.

4 Spread the sponge mixture evenly in the mould. Microwave at 100% [High] for 7-8 minutes, or until springy when lightly pressed. Stand for 5 minutes before turning out on to a rack to cool slightly. Clean the mould.

5 To make the syrup, put the coffee and sugar into a jug and add the water and liqueur. Microwave at 100% [High] for 2-2½ minutes, or until boiling.

6 Return the warm cake to the cleaned mould and pour over the hot syrup. Cool.

7 Turn the cake out on to a serving plate. Whip the cream together with the coffee essence, if using, until firm. Use to pipe rosettes at intervals around the ring cake. Sprinkle with the coffee or cocoa powder and serve any left-over cream separately.

Serve Austrian ring cake slightly chilled with strong after-dinner coffee. To save yourself time – and washing up – use a spray can of decorating cream and spray or pipe around the cake, if preferred.

DEVIL'S FOOD CAKE

Devil's Food Cake is a rich, dark chocolate cake with a fudgy icing. It can be made in the microwave in a matter of minutes. Making the icing is also speeded up when you can melt the chocolate in the microwave. It is often served with a glass of very cold milk.

MAKES 8-10 SLICES

300 ml [11 fl oz] milk
5 tablespoons cocoa powder
100 g [4 oz] butter, softened
350 g [12 oz] caster sugar
½ teaspoon vanilla essence
2 medium-sized eggs
250 g [9 oz] self-raising flour
pinch of salt
½ teaspoon baking powder

For the icing:
350 g [12 oz] plain chocolate, broken up
175 g [6 oz] unsalted butter, softened
350 g [12 oz] icing sugar, sifted
3 egg yolks

This selection of cakes can be made quickly and easily in the microwave. Left to right: Poppy seed cake, Devil's food cake and Madeira cake.

1 Grease and base line two 23 cm [9 in] round cake dishes. Place the milk in a jug and microwave at 100% [High] for 1½ minutes, or until hot, stirring once. Whisk in the cocoa and leave to cool until tepid.

2 Cream the butter and sugar until light and fluffy. Add the vanilla essence, then the eggs, one at a time, beating well after each addition.

3 Sift together the flour, salt and baking powder and fold into the creamed mixture alternately with the flavoured milk.

4 Divide the mixture between the dishes and cook, one at a time, at 100% [High] for 4-6 minutes, or until well risen and shrinking slightly from the sides of the dish, giving the dish half a turn every minute. Leave to stand for 5 minutes, then turn out on to a wire rack, remove the lining paper and leave to cool completely.

5 Make the icing. Place the chocolate in a small bowl and microwave at 50% [Medium] for 4-6 minutes or until nearly melted, stirring halfway through and again at the end. Cream the butter and icing sugar until soft and fluffy. Beat in the egg yolks, then the melted chocolate.

6 Sandwich the cakes together with a little of the icing and spread the remaining icing evenly on the sides and top.

MICROWAVE MADEIRA CAKE

A Madeira cake is usually baked in a round tin, but a ring mould gives a better result when cooking it in the microwave. It is important that the ring mould is rotated so that the cake cooks evenly. As the cake does not brown well in the microwave, it is given a coating of biscuit crumbs. Although not traditional, this helps to improve its appearance.

6 slices citron peel
175 g [6 oz] butter, softened
grated zest of ½ lemon
225 g [8 oz] caster sugar
4 medium-sized eggs
275 g [10 oz] plain flour
2 teaspoons baking powder
75 ml [3 fl oz] milk

For the coating:
15 g [½ oz] butter
40 g [1½ oz] digestive or plain sweet
    biscuits, crushed

1 Place the butter for the coating in a 1.1 L [2 pt] bowl and microwave at 100% [High] for 30 seconds, or until melted. Brush it all over the inside of a 2.3 L [4 pt] ring mould. Arrange the peel carefully in the base of the mould, then sprinkle the crushed biscuits evenly over the base and up the sides of the mould.

2 Cream the butter with the lemon zest and sugar until light and fluffy. Beat in the eggs, one at a time, beating in a sprinkling of the measured flour with each egg and beating well after each addition.

3 Sift the remaining flour with the baking powder and fold into the creamed mixture with the milk. Pour into the prepared mould and microwave at 100% [High] for 6-8 minutes or until a skewer inserted in the centre comes out clean, rotating the mould a quarter turn every 3 minutes to ensure the cake cooks evenly.

4 Leave to stand for 5 minutes, then turn the cake out on to a wire rack and leave to cool.

Variations

The same variations can be used for the microwaved version of Madeira cake as for the conventionally cooked one (see page 77).

HANDY HINTS

Freezing cakes

To freeze Madeira cake, slice thickly, interleave with greaseproof paper, place in a polythene bag, seal and freeze for up to 3 months. To defrost four slices: put on plate, cover and microwave at 100% [High] for 30-60 seconds, or until no longer icy. Stand for 5 minutes.

Freeze Devil's food cake for up to 3 months. Defrost at room temperature for 4 hours.

JAM SWISS ROLL

MAKES 6 SLICES

2 large eggs
50 g [2 oz] caster sugar, plus extra for
    dusting
50 g [2 oz] plain flour

For the filling:
4-5 tablespoons jam

1 Grease the base and sides of an 18 × 28 cm [11 × 7 in] shallow baking dish and line base with oiled greaseproof paper, leaving a handle of paper at each end.

2 Place the eggs and 50 g [2 oz] sugar in a bowl. Using an electric whisk, beat them well until very thick and foamy. Sift the flour over the surface of the egg mixture and fold in gently.

3 Pour the cake mix into the baking dish. Microwave at 100% [High] for 2½-3 minutes, or until cooked.

4 Leave the cake to stand for 2-3 minutes, then turn it out on to a piece of greaseproof paper lightly sprinkled with caster sugar. Peel the lining paper away from the cake. Using a sharp knife, trim 6 mm [¼ in] from the edges of the cake. Place a sheet of dampened greaseproof paper on the sponge.

5 Starting with the far edge, roll the sponge towards you, with the dampened paper on the inside. Place seam side down on a wire rack and leave until cold.

6 To fill, place the cold cake on a flat surface and unroll it. Remove the

paper, spread with jam and roll up again. Sprinkle with caster sugar, then leave to chill for 10 minutes. Slice to serve.

Variations

● Hazelnut sponge roll, replace 25 g [1 oz] of the flour with 25 g [1 oz] ground hazelnuts. Sprinkle the nuts over the whisked egg mixture and fold in with the flour. Microwave as in step 3 for 2½-3 minutes. Turn the cooked sponge out on to paper sprinkled with 25 g [1 oz] ground hazelnuts.

For the filling, soften 50 g [2 oz] butter at 30% [Low] for 15-20 seconds; beat in 50 g [2 oz] sifted icing sugar. Microwave 2 teaspoons instant coffee granules with 2 teaspoons milk at 100% [High] for 10-15 seconds. Stir well, then beat into the

butter-cream. Spread on the cold cake and roll up as for Jam Swiss roll.
● Chocolate arctic log, replace 1 tablespoon flour with 1 tablespoon cocoa powder. Microwave the mixture as in step 3 for 2½-3 minutes. Turn out and roll up as in steps 5 and 6. Unroll the cold cake and spread with 275 ml [10 fl oz] soft scoop vanilla ice-cream. Roll up again. Wrap quickly and freeze 15 minutes to firm before slicing.

GINGER CAKES

MAKES 15-20 CAKES

150 g [5 oz] plain flour
100 g [4 oz] caster sugar
½ teaspoon bicarbonate of soda
½ teaspoon salt
½ teaspoon ground ginger
¼ teaspoon grated nutmeg
¼ teaspoon ground cinnamon
2 medium-sized eggs, beaten
50 g [2 oz] soft margarine
4 tablespoons golden syrup
60 ml [2½ fl oz] boiling water

For the frosting:
25 g [1 oz] butter
2 tablespoons orange juice
1 teaspoon grated orange zest
pinch of salt
225 g [8 oz] icing sugar, sifted
few drops of yellow food
    colouring

1 Line the wells of a microwave bun tray or individual ramekins with two paper cake cases.
2 Place all the cake ingredients in a bowl and beat together using an electric whisk, until well mixed and smooth. Use to fill the paper cases to about one-third full.
3 Cut through the top of each one with a cocktail stick to prevent large air pockets forming, then microwave for times according to the chart (see page 305), rearranging halfway through the cooking time.
4 Leave the cakes to cool on a wire rack.
5 To make the frosting, combine the butter, orange juice, zest and salt in a mixing bowl and microwave at 50% [Medium] for 1-2 minutes, until bubbling. Add the sugar and colouring and beat until the frosting has a smooth consistency.
6 Spread the frosting over the top of the cooled cakes.

HANDY HINTS

Freezing Swiss rolls
To freeze the Hazelnut sponge, slice the cake and freeze the individual portions. Place the slices in a freezer container with a sheet of greaseproof paper between each one.

To defrost, microwave four slices at a time on a plate at 30% [Low] for 1-1½ minutes, turning once.

The plain Swiss roll is not suitable for freezing as the jam would make it soggy, and the ice cream in the Arctic log should not be refrozen.

Years ago, if anyone said you could produce a batch of small cakes in 6 minutes, the reaction would have been one of stunned disbelief! Microwave cooking has revolutionized baking – small amounts of mixture will cook and rise before your eyes to make soft, light cakes. As they are so quick to cook, you can make them fresh, as you need them. Store the mixture in the refrigerator (bicarbonate of soda ones will keep for up to a week, baking powder ones, 3-4 days.)

PLAIN SMALL CAKES

Small cakes are particularly quick to mix and microwave, but remember that microwaved plain cakes will be very pale in appearance. For extra colour, add ground cinnamon, chopped nuts or cherries.

MAKES 20-24 CAKES

100 g [4 oz] soft margarine
100 g [4 oz] caster sugar
100 g [4 oz] self-raising flour
½ teaspoon baking powder
2 medium-sized eggs
2 tablespoons water

1 Place two paper cake cases in the wells of a microwave bun tray or in small ramekin dishes. (Cakes keep their shape better in containers.)
2 Blend all the ingredients together using an electric whisk. One-third fill the paper cases, using less if using cases without any support.
3 Cut through the cakes with a cocktail stick to prevent large air pockets from forming due to the very quick rising process.
4 Arrange the ramekins in a ring in the cooker. Microwave at 100% [High] for times according to the chart opposite. Rearrange as indicated.
5 Microwave until almost dry on top. Small moist spots will dry out on standing. Overcooking will make the cakes dry and tough.
6 Remove the cakes from the dish or tray as soon as they are microwaved, then leave to cool and dry a little on a wire rack.

Variations

Top these small cakes with icing or frosting for a colourful finish. Use any of the frosting or icings on pages 144-153. Alternatively, top the cakes with glacé icing either plain or flavoured (see page 14). Decorate with shredded orange or lemon rind, hundreds and thousands, toasted desiccated coconut, grated chocolate, glacé cherries, or chopped toasted nuts.

CHERRY WALNUT CAKES

MAKES 20-24 CAKES

100 g [4 oz] soft margarine
100 g [4 oz] caster sugar
100 g [4 oz] self-raising flour
½ teaspoon baking powder
2 medium-sized eggs
2 tablespoons water
50 g [2 oz] glacé cherries, chopped
3 tablespoons chopped walnuts

1 Blend together all the ingredients except the cherries and walnuts, using an electric whisk. Stir in the cherries and walnuts.
2 Line the wells of a microwave bun tray or individual ramekins with two paper cases and fill them one-third full with the mixture. Cut through the tops with a cocktail stick.
3 Microwave at 100% [High] for times as indicated in the chart, until the tops are springy to the touch. Rearrange halfway through the cooking time.
4 Remove from the tray and leave to cool on a wire rack. Repeat with the remaining mixture.

PEANUT BUTTER CAKES

MAKES 20-24 SMALL CAKES

150 g [5 oz] plain flour
150 g [5 oz] soft brown sugar
1 teaspoon baking powder
½ teaspoon salt
½ teaspoon vanilla essence
50 g [2 oz] soft margarine
3 tablespoons peanut butter
2 medium-sized eggs, beaten
125 ml [4 fl oz] milk

For the frosting:
1 tablespoon butter
2 tablespoons peanut butter
2 tablespoons milk
pinch of salt
225 g [8 oz] icing sugar, sifted

1 Line the wells of a microwave bun tray or individual ramekins with two paper cake cases.
2 Place all the ingredients in a bowl and mix thoroughly. Fill the paper cases to about one-third full with the mixture. Cut through the top of each with a cocktail stick, then microwave

at 100% [High] for times as indicated in the chart.
3 Repeat this procedure with the remaining mixture, and allow to cool on a wire rack.
4 To make the frosting, combine the butter, peanut butter, milk and salt in a large bowl.
5 Microwave at 50% [Medium] for 1-2 minutes, or until bubbling and melted.
6 Add the sugar and beat until smooth and of a spreading consistency, adding a few drops of milk if required to make it thinner. Spread the frosting over the cooled cakes.

Microwave times for small cakes

QUANTITY	650/700 WATTS	600 WATTS	500 WATTS
1	25-30 secs	30-45 secs	30-45 secs
2	45 secs-1¼ mins	45 secs-1¼ mins	1-1½ mins
3	1-1½ mins	1-1½ mins	1¼-1¾ mins
4	1¼-1¾ mins	1½-2 mins	1¾-2¼ mins
6	1½-2 mins	2-2½ mins	2½-3 mins

*Rearrange after half the cooking times, except when cooking one at a time.

HANDY HINTS

Microwaving small cakes

When microwaving small cakes, double layers of paper cake cases will absorb moisture. Place these in a microwave bun tray or in ramekins for support. Small cakes will rise higher than with conventional baking, so only fill the cases to about a third full. (Judge the amount of mixture needed according to the spreading room allowed by the containers – use less for bun trays than ramekins.)

To ensure that you have equal amounts of mixture in each case, you could use an ice cream scoop as a handy measure. Follow the instructions for small cakes and use the chart (above) to calculate the microwaving time required for the number of cakes you wish to cook. Check cakes after the shortest time to avoid overcooking.

SAVARIN CHANTILLY

SERVES 6

165 g [5½ oz] 81% plain wholewheat flour
15 g [½ oz] caster sugar
1 teaspoon easy blend dried yeast
125 ml [4 fl oz] milk
2 medium-sized eggs, beaten
50 g [2 oz] butter, softened
pinch of salt
canned pineapple pieces and angelica, to
    decorate.

For the syrup:
100 g [4 oz] caster sugar
2 thin strips of lemon zest
2 tablespoons rum

For the Chantilly cream:
275 ml [½ pt] double cream
4 teaspoons caster sugar
few drops of vanilla essence

1 Sift the flour into a warmed bowl. Mix in the sugar and yeast. Pour the milk into a jug and microwave at 100% [High] for 1 minute to heat.

2 Stir the milk and eggs into the flour mixture, then beat vigorously by hand for 5 minutes. Put the mixture into a large greased mixing bowl, cover and microwave at 30% [Low] for 1 minute, then leave to stand in a warm place for 10 minutes to rise the mixture. Repeat this process.

3 Microwave the butter at 30% [Low] for 30-45 seconds, or until very soft but not melted, then beat into the yeast mixture with the salt. Beat well for 5 minutes.

4 Butter an 18 cm [7 in] ring mould, pour in the mixture and microwave at 30% [Low] for 1 minute. Leave to stand for 5 minutes. Increase power to 100% [High] and microwave for 4-6 minutes, or until firm and a skewer inserted in the centre comes out clean, turning once.

5 To make the syrup, place the sugar and 150 ml [¼ pt] water in a 575 ml [1 pt] jug and microwave at 100% [High] for 2 minutes. Stir to dissolve the sugar; add the lemon zest and microwave for a further 2 minutes or until syrupy. Remove the lemon zest and add the rum.

6 Turn the savarin out on to a wire rack over a deep plate and baste the warm cake with the hot syrup until it is thoroughly soaked. (It is important to use up all the syrup.) Leave to cool.

7 Whip the cream with the sugar and vanilla. Place the savarin on a serving plate. Pile half the Chantilly cream in the centre; pipe the rest around the base. Decorate with pineapple and angelica.

HANDY HINT

Let the microwave soften butter to use in cakes and frostings. To soften 100 g [4 oz] butter: place in a bowl and microwave at 30% [Low] for 10-15 seconds or until just softened, giving the bowl a half turn once, use immediately.

Sweet yeast breads are traditional throughout Europe, and different countries have variations on the same recipe. The savarin mixture is typically French. As it is always cooked in a round plain ring mould with a large hole in the centre, it adapts easily to microwaving. Wholewheat flour is used to give a richer colour. Savarin chantilly, soaked in syrup but undecorated, keeps in the refrigerator for 2-3 days.

CHOCOLATE CHIP KUGELHOPF

SERVES 8-10

175 g [6 oz] butter
50 g [2 oz] digestive or plain sweet biscuits, crushed
18 blanched almonds
285 ml [10½ fl oz] milk
500 g [1 lb 2 oz] plain flour
2 tablespoons caster sugar
1 tablespoon dried yeast
3 large eggs, beaten
½ teaspoon salt
75 g [3 oz] sultanas
40 g [1½ oz] raisins
40 g [1½ oz] chopped candied peel
50 g [2 oz] chocolate chips
icing sugar, for dusting

1 Lightly grease a 23 cm [9 in] fluted microwave ring mould using a little of the butter. Sprinkle with the biscuit crumbs to coat evenly and arrange the almonds in a pattern in the base.
2 Place the milk in a jug and microwave at 100% [High] for 1-1½ minutes, or until hot.
3 Mix 175 g [6 oz] of the flour with 1 teaspoon of the sugar and the yeast. Add the hot milk and beat well to blend. Cover loosely with stretch wrap and microwave at 30% [Low] for 1½-2 minutes. Stand for 10-15 minutes, or until well risen and frothy.
4 Place the remaining butter in a bowl and microwave at 100% [High] for 1-1¼ minutes, or until melted, stirring once. Add to the risen mixture with the remaining sugar, flour, eggs and salt, beating until evenly mixed.
5 Stir in the sultanas, raisins, candied peel and chocolate chips. Spoon into the prepared mould, taking care not to disturb the almonds.
6 Cover loosely with stretch wrap and microwave at 30% [Low] for 8-9 minutes, or until the batter has started to rise. Leave until it has risen to the top of the mould.
7 Microwave, uncovered, at 100% [High] for 6 minutes, or until just firm to the touch on top, giving the mould a quarter turn twice. Stand for 5 minutes, then turn out to cool on a wire rack.
8 Serve the kugelhopf, dusted with a little sifted icing sugar and cut into chunky wedges.

Chocolate chip Kugelhopf is a moist yeast cake which will keep for 3-4 days in a cool place. Wrap closely in stretch wrap or foil for maximum freshness.

HANDY HINT

Making dough rise
When microwaving the dough to make it rise, stand about 15 minutes after the first 8-9 minutes, then if necessary, repeat once more to speed rising.

CHOCOLATE ICE CREAM CAKE

This rich moist cake with its chocolate coating and surprise ice cream and raspberry filling makes a truly delicious treat. For a special occasion, stir 1-2 tablespoons of kirsch into the softened ice cream and mix well before stirring in the frozen raspberries.

Alternatively fill the cake with choc-mint ice cream and decorate the top with chocolate coating, then sprinkle with chopped mixed nuts. The centre of the cake can also be filled with orange sorbet.

SERVES 8

175 g [6 oz] caster sugar
175 g [6 oz] soft margarine or softened butter
3 medium-sized eggs
175 g [6 oz] self-raising flour
pinch of salt
75 g [3 oz] cocoa powder
150 ml [¼ pt] milk
500 ml [17 fl oz] vanilla ice cream
125 g [4 oz] frozen raspberries

For the chocolate coating and decoration:
125 g [4 oz] plain chocolate
4 tablespoons golden syrup
1 tablespoon thin cream
65 ml [2½ fl oz] thick cream, whipped
few frozen raspberries, defrosted

HANDY HINT

Chocolate ice cream cake has been tested on all four standard wattages. See the cooking times below.

700 watts   8½ mins
650 watts   10 mins
600 watts   10-12 mins
500 watts   12-13 mins

1 Cream the caster sugar and soft margarine or softened butter together in a large bowl using a wooden spoon or electric beater, until the mixture becomes light and fluffy.

2 Add the eggs to the creamed mixture, adding them one at a time. Beat the mixture well with a wooden spoon or electric beater after each addition to ensure the eggs are well blended.

3 Sift together the flour, salt and cocoa powder. Using a spatula or metal spoon, fold the sifted ingredients into the creamed mixture, a little at a time, alternately with the milk, until completely combined.

4 Pour the mixture into a greased 2 L [3½ pt] decorative ring mould (or use a glass bowl, see next step). Smooth the surface of the mixture with the back of a spoon or a knife until quite even.

5 If you have no ring mould, use a 2.3 L [4 pt] bowl and stand a straight-sided glass or jar, open end up, in the middle of the bowl. Grease both bowl and glass and pour the mixture round the glass.

6 Stand the mould on an upturned plate and microwave at 100% [High] for 8½ minutes, rotating the mould ¼ turn every 3 minutes. Leave to stand for 10 minutes, then loosen edges with a knife and turn out to cool on a rack.

FILLING CHOCOLATE ICE CREAM CAKE

1 Cut off bottom quarter of cake and set aside. Remove centre by cutting 12 mm [½ in] in from inner and outer edges. Scoop out centre with a spoon leaving 2.5 cm [1 in] on the top. Freeze for 1 hour.

2 Place the ice cream in a bowl and microwave at 30% [Low] for 30-60 seconds. Stir in the raspberries. Spoon the ice cream into the cake, replace the base and carefully turn the cake over.

3 Break the chocolate into a small bowl and microwave at 50% [Medium] for 4 minutes. Add syrup and thin cream; spoon over cake. Freeze. Transfer to the refrigerator 45 minutes before serving. Decorate just before serving.

To some people, a gâteau is not really a gâteau without chocolate. Here a chocolate sponge is sandwiched with butter-cream and peach slices and the sides are coated with flakes of chocolate.

LAYERED PEACH GÂTEAU

MAKES 8-10 SLICES

4 eggs
100 g [4 oz] caster sugar
100 g [4 oz] plain flour
2 tablespoons cocoa powder
pinch of salt
50 g [2 oz] butter
crystallized yellow rose petals to decorate
  (see steps right)

For the filling and topping:
225 g [8 oz] butter
450 g [1 lb] icing sugar, sifted
425 g [15 oz] can peach slices, well
  drained, chopped
75-100 g [3-4 oz] plain chocolate
  flakes

1 Lightly grease a 20 cm [8 in] round cake or soufflé dish and line the base with a circle of greaseproof paper. Grease the paper lightly.
2 Whisk the eggs with the sugar in a large bowl until light and creamy and have more than trebled in volume. Sift the flour, cocoa powder and salt together into a separate bowl.
3 Place the butter in a small bowl and microwave at 100% [High] for 45-60 seconds to melt. Sprinkle the flour mixture over the egg, pour the butter in, in a steady stream, and fold into the mixture carefully using a large metal spoon.
4 Pour the mixture into the prepared dish and microwave at 100% [High] for 4½-5 minutes, giving the dish a quarter turn twice. Test for doneness (see pages 292-3). When cooked, stand in the dish for 5-10 minutes, then turn out on to a wire rack to cool.
5 Cut the cake horizontally into three layers, using a large, sharp knife.
6 To make the filling and topping, place the butter in a large bowl and microwave at 30% [Low] for 15-30 seconds, or until just soft. Beat the sifted icing sugar into the softened butter until light and fluffy.
7 Set aside two-thirds of the butter-cream and add the chopped peaches to the remaining third. Use the peach mixture to sandwich the three layers together. Use half of the plain butter-cream mixture to coat the base and sides of the cake, spreading smoothly and evenly.
8 Coat the sides of the cake with chocolate flakes and put the remaining butter-cream into a piping bag fitted with a large star nozzle. Pipe rosettes around the top of the cake and decorate each one with a crystallized rose petal. The gâteau is best eaten the same day – otherwise keep in a cool place for no more than 2 days before serving.

Variation

● Instead of crystallized rose petals, decorate the top of the gâteau with chocolate-coated coffee beans, thin mints or chocolate leaves.

MICROWAVING CRYSTALLIZED ROSE PETALS

1 Select 16 perfect pale rose petals and wipe them gently with a soft cloth. Beat the white of one egg lightly and spread about 4 tablespoons caster sugar on a small plate.

2 Dip each petal in beaten egg, letting any excess drip off, then in the caster sugar to make an even coating all over. Arrange on a piece of greaseproof paper in the microwave.

3 Microwave at 20-30% [Defrost] for 4 minutes, turning over every minute; transfer to a wire rack. Leave for 15 minutes to dry, then sprinkle both sides with more caster sugar.

COCONUT JEWEL CAKE

MAKES 8-10 SLICES

175 g [6 oz] butter
175 g [6 oz] caster sugar
finely grated zest of 1 lemon
3 large eggs, beaten
200 g [7 oz] plain flour
1 teaspoon baking powder
50g [2 oz] desiccated coconut
2 tablespoons lemon juice

For the decoration:
5 tablespoons desiccated coconut
6 tablespoons apricot jam
100 g [4 oz] mixed glacé fruits
preserved ginger, maraschino cherries,
    and angelica

1 Grease a 22 × 12 cm [8½ × 4½ in] loaf dish that is 7.5 cm [3 in] deep and line the base with greaseproof paper. Grease the paper.
2 Soften the butter in a large bowl at 30% [Low] for 15 seconds (500 watts: 30 seconds). Cream the butter with the sugar and lemon zest until light and fluffy. Beat in the eggs, a little at a time, beating well after each addition.
3 Sift the flour and baking powder into the creamed mixture. Add the desiccated coconut and lemon juice and fold in lightly with a large metal spoon. Turn the mixture into the prepared dish and smooth the surface.
4 Stand the dish on an inverted saucer and microwave at 100% [High] for 7 minutes (500 watts: 7-8 minutes) or until very nearly done and only slightly moist on top, giving the dish a quarter turn every 2 minutes to ensure even cooking. Let stand for 5 minutes.
5 Turn the cake out on to a wire rack covered with greaseproof paper to prevent the grid marking the cake. Remove the greaseproof paper lining. Turn upright and leave to cool.
6 Meanwhile, place the desiccated coconut for the decoration in a roasting bag and tie the top loosely with string or an elastic band. Microwave at 100% [High] for 1½-2 minutes, (500 watts: 2-2½ minutes), or until just coloured, shaking the bag every 20 seconds. Tip the coconut on to a plate and spread evenly.
7 Sieve the jam into a small bowl and microwave at 100% [High] for 1-1½ minutes (500 watts: 1½-2 minutes), or until smooth and runny, stirring once.
8 Spread one-third of the jam evenly over the warm sides of the cake. Coat sides with toasted coconut. Spread top with half the remaining jam and arrange the glacé fruits on top, with the preserved ginger, maraschino cherries and angelica. Brush with the remaining jam to glaze. Leave to cool.

HANDY HINTS

To decorate the sides of the coconut jewel cake, brush the two long sides with jam; then, holding the top and bottom of the cake between your hands, press each jammy side in turn into the toasted coconut to coat. Repeat with short sides.

The undecorated cake can be frozen for up to 4 months. Allow it to cool completely and wrap it well in foil or a freezer bag. To defrost, unwrap the cake and place on a plate. Microwave at 20-30% [Defrost] for 4 minutes (500 watts: 4½ minutes), or until spongy to the touch and just warm. Stand for 5 minutes, then brush with jam, decorate and glaze.

Quick fruit cake has a delicious and colourful decoration of glacé fruits and walnuts.

HANDY HINTS

Store microwaved fruit cakes closely wrapped in stretch wrap or foil in the refrigerator for best keeping. Remove from the refrigerator and allow to reach room temperature before serving.

Unlike conventional fruit cakes, these are ready to eat as soon as they are cool, and do not improve particularly through keeping. Allow cakes to cool completely (they hold the heat for up to 2 hours) before wrapping. The cakes will keep for up to 3 weeks, provided they are well wrapped.

QUICK FRUIT CAKE

This is the age of the one-hour fruit cake. Microwaving makes it easy to produce full-flavoured fruit cakes at short notice with no trouble at all.

MAKES 8-10 SLICES
175 g [6 oz] self-raising flour
½ teaspoon baking powder
pinch of salt
100 g [4 oz] dried apricots, chopped
6 tablespoons water
100 g [4 oz] glacé cherries
100 g [4 oz] cut mixed peel
100 g [4 oz] walnut pieces
100 g [4 oz] margarine, softened
100 g [4 oz] dark soft brown sugar
2 large eggs, beaten
½ teaspoon vanilla essence

For the decoration:
5 tablespoons water
100 g [4 oz] caster sugar
few drops of lemon juice
glacé pineapple rings
red glacé cherries
green glacé cherries
walnut halves

1 Oil the base and sides of an 18 cm [7

in] soufflé dish. Line with oiled greaseproof paper.
2 Sift the flour, baking powder and salt into a large bowl.
3 Place the apricots in a bowl with 3 tablespoons of the water. Cover and microwave at 100% [High] for 2½ minutes. Allow to cool. Add to the flour with all the other ingredients, beating well.
4 Spread the mixture in the prepared dish. Place on an inverted saucer in the cooker and microwave at 30% [Low] for 28 minutes, or until cooked, giving the dish a quarter turn every 5 minutes.
5 Stand for 10 minutes, then turn out on to a wire rack.
6 To decorate, microwave the water, in a small covered bowl, at 100% [High] for 1½ minutes, or until boiling. Add the sugar and lemon juice. Stir to dissolve, then microwave at 100% [High] for 3 minutes. Leave to cool.
7 Brush the cake with syrup. Arrange the pineapple rings, cherries and nuts on the cake. Microwave remaining syrup at 100% [High] for 30 seconds, then brush over the fruit.

GLACÉ FRUIT RING

This luscious and unusual fruit cake is cooked in under 10 minutes. Made with a tempting mixture of glacé and dried fruits which produce a wonderfully moist textured cake, it has a really festive flavour. Choose a colourful combination of glacé and dried fruit for the mixture.

MAKES 12 SLICES
175 g [6 oz] mixed glacé fruit, chopped, rinsed in boiling water, drained and patted dry
200 g [7 oz] mixed dried fruits, chopped where necessary
2 tablespoons brandy
2 tablespoons sweet sherry
150 g [5 oz] butter or margarine, softened
65 g [2½ oz] soft light brown sugar
65 g [2½ oz] caster sugar
95 g [3 ½ oz] self-raising flour, sifted
3 large eggs, beaten
50 g [2 oz] chopped mixed nuts
2 tablespoons mincemeat
2 tablespoons lemon juice
glacé cherries, to decorate

For the soured cream icing:
100 g [4 oz] icing sugar
2 tablespoons soured cream

1 Put the glacé and dried fruit in a bowl. Stir in the brandy and sherry; cover with cling film and leave the mixture to stand for at least 3 hours, stirring twice.

2 Put the softened butter in a bowl, add the sugars and mix lightly with a wooden spoon. Add the sifted flour, beaten eggs, soaked fruit mixture, chopped mixed nuts, mincemeat and lemon juice.

3 Mix well with a wooden spoon, stirring rather than beating the mixture, until blended. Well grease a 1 L [2½ pt] microwave kugelhopf ring mould. Turn the mixture into mould; level surface.

4 Microwave at 100% [High] for 8½-9½ minutes, giving a half turn after 2 minutes, then after each minute, until the surface of the cake is soft but dry and the cake is shrinking away from sides of the mould.

5 Leave the cake to stand in the mould for 20 minutes, then turn out on to absorbent paper on a cooling rack and leave to cool completely. Cover loosely with cling film to prevent drying out.

6 To make the icing, sift the icing sugar into a bowl, add the soured cream and mix with a fork to make a smooth, fairly soft icing.

7 Spoon the icing over the cake, allowing some icing to trickle down the sides. Decorate the top of the cake with quartered green, red and yellow glacé cherries (see *Handy Hint*).

HANDY HINT

Decorating Glacé fruit ring

For a festive decoration, quarter 5 glacé cherries (using an assortment of colours). Arrange on the iced cake while the icing is still moist and leave icing to set before serving. Alternatively, roll 8-10 red and green glacé cherries (with their syrupy coating) in caster sugar until evenly coated with a sparkling white frosting and arrange on the iced cake.

DECORATING THE WEDDING CAKE

1 Turn the cakes upside-down. Trim the edges of the ring cake so they are straight. Fill the centre with the trimmings. Add a little marzipan to the centre to level it evenly if necessary. Prick the cakes all over and sprinkle with the brandy.

2 Sprinkle a work surface with icing sugar and roll out about two-fifths of the marzipan to a circle large enough to cover the top and sides of the small cake. Brush cake with egg white and lift the marzipan on to the cake, smoothing with a palette knife.

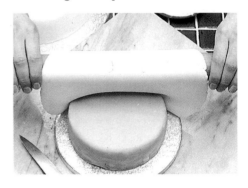

3 Use the remaining marzipan to cover the large cake in the same way. Trim the edges of the cakes neatly with a sharp knife. Lift the two cakes on to the centre of the two boards and leave overnight for the marzipan coating to harden and dry.

4 Sprinkle a surface with icing sugar and roll out about two-fifths of the fondant icing to cover the smaller cake. Smooth the corners and trim the edges. Use remaining fondant to cover the larger cake, moulding the icing right down to the board.

5 Mark six equidistant points around the top edge of both cakes. Measure the distance between these points and use to make two paper templates with a scallop shape. Mark out scallops. Tint a fifth of the royal icing peach.

6 Pipe, using a small writing nozzle, in a peach trellis pattern below scallops and attach silk flowers and leaves at points of scallops. Use white royal icing to pipe shells around both cake bases. Trim with flowers.

WEDDING CAKE

SERVES 40

275 g [10 oz] butter
275 g [10 oz] dark soft brown sugar
6 medium-sized eggs, beaten
3 tablespoons milk
½ teaspoon vanilla essence
225 g [8 oz] plain flour
200 g [7 oz] self-raising flour
large pinch of salt
1½ teaspoons ground mixed spice
1½ teaspoons ground cinnamon
275 g [10 oz] each currants, raisins and
    sultanas
100 g [4 oz] cut mixed peel
175 g [6 oz] glacé cherries, washed,
    drained, dried and chopped
225 g [8 oz] blanched almonds, chopped
8 tablespoons brandy

For the decoration:
900 g [2 lb] marzipan or almond paste
    (page 194)
icing sugar, for dusting
1 egg white, beaten
20 cm [8 in] round silver cake board
28 cm [11 in] round silver cake board
1 kg [2lb 3 oz] white fondant icing
175 g [6 oz] royal icing mix, made up
    according to instructions (page 200)
peach food colouring
2 semi-circular paper templates
    (see recipe)
12 small peach silk flowers
silver cake leaves
3 pillars
spray of small silk flowers

1 Grease and base line a 15 cm [6 in] round soufflé dish and a 23 cm [9 in] ring mould.
2 Place the butter in a large mixing bowl and microwave at 30% [Low] for 30 seconds, until soft, turning once. Add the sugar and cream together until light and fluffy. Beat together the eggs, milk and vanilla essence, then gradually beat into the creamed mixture. Sift the flours with the salt and spices and fold into the mixture. Add dried fruit, peel, cherries and almonds.
3 Spoon the mixture into the prepared containers, to the same depth, then smooth the tops.
4 Microwave the ring cake at 30% [Low] for 45-50 minutes, or until just firm at the edges, but slightly moist towards the centre, giving the dish a quarter turn every 5 minutes. Stand for 10 minutes; cool on a wire rack.

5 Microwave the second cake at 30% [Low] for 20-25 minutes, giving the dish a quarter turn every 5 minutes. Stand in the dish for 10 minutes, then cool on a wire rack.
6 Turn the cakes upside-down. Trim edges of ring cake so they are straight. Fill centre with trimmings. Prick cakes all over and sprinkle with brandy.
7 Sprinkle a work surface with icing sugar and roll out two-fifths of the marzipan to a circle large enough to cover the top and sides of the small cake. Brush cake with egg white and cover with the marzipan.
8 Use remaining marzipan to cover the large cake. Leave to dry.
9 Sprinkle a work surface with icing sugar and roll out fondant the same way as the marzipan and cover the two cakes.
10 Tint a fifth of the royal icing peach and decorate cake according to the step-by-step instructions (left). Use remaining royal icing to pipe shells. Assemble according to the instructions on page 231.

The cake is the centrepiece of any wedding table — it should look fabulous and taste perfect. This adaptation of a classic royal-iced cake makes a professional-looking finish easy, even for beginners. Microwaving the rich fruit cake takes far less time than conventional baking. Decorating, too, is easier if the covering for the cake is made of rolled-on fondant icing — this makes it quicker to make a smooth surface which can be decorated almost immediately. Fondant is used instead of traditional royal icing which has to be applied layer by layer and allowed to dry.

The christening cake is the focal point of the buffet table and served with champagne, it rounds off the festivities perfectly. Simply but attractively decorated, even beginners can achieve professional results with this cake.

To save time before the christening, this rich sponge cake can be made ahead and frozen for up to one month. Defrost it, wrapped, at room temperature before decorating.

CHRISTENING CAKE

MAKES 20 SLICES

225 g [8 oz] caster sugar
8 medium-sized eggs, beaten
100 g [4 oz] butter at room temperature
225 g [8 oz] plain flour
large pinch of salt
9 tablespoons lemon curd

For the icing and decoration:
700 g [1½ lb] marzipan
icing sugar, for dusting
900 g [2 lb] fondant icing
1 egg white, lightly beaten
yellow and green food colouring
225 g [8 oz] royal icing (page 200)
25 cm [10 in] round cake board
1 rosette, made of thin cream and yellow
  ribbon

1 Whisk sugar and eggs in a large bowl over hot water until mixture holds a trail for 3 seconds.
2 Microwave butter at 100% [High] for 1-1½ minutes, until melted. Sift flour and salt together three times, then fold into egg mixture alternately with melted butter.
3 Divide equally between three greased and base-lined 20 cm [8 in] cake dishes. Microwave each dish at 100% [High] for 3-4 minutes, or until just firm in the middle, rotating, half a turn once. Stand for 10 minutes, then turn out, remove paper and cool on a rack.
4 Spread tops of two layers with lemon curd and stack together. Top with remaining cake; coat the top and sides with lemon curd.
5 Sprinkle work surface with icing sugar. Roll out marzipan to a 40-45 cm [16-18 in] circle, large enough to cover top and sides of cake. Smooth marzipan over cake to cover completely. Trim excess, place cake on a cake board and leave overnight to set.
6 Reserve about 25 g [1 oz] white

fondant. Colour remainder pale lemon, roll out as with marzipan. Brush surface of cake with egg white; cover with icing. Reserve trimmings.

7 Colour half the royal icing pale lemon, and the rest palest green. Fill a piping bag fitted with a small star nozzle with lemon royal icing and pipe a row of shells around the base. Pipe tiny flower sprays with fine writing nozzle on top and sides of cake.

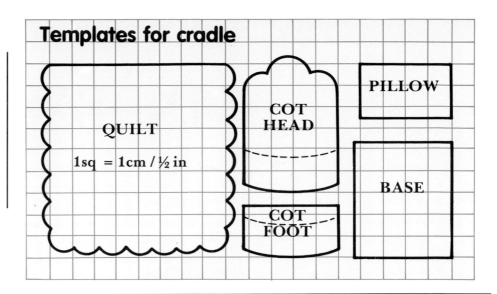

Templates for cradle

QUILT

1sq = 1cm / ½ in

COT HEAD

COT FOOT

PILLOW

BASE

MAKING THE CRADLE

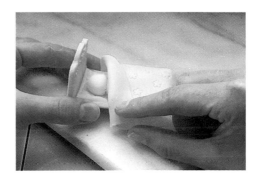

1 Make templates for cradle parts from greaseproof paper, see above. Roll out reserved fondant trimmings and cut out cradle pieces with sharp knife. Wrap remaining fondant and set aside. Shape white fondant into a 5 cm [2 in] roll for the baby.

2 Lay base of cradle over a small glass jar so it dries slightly curved. Leave all pieces to dry, then use palest green icing and a fine writing nozzle to pipe decorations on them. Stick the cradle pieces together with small amounts of royal icing.

3 Roll out reserved fondant and cut out quilt. Decorate with tiny flower shapes. Place 'baby' in cradle; drape quilt over, folding back one corner. Decorate with ribbons; leave to dry. Secure the cradle to the cake with a ball of icing, pressing on lightly.

MAKING THE FRILL

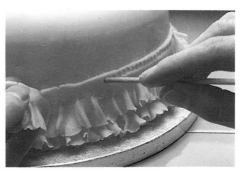

4 Roll out the remaining fondant thinly and cut out eight circles with a 8.7 cm [3½ in] fluted cutter. Work with one at a time, wrapping the rest to prevent them from drying out. Cut a 2.5 cm [1 in] round from the centre of the circle of fondant.

5 Cut through circle once at any point. Using a wooden cocktail stick, roll the point over the scalloped edges until the fondant circle puckers slightly at the edge. Work round the circle quickly to make the frill while the fondant is moist.

6 Dampen a line about 2.5 cm [1 in] from the base of the cake with a small brush. Carefully stick on the frill, gently pressing it into the cake. Scallop remaining circles one at a time. Place second frill 12 mm [½ in] above the first.

INDEX